Forgotten First Citizen:
John Bigelow

JOHN BIGELOW AT SEVENTY

*This photograph was taken in 1888 by Albert in Brussels when
Mr. Bigelow was United States Commissioner at the
International Exposition*

Forgotten First Citizen:

John Bigelow

By MARGARET CLAPP

Little, Brown and Company · Boston

1947

*Published simultaneously
in Canada by McClelland and Stewart Limited*

PRINTED IN THE UNITED STATES OF AMERICA

To A. R. C.

Acknowledgments

I T IS a pleasure to express my gratitude for the help given to me in the preparation of this biography, especially by Professor Allan Nevins who proposed the subject, generously encouraged the research, and suggested substantial improvements in the text. His stimulating comments have enriched my understanding of the nineteenth century. For expert criticisms of the manuscript I am indebted, also, to Professors John Mantle Clapp, Henry Steele Commager, John A. Krout, Dwight C. Miner, and Lionel Trilling. I should like to thank Mrs. Bryan Conrad and Princess Simon C. Eristoff for unrestricted use of the Bigelow papers; Mrs. Charles E. Tracy, Mr. Poultney Bigelow, and Mr. Oswald Garrison Villard for the very helpful information they gave me; the librarians of the New York Public Library, especially Mr. Robert W. Hill, Mr. Wilmer R. Leech, and Mr. Edward B. Morrison, for assistance over a long period of time; the librarians of Columbia, Harvard, and Princeton Universities, the Library of Congress, and the National Archives; and Miss Rita E. Shaw, who kindly typed much of the manuscript.

M. C.

Forgotten First Citizen

[*1817–1911*]

THE POLICEMAN on the block straightened his shoulders and saluted heartily when John Bigelow passed him. Citizens bowed with a shade more courtesy when they met the old gentleman. New Yorkers liked to see him striding down Madison Avenue, vigorous and erect at ninety years of age, a tall figure meticulously clad in old-fashioned garb, a shock of white hair reaching down in trimmed side-beards on ruddy cheeks, gray eyes bright with eager curiosity. Their "First Citizen," they called him in the early years of the twentieth century.

He was born in 1817, when James Monroe was President of a farmer republic sprawled along the Atlantic and westward into portions of the Mississippi Valley. Ninety years later, in the close-knit industrial nation of President Taft's days, John Bigelow was still alive — and not merely alive, but actively engaged in public life. In the 1840's, the distant time when the city first brought running water into its better homes and turned to horse-drawn buses to solve the transportation problem, young John Bigelow, then in his twenties, had helped to reform the worst of the state's prisons. In the 1850's, he had helped to create the Republican party. In 1861, having put the *Evening Post* on a paying basis, he had retired from business, not wealthy but with enough, to the study and writing which he loved, only to be called into the service of his country throughout the Civil War. As consul in Paris, then as Minister to France, he did more than any other man to ward off dreaded French intervention on behalf of the Confederacy; and in the doing showed a breadth of vision, a sense of timing, and a capacity for practical action. The six momentous years in France were followed by seven years of private life as writer and editor in America and Germany. Then he returned to politics to help Governor Tilden crush the Canal Ring and to assist in the presidential campaign of 1876. For thirty-five years thereafter, an elder statesman who never lost faith in the slow unfolding of democracy, he aided with kindly counsel the

stream of inquirers who sought him out, public leaders and young no-
bodies alike; and at the same time he labored at far-reaching projects
— one of them the creation of the New York Public Library, another,
the Panama Canal. (In his home, in his eighty-seventh year, he watched
the sewing of the first flag of the Republic of Panama, some weeks
before that Republic was born.) Moreover, throughout the active
years, he never ceased participation in current debate of social and
political issues, through articles, editorials, books.

It is not strange, then, that a list of John Bigelow's friends should
be a roll call of the leaders of his time, American, British, European.
Nor is it strange, though it is impressive, that the tributes to his memory after his death in 1911 dwelt less upon specific achievements —
there were so many of them — than upon the character of the man himself. Joseph Choate stressed his "unfailing public spirit. . . . He was
always alive to every public question, and his unpaid services to his
countrymen, in studying and expounding them, were quite as valuable
as if he had spent the last forty years of his life in some great office
or in making more money." William Milligan Sloane, the historian, before the American Institute of Arts and Letters to which Bigelow had
belonged, emphasized his "genius alike for leadership and co-operation."
Perhaps the feeling of those who knew him best was summed up by
Henry van Dyke before the Century Association, which had chosen
Bigelow as president for the preceding six years, when he said: "He
was a human fountain of sanely directed energy. He loved to be in
the thick of things. . . . But at the same time he was a follower of
the contemplative life. . . . He was, in fact, a *common-sense* mystic.
. . . He belonged to the double tribe of Joseph, both dreamers and
doers, men of the type of Milton, Lincoln and Pasteur, who are better
citizens on earth because they hold fast to their citizenship in Heaven." [1]

Shrewdly practical, and an intellectual; worldly, yet with other-
worldly interests; a natural aristocrat who believed in democracy —
such a man was John Bigelow.

Contents

Forgotten First Citizen:
John Bigelow

CHAPTER I

Upriver Lad

[*1817–1835*]

BELOW Albany the broad Hudson flows placidly southward, not yet cutting its way through the rocky barriers of the Highlands. Its banks touch gently a narrow plain that sheers upward, some fifty yards back from the water, to an elevation of two to three hundred feet. Even today, maple, larch, oak, and poplar thrive on the steep slopes as far as eye can see, and give the river, tranquil as a lake, a soft, rolling, green border. It is a serene region, inviting and soothing. In the old days Dutch patroons, and later the favorites of English kings, held great estates on the eastern shore, from which they could look across to the western bank to a scene almost untouched by human habitation.

In 1813 a Connecticut trader named Asa Bigelow came to a stretch of that western shore known at the time as Bristol, forty miles south of Albany, and bought some acres with his hard-earned cash. The newcomer cleared a space fifty feet from the hill's edge where the view was best, and made a home for his wife and daughter and son. Within a few years the trees that surrounded the first clearing gave way to vegetable gardens, hayfields, orchards, and pasture land, later to flower gardens and an open summerhouse. Behind his home Asa Bigelow built a huge barn. Gradually he wore a dirt road, wide enough for his carriage, winding up the steep hill from the shore to a driveway flanked by maple striplings which one day would form a stately row. Inside the two-story-and-attic farmhouse, a narrow hall opened on the left into two comfortable, low-ceilinged living rooms, and on the right into the modest dining room and the huge, busy, well-stocked kitchen. There were thousands of homes like this in the early nineteenth century, in New England and parts of New York. It is to be noted, however, that this was not the cabin of a pioneer, but the substantial house of a man already settled in his business, prospering, and looking forward to prosperity.

Five generations of his name had preceded Asa Bigelow in America. John Bigelow or Biglo or Bigulah, baptized in England in 1617, had crossed the sea by the mid-seventeenth century and had settled in Watertown, Massachusetts, where he became a prosperous blacksmith, a selectman, owner of sixty acres of land, and founder of the Bigelow family in America. His grandson, another pioneering John, left Massachusetts for the richer, freer land of Connecticut, settling in Colchester, where he farmed and lived quietly into his ninety-fourth year, and where his oldest son remained for ninety-two years — through Queen Anne's War, King George's War, the French and Indian War, the Revolution. In the fifth generation, David Bigelow, born the same year as George Washington and still active in 1817, moved to near-by Glastonbury where, high on a hill, he built his home. There Asa Bigelow grew up. He did not know much about his ancestors, nor did he care that they had intermarried with Warrens, Flaggs, Footes, and Days, all of Anglo-Saxon stock. Like them and like his son John, he was too concerned with the part he was playing in the world to give much thought to genealogy. Yet the stern traditions of his long-lived, shrewd, devout forebears — hard work and godliness — shaped his life and were to shape his son's.[1]

Lucy Isham, Asa Bigelow's childhood playmate and later his wife, had a similar heritage to pass on to her children. Ishams had settled in Barnstable, Massachusetts, in the seventeenth century; in the early eighteenth century they had pioneered to Colchester, Connecticut, and there, before the Revolution began, Lucy's father, Samuel, was making a profitable living from a farm, a tavern and a general store. In only one respect did John Bigelow's maternal ancestry differ markedly from the paternal side. From either he could have derived the practical sense and the physical vigor which characterized his maturity, but only in his mother's family was there a strain of nonconformity in religion which was to recur, in another guise, in his own life. Early records of Barnstable list no Ishams among the baptized or the church members, nor did the John Isham who first lived there become a freeman until 1691, after religious qualifications for citizenship had been removed. In days when nonconformity was perilous, he may even have been a Quaker; certainly he counted Quakers as his friends. His son and his son's son remained equally apart from the organized churches of their communities, though in the fourth generation Samuel Isham, John Bigelow's grandfather, joined the Congregational church in Colchester.[2]

Asa Bigelow, apprenticed at fourteen as a clerk, became a capable storekeeper. Working hard and living frugally, he saved up several hundred dollars. Then in 1802 he and Lucy Isham were married, he being twenty-three years old and she not quite twenty-two. Together they decided that the future lay to the west. But not far west, they cautiously determined; only across the border into New York State. When Asa Bigelow placed all his cash in his saddlebags in 1803, mounted his horse, and with his brother-in-law rode off to the Dutch town of Saugerties, two miles beyond the Hudson, he was not making much of a break with the past. Rather he was seeking the best center in which to carry on a familiar way of life, much as his ancestors had done in their day.

Soon he found employment in a Saugerties store and brought his wife to settle in the thrifty little town. Then he went into business for himself. He opened his own store and freighted crops to New York City. He saw, however, that if he was to make much of his business he must have access to the river. His wife's father and her two brothers thought as he did. So together, in 1808, they purchased two hundred acres along the western bank of the Hudson in what was commonly called Bristol, paying $6000 in cash (never in his life did Asa Bigelow buy an article for which he did not have ready money). Only a deserted fish-depot remained of an earlier Dutch settlement, but within ten years thirty farmer families were settled in Bristol, some of them of Dutch descent, some of them like the Bigelows transplanted New Englanders, all of them rooted Americans who drew their sustenance and strength from the land.

In 1817 Asa Bigelow was thirty-eight years old, an established merchant, and the hamlet's leading citizen. He had docks on the Hudson, ships plying between Bristol and New York, and, housed in one large brick building, a post office, a general store, and the headquarters of his Blue Stone Trading Company. He was convinced that there was a future in the stone business and that Bristol, called Malden after 1823, would one day be a thriving metropolis. He had also the farm on the hilltop where he and his capable wife made a home for their children: twelve-year-old Emmeline and the three boys — Edward, seven; David, two-and-a-half; and the baby born on November 25, 1817, John, who was never to lose his affection for his birthplace or permit it to pass from family ownership. Perhaps the memories it evoked of his parents represented abiding strength, self-respect, and moderation, qualities which Asa and Lucy Isham Bigelow instilled in son and home alike.[3]

The boy's early years were much the same as those of other upstate country children, except for one odd interruption when he was about six. Then his father, ambitious for his boys, took David and John to a highly recommended schoolmaster in Sharon, Connecticut. David learned a little there, but when the master discovered that six-year-old John was wholly unlettered, he found it simplest to excuse him from classes. Left to his own devices, the child entertained himself, and, without his mother to stop him, taught himself to swim. It was not strange, therefore, that when their father came to inquire into their progress, he was irate at the waste of his money and their time, and it was like him to take his little sons home that same day, cold though it was and with night coming on. Their mother, surprised when they walked in, was even more delighted to have them home where she felt small children belonged. Hastening to seat the chilled lads near the fire, she went to the high-doored mahogany sideboard and brought out a mysterious bottle. The drink John got, rum and sugar he later learned, warmed him through and through. He would have liked more, but he dared not ask for it. That bottle contained medicine which he was not supposed to like. His home, as he seemed always to know, was a temperance home; indeed, all Malden perforce practised temperance simply because the only stores in town were owned by John's father and uncles, all of whom had taken the pledge.[4]

Thereafter John returned to the district school and to the wholesome discipline of a farmboy's chores. When he was seven and no longer the baby, for another sister was born in 1823, he took his turn at driving the half-dozen cows to pasture and filling the woodbox. The next year he helped to milk the cows morning and evening. Soon he drove the horse at plowing time, then learned to rake and stack hay. He was part of a world where everyone worked and took pride in that fact. His mother, sister, and the hired girl cooked, cleaned, spun, wove, knitted and sewed, made candles, soap, butter and cheese, and preserved the fruits of the garden, while the sons and the hired men tilled the one-hundred-and-fifty-acre farm under the rigid supervision of Asa Bigelow, or helped him in the store.

Sundays were days apart. When John was little the whole family used to climb into the big carriage and drive two miles to meeting in Kaatsban. There in the old stone Lutheran church stern, dark-eyed Dominie Ostrander thundered at them in what was a terrifying fashion to a small child, one week in English, the next week in Dutch. But when Asa Bigelow decided that a turnpike was needed and the Dominie joined the opposition, the family left the congregation. They were Presbyterians, after all, and had attended the Lutheran church only because no other was at hand. Asa Bigelow paid to have his turnpike built. Then with the help of his wife's brothers he had a Presbyterian church erected in Malden and selected his own pastor with views, undoubtedly, that were unexceptionable as regarded the joys of heaven, the horrors of hell, and the wisdom of modern improvements.

Between his seventh and his tenth years John grew tall and robust. Moreover, he took to learning with the same agility and competitive zest that he showed in sports. In fact, by the time he was eleven he had outstripped the others in the district school. So his mother took him upriver to Troy, to the alien atmosphere of a city of eleven thousand people, one of the largest cities in New York State, where his sister Emmeline, now grown up and married, took care of him during the next two years. At first he felt loutish alongside the city boys in Allen Fisk's Walnut Grove Academy. They dressed in store clothes, while he wore the drab, ill-fitting garments he had so admired when the local tailor had made them from his mother's woven goods. He felt like fighting every boy who saw his self-conscious confusion. Instead he stiffened his chin and determined to "show" them. Actually his family was as "good," as well-to-do, as any of his new classmates', and he himself was quite capable of holding his own in lessons and sports. Before long he stood near the head of his class, although he was by far the youngest, and on the playground he was always one of the first chosen for a team.

In 1831 several of his classmates decided to go to Washington College, later to be known as Trinity College, which had been established just seven years before in Hartford, Connecticut. Young Bigelow's dearest wish was to go with them, to have four more years of study. His father, proud of the boy's ambition, had him taken to Hartford for entrance examination, where Dr. Brownell, president of the college and Bishop of Connecticut, accepted the thirteen-year-old as one of twelve members of the class of '35, in a college frankly interested in supplying the Episcopal ministry.[5]

Two months before his fourteenth birthday, John Bigelow commenced his college career, intensely eager to be part of the new world and wholly confident that he would succeed in it. But his hope of a community of brilliance was soon extinguished in the narrow if high-minded atmosphere so typical of American colleges at the time. During his freshman year he had to plod through routine drills on advanced grammar. Later he read classic rhetoricians, historians and poets, not to expand his knowledge of the world, but to achieve "elegance of translation." The mathematics which he studied term after term bore even less relation to life. Frankly admitting that the students would forget most of it, the authorities scheduled it as a means of training the reasoning faculties.[6]

The boy turned hopefully to the college library for the stimulation which he missed in his classes, but the library was pitifully small. He read the sprinkling of history and the nineteen biographical works which the college possessed. And, though the poetry shelf never attracted him, from sheer curiosity he undoubtedly browsed through the works listed alphabetically under "Miscellanies," among them *The American Constitution, Correspondence of Louis XIV, Milton's Complete Works*, and *Niles' Weekly Register*. That was about all he found worth reading in the library, for it contained no fiction, and he had no desire to devote his free hours to a perusal of the theological works and the Greek and Latin classics which together formed almost half of its stock. So he disregarded the interdict on books not owned by the college — as did other students evidently, for one of their fellows in the debating society publicly reproved those who read "the duodecimo volumes of Scott, Cooper, or Washington Erving [*sic*]." It was here that young Bigelow reveled in the romantic novels of Scott and was profoundly stirred by the social novels of Maria Edgeworth.[7]

He did not need to attend college in order to read contemporary novels, however. Wasted years, he was later to call his fifteenth, his sixteenth, and that part of his seventeenth year which he spent at Washington. Yet perhaps it was to those years of dull, classroom catechisms that he owed the foundation of his wide knowledge as well as the habits of thorough preparation and close reading which were to play so important a role in his life. And though he was never to say a word in praise of his instructors at Washington, nevertheless, forty years after Bishop Brownell delivered his farewell speech in 1831 upon resigning the presidency of the college, Bigelow gave his sons the same advice the Bishop then had given: Be careful in choosing companions; avoid the evils of idleness; use leisure time for cultural interests.[8]

Young Bigelow's dissatisfaction with his college culminated in his junior year when he alone in his class of twelve failed to receive a junior appointment. That was an academic honor which he coveted and which he deserved as one of the top men in his class, but the faculty decided not to award it because of his boyish prank one cold winter night, a few weeks before appointments were read out, when a fire broke out in his room. The fire was not his fault, nor was his prompt action in leaping downstairs for the ever-ready pail of water anything but praiseworthy. What the faculty did object to, with cause, was that when he returned with the water and found a crowd gathered, including a barefoot, nightshirted professor, he took too obvious care to have the shivering professor directly between himself and the fire before he hurled the water toward the flames. The academic consequence of his horseplay infuriated him. Had they deprived him of free time or meted out to him some social penalty, he would have felt no resentment, but when they kept him from his merited academic distinction, his sense of justice was outraged.[9]

He began to consider seriously the repeated invitations of his brother David, who though two years his senior was behind him in school, to join him at Union College in Schenectady. Provided a lad was sixteen, and John was just that, he could enter Union as a freshman, or, if he qualified, as an upperclassman. David said that the transition to Union should not prove difficult; President Eliphalet Nott's ability to meet the needs of students dissatisfied elsewhere was already famous. So many boys transferred to Union as juniors and seniors that a considerably larger enrollment in the last two years was customary. It would be a distinct advantage to leave a community of forty-three students for one of two hundred and sixty. There would be stronger competition, a larger and abler faculty of ten professors, and an incomparably better library containing approximately 13,000 volumes as against the 880 books at Washington. Perhaps at Union he would find the intellectual stimulus he wanted.[10]

Finally his father permitted the shift in spite of misgivings about sending a boisterous, cocksure youngster to the big, open city of Schenectady, for at the same time his third son was unquestionably a student and deserved the best possible instruction. After the brief April holiday of 1834, John Bigelow, at sixteen years an attractive, upright, confident lad, almost six feet tall and still growing, accompanied his brother to Schenectady. Through the splendid, modern city the two youths went, past the dominating four-story courthouse and the equally high Mohawk bank, along the main street lined with brick stores, through a residential section where the square, solid houses suggested permanence and large, comfortable families, and on up a hill not far from the center of town to Union College and South Hall, a trim three-story brick building where upperclassmen lived.[11]

John found it easy to fit into his new surroundings. He arose about 6:30 A.M. when the rising bell clanged, had breakfast, attended prayers, and was ready for his first class at 7:30 or 8 A.M., according to the season of the year. Then he studied for two hours before going to his second recitation at eleven. Afternoons were less exacting; one study hour, one recitation and prayers were all that were scheduled. In the intervening hours he could do what he wished, provided he did not wish to do the wrong things such as "avowing or propagating infidel principles," "playing at cards, billiards or other unlawful games," "using intoxicating liquors, or giving entertainments," "combining to resist the government of the college," "throwing water or other things from the windows," and so on.[12] Those restrictions did not bother John. He did not smoke or drink, though smoking was permitted if parents allowed it, or gamble. Before he had entered college, his mother had exacted one promise from the precocious thirteen-year-old: not to play cards. At the time that had been an easy promise, because John knew nothing about cards; thereafter it was worth keeping because it meant so much to her. Nor did he have time or inclination for frivolity. He was determined to prove to his father the wisdom of the removal to Union.

The classical course for the third term of the junior year covered three fields: political economy, natural philosophy including dynamics and hydrostatics, and a study of Medea and other classic plays. The newcomer worked hard and had reason to be satisfied. His marks were good; he was elected to Sigma Phi, one of the earliest Greek letter fraternities established in America, and, what meant most to him, he was among thirty-eight upperclassmen invited to join the Philomathean Society. This was one of Union's two literary organizations, each of which had its private meeting room and library, the latter young Bigelow's mecca. He attended the debates, listened to his older classmates argue such issues as: "Does political excitement, such as exists at the present day, contribute to the benefit of the country?" "*Resolved:* That this country should encourage foreign emigration"; "*Resolved:* That the proceeds from the public land should be devoted to advancing the cause of common school education throughout the country." But he himself did not take part.[13] He preferred less formal discussions where, in his cultivated tones, he would proclaim himself an advocate of democracy, equality and free enterprise. President Jackson, whom he had seen once when Jackson and Van Buren drove through Hartford, was his hero.

By the fourth Wednesday of July the long routine of summer was established; Union, after impressive closing exercises, sent her students home. In Malden John helped his father and his older brothers; then in the fall of '34 returned to college as a senior. Expenses for room, board, fuel, light, and laundry had gone up from $112.50 to $116, but $200 was still considered sufficient for all the needs of economical students. The enrollment had risen to 268 men, 89 of them in the class of '35, the largest class since Union's foundation in 1795. Most of the seniors were, like young Bigelow, eager to profit from their last year, to immerse themselves in the course which reflected President Nott's own interests.[14]

Eliphalet Nott, Presbyterian minister, temperance reformer, abolitionist, was a vitalizing force in nineteenth-century American education. Under his leadership, which lasted from 1804 until he was well along in his nineties in 1868, Union became a foremost American college, pioneering in scientific education, one of the first colleges to offer a scientific course and to steep even its classical students in science. Dr. Nott himself experimented with the combustion of anthracite coal and held some thirty patents for his inventions, including his popular Nott stove. Far in advance of most college presidents he urged upon his students awareness of the tremendous impact science would have upon their world. He had seniors study electricity, magnetism, optics, astronomy, and hear lectures on chemistry, botany, and mineralogy. Moreover, he himself lectured to them on Kames's *Elements of Criticism*, using it to give, in effect, a course in psychology and ethics and to teach the futility of unquestioning acceptance of authority.[15] The impact on John Bigelow of this strong-minded liberal who demanded critical scholarship not for itself but in order to apply it to practical accomplishment must have been enormous. For the first time in his life young Bigelow was in close touch with a scholarly man of action. As such a man he himself was later to make his mark. Significantly, he was to choose as the topic of his first public lecture, in 1842, "The Reciprocal Influences of the Physical Sciences and Free Institutions."

The young student enjoyed all of the senior subjects, which included, besides the science, lectures on rhetoric and political economy, study of intellectual philosophy, moral philosophy, and the Greek and Hebrew Testament. However, one episode at the end of his course rankled, and affected forever his estimate of his schooling. He had stood *maximus* in most subjects throughout the year and close to that in others. So, when he went home for the April vacation, he was proudly confident that he would be chosen to deliver a commencement address. It was an old custom at Union for seniors to take an extra few days on their spring vacation, presumably to prepare for their coming share in commencement activities. Young Bigelow followed that custom and was still in Malden, mulling over plans for a speech, when a note from a classmate informed him that he had not been assigned a place in the exercises. The explanation, for which he hurried to Union, that the authorities had decided without serving warning to give no appointment to seniors who overstayed their vacation, seemed to him outrageous. If they had said he was too young, if they had said he did not reach their standards, he would have accepted the decision. Under the circumstances, however, his sense of logical justice was outraged just as it had been at Washington College; indeed, he was still seething about it as he traveled home to Malden in July 1835.[16]

However, the important thing was to look ahead. What was he to do with his life? He was now seventeen years old, a college graduate, the first in his line to hold a degree. Probably he could enter his father's stone business if he wished, but with two older brothers already in it there would be little future for a third. Besides, Malden was a tiny spot, a sleepy village of fifty families; after six years of city life young Bigelow had no desire to rusticate where no one could talk books with him or share his zest for learning. Yet if Malden for life was a dreary thought, it was good to come home for the summer. Near his father's docks the water lapped at the shore as lazily as ever. There was the spot on the bank from which he used to cast a fishing line, and the dock from which he rowed out into the current for a white bass or shad. All his childhood memories were centered in Malden, memories of home, chores, school and, above all, of the river. He recalled shooting ducks and pigeons as the great flocks soared over it in the spring, canoeing and sailing in the summer, in the winter skating or paddling hilariously on cakes of ice, and endlessly teasing the sailors for stories of the places where they traded all the way to the big city at the river's mouth. The river had always fascinated him. It seemed to him that he, like its waters, must move on.

He thought of ways to apply his college education. He could study for the ministry or become a doctor, but neither calling attracted him. He had seen too many doctors who were quacks, too many ministers wearing the blinders of dogma. Law seemed to be the only field which offered possibilities. By midsummer he had decided to become a lawyer — his father, who believed that a man must choose his own career, having neither encouraged nor discouraged him. Once the profession was settled, the question of method arose. Obviously he must study in someone's office, but the family knew no lawyers who seemed to suit; neither father nor son had any idea that there was a school of law in Litchfield, Connecticut.[17]

The young alumnus temporarily solved his problem by going to Hudson, the county seat, where President Van Buren and Attorney General Butler had once practised and where many famous Democrats had their offices, and applying to one of the best firms, that of Bushnell and Gall. They had several students but were willing to take on another; so, early in September, John Bigelow's new routine commenced. He arrived at the small, one-story building at 7 A.M., swept it, lighted the fire, and returned to his boardinghouse for breakfast. By 9 A.M. he was back in the office to start the day's work, which consisted of doing whatever he was told to do, reading whatever book was put into his hands, and remaining, except for the dinner and supper hours, until his employers left at nine or ten o'clock at night.

The routine was pleasant, but it was to last only a few weeks. The firm of Bushnell and Gall was abruptly dissolved, Mr. Bushnell, the abler partner, joining Charles B. Butler in New York city, and Mr. Gall remaining in Hudson, where he invited young Bigelow to continue. By this time, however, the youth had caught a vision of a still wider field. His father, as before, approved the daring course, and with scarcely an acquaintance in the city, Bigelow went to New York to make his way.[18]

CHAPTER 2

Young Man in Manhattan

[*1835–1844*]

THE *Chief Justice Marshall*, Hudson river steamboat, nosed into the slip on lower Manhattan. Standing at the rail, young John Bigelow scanned the expanse of tall buildings, smokestacks and church steeples, behind him the broad river and the cities and villages past which he had come, farther south the waters of the harbor, busy with graceful sloops, dirty useful barges, tall-masted ships from overseas. On the wharf below, kegs and bulky crates were being hoisted by sweating, rough-voiced stevedores from the open hatches of ships, to be wheeled in barrows and wagons up the cobblestoned street. Countless times, at home, he had seen his father's sloops unloaded in the same way; but here the familiar process took on new significance from the number of ships, the confusion and bustle, and the tang of the ocean in the October air.

Making his way up from the river, he got his first glimpse of Broadway, lined with massive flat-topped buildings, four, five, and even six stories tall, jammed one against another as far as he could see, in both directions. Important-looking businessmen strode past; shouting urchins dashed across the path of fast-moving carriages; a wretched old woman, mumbling crazily, stumbled along; countrymen and foreigners went gaping by. This was New York, the city of his dreams, to whose bustle and life lads by the hundreds and thousands were flocking from upstate, from New England, and across the ocean from old England and Ireland and indeed all Europe.

This city of 250,000 people was the world Bigelow wanted, the place, it seemed to him, where an educated gentleman, able and willing to work, could prosper. His thoughts, his manner and speech, he knew, were those of a gentleman, and the weeks of sweeping Mr. Bushnell's office were at least indication of willingness to work. He did not doubt his ability to succeed. He had never flinched from competition with his fellows but rather had sought it out, exulting in the strength of his big frame, and no less in the quickness of his intellect. True, he had not received high honors at college, but he had held his own in classes and in evening-long discussions of religion, ethics, and politics with lads four or five years his senior. Never had he been afraid to speak his mind, or to act. What he felt strongly he expressed boldly, let the chips fall where they might. And not many lads at eighteen, or more precisely at seventeen years and eleven months, had graduated from college, had embarked on a profession, and had deliberately left the security and friendliness of a familiar region for the chance of greater success in a strange place. On the other hand, as the young man in his honesty did not forget, not many lads in 1835 had fathers able and willing to pay for such a gamble.

Somehow he selected a boardinghouse from among the hundreds that offered to lodge and feed him for four or five dollars a week. Then, armed with the letter of introduction which Mr. Bushnell had given him, he went to the law office of Dey and Bonney on the corner of Cedar and Nassau Streets, where he was presently taken on as an unpaid apprentice to make himself useful and learn the law. But no one gave him books to read or suggested legal points for him to consider. All he got was an endless series of papers to be copied in a fair, round hand. Gradually, as he sat, cramped, physically and mentally, behind a narrow desk, the earlier elation at being on his own gave way to discouragement. He asked himself bitterly if this was why he had gone to college and moved to New York City. As the weeks went by he looked in vain for training which would carry him ahead. Moreover, he was warm-hearted, gregarious, fond of sports and parties, but he met no young men whose company he could enjoy. He had no desire to rub against all kinds or find a brother in every man. It seemed far preferable, that dreary winter, to spend solitary evenings mulling over Blackstone or reading and answering letters from home. He was sure he would eventually meet men whose friendship he would prize, but at times he was intolerably lonely.

He stayed with Dey and Bonney for a year and a half and then in the spring of '37 suddenly resigned, infuriated. Mr. Bonney, for whom he had slaved for eighteen months, who paid him nothing and taught him little, refused to lend him fifteen dollars to tide over until he could get funds from home. Burning with indignation — cool self-control was never a virtue of Bigelow's — at nineteen seeing everything in black and white, refusing to consider that Mr. Bonney may well have been caught short in the financial crisis that had suddenly gripped the country, he stalked out and looked for another office. At this point the tide turned. After a brief interval, he had the good fortune to be accepted by Robert and Theodore Sedgwick, II, outstanding members of the New York bar. Here, though the monotony of unpaid copying continued, it was varied by more responsible duties and relieved by occasional glimpses of the Sedgwicks' literary friends. William Cullen Bryant, the nationally known poet and editor of the intellectual *Evening Post*, often walked through the outer office where the tall youth, pushing back his unruly thatch of hair, looked up from dull papers to envy the colorful life of the journalist. Young John Bigelow, however, was too insignificant a part of Sedgwick brothers to receive more than a nod; in 1837 neither Bryant nor Bigelow had any premonition of the good fortune each would one day bring the other.

In every way the year and a half he spent with the Sedgwicks was happier than his bleak first year in New York. His studies were progressing satisfactorily, and his employers, at least during office hours, were cordial. They were true mid-century liberals, free-traders of the English classical school, and Democrats. Robert Sedgwick had introduced Bryant to English liberal thought, and likely enough it was in the office that young Bigelow gained a smattering of Manchester liberalism, for before he was twenty-five years old he was on record as a thoroughgoing free trader. He would have liked to frequent the Sedgwick home, where Bryant, Cooper, James Hillhouse, the poet, Robert C. Sands, Samuel Morse, and Fitz-Greene Halleck were welcomed guests. But clerks had no place in that circle, though echoes of Sedgwick doings were bound to reach the office and their interests were apt to influence the young men around them.[1]

Yet Bigelow was no longer lonely. Between his nineteenth and twenty-first birthdays he formed lasting friendships which were to prove far more important to his career than his legal studies. Not only young men of talent but older men who had already made their mark recognized his intellectual capacity, and he won and held their affection by his ever-fresh appreciation of their powers and his ability to make allowances for their weaknesses. Of necessity he associated with his seniors, since most lads of his age and with his interests were still college students. In that respect he considered himself fortunate; despite an occasional flash of temper and a sharp tongue, young Bigelow had the good sense to prefer a lesser seat in a talented circle to a high place among mediocrity.

One evening he dropped in at the Café Français on Warren Street, having heard that Fitz-Greene Halleck, who worked for John Jacob Astor by day and indulged in poetry and conversation by night, almost always sipped a brandy and water there between six and seven o'clock. It was Bigelow's first taste of the old world. The walls were lined with pictures of the barricades of Paris, with the tricolor flying above. Small groups of men bent intently over marble-topped tables — foreigners, mostly French or German — with glasses of absinthe or brandy comfortably at hand. One heard only the rattle of dominoes turned out on the board, the dim staccato of billiard balls from the back room, the rustle of a newspaper, an occasional "Check" punctuating the earnest chess games, but nothing of the shrill or hoarse voices, the bedlam of pointless phrases, the noisy clatter of dishes of most New York taverns. There Halleck held forth, drawing from years of wide reading the apt and unusual allusion, compounding his humor of sarcasm and sentiment. There Bigelow returned, as frequently as his slender allowance permitted, to talk with the poet, clarifying his own views and gaining confidence from the older man's kindly attention.[2]

Most of his friends, of course, were more nearly his age. The ones he loved dearly and long were chiefly of the caliber of Frederick Sheldon, later to be known as a generous lawyer of unblemished reputation, devoted to quiet acts of good citizenship. In a class by himself was another young man who was to be a lifelong friend, exercising a tremendous influence upon Bigelow, to a large extent shaping his public career, and whom he was later to address as "Mr. President." This man Bigelow met when Mrs. Polly Barnes, keeper of a boardinghouse on Fifth Avenue and Eighth Street to which he had moved, introduced him to her nephew, Samuel Jones Tilden. Like Bigelow, Tilden was from a well-to-do upstate family, a law student, and an ardent believer in democracy and the Democratic party. At first, it is true, Bigelow was not attracted to the cold, unbending youth, who seemed subject to emotion only when he discussed his bodily pains and illnesses and who, aside from these, had only two interests, his law business and politics. As the young men met at breakfast, however, morning after morning, Tilden talked politics, practical politics in which he had dabbled since he was a child. Bigelow listened attentively and inquiringly. His respect for the other's knowledge and unswerving strength of purpose mounted with each conversation, and even after leaving Mrs. Barnes's home he continued seeing Tilden, though never for a frivolous evening or for intellectual exercises which had no practical bearing. For all these he turned to other friends who, like himself, had many-sided interests.

Acting upon the theory that variety lessened the discomforts of cheap accommodations, Bigelow moved frequently during his first years in the city. He came at last to a house on Grand Street which proved to combine almost every known disadvantage, not least of them the proprietress, a thin-lipped, sharp-featured woman with garish red hair, forever clad in a black bombazine dress as dirty as the house she kept. In these unpromising surroundings, however, he found a kindred spirit in Charles Eames, a nimble-witted Harvard graduate five years his senior, later to be a lawyer, newspaper editor, and Minister to Venezuela under Presidents Pierce and Buchanan. Eames had no money, but he was the sort of man who made friends wherever he went. With a young man's love of discussion, he had discerning literary taste, and marked personal charm. Before long he and Bigelow decided to become roommates, anywhere so long as it was not on Grand Street.[3]

They moved to the Chambers Street home of a genteel English family, not far from Columbia College on Park Place. It was a pleasant residential section of town which had been the center of fashion until the wealthy deserted it in the early 1830's for more spacious quarters farther uptown around Washington Square. Then a new class began to move in, lawyers, journalists, doctors, and junior partners of the great merchants. In Chambers Street Bigelow found his proper milieu, with other well-bred, educated, and ambitious young men, and in this neighborhood, though in different boardinghouses, he remained for the next ten years.

Eames belonged to the unpretentious but intellectually exclusive Column Club, started in 1825 by a few alumni of Columbia College who wanted a center for sociability and discussion. Bigelow was invited to join in 1838; thereafter he attended the weekly literary meetings in a small upper room on Canal Street and the gaily earnest monthly suppers, little thinking that one day he would be the sole surviving member, or that sixty-three years after his admission he would preside at the symbolic merging of the Column Club with the Century. Among the members he made lasting friends of such men as Edgar S. Van Winkle, Anthony Robertson, Charles G. Havens, Richard Lawrence, George B. Butler, Augustus Schell. They would disagree on religion, politics, and economic beliefs as the years molded them in different forms, yet the long acquaintance itself was to prove an ever-growing bond. Within a few years two others joined the club, William Evarts — destined to become one of the great lawyers of the century, United States Senator, Secretary of State under Hayes — and Parke Godwin of the *Evening Post,* both of them men whose paths would cross Bigelow's more than once.[4]

Now life was rich and satisfying, even though Eames had asthma and kept their rooms choked with the fumes of burning nitre paper. In the evenings after Eames had prepared his lectures for the young ladies' seminaries which supported him, and perhaps had written an article for one of the papers, and after Bigelow had closed his law books for the day, they often brought together several young intellectuals to read a Greek classic — Aeschylus was the favorite — and to argue the mores and philosophies of other times and their own. Sometimes they heard a concert or went to Niblo's Garden. Or at home they studied and read quietly, filled with a zest for learning and for using their learning in balanced expression.[5]

When Bigelow was admitted to the bar shortly before his twenty-first birthday in 1838, the immediate goal of the last three years was accomplished, but when it came to converting knowledge into money, he found that teaching offered more security than the law. So he accepted a teaching position in Madame Chegary's seminary for girls in Madison, New Jersey, for which he was to be paid $500 and board. He leaned heavily on Sismondi's books while preparing his lectures, on Stewart's *Elements of the Philosophy of the Human Mind*, and on the *Encyclopedia of Geography;* he made use of Gibbon's *History of the Decline and Fall of the Roman Empire*, Chateaubriand's *Études Historiques*, and Guizot's *Histoire de France*. Yet he was thinking while he worked; his lectures were not mere parroting of others' ideas. One lecture, "Newspapers as Civilizing Agents," undoubtedly held a personal interest for him, the Column Club and the heady discussions of his young journalist friends having appealed far more than the sobriety of the law. In it he described how newspapers made public agents accountable, created more equality between classes, and formed public opinion. His feelings rather carried him away, for he concluded sophomorically: "When society shall dispense with legislation as I hope it soon may newspapers will doubtless be the substitute." [6]

He gave the girls for a competition subject: "Cards as a Civilizing Agent," which may have surprised some of their mothers and certainly would have surprised his own mother. Another day he spoke in "Defense of Novels," a topic sure to hold an audience in a society that deplored time wasted on light reading. His lectures on history, a subject he defined as "the record of the deeds of men among men written by antiquity for posterity in human alphabets and subject to human confusions," had little topical or chronological sequence. They had, however, a unifying thread in their invariable concern with man's influence upon man, presenting social utility as the sole measure of worth. From history he turned to geography, "the lesson of the Almighty written in legible characters upon this earth in the shape of rivers and mountains for all time." He described climate, soil and hydrography with equal regard for established facts and for the moral lessons they reflected. It seemed quite proper to Bigelow to consider in a

geography lesson why there should be differences in physical surroundings if there was an impartial Providence. And it was almost inevitable
that he should deduce from the gradual erosion of mountains and the
filling-up of valleys that democracy was part of the universal pattern.[7]

Madame Chegary wanted to engage him for the following year. The
girls were quite as eager as she to have him return; it was not often
that they had as an instructor a robust young six-footer with wavy
hair, blue-gray eyes, and a most attractive smile. However, though
pleased with his success in his first job and though aware that he
learned what he taught as he never had learned what his professors
taught, Bigelow missed the stimulation of his mental equals and betters.
He was bored in Madison. As soon as his contract was up, he returned
to what for him was life.

Having saved most of his salary, he could afford to begin the practice of law. Edgar S. Van Winkle, an older member of the Column
Club and an established lawyer with an office at Wall and Nassau
Streets, gave him deskroom, and there Bigelow hung out his sign and
waited for clients. He expected little business at first, because New
York was almost as well-supplied with lawyers as it was with grocers
and porterhouses. Moreover, most of his friends were young men who
had neither the need nor the money for lawyers or else were themselves lawyers looking for clients. Accordingly, he determined, while
waiting for business, to indulge his other interests. Charles Eames was
ready to join him and again they took rooms together, this time at
New York University on Waverley Place, in Professor Da Ponté's
wing.[8]

At the end of the '30's, New York was growing fast. The flood of
immigrants steadily increased as the financial depression began to lift,
and though the city pushed northward like a giant amoeba, the population grew denser every year. Unfortunately, few people were as yet
aware of the complex problems of sanitation in a large city, with the
consequence that filth seemed to multiply faster than the inhabitants.
The streets were disgusting; crossing them in wet weather was a hazard. Yet there were few complaints. People accepted philosophically
what they were used to, and chuckled over current tales of the small
boy submerged and lost when he did not hold his mother's hand as he
should, of the old lady gazing from her window during the murderous
epidemic of 1832 when the desperate city fathers had all the streets
scraped and cleaned. "Cobblestones at the bottoms of the streets!" she
exclaimed. "How very droll!" [9] The frequent epidemics, however,
were indeed serious. The free pumps at the street corners were every-

where a source of danger. Bigelow, and all but the very poor, got along passably with baths in rainwater collected on roofs and by using "Knapp's safe drinking-water," hawked through the streets at a penny a gallon, but in the Five Points district, where people had no money for peddled water, typhus, typhoid and dysentery took a constant toll. Yet in this matter the outlook for the future was better; within a few months, a year or two at the most, the Croton Dam would be completed and clear water could be piped into the better houses and to the street corners of the poor. Growth in size was compelling improvement in living conditions, however slowly.

And what were dirt and even pestilence compared to the charm of the city, even to such a fastidious person as Bigelow! He and his friends had the latest news, the newest gossip, heard the greatest actors and singers and lecturers, knew all they deemed important of the European world, and spoke with final authority upon every aspect of life. In compensation for the dragging days in his empty office during the early 1840's, Bigelow's evenings were filled with variety. Even with his limited funds he managed each year to see most of the current plays and several Shakespeare revivals at the Park Theater or the National. There were other theaters, but those two offered the best and drew the nicest people, which appealed to Bigelow. He saw Fanny Elssler dance in 1840 when all New York went wild about her. Later he heard Ole Bull give his first American concert and joined the throng in tumultuous acclaim. Occasionally he heard operas which he enjoyed enormously, or so he said, especially the Italian company, though with suspicious frequency more important matters forced him to leave before the end. But he was never called away when the "Ethiopian Singers" were giving New Yorkers their first taste of minstrel harmonies and Negro voices.[10]

During an average week he saw a play, heard a concert or a lecture, attended a dance or reception or a round of parlor games, and regularly on Saturday nights he turned up at the Column Club. Occasionally he spent an evening reading at home, though he had time enough for that in the office, or writing lightsome notes to arrange theater parties or picnics, or counseling his roommate, Eames, on how to woo a girl against her parents' protests. He himself had no thought of marrying now nor could he have afforded to if he wished, for he still was largely dependent upon his father. He did enjoy escorting an attractive girl, however, and as a personable bachelor in his early twenties, he knew a full measure of carefree popularity. Hostesses liked to have at their parties a young man who made a splendid appearance in a ballroom and who could be amusing or impressively erudite as the occasion de-as to his position. His words came in crystal phrases; his opinions rang forthrightly. Bryant thundering against the tariff was not the gentle household poet.

Bigelow's interest in magazines was more catholic. At any time during the 1840's there were twenty-five current magazines of some merit, not many of them long-lived, but as one went under another replaced it, keeping the number fairly constant, while the same editors shifted from one venture to another, undaunted.[2] Who the editors were, who were planning new magazines, what material they wanted, how their finances stood, provided the conversational staple of the men and women Bigelow knew. Most of his friends, older than he, gave much of their leisure time to the writing of stories, sketches, poems, book reviews, gossip, essays, pouring out words to fill all the magazines. A few of his acquaintances tried to make a career of such writing, but most of them knew that it promised but a shabby living, pleasant though it was as an avocation.

Tentatively, Bigelow stepped into the world of writers. The *New York Review*, the most distinguished literary magazine in America save the *North American Review* of Boston, accepted for the July '41 issue his first effort, "The Profession of Law at Rome before the Empire." The fluent prose, the logical sequences, the careful documentation of this unsigned essay gave promise of a writer who might in time take his place as an authoritative spokesman for the past or the present. And the forthright condemnation of Gibbon's treatment of Rome, in part reflecting a youthful dogmatism which might be outgrown, also suggested critical rather than creative ability.

The sip of success was intoxicating. Bigelow took to writing in office hours. The following month the *Democratic Review*, peppery John O'Sullivan's magazine, carried a nine-page review by Bigelow, of Charles Anthon's edition of Lemprière's *Classical Dictionary*. The still anonymous young critic wrote once more with all the accuracy of a scholar, but this time without a scholar's restraint. That was because, in youthful exuberance, he entered wholeheartedly into the fun of tearing apart the Columbia professor's work, at the request of the publisher of a rival dictionary. In his maturity he was to dismiss as a "squirrel hunt" this review, which seemed to him, at twenty-three, a triumph.[3] Yet though his criticism was unnecessarily severe — as he himself realized before many years passed — he had a point worth making. The professor's statement that he had included nothing that "shall bring a blush to the fairest cheek . . ." touched Bigelow off. "We protest," he said, "against emasculating history for the purpose of favoring prudery or tickling the moral self-complacency of any class or sect. A fact, wherever and whenever and however begotten, should be inviolable." Furthermore Bigelow remarked upon the omission of some twenty-four names and gratuitously told Dr. Anthon for what each was noted. The nettled professor retorted in the columns of the *New World*, thereby opening himself to another blow which Bigelow made haste to deliver after arming himself with a careful scrutiny of reference books and the approval of Professor C. C. Felton of Harvard.[4]

Henceforth O'Sullivan was Bigelow's friend. A year later the editor made an anonymous article, "Lucian and His Age," the leader in his magazine. "My Lucian," was the way Bigelow proudly referred to the essay. It proved the wisdom of the exercises in style which he had set himself. Indeed, few people could have realized that the bombastic articles about Dr. Anthon came from the same pen as this essay, one of the best-written papers which the *Democratic Review* carried in the '40's, when Whitman, Poe, Hawthorne, and Thoreau were among the contributors. In the paper Bigelow gave, briefly, biographical data about Lucian; then more fully, though the essay was too short to be more than suggestive, he entered upon a study of Lucian's writings. Yet he had no desire to write for antiquarians. Active, quick of mind and spirit, his pleasures ranging from legwork for the Democratic party to repeating bad conundrums for the amusement of young ladies ("When is Edgar A. Poe always a poet — Do you give it up? after taking T. Don't you tell on me — it injures a lawyer in this city to be reputed a wit . . ."),[5] this youth who crowded his life with political discussions and social parties, with a search for knowledge and money, had no use for a return to the past. Though he was interested in ancient history, he was more interested in ward politics. He agreed with Emerson, as he wrote in his article on Lucian, that in twenty years Americans would be the leading students of antiquity but they would never be its slaves.

> And herein lies the error of all the idolators of the past. Because the ancients did well in their day with their means, therefore we should do like them in our day with our means. Instead of qualifying our institutions to the changes taught by time and reflection, they would have us translate the institutions of Greece and Rome into American forms. They have no sympathy or taste for native virtues.[6]

Here was an American of the main current. Bigelow believed that Lucian, of all the ancients, had the most to offer American students of politics and society. He studied the Roman's writings not as literary

literary work and commissioners fees. My prospects look dark.
I have tried in vain to be in good spirits today I never remember
to have been so dispirited on New Year's day before.

He heard that Duff Green was starting a new magazine, the *Republic*. Perhaps Green would like a weekly review for ten dollars,
similar to the ones Bigelow had written regularly for the *Plebeian* two
years before and more recently for the *Pathfinder*. It was worth inquiring into, but apparently nothing came of it. Weeks went by with
occasional wills to draw and small cases to handle, with hours at the
office free for reading Pascal's *Pensées*, Adam Smith, Alison's *French
Revolution*, Tennyson's "Locksley Hall" — there was a good poem,
that of a poet only less than first rate. But it was a desultory life.
Parties in the evening or chess, a game he used to detest as a time-
waster but now played avidly, could not fill his need for purposeful
activity. It was time to buckle down. Again he resolved "to go to
studying law and doing law and making money — I wrote home last
week (for) $250 I have recd no answer I trust the old gentleman does
not intend to stop the supplies — ." He took a partner and a new office
at 84 Cedar Street and was glad when his brother David sent the money.
However, the new office brought little new business because his partner
was neither deeply versed in law nor interested in it, while Bigelow
himself was soon engaged upon another literary venture.[10]

Bryant must have been satisfied with the editing of *Rambles in
Yucatan*, for he recommended Bigelow for another, similar job. This
time it was to help Josiah Gregg write *Commerce of the Prairies, or
Journal of a Santa Fe Trader*. Gregg was an unhappy little man in a
city; Bigelow alone among the New Yorkers he met was able to pierce
the thick layers of his shyness; yet he was as keen an observer, as
tingling alive as any man of his time once free on the prairies. He had
come East to find a publisher, after shaping his notes on a trader's life
into a painstakingly accurate account, and had hired Louis Tasistro to
polish the manuscript. But when the literary man sacrificed facts to
phrases, Gregg discharged him and, upon Bryant's suggestion, hired
Bigelow to complete the revision. If Bigelow tried any literary "notions," the unimaginative Gregg stood ready to stop him, anxious only
for as plain and correct English as possible.[11]

So it was Gregg's book, on which Bigelow deserved credit merely
for the "laundry work," as he called it. He received no public acknowledgment for his share in the book when Langley's published it in June
1844. Yet it is inaccurate to say that "It is scarcely conceivable that
Bigelow did not wish his name used in this connection. Naturally a

young man of twenty-seven, thirsting for literary fame, would have welcomed some acknowledgment of his scholarly work in Gregg's preface." [12] No doubt Bigelow's yearnings were for literary fame, but his Yankee sense of the practical had kept him before this from attaching his name to any of his writings. He was a lawyer, if a half-hearted one, just now; and he could not afford to jeopardize a probable future position of wealth and standing at the bar for the unsubstantial satisfactions of the artist.

For several months the book absorbed him. The two hundred dollars he was to receive would be pay at the highest rate he had yet made.[13] Aside from that, the subject matter alone was worth his time. Gregg gave Americans their first insight into Western Latin culture, his exact portrayal colored only by typical American biases. When he deplored the gambling, the superstitious religion, the lack of justice as an Anglo-Saxon conceived it, Bigelow, too, accepted those as evils. He saw, also, another evil: "In nothing was the deplorable state of things already noticed made more clearly manifest, than in the absence of a public press. . . ." [14] That was one of Bigelow's fondest convictions and never a matter of much concern to Gregg; Bigelow's hand at this point, at least, seems obvious.

When the book had gone to press, Bigelow reviewed it in the *Democratic Review* and gave Eames material to do likewise in the *World*. Certainly Bigelow, anonymously, should have been able to compose a favorable account of a book which he, anonymously, had edited. But Gregg was not satisfied. He wrote to his brother, enclosing copies of Bigelow's articles:

> . . . I find it not a very good one. The young man who wrote it stands high as a literary character, and had examined my book thoroughly; so that I thought he could have made a better selection than he did from it.[15]

In truth, Bigelow's review was hampered by modesty and colored by his own interests. Not a word did he say of the readability of *Commerce of the Prairies,* for that would have been self-praise. He contented himself with stringing together copious excerpts depicting the life of a trader, the evils of Western Catholicism, and some of the picturesque aspects of Western life. For his part, he regretted the meagerness of Gregg's data upon the government of New Mexico, yet he recommended the book without equivocation:

> It presents by far the most complete and reliable account of the origin of our overland commerce with Mexico and the kind of life led by those who engage in it, of any work that has ever been

printed, to our knowledge. We say reliable, because, in the first place, the work is throughout marked by a cautiousness of expression and an indisposition to exaggerate or overstate, which at once commands our utmost confidence in the author's fidelity. In the next place, Mr. Gregg's statements are entitled to special consideration at this time, because he has, probably, a larger experience in this trade than any other living writer.

Bigelow concluded by noting that Santa Anna had closed United States–Santa Fe trade in August 1843 and that in private conversation Gregg had predicted a rebellion in Mexico unless the ban were lifted. That being so, trade would be resumed, Bigelow stated, but he foresaw a serious obstacle to its growth in the dangers of crossing the wide, unpoliced lands of Mexico. He expected years, almost centuries, to pass before settled communities in those areas would provide effective protection for travelers. So, being practical-minded, he proposed the establishment of a *mare liberum*, so to speak, over which Mexico would grant to the United States the right to convoy caravans to Santa Fe, at the expense, as any Democrat would agree, of those so escorted. Of a possible U. S. grab of those lands, already advocated here and there, Bigelow took care to say nothing. Such an act he would always consider evil.[16]

Once the book was completed, he picked up the threads of his normal life. Business was so bad that he told his father he would quit if it did not improve soon. Yet he did not sound depressed. The fact was that another interest, gradually developing, not superseding his devotion to letters but determining his subject matter, was leading him further from the law. John O'Sullivan, editor of the *Democratic Review*, wanted to start a daily paper to help swing their doubtful state into the Democratic column in the elections of 1844. He hoped to get Tilden to join in such a venture. In that case, Bigelow thought, possibly O'Sullivan would let him run the *Review*. "I would leave my profession for such a berth. Oh how quick!" Or perhaps he could have a share in the newspaper. Work on either publication would give him a chance to write and to help form opinion, which in a democracy, he had come to believe, should be the chief end of an educated man.[17]

It seemed to him that an American should place first on his list of duties the intelligent use of his vote; if he could do more than use his single vote wisely, so much the better for him and his country. Bigelow had cast his first vote in 1840 for Van Buren, and Van Buren had lost. Tilden then analyzed the reasons, for Bigelow's benefit, though Bigelow needed no help to see that the crippling depression of 1837, not yet fully overcome, was largely to blame. Tilden also lectured him on the pointlessness of discouragement — a decidedly useful first political lesson, for in the eighteen presidential elections which clocked Bigelow's adult life, the party he supported was to win the highest office only eight times, and of those eight times, not once was the man whom the party chose as leader the man Bigelow thought best suited for the position.

In 1840 Tilden said that they could do what countless others did: ridicule, snipe at, hate the Whigs, and hope that the country would come to its senses within four years. Or they could do all that and work for the change they wanted. That was Tilden's idea of proper reaction to defeat: start at once to organize for the next campaign. Yet even Tilden had to admit that the outlook was bleak. Whigs for the first time controlled the Federal government; they had recaptured the governorship of New York, had gained control of its legislature, and were even threatening Tammany's stronghold. Van Buren had been defeated by William Henry Harrison in a noisy, utterly stupid campaign. More properly stated, so far as New York State was concerned, the Whig triumvirate composed of William H. Seward, Thurlow Weed, and Horace Greeley had beaten little Van. Tilden and Bigelow admitted that those three men had brains and money, but they considered their methods despicable, and their program, of government aid to canals, railroads, charities, and education, downright dangerous.

The next year, 1841, Democrats saw one encouraging rift in the national darkness when Vice-President Tyler became President upon the death of Harrison. An ex-Democrat, Tyler was soon quarreling with Congress and might well split the Whigs by '44. Perhaps the Democrats could help that good work. Their outlook in New York, where they regained control of the legislature, likewise brightened. The following year they succeeded in electing William C. Bouck as Governor. In so far as that broke Whig control, all Democrats were satisfied, but not all of them were pleased to have Bouck as their leader, because he was a Conservative — that is, a Democrat who went part way with the Whigs in their advocacy of state-financed public improvements — while the Radical wing, to which Bigelow and his political friends belonged, stood for a minimum of government and economy in that. The split between the two factions of New York's Democratic party widened in 1843. Governor Bouck realized the Radicals' worst fears when he called for resumption of work on the Erie Canal. The Radicals at once prepared to fight back under John Van Buren — "Prince John," the ex-President's son, New York's Alcibiades; Michael Hoffman, energetic Assembly leader from Herkimer; Silas Wright,

United States Senator from New York; and Azariah C. Flagg, the politically astute Comptroller.

These men were friends of Tilden, whom Bigelow frequently met in Tilden's rooms where he went to follow the progress of their planning. Yet in sober fact Bigelow was only a listener, just another young man eager to serve, a young lawyer who found business slow. However, it was not in him to remain passive; he felt strongly that he, too, must contribute. Presently he found his opportunity in one of the major problems before the Radical Democrats: should they seek a constitutional amendment embodying their Suspension Act of 1842, which banned state borrowings for internal improvements, or should they call for the drafting of a new Constitution, in order to make other than financial reforms? An amendment required approval by a majority of each branch of the legislature, confirmation by two thirds of each branch of the successive legislature, and popular ratification — a difficult task at best, and doubly so when the majority party was divided into factions. Would it not be easier and wiser to revise the entire Constitution? Bigelow became one of the many who considered that question, and one of the few who began by a scholarly study of the background of American Constitutions.

First he made a careful review of Jefferson's theories of government. Next he talked with old Peter Livingston, who had been influential in drafting New York's Constitution of 1821. Soon he was absorbed in the subject of American Constitutions. He noted in his diary on November 24:

> Our political institutions are almost the only product of the intellect in this country of which we may feel proud and for a knowledge of which there is no substitute. At almost any court in Europe may be found better poets better historians — (Bancroft's merit is derived from the political system about which he writes. His historical style is founded upon European models) — profounder philosophies more accomplished naturalists — but there are no such constitutions in the world as those of the U. S.

He began to construct two essays: "The Origin and Theory of American Governments" and "Constitutional Reform." The latter was completed first, because, as he observed: "I am disposed to think that I shall do my best henceforth to use my pen if at all upon subjects of immediate public concernment. I shall probably never be paid for the labor my Lucian cost me though its literary merit is much greater than this." When the *Democratic Review* appeared with his name attached as author of "Constitutional Reform," he was surprised and at first indignant. He had not authorized the use of his name, and

John O'Sullivan knew that he preferred anonymity lest a literary reputation should scare off possible clients. But upon reflection Bigelow
concluded: "I do not know that I regret it. It is not a topic foreign
to my profession and perhaps may serve me." [18]

Among friends of reform the paper was well-received. The *Post*
called it "one of the most persuasive and well considered arguments
that has appeared upon the topic"; the *Herald* also praised it; and
though the fee of ten dollars which Bigelow received was small, he
did not spurn it. Moreover, that article was to form the first of a
series upon constitutional reform which he would write during the
next four years, and of which the *Democratic Review* would one day
say: "We are glad of this occasion . . . of congratulating him on being the first writer to draw public attention in this country to many
radical changes and improvements since adopted in various states of
the Union." [19]

However, the story of constitutional reform in New York belongs
later, for before it could make headway it was eclipsed by the presidential campaign of 1844, in which Bigelow had a small share. New
York Radicals were sure that ex-President Van Buren would return
to the White House in 1845, until, a month before the national Democratic convention assembled in May '44 he put frankness before discretion on the major question of the day, flatly opposed the annexation of Texas, and thereby lost the support of the South. In the ensuing
scramble for the nomination, James Knox Polk, a little-known Conservative from Tennessee, came out victorious. To hold the party together, the Conservative wing then offered the Vice-Presidency to
New York's Radical senator, Silas Wright, but he bluntly refused to
"ride behind the black pony," and the second place went to George
Mifflin Dallas, the Conservative leader of Pennsylvania, a district attorney in Andrew Jackson's day but later a protectionist and an advocate of the second United States Bank. The mood of New York Radicals darkened; their earlier zeal to win the Presidency abated. Tilden,
who had encouraged O'Sullivan's project of a campaign newspaper,
now became dubious. On July 5 he walked into Bigelow's rooms before his leisurely friend was up and remained there until 8:30 that
evening, deliberately checking the pros and cons of the newspaper
venture, weighing the possible advantages to party and self against the
possible failure of a paper and the sure loss of income from the law.
The sheer persistence of his thinking, "the clearness and foresight and
judgment" made a tremendous impression upon Bigelow. He, of course,
urged the paper; so, too, did O'Sullivan when he dropped in from
10 A.M. to 3 P.M.[20]

Later when Senator Silas Wright was persuaded to seek the Democratic nomination for the governorship, as the one man who could defeat the Whigs in New York, Tilden decided to go ahead with the paper. In August the *Morning News* came into being. Within a week it had 3000 subscribers. O'Sullivan served as its editor, but he kept his hold on the *Democratic Review* as well, which effectively blasted Bigelow's hope of running the magazine. Yet he had few regrets, because he immediately became third man on the *Morning News*, had full charge of the literary, drama, and music notes, and was assistant on political sections. He could even conclude that it was good that he was poor and had an uncongenial profession, a usual sign of a brightening future. If all youths had to overcome the difficulties of poverty and low social position, he now philosophized, there would be free competition in every field. They would learn to tolerate and to appreciate differing qualities, would have their fixed prejudices rubbed off, and having learned to give every opinion a fair hearing, would in their day of power make America a truly democratic land.[21]

With more to do in politics, law, and society, he still found time for reading. He reread Jonah — "What nonsense to call that an inspired book." He read Sismondi's *Études sur les Constitutions des Peuples Libres* and decided that it would pay Sismondi to take lessons from Tammany Hall. Vail's *Life of Paine*, though poorly written, convinced him that no man except Jefferson did as much as Thomas Paine to establish democratic institutions in America. Of course he kept up with the magazines and the latest books. Some of this reading was done on trains, for new law cases were coming his way and they as well as political affairs often required his presence in Albany. Now, if he would have time for all he wanted to do, he must watch the minutes, utilizing every one for pleasure or profit.

Business took him to Schenectady one week end of that summer, where he lunched with one of his former professors and with ex-Governor William H. Seward, who, to Bigelow's scorn, proclaimed Philip Hone a greater orator than Daniel Webster. Bigelow took private revenge in his diary, describing his famous fellow alumnus as "a very mean-looking man. His temperament is sanguine, nervous. Hair very dirty colour — if clean it would be nearly red. His complexion is much of the same hue." Seward, one must remember, was a Whig and Bigelow a Democrat. The description changed later when both were of the same party.[22]

The Democratic state convention met in Syracuse in September. Bigelow and Tilden, sitting in the press section, saw their man, Silas Wright, win the nomination. They were jubilant, because even the

Conservatives would now work for Wright's election as the one means of carrying the state for Polk. Daily in the *News* Tilden and O'Sullivan, with Bigelow helping at every turn, pounded home their faith in the Democratic party and in Wright. Bryant on the *Post* was sending the same message to his smaller and more select audience. Those two papers alone fought the powerful Whig press in New York City, and in their common cause the friendship between Bryant and the younger men, Tilden, O'Sullivan, and Bigelow, was cemented.

Though the weeks were crammed with activity, Bigelow never let himself become so absorbed in the moment that he forgot his own future. Looking ahead, he knew that the *News* would soon cease to exist, for Tilden had no ambitions which journalism could satisfy. He knew, too, that though he himself intended to devote to his law practice, at last firmly established and modestly growing, all of the time he profitably could, he would have some spare hours every day. Those, he wanted to fill with some project which would combine his writing and his political interests. Then it was that E. P. Hurlbut, his roommate since Charles Eames had married and moved to Washington, came bursting into the boardinghouse with an idea he had to share: what America needed was a political cyclopedia. He proposed that he and Bigelow publish one. It would lead them into fascinating bypaths of the past, would place them in the midst of momentous questions of the day. But they were poor in 1844; they each paid just five dollars a week for room, breakfast, and tea, living with a worthy woman whose colloquial English they could pardon but whose inability to cook an egg decently they deplored. This was the best they could afford, and now Hurlbut was suggesting a work which would take at least two years to complete and then might or might not pay cash dividends. Bigelow talked sensibly and discouragingly about it, but he could not forget it.[23]

On October evenings after his law cases and his articles for the *News* were prepared, he worked with Hurlbut on a list of topics for the cyclopedia. By the time the Democrats swept New York and the nation in the November elections, Bigelow had completed the whole scheme of the work. He planned to pay contributors ten dollars a page out of the profits, and, to get strangers to work for a young nobody on such a basis, he asked John O'Sullivan and Benjamin F. Butler, the famous former Attorney General, whom he now knew well and who was to remain a friend until his death in 1858, to serve as auditors. Both men immediately accepted that responsibility; both men offered to write articles; O'Sullivan even offered to get a contribution from Martin Van Buren. Theodore Sedgwick and other prominent New Yorkers agreed to help.[24] The outlook was promising indeed for Bigelow, who nine years before had not known a person in New York. Now, established men had sufficient faith in him to work for him and to lend him their credit. The occasion served to strengthen his self-confidence and to mark the time when he gained at least journeyman standing among writers and politicians.

CHAPTER 4

Prison Reformer

[1845–1848]

No one knows what makes some eras seethe with new ideas or old ones newly uttered. At the time the pattern is not complete, and later when the shape is clear the small details are missing. The 1820's, 1830's, 1840's, the years which molded Bigelow, were young, cocksure years, dominated by men and women who sought one goal, to better man's life with man. But they had no one formula to reach it. There were those who wanted equal political and legal rights for the poor and the rich, even among women. There were temperance advocates. There were some who sought a richer life through communal living, in socialism, Fourierism, or with the Mormons or Shakers. Others found that richer life in reliance upon the soul's capacity to sense the universal pattern. Still others through science and industry looked to material progress to enrich everyone, or through institutional reforms sought to equalize opportunities. Some worked among the educated to bring them a more complete life or among self-respecting laborers to bring them economic good. Others were concerned with the derelicts, with orphans, slaves, drunkards, criminals, or the insane. Yet all worked with the same belief that man's instincts were good, that he could achieve mightily given opportunity, that he could better his world given education.

Far from being amazed at the strength of these reforming elements, Bigelow found his world quite normal. He had known little, as a child, of the flow of eager projects for the reconstruction of society; certainly he had felt none of the turbulent, driving spirit behind them. With his own home a temperance center, reform was an accepted part of the boy's life, like going to school or playing along the Hudson. As he grew older, though he could realize somewhat that he lived in a period of ferment and change, he absorbed without query the current belief in the perfectibility of man and the importance of education to the success of a democracy. But it was not in him to be a crusader

or a martyr to a cause. He was a student of history and trained in
the law; he had too much balance, too healthy a body, too critical
and reflective a mind to be swept off his feet by any current "ism."
He had his own future to consider as well as his duty to his fellow
men. The two were compatible, in his opinion, but they were not
synonymous. Moreover, he believed that lasting progress was achieved
not by momentary zeal but through the patient work of intellectuals
slowly spreading the philosophy of the rights of man and through
the practical, specific improvements which men of action could intro-
duce. Therefore he considered it his pleasant duty, during his late
twenties, between 1845 and 1848, to devote to civic improvements the
bulk of his time not consumed in earning a living. As a practical reformer he served in New York's prison system, and, as a reforming
publicist, he applied his writing talent to other problems of the day.

His opportunity to enter upon such work came through influential
friends who judged him to be one of the few young men in New York
who could both understand a principle and carry through a job.
Samuel Tilden, a member of the Assembly and a power in the state
since the November Democratic victory, took him to Albany to meet
Governor Wright. It was a complimentary act though at the time the
visit seemed more ridiculous than propitious, for after some general
conversation, Tilden hitched his chair close to the Governor's and
started speaking in the near-whisper he invariably adopted when he
turned specifically to one person and was concerned only with that one
person's response. Bigelow, sitting across the room, was completely
ignored. Finally, irked, amused, embarrassed, he arose and interrupted
with a "Mr. Tilden, I leave you now with the Governor"; but Tilden
would have none of it. So he sat down again, and again they forgot
his presence. Three times that evening he tried to withdraw politely,
but each time Tilden made him stay, and the indistinct murmur of
voices went on. Finally they departed, Tilden quite satisfied with the
visit, Bigelow filled with wry amusement. He had come at Tilden's
request to see the Governor and that was precisely what he had done
— he had seen the Governor.[1]

Yet the visit bore fruit. In March his friends began talking to him
about an executive appointment to one of the five inspectorships of
Sing Sing State Prison. The job entailed establishing rules concerning
discipline, work, finances, and other matters, within a framework set
by legislative enactment; making monthly inspections of the prison's
condition as well as annual reports to the legislature, and selecting
prison officials whose day by day actions would give shape to the
inspectors' policies. For two equally valid reasons Bigelow was inter-

ested. As a believer in the possibility of reform, he could render practical service in such a post. Moreover, he saw in an inspectorship an avenue to a wider reputation, useful either in his law practice or in politics, should his interest in that line develop. Tilden urged his appointment, and Tilden was Wright's adviser; O'Sullivan recommended him, and O'Sullivan carried weight in Albany. Yet week after week went by and nothing happened. Finally on May 10 the appointment came through.[2]

Prisons needed reform in 1845, in spite of the improvements already made by pioneering penologists. The record of brutality in prisons throughout the country was shocking whether they were built on the Pennsylvania plan or the Auburn. The former treated all inmates to solitary confinement, day and night, as the surest way to eliminate plottings and rebellions, for concerted action was impossible where keepers could overhear all talk between cells. The latter, economically a more profitable system, initiated in New York's Auburn Prison and then applied to Sing Sing, also provided small individual cells into which prisoners were locked at night, but during the day they were allowed to work together, getting some comfort from comradeship, though no word of conversation was permitted. In either case, men were forced to live in damp, foul-smelling, vermin-infested places, whipped to hard labor, and fed a monotonous, rotten diet. They had done wrong; they were to be punished. The sole purpose of prisons was to keep criminals away from respectable taxpayers, and while away, it was up to the prisoners to support themselves and their keepers through contract labor. Women fared no better. Not until 1832 was a matron appointed in a New York prison, and then the woman was typical of what could be hired for sixteen dollars a month.[3]

For four years Dorothea Dix had been visiting prisons throughout the country, keeping notes on what she saw and dinning reform into the ears of everyone she met. In 1844 she published the facts in *Remarks on Prisons and Prison Discipline in the United States* and the next year issued a revised edition. She added to her first report on the Mt. Pleasant Prison at Sing Sing a description of a revisit in November 1844 when, in the thousand cells, seven by seven by three and a half, built in "tiers of two ranges on a story, back to back, surrounded by an area nine feet wide, lighted by windows through a wall three feet in thickness," she found "the governors of both the men and women's prison determined to maintain order through the mildest possible influences; but all their exertions, up to that time, had not exempted them from the painful duty of imposing severe sentences. . . ."[4]

Her pioneering aroused decent citizens especially in Philadelphia,

Boston and New York. A group of philanthropic New Yorkers, among them Bigelow's friends Benjamin F. Butler, John O'Sullivan, Theodore Sedgwick, and John Edmunds, formed the New York Prison Association in 1844 to inspire the use of prisons as centers for retraining programs and to help ex-convicts find an honest place in the world. "Soft-headed idealists," many people called them, while contractors and brutal keepers jeered softly and waited for the furore to subside. But the Prison Association was there to stay. Two years later, when Bigelow was an active member of its committee on detentions, it was incorporated by the legislature; it inaugurated a women's committee to consider the needs of female convicts, and it arranged for periodic fact-finding surveys, the first such attempt to be made in New York's four State Prisons.[5]

These four prisons were located in Auburn, Sing Sing, and Clinton. Clinton Prison, but partially completed in 1845, housing only about 100 convicts and blessed with new equipment and an enlightened head keeper, had little in common with the other state prisons, and because its problems were as yet primarily constructional and financial, an act of 1844 provided that the governor, the attorney general, and the comptroller should serve as its inspectors. Auburn and Sing Sing, on the other hand, were large, fully established institutions, the former built in 1816, the latter erected ten years later by convict labor brought over from Auburn. Each of them was governed by its own board of five appointed inspectors. Of the two, Sing Sing was by far the worse. While Auburn had 500 inmates, Sing Sing housed 1000 men and knew all the attendant evils of size: enormous managerial burdens, constant danger of riot, and well-nigh insuperable obstacles to experimentation. The men at Sing Sing, chiefly from New York City, were, according to Dorothea Dix: "the most corrupt, the most degraded, most desperate class of prisoners, in any prison north of Mason and Dixon's line." [6]

Moreover, Sing Sing alone faced the problem of running two prisons in one plant, a men's prison and a women's. In 1839, eighty-one cells were built in a separate wing at Sing Sing in which all the female prisoners of the state were lodged. Here half-wits and insane mingled with the vicious during the day, as they did in all prisons on the Auburn plan, but here, by 1845, there was no separation for some of the women even at night, for there were not enough tiny cells. And though there was a law calling for the segregation of the sexes, it was openly flouted. To complete the dark picture, medical care was so haphazard that while wretches who gave birth to children in Sing Sing had some chance of survival, prior to 1846 not a child born in the jail lived more than a few months.[7]

Sing Sing, where conditions were worst and numbers greatest, naturally became the center of the battle between aroused reformers and advocates of the *status quo*. Soon in the midst of that battle were Bigelow and four other inspectors appointed by Governor Wright for a three-year term commencing in May, 1845. Two of them, elderly Judge Powers of Catskill, who served as chairman of their board, and Benjamin Mace, an energetic young lawyer from Newburgh, were as keen for reform as Bigelow. The other two, antireform Westchester politicians, contractors' representatives, did not matter at this time, for they formed the minority and were invariably outvoted.

Shortly after his term began, Bigelow took an unusual trip for a political appointee. He toured state and country prisons for two weeks with Harmon Eldredge, head keeper at Sing Sing, to discover for himself what practical improvements his board might undertake. Soon he was engrossed in the problem of discipline. He learned that theories concerning the treatment of convicts varied widely in respect to work, food, and punishment. He found that little problems, such as whether to allow the use of tobacco — a matter of more concern to the average prisoner than any amount of theory — were apt to be tossed aside by reformers intent upon the major issues: should prisons exist to punish or redeem men? What effect did prison labor have on convict morale? Upon the free labor with which it competed? To discuss a weekly plug of tobacco was descending to the ridiculous. Yet Bigelow was willing to descend; he canvassed the keepers of the prisons, and on the basis of their replies he campaigned in reports to the Assembly and in the columns of the *Democratic Review* and the *Evening Post* until in 1846 weekly rations of tobacco were permitted.[8] It was no great achievement, but it was a practical blessing to many human beings.

The officers of the prison and the men and women confined there soon knew that this board of inspectors was unlike most. It worked and it accomplished much of what it set out to do. It appointed keeper, agent, and chaplain on the basis of ability to serve. It accepted the reformers' view which Bigelow expressed in the words: "all punishment which merely insults, depraves," and it required that all offenses be reported in writing to the head keepers who alone were allowed to set punishments. "In consequence of this, the accomplishments of reading and writing were added to those which had previously been esteemed sufficient for this class of officers." [9] The antireform minority on the board at once had backing as the old group of illiterate assistant keepers, hardened brutes all of them, lost their jobs. Local contractors sided with them too. For years they had battened on sales to the prison and on overworked, underpaid contract prison labor. Now the board

of the Mt. Pleasant Prison at Sing Sing saved money by placing whole-
sale orders with reputable out-of-town firms. It was convinced, always
by a three-to-two decision, that separation of prison from town interests was essential to the welfare of the inmates and the economy of
state funds. Graft was out of vogue.

At the head of the women's prison the inspectors retained Mrs. Eliza
Farnham — an amazing woman, strong-minded, sensitive, committed to
the cause of penal reform. "The most sacred duty which can attach to
the administration of any penal institution is the reformation of its
inmates," she reported to the inspectors; and they for the first time,
in January 1846, included the matron's statement in their report to the
legislature. Bigelow, Powers, and Mace heartily agreed with her revolutionary views, though she astounded many honest men and her report
brought sneers and recriminations from prison profiteers. Soon the
resolute woman brought out an American edition of M. B. Sampson's
Rationale of Crime, relying upon Bigelow and her friend, William
Cullen Bryant, for counsel in planning the form of her work and in
arranging for its publication and favorable reception. By permitting
an artist to visit Sing Sing, Bigelow made possible the inclusion of outline drawings of the head formations of American criminals, which
Mrs. Farnham considered her most important addition to the original.
So he materially assisted the making of a book which stimulated a
more scientific attitude toward penology, though, it is equally true, it
nourished curiosity about phrenology.[10]

Yet reform moved slowly. It would move slowly, these lawyer
inspectors knew, for reform was the slow-changing attitude of a
whole people. They could not expect much to result from the little
kindnesses they had so recently brought to New York's prisons.
Vicious hate stored for years would not dissolve at once, as a letter
Bigelow received in July 1846 proved. The writer was a good citizen
and a delightful speller, who put responsibility for the welfare of
strangers above a normal distaste for telling tales on himself. His letter
began: "Jefferson Addams to the Jentilman inspectors of the new york
States prison." This seemed a promising opening. Bigelow read on:

> Sirs i am a native of portland and i giniraley viset the city onse
> or twise evrey six months, the reason that i take this liberty is i
> thinck that it is no more than my duty to inform you all that there
> is a snare prepareing for someone of you. . . . Sirs previous to my
> departure i was on what the saylor turmes it a cruze laust night
> and to my disgrace i will relate to you in what port i past the night
> it was in little warten Street. . . . Sirs about half past one oclock
> two females entered my apartment and than passed to the next

and closed the door arfter them i arose from the Bed to watch there movements through a hole in the dore one of them drew a latter from her bossom and delivered it to her companion stating that it was from up the river. . . . i am ashamed to relate the whol contents but the names of the inspectors and matrons ware roughly handled. . . . the letter requested her to inguer enny of the inspectors by heaveing some poisonous lickwid upon them or setting on fire some of there dwellings it did not matter which one But to do her work clean. . . .[11]

There was no way to reason with such women, even though Addams supplied the names of the two who swore to "inguer" the inspectors. They could only take precautions.

On the other hand some prisoners turned to them as friends. One man, for example, who had completed his term wrote to Bigelow preferring charges against the prison doctor. He had faith that this board of inspectors would improve conditions if upon investigation his charges proved true, for, he wrote:

I know from the reformation that you & the other members of the board of Inspectors has made in that Institution it gives me to know that you are men possessed of feelings of simpathy, for the afliction of your fellow men.

Another ex-convict wrote to Bigelow along similar lines:

Sir I take the pen to inform you that I am in trubles and without your asistance things will gou hard with me although I am inosent Sir.[12]

Meanwhile the antireform group was not idle. In 1845 they tried to discredit a new and honest agent. In 1846 they started a whispering campaign against Mrs. Farnham, when their favorite chaplain was dismissed to be replaced by a reformer, Matthew Gordon. In 1847 they joined Keeper Eldredge in protest against the novels Chaplain Gordon and Mrs. Farnham brought to the inmates, objecting particularly to *Oliver Twist* and *Nicholas Nickleby*, the dangerous social novels of Dickens, and they were incensed, as Eldredge was, when the reformers advocated teaching the illiterate to read and write. Finally, when the honest but tradition-bound head keeper said he would resign unless all the prison officials were made to realize that prisons were to punish, the majority on the board hastened to accept his resignation before he could retract it. It fell to Bigelow to examine candidates for the position. He decided to select a man already acquainted with the problems of Sing Sing instead of bringing in a stranger. At his insistence, the board took the unprecedented step of appointing the much-talked-of chaplain, Matthew Gordon, as head keeper. A reforming cleric was at the head of New York's largest prison.[13]

That was the last major change of the inspectors of 1845 to 1848. They had successfully striven for small comforts for the men behind bars; they had raised the standards which assistants must meet, had made one person accountable for all punishments, and had put reformers in control. They had induced the legislature to appropriate $100 for books, which with contributions from friends provided the beginnings of an attractive library. What they now urged, in conjunction with the Prison Association, was full-time employment of a teacher. Unfortunately the term of their board was expiring by the time they secured the necessary legislative permission in 1847. Bigelow determined, therefore, to seek another term, in spite of the hard work and enmities it meant, in order to see to it that the education of prisoners was commenced. But the state prison inspectorships had become elective positions under the new state constitution adopted in 1846. Bigelow, now a Free-Soiler, could not buck the party machine sufficiently to win a nomination; his friends were powerless to help him, and antireform men took over.[14]

Benjamin Mace did not care. He wrote to Bigelow:

> I am rejoiced that I am clear of the whole concern, and would not endeavor for the next what I have for the last three years for the whole of Sing Sing and parson Lucky to boot — and how in the name of *common sense* you could ever have permitted your name to be used a second time was to me a perfect mystery — It would have been worse than a death and burial. . . . Take the advice of a friend, and never or at least for ten years to come permit your name to be used in connection with any office *whatever* except that of "J Bigelow's law office." . . .[15]

Sound financial advice though it was, Bigelow remained bitterly disappointed. He had wanted to see through this job undertaken for the benefit of his fellow men. Though that had become impossible, one last chance remained to set forth his beliefs. Their third and last annual report to the legislature must be drafted. Bigelow, the most facile writer on the board and the most energetic worker, assumed that burden, as he had for the past two years. He pointed out that prison earnings in 1847 had increased while expenses had been cut. Insinuation could blur but not blot out the fact that their board had markedly improved prison finances, which had been the chief problem confronting it, according to its first report in 1845, signed by all five members.[16]

How had the saving been accomplished? That was the question which interested reformers. Decent treatment and a minimum of degrading punishments, Bigelow asserted, had obtained from the convicts the most orderly conduct and the best work record in the prison's history. Yet that had not saved the reformers from vituperation, and against the lying rumors Bigelow vented his rage:

. . . We should hardly be excused, however, if we were to pass over in silence the fact, of which we could scarcely affect to be ignorant, that widely different views from these, of the character and results of the present Board of Inspectors, have been entertained by some and expressed by more, and that efforts have been made by ignorant and designing persons to prejudice the public mind, and especially the legislative authorities against every effort which has been made by this Board, as well as by philanthropists throughout the State, to meliorate the discipline of our prisons, and to subject it to the supremacy of the same intellectual and moral influences which are found most available in the government and training of free citizens. From such sources have emanated statements reeking with falsehood, absurdity and brutality, which have passed from mouth to ear, until they have found expression on the floor of the legislature, from whence they have issued with disastrous currency over the land, threatening to cover with an overwhelming popular prejudice all our labors, and the efforts of those who have labored with us, for the establishment of an enlightened penitentiary system.[17]

It was December 1847 when Bigelow completed this hard-hitting report and submitted it to his colleagues. Powers and Mace promptly signed. Fisher and Dean promptly refused to sign. The legislature had not asked for a full description of the new system of penal discipline; certainly those two men did not intend to assist the spread of reform propaganda. In fact, and not without intent, Bigelow had made their position awkward. To combat charges of relaxed discipline and consequent financial loss, he had compared conditions in 1847 with 1839–1840. In that notorious year Fisher had been an inspector and Dean an assistant keeper. If the two men should sign Bigelow's report, they would indict their own earlier conduct. Therefore they turned in to the Assembly a separate minority report, seeking to prove by twisted figures that prison discipline and earnings had steadily declined since 1839–1840, and objecting to the majority statement that "the cardinal object of all penal discipline we have supposed to be the reformation of the offenders."[18] To them the cardinal object was the protection of the community.

Within a month came another and totally unexpected attack upon the retiring board of inspectors. Its chairman, old Judge Powers, was overcome with grief and shock and pain. He wrote a long, helpless letter to Bigelow, praying him to do something: "Nothing has occurred in my official relations with the prison before . . . which makes me *feel* that *our characters* were touched by the conduct of others, who had office under us." Mace received a similar letter from the Judge, and gaily soothed him: ". . . the acceptance of the office of State Prison Inspector presupposed a total absence of all character, and therefore we should not trouble ourselves upon that point." Mace was troubled, however, and so was Bigelow. On February 8 the new board of inspectors had petitioned the Assembly for $75,074.11 to enable them to carry on their work. It was a huge sum, completely discrediting the accounts submitted by Bigelow's board; if warranted, it would disgrace the whole reform movement. The worst discrepancy was one item of $20,000. Were the inspectors of 1845–1848 thieves or gullible fools unfit for responsibility? [19]

Bigelow wrote to Hiram Rowell, the financial agent his board had hired, for information. Again he wrote: "Come down tomorrow if you value your character or ours and have anything to defend yourself with." Meanwhile Judge Powers deluged Bigelow with letters — he was convinced that they had been deceived — he was in the dark — why didn't Rowell answer? — what were they to do?

At last Rowell offered some hope. He thought he could untangle the charges and clear both himself and the board, but he needed time. Bigelow worried and waited, unable to prepare a counterattack without more information. That came two weeks later, in the form of pages of figures refuting the new board's statements. Bigelow shaped them, wrote some pertinent letters, talked with William Cullen Bryant. The next day the *Evening Post* came out on their side; other friends followed suit, and vindication surged forward. "God bless you," wrote Mace. "You have taken the hide entirely off from Esquire Spencer" — member of the new board. "But I doubt whether he has brains enough to realize it." [20]

To A. K. Hadley, Speaker of the Assembly, Bigelow sent a detailed answer to the charges. All of his legal training in logic and analysis, all of his self-training in literary exposition, he put to the test in this paper which must clear his own reputation and that of the cause for which he had labored. The result was a statement unexceptionable in every way. He proved beyond doubt fraud in the new board's listing of unpaid debts until that figure dropped close to what his board had estimated. Next he proved the existence of sizable assets which the new inspectors had failed to mention. Finally, he proved once more that their disciplinary measures had not hurt finances. There was nothing more to say. After a legislative inquiry [21] and after widespread newspaper publicity redounding to the credit of the board of 1845–1848, the matter was closed and Bigelow's official connection with prisons ended.

CHAPTER 5

Reforming Publicist

[*1845–1848*]

THE THREE YEARS during which Bigelow served as a prison inspector
marked the period in which he achieved financial independence
and an established position among reforming publicists. Little need be
said of his law practice, for, though it provided a steady income, it
never engrossed his attention. He rarely mentioned cases in letters to
friends and he rarely had legal propositions on his mind when he sat
down to his diary in the late evening. Several months before he became
an inspector at Sing Sing he did accept with alacrity an offer of a law
partnership from Edgar H. Seeley, an established, reputable lawyer
who had approved Bigelow's capable handling of small cases and had
observed his acquaintance with political bigwigs. But he accepted it
solely for the sure footing in his profession and the sure income Seeley
offered. The details of most cases bored him as much as ever; the law
still seemed as confining as that narrow desk he once had occupied in
Dey and Bonney's office. Within a few months he was to publish,
anonymously of course, the summation of his views upon the place of
a lawyer in America:

> It is scarcely too much to say that the great mass of his pure law
> learning, might be erased from his mind, without materially im-
> pairing his interest as a companion, or his usefulness and value
> as a citizen; and yet we are well satisfied that the members of no
> other literary profession undergo the same amount of sheer in-
> tellectual labor, as the same numbers of lawyers. . . .
> The preliminary study and thought which are necessary to
> qualify a young lawyer to hold his first brief, would suffice to
> master the learning of almost any of the practical sciences, and
> then he would have the best of his mature life to widen its circle.
> His labors, too, would then be sustained by the consciousness that
> he was enlarging the sphere of human intelligence; that his indus-
> try, and perhaps his name, would go down to posterity, associated
> with the causes or the instruments of some of its most substantial
> enjoyments.

If parents, and the friends, whose duty it is to direct the education of our young men, would properly consider these things, we are persuaded they would spare themselves and their charges much of the mortification and anxiety, which always pursue defeated hopes.[1]

The bitter words mirrored his own frustration. He was a student of American institutions and American conditions, and while he believed them the best in the world, he wanted to see them improved. More than that, he wanted a hand in their improvement. The work he was doing at Sing Sing was in the right direction but prison reform concerned only a small per cent of the people. What he earnestly desired was an opportunity to publicize other reforms which needed the enlightened support of the mass of Americans in order to become part of the American way. So when O'Sullivan asked him, later in '45, to give full-time service to the *Democratic Review* as managing editor — the position Bigelow had day-dreamed about the previous year — he was sorely tempted. Here was not only an opportunity to further the cause of reform, but, more selfishly, a chance to know well all the writers of the day. Already Bigelow had bowing acquaintance with many contributors to the magazine; with, for example, William Gilmore Simms, whom he met at the Duyckincks' home. He did not like Simms; as he noted in his journal, the Southerner was too full of

. . . pride and intolerance of conflicting opinion. He looks upon his particular section of the south as the geographers of the fourteenth century looked upon Jerusalem. . . . His style in society . . . is overbearing but energetic — He scatters terribly and talks elements. This is partly attributable to his habits of talking with uncultivated people whose ignorance of elements force him to leave the line of his conversation continually to instruct them and partly to a defective discipline. At present he has no concentrativeness.[2]

Yet though he did not like him, he liked meeting him, just as he liked meeting Edgar Allan Poe and hearing the rumor, which proved to be false, that Poe was including him in his articles upon "The Literati of New York." If he became managing editor of the *Review* he would meet other writers. He would drop in frequently at the Duyckincks', for Evert A. Duyckinck was literary editor of the *Review* and, as everyone knew, his home was a center for authors.

Yet though he would gladly forsake law, he would not embrace poverty. He offered to work on the *Review* for $2000 a year and a contingency fund, knowing as he made the offer that O'Sullivan could not afford him. In effect he chose Seeley and security rather than O'Sullivan and letters, chose future power through accumulated wealth in preference to the present power of influencing others through the written word. Then O'Sullivan offered the perfect straddle, the chance to pursue the will-o'-the-wisp while maintaining his law partnership with Seeley. He offered, and Bigelow accepted, $500 a year for twenty pages a month and management of the political department of the magazine — that is, pay at the rate of about two dollars a page, twice what Boston's *North American Review* paid its contributors.[3]

Days became minutes; parties, music, planning the cyclopedia, browsing through books, all belonged to the leisurely past. Bigelow still read prodigiously, but he read only for an immediate purpose upon subjects related to penology, to some article or project he had in mind, or to the law. Except for *Martin Chuzzlewit* he did not look at a novel for over a year; limited time required a prompt return from its investment. He had a new law office, a decent income from it, and more legal work than ever before. He had a political appointment which kept him commuting several times a month to Sing Sing, planning reforms, drafting reports. He was now Recording Secretary of the New York Historical Society, which took time but was worth it, because as an officer he had full use of its reference library. Best of all, he had a steady position on New York's finest literary political magazine with an opportunity to advocate improvements in which Jacksonian reformers believed.

While this arrangement lasted, and it continued even after O'Sullivan sold the magazine to T. P. Kettell and H. Wykoff in 1846, Bigelow had freedom to choose his own subjects, provided he kept politics in the foreground. Hence what appeared in the *Review* revealed the trend of his thought during his late twenties. Many of his pages were filled with book reviews, not gentle, temporizing comments upon subject matter and style, but vigorous essays on beliefs. A book, if effective, led to reflection, and his own reflections upon the mores of contemporary America were primarily what Bigelow offered the public. A reader of his review of Horace Twiss's biography of Lord Eldon, Chancellor of England, forgets the author, indeed, almost forgets Lord Eldon as someone other than Bigelow might have judged him. He remembers Bigelow's decision: intellect, excellent; moral character, bad: "selfish, avaricious, and deceitful; a hypocrite, a sycophant, and a coward." The conclusion is worth quoting in full, for as he sat down to his diary evening after evening or perhaps after a lapse of months, the same thoughts often found their way to the paper:

There are more Eldons in the world than Mr. Twiss has written the life of. We have them in our country, and in every party and sect of politics and religion. . . . They are called prudent and safe men. They usually spring from poverty rather by meanness than talent, and become rich, and cut all their relatives and acquaintances less wealthy than themselves; they are generally officers of some church and sundry benevolent societies. . . . In politics they are conservative. They like low taxes but liberal monopolies, sound currency but high interest. . . . Offenses against property they think much more serious than those against the person. Capital punishments they believe to be necessary to the very existence of man in society, and imprisonment for debt indispensable to his prosperity and virtue. They foresee anarchy in every popular demonstration, and public ruin in every reform. In short they bear the same relation to society that the vis inertia does to matter. They have always to be overcome before there can be any progress.[4]

In another review he urged a liberal reform party, first penning an orthodox summary of Michelet's *The Priest — The Wife — The Family*, then forgetting Michelet as he enlarged the meaning of "Jesuitism" to suit what he wanted to say to Americans. Jesuitism, he said, referred ". . . to all those of every religious denomination who are more zealous for their church than for Christianity, more particular about ends than means, who resist the teachings of their instincts as solicitations from the devil, who estimate their virtue by what they suffer rather than by what they enjoy . . . and who, in time, form a habit of deception that spreads over the whole surface of their character, perhaps without their ever suspecting its existence." Look at our colleges, he continued:

Have we a single college which is not sectarian — which is not commonly spoken of as an Episcopal, or Presbyterian, or Unitarian, or Catholic college. . . . Why is it that all our young men who enter college without any fixed political opinions, invariably leave conservative upon all — wrapt in admiration for the past and full of contempt for every tendency which indicates the future? While almost as frequently, those who take to the active pursuits of life at the usual time for entering college, are so generally liberal and appreciative of whatever about them is indicative of progress or favorable change.[5]

Bigelow placed the blame on those priests of every faith who followed, even obstructed opinion, instead of leading it. Nor did he have much more use for socialist reformers, particularly the agrarians who demanded periodic equalization of landed property. They were too distant from reality. Bigelow was interested in practicable reforms such as scientists and artisans could accomplish. They alone, in his opinion, could strike at the core of social disorder — the deadening struggle for material possessions. They alone could teach men how to increase the product of their industry and how to measure their true necessities that they not become prey to conventional tastes. At the same time he believed that scientists and artisans could flourish only where civil liberty and ample recognition of individual independence existed. So he found a role for political reformers, who by guarding and enlarging the rights of individuals served as forerunners of an age of science.[6] Hence his advocacy of equal suffrage for men and women, rich and poor, white and black, and his call for the election of all public officials.

His article on the latter subject was the leader in an issue of the *Democratic Review* which carried contributions from Walter Whitman (he was not to be "Walt" for several years), from Whittier, Hawthorne, G. W. Curtis, and G. P. Putnam.[7] Bigelow's essay, like all of his, was not signed, yet some New Yorkers, among them William Cullen Bryant, knew who the fiery young democrat was, and knew him as a man who felt strongly, thought clearly, and worked indefatigably, whose days and evenings were so crowded with legal work, writing, and prison reform that he rarely had time for the pleasures he loved so much, for a picnic sail up the Hudson or for a ball or theater party with Miss Granger or Miss Selden or Miss Bayard.

It was during this period that Bigelow came to know Bryant well. To a slight degree, proximity was the cause, for Bigelow had moved to Amity Place and had taken comfortable rooms on the second floor of the two-story house where the Bryants lived. Bigelow's movable shower bath proved irresistible to Bryant, who before long shared it on a schedule satisfactory to both, since the poet invariably was up and dressed before the lawyer was awake.[8] Fundamentally what drew them together was a similarity of viewpoint. Both men were seriously concerned with man's progress on earth; both had a living faith that improvement was possible. Neither was attracted by the panacea of any one "ism"; neither had any use for a perfectly drawn chart of a revolutionized world. They were distrustful of fanatics and antagonized by the flagrantly experimental, preferring a practical, evolutionary approach to reform. Each believed that as a publicist he could best serve society. Moreover, in politics both were Jacksonian Democrats of the free-trade, sound-money school, and Radicals who objected to President Polk's expansionist schemes and considered the proposed annexation of Texas the equivalent of an unjustifiable declaration of war against Mexico.

The moral evil of such a war did not concern Bigelow so much as the danger of expansion to the welfare of the United States. If Polk could make political capital of the annexation of Texas, what was to hinder another from advocating the annexation of all Mexico, and still another from seeking position by calling for the annexation of Canada? Moreover, there was every reason to expect New Mexico, Chihuahua, California, and Yucatán to follow the lead of Texas, and, throwing off the Mexican yoke, declare their independence and seek entrance into the United States. At the risk of being labeled an alarmist, Bigelow faced the issue of territorial aggrandizement in the October 1845 issue of the *Democratic Review*.[9] He saw no constitutional objection to the unlimited extension of the United States; he saw no moral objection to the unlimited expansion of democracy. But to lose democracy in the process of spreading it would be tragedy. He thought eventual annexation of Mexico was inevitable, but to move too rapidly would be suicide.

Should Mexico in its present stage of political development, or sections of Mexico, be added to the United States, the average political intelligence of the enlarged republic would be reduced. Untrained in self-government, Mexicans would require direction from Washington, which would result in precisely what Radicals wanted to avoid: greater centralization of government and an unprogressive period in the old states while the new ones slowly approximated their political level. Far preferable for Mexican and American alike would be conquest by moral agencies alone. Let the United States continue to develop democratically. Let Mexicans see for themselves the advantages of democratic institutions; let them voluntarily adopt similar ones and in the process train themselves in self-government. Then, if of their own volition they should ask to join the Union, they would be able to take a place in it without destroying its capacity for continuous growth in freedom. So Bigelow believed. So, too, did Bryant.

On still other issues Bigelow's views proved similar to Bryant's. Since his first essay on constitutional reform in 1843, Bigelow had continued to study the constitutional needs of New York and the importance of constitutional guarantees to democracy, collecting copies of other states' constitutions, poring over the revisions so many states were in the process of making, publicizing his findings and his opinions in his column in the *Democratic Review* and in Bryant's *Evening Post*. He wrote almost every item on that subject carried by either of those journals in the '40's. In no instance was he the first to suggest a needed revision; most of the weaknesses in the New York Constitution of 1821 had been pointed out long before he reached his majority, and some lawyers and politicians had urged revision years before he began to study the subject. Yet probably no man, initiator or publicist, deserved more credit than he for interesting educated but ordinarily apathetic citizens in the need for action or for stating possible changes in terms intelligible to laymen.[10]

New Yorkers finally called for a constitutional convention. The delegates assembled in June 1845, whereupon anti-renters, locofocos, and judicial reformers urged their special interests. Bigelow, also, through a pamphlet reprint of an article of his in the *Democratic Review*, pressed his views upon the Radical majority of the convention. A number of the changes which he advocated were adopted: wider suffrage, direct election of officials formerly appointed (including judges, which Bigelow lived to regret), elections to the legislature from separate districts, end of the legislature's power to contract debts at will, a ban on all inspection laws which interfered with the liberty of trade or business, a simplified method for amending the Constitution, and a reorganized court system consolidating law and equity courts.[11]

Other changes which Bigelow urged in print and in private correspondence with leaders of the convention failed to carry. He urged the extension of suffrage to all men eighteen years and over, be they black or white. If an age limit must be included, it would be better, he said, to disenfranchise men over seventy than to keep the youths who had their whole future before them from having a say in the shaping of their world. He believed that the common-school fund should be applied to the present crippling state debt and that thereafter the state should cease to propagate any science, art, trade, or religion among any class of people. He wanted an end to the death penalty. He wanted individual liability clauses written in all corporation charters and all incorporations to be made under general laws. But in these, as in other measures, he was too radical for the Radical convention.

Yet in spite of his disappointment he favored adoption of the Constitution drafted in 1846. A half loaf was better than none. So he wrote in the *Democratic Review* and the *Evening Post* just before the vote was cast, urging his readers to vote "yes." Once the Constitution was accepted, Bigelow took an active part in preparing for the judicial election authorized for the spring of 1847. He issued a call for a meeting of the bar association to consider how it could render effective the new judiciary system, and became one of a committee of thirteen asked to draft recommendations. He worked almost singlehanded for the nomination of his friend E. P. Hurlbut to the Supreme Court, winning thirty-seven votes for him at the Democratic convention, where but six men knew Hurlbut, and later helped in his election.[12] He continued his study of constitutional revision. He continued to fear centralized government, and the tendency of legislators to grant corporations freedom from personal liability, writing:

> Too much government has a direct tendency to aid one man or one set of men in the "pursuit of happiness," and in the "acquiring, possessing and protecting property," if not at the expense of the rest, at least without rendering them the like assistance. As far as the conditions of animal existence go, there is very little difference in the ability of all men to provide for themselves and families; and if all were left without any special aid from government, both land and the products of industry would be far more equally distributed than they are. . . . It is, however, the case, that four-fifths of the action of all legislation, is, by law, to promote the accumulation of prosperity in a few hands.[13]

And constantly he reiterated his contention that "change as men and factions may there will still remain but two parties, the one of progress & reform, the other of conservatism & monopoly." [14]

CHAPTER 6

With Bryant on the *Evening Post*

[*1848–1849*]

ANNE CHARLOTTE LYNCH, the poetess who taught school to support herself and her widowed mother, lived in a charming, unpretentious house on East Ninth Street. There she was at home every Saturday evening to her friends, and there she created, in the late 1840's, the one true salon in America, vastly different from the competitively ornate, banal receptions of the stylish. Bigelow was pleased to be of the group who had a standing invitation to come whenever they could, for in a sense that placed him among the leading figures of New York's literary and artistic worlds. There he frequently met his friends the Duyckinck brothers, Bryant, Halleck, Theodore and Catherine Sedgwick, Parke Godwin, and N. P. Willis, and there he became acquainted with Poe, Rufus W. Griswold, Grace Greenwood, George P. Morris, George Bancroft, and Bayard Taylor. Sometimes Anne Lynch read a poem she had just completed, or one of her guests read something of theirs; it was at her home, for example, that Poe's "The Raven" was introduced to the world. And the talk and music were always good.[1]

As Bigelow was escorting Mrs. Farnham home from such an evening in February 1847, the reforming matron of Sing Sing intimated that she had been asked to sound him out about joining the *Evening Post*. Bigelow responded with leaping heart and that caution typical of his father; he was interested, of course, but he doubted if the *Evening Post* could improve his prospects. If Bryant thought it could, Bigelow would be glad to hear from him. Within a month Bryant made a direct overture. Repeatedly during the following year he urged Bigelow to name his own figure and become a salaried employee. Each time Bigelow returned the same answer: if Wm. C. Bryant & Co. really wanted him, they would make him a partner; anything else for him would be a step backward. He had realized, he wrote Eames somewhat later, "the folly of any persons attempting to do anything for himself or anybody else without money. . . . I shall be a very great fool to let any more of my life step away without garnering up for the future some of that power which is *power*." [2]

It was evident that Bryant wanted him, even if he could not at the moment offer a partnership. During his twenty years on the *Post* the poet had longed time and again to escape its irksome duties. Now in his fifties, he wanted leisure more than ever, yet with his income wholly dependent upon the paper he could not afford long vacations unless he left in his place a man he could trust. Parke Godwin, his son-in-law who worked for him, was in many ways an asset, but there was always a fear in Bryant's mind that, given a free hand, Godwin might repeat with some current equivalent his earlier stunt of inserting Fourieristic propaganda after having been expressly forbidden.[3] Of all the men Bryant knew, young Bigelow seemed the most desirable for the *Evening Post*. His political and economic views, similar to Bryant's, would insure continuity of policy. His distinguished style measured up to Bryant's high standards. His ability to concentrate, his wide acquaintance with books and people, his studies of political theory combined with the practical experience in politics that he had gained in the campaign of '44, all pointed to him as the man for the place. Moreover, Bigelow accepted Bryant's philosophy of journalism. He disdained the sensational appeal of the penny *Sun*. He considered the emphasis upon news-gathering and gossip which characterized James Gordon Bennett's *Herald* a regrettable departure from the function of a journal which should inform opinion, not reflect it; interpret, not narrate. And though he acknowledged the brilliance and compelling vigor of many of Greeley's editorials, he mistrusted Greeley's untempered enthusiasms and of course disagreed with his Whig political principles.

With each passing month Bryant's need for an assistant became more acute. In September 1847, six months after he first asked Bigelow to work for him, the New York Democratic party split wide apart at the annual state convention where the majority were Conservatives, derisively called "Hunkers" after their avid "hunkering" for patronage led them to approve of the annexation of Texas. In a tense session they tabled David Dudley Field's resolution approving the Wilmot Proviso (which forever forbade slavery in the territories acquired from Mexico), declared the motion out of order when the Radicals offered it a second time, and in the ensuing tumult slipped from the room to avoid a roll call. A new era was commencing. The issue of human freedom in the territories had become paramount. Aroused Radicals, refusing to sacrifice the principle of the Proviso, seceded in a body,

Post, had served on his local Committee of Organization and Correspondence, had helped set up a Free-Soil speakers' bureau; he had even made a few speeches.[6] Nevertheless, it was apparent that the life of the new party depended upon stronger organization, larger membership, and a supporting press. In New York City, when Greeley swung his *Tribune* to Taylor, only the *Evening Post* was left to support the antislavery party. And the *Evening Post* needed someone to assist Bryant, someone more willing and able than he to leave the desk and move from principles to immediate areas of conflict. During the campaign Bryant and Tilden pressed Bigelow to leave the law. But he wisely stood his ground: first let a partnership be offered to him. Finally, in the last phase of the campaign, William Boggs, the amiable but uneducated printer who held three tenths of the *Post* shares, was persuaded to sell.

There remained just one obstacle; Boggs's shares were worth $15,000, and Bigelow had no money. Bryant guaranteed Boggs $12,500 in regular installments at seven per cent interest, which Bigelow was to pay, and agreed to let Bigelow repay the principal at his convenience out of his earnings. But Bryant could not raise the $2500 in cash which the retiring partner needed immediately; the credit of Wm. C. Bryant & Co. was too shaky for the company to borrow at the banks. So it was up to Bigelow somehow to raise the money.[7] If he succeeded, he would be part owner and co-editor of the paper which had always seemed to him unequaled in America, partner of the man he respected more than any man he had ever known, and established member of the profession he had wanted to join for ten years. Put another way, if he raised the money, he would give up the honorable and lucrative profession of law to join a limping paper which was itself unable to raise $2500.

Bigelow took counsel with Tilden, who tried to borrow the money on his own note from his lifelong friend William F. Havemeyer, Mayor of New York, soon to be president of the Bank of North America. When Tilden was turned down, Bigelow was dismayed. One by one he thought over his list of acquaintants. Those who had money had no reason to gamble it; those who would be glad to help had not so large a sum of money. Then he thought of Charles O'Conor, at forty-four one of New York's truly great jurists. As a member of the constitutional convention, O'Conor had written Bigelow frequently about possible judicial changes. Moreover, he was always friendly, though they met only on business or as fellow members of a bar association committee; he seemed to respect the younger man; he had money beyond his needs, and he had an integrity which would never demand a *quid pro quo*. On the other hand, he had fought against acceptance of the Constitution of 1846; he had opposed the three major changes made in the judiciary which Bigelow had supported — election of judges, union of equity and law cases, abolition of county courts. And, as a Conservative Democrat, a Hunker, at the very moment running for the lieutenant-governorship on the ticket which the *Evening Post* had sworn to defeat, he certainly would have every reason to refuse. Yet Bigelow could think of no one else who might help him — except his father, to whom he did not wish to apply: he had received $2000 from Asa Bigelow before he had established himself in the law; now, if he went home to say he was throwing aside his legal training and added that after ten years in New York he was unable to get credit, his father, who had never borrowed a cent, would have every reason to doubt his son's capabilities. So he approached O'Conor. Before he could complete his statement, the older man interrupted with a hearty: "Of course. Bring the notes around." From that day to the end of his life Bigelow called O'Conor "my greatest benefactor." [8]

Readers found at the head of the *Evening Post's* editorial column on December 5, 1848:

Notice
The co-partnership heretofore existing between Wm. C. Bryant, William G. Boggs, and Timothy A. Howe, is this day dissolved by mutual consent.
Dated November 15, 1848.

Card
The undersigned have pleasure in announcing that John Bigelow has been this day associated with them as one of the editors and proprietors of this paper.
All business with the printing or publishing departments of the *Evening Post* office will continue to be transacted in the name of
WM. C. BRYANT & CO.
Dated December 5, 1848.

Bryant retained control of policy, four tenths of the *Evening Post* shares and three tenths of the job office. Bigelow, owning three tenths of the *Post* and two-tenths of the job office, was to share with him the editorial tasks, while the third partner, Timothy Howe, whose financial interest equaled Bigelow's, continued as business manager.

Bigelow, just turned thirty-one years of age, was for the first time contented with his position in the world. Yet even for a partner who had little capital involved, the *Evening Post* was a gamble, as he very

With Bryant's permission he wrote out a card which he inserted at the head of the editorial column on January 24, 1849, and thereafter ran almost daily:

> We beg our subscribers and friends to bear in mind that, attached to the *Evening Post* Office is a well appointed Book and Job Printing establishment, prepared to execute any kind of printing that may be required.
>
> Special attention will be given to the printing of law cases and points, with accuracy, neatness and dispatch. We trust that our claims upon the good will of our personal, political and professional friends, may not be overlooked.

Widely acquainted with lawyers and judges, Bigelow energetically went after the business. He told his former colleagues that his company could render better service than any other outfit, for with a lawyer on its staff it would make no mistake in setting up forms which to most printers were strange and complicated. His salesmanship succeeded. Once jobs started coming their way, others followed until the *Evening Post* handled almost all the legal printing in New York City. To ensure holding his customers, Bigelow laid down a hard and fast rule: no job was to be turned away for lack of time, even if it were necessary to sublet work to every paper in town. Steadily net profits rose in the job office from less than $100 the year before Bigelow became a partner to more than $10,000 ten years later, and that increase, after Bigelow's initial aggressiveness, came without either Bryant or Bigelow putting in three days' work a year in that end of the business. It was no wonder that Bigelow was remembered for decades after he left the *Post* as the man who could wring profits from an intellectual enterprise.[12]

While Bryant was away in '49, Bigelow wrote almost all of the paper. Parke Godwin, who had intended to fill in for Bryant, caught the fever, so that Bigelow was left with only a youth who read exchanges and the marine reporter. Finally he hired a man for sixteen dollars a week and wrote to Bryant of the relief it was to have an energetic, though inexperienced, helper. Bigelow himself kept in condition with cold baths, plenty of water, no medicine; drove himself relentlessly, and looked with pride and optimism upon his management of the *Post*. "I have not had a fight since you left," he wrote Bryant gaily in the fall; as to the paper: "I have heard no complaints or of any having been made about it."[13]

In fact, a growing subscription list and a voluminous private correspondence rewarded his maintenance of the Free-Soil line. Gossip came to him from Albany, Washington, Boston, the West. Much of it libelous, it could not appear in editorials or over a signature. So, early in the year he had invented "John Brown, Ferryman," and with impudence, sarcasm and humor, John Brown, New Jersey ferryman, commenced writing to the *Post* on February 17, relating what politicians told him as they crossed the river on their way to and from Washington. He described patronage deals, plans for the Cabinet, and the growing feud between Vice-President Fillmore and William H. Seward, New York's ex-Governor whom Bigelow had so uncomplimentarily described in his diary five years before and who had just been elected to the Senate. He explained quite accurately how Seward and Thurlow Weed, editor of the *Albany Evening Journal*, ran New York, city and state, without the President's knowledge.

> They have filled nearly every post office in the state with their men, without letting the President know it, and they are now working for the same results in other states. . . . This has been their game. They knew it would never do for them to play an open hand. Instead of that it has been, and continues to be their practice to press particular candidates, for whose success they are not solicitous, and to send on at the same time, cunning men to press other candidates of their own selection and their preference, though professedly opposed to them, for the double purpose of drawing off, and thereby weakening the strength of the real opposition, and also of throwing dust in the eyes of the President. The old man who has no more comprehension of such a phenomenon as the editor of the *Evening Journal*, than a shad has of steam navigation, fell right into the trap that was laid for him, and in trying to thwart the scheme of the priesthood at Albany, has given them all they want.[14]

He reported Abbott Lawrence en route to Washington to prove "the higher the duty the cheaper the article," asserted correctly that Lawrence refused a seat in the Cabinet when he heard Taylor's views on slavery, said that Hannegan, "the most abject of all the doughfaces in the heavens above, or in the earth beneath, or in the waters under the earth," was appointed Minister at Berlin as a reward for selling Indiana South. Clayton he dubbed "a phenomenon of laziness." Then he innocently wondered why there were so many flare-ups over his letters. To be sure, his data was not always accurate, but how was a poor ferryman to know? He passed on what he heard and always corrected himself later if better advised — of course after the damage was done. Yet John Brown's per cent of accuracy was astonishingly high, and the spicy gossip column became one of the first parts of the paper to read.[15]

By the spring of '49 it was painfully evident that the Hunker–Free-Soil feud in New York was strengthening the Whigs without helping either faction of the Democratic party, which, if it worked in unity, could control the state. So the politically wise young Hunker, Horatio Seymour, engineered a movement to reunite the party. Bigelow, as an editor of the leading Barnburner organ, took a major share in the negotiations, though he had no intention of sacrificing to party expediency his views on slavery. He served as a delegate to a special Barnburner convention which met in Rome, New York, on August 15, in the same city and on the same day as the Hunkers met, one group holding forth in the Presbyterian church, the other in the Baptist, in a mutual effort to compose their differences. Both factions agreed that slavery was evil. The Conservatives even accepted the Barnburners' contention that Congress had the power and the duty to prohibit the spread of slavery into free territory, unless local laws were already sufficiently prohibitory. Conflict arising at the usual point, however, over the application of the principle, the conventions adjourned after four days, no nearer unity than before. In the case of California, where thousands of gold-crazed people were pouring, Hunkers honestly believed that old local antislavery laws provided sufficient guarantees of freedom. Consequently they maintained that Congressional action would serve merely to irritate the South, while Barnburners, to the contrary, were convinced that without stronger antislavery legislation, freedom on the West Coast would be lost.[16]

What Bigelow thought of Hunker-Whig reasoning he described in the *Post* on August 30:

> . . . When we read of the princes of Dahomey or Gaboon entering the villages of their neighbors, burning their homes and carrying off their people to be sold into perpetual slavery, none can be found here so stolid or so politic as not to shiver with horror at the tale, but when it is proposed to open a new market for property thus acquired in a vast territory which we found free, and by force of arms have subjected to our rule, we find even in the state of New York, a party unwilling to express any opinion on the subject by which, as a party, they will be bound lest they peril thereby their political fortunes. It is a saddening reflection, that with all the political and social advantages which are enjoyed under American institutions, there should be so little difference, morally, between Gaboonism and Hunkerism, between the leaders in Dahomey and the leaders at Rome.

In September '49 Bigelow was a delegate to another Barnburner convention, this one meeting in Utica. Again a compromise with the

Hunkers was sought. This time it was effected. Not until later did most Free-Soil adherents realize the setback they had given their cause; that John Van Buren's antislavery views had become, through Seymour's skillful tailoring, a coat to be doffed when convenient; that for patronage and power and the right to verbalize their principles, they had surrendered to Hunkers control of their actions. At the moment many a Free-Soiler like Bigelow felt some misgiving yet on the whole was glad for the reunion. They reasoned that as a third party, a minority party, they would be powerless to set up free institutions in the territories, whereas if they worked with the Conservative Democrats, there was at least a chance that their views would prevail. Certainly few Barnburners who returned to the Democratic fold meant to compromise their Free-Soil tenets. Moreover, they were convinced that Southern threats of secession, should Free-Soil beliefs prevail, were utterly ridiculous. Bigelow editorialized:

> . . . the impotence, inconsistency and folly of those who make such threats, are becoming more conspicuous every time they are repeated. And yet there are those at the north who think we ought not to agitate any question about which the south differs from us, because it irritates the feelings of southern people and provokes sectional controversies. Then we may as well withdraw our northern representatives from Congress. The southern people are not educated to abide by the will of the majority. — They cannot reconcile themselves to the supremacy of any law by which they imagine their own interests are not to be promoted. And it is idle to suppose that the rights of the north can be preserved, if northern statesmen are to be silent, whenever southern politicians threaten disunion.[17]

If only Northern Democrats would drop appeasement!

CHAPTER 7

The Work and Opinions of a Liberal Editor

[*1850–1853*]

WHEN BRYANT returned in December, Bigelow departed for his first vacation, an even more pertinent busman's holiday than Bryant's, for he was going to Jamaica to write letters to the *Post* about the conditions and the capabilities of the free Negroes there and by implication to point the moral for the United States. He expected the hundred dollars he drew for the trip to give him a rest, a change, and a supply of antislavery ammunition. At three o'clock on the wintry afternoon of January 3, 1850, the ship on which he had passage, the *Empire City*, left its Hudson River pier. Thirty-two years before, Bigelow had been born near this same river. As a child playing by its bank, he had watched his father's laden ships edge slowly to the dock and watched the *Phoenix*, his father's pride, speed by every sloop in the region. Later he had sailed upriver for his schooling; then, for his fortune, downriver to New York. Now for the first time he was out on the ocean, seeking more schooling, more fortune.

The fifth day, the *Empire City* sailed into Kingston harbor, Jamaica, into a new world – the ship suddenly surrounded by shouting, grinning Negroes, bobbing up and down in their little boats, "some dressed decently and some dressed indecently and some not dressed at all." One energetic, gesticulating "commodore" took Bigelow ashore in a rowboat propelled by homemade oars fastened clumsily to its sides. He made a good "spot" for a reporter with his stout defense of his odd contraptions, showing "a force of logic which required nothing but a stupidity among his hearers, corresponding with his own, to render perfectly conclusive."

The town itself was dismal. Mean, one-story houses crowded both sides of roads so worn by rain and travel that the centers were one to three feet lower than the sides. Except for the insane asylum, closed for lack of funds, not a building was modern; all were as slovenly and dilapidated as the listless people slouching along the way.

Bigelow was not surprised. He had known that the once productive island was poverty-stricken, and he had come to see for himself and for readers of the *Post* that this was not the result of emancipation as so many Americans believed.

First he examined the government buildings, visiting the Jamaican House, where he found twenty-five bored men in a huge, scantly furnished room, gazing indifferently at one another or at the Speaker. Elected? Certainly they were elected; they represented the property owners of Jamaica. Admittedly that meant that less than one per cent of the people voted and that the interests of the commercial, industrial, and mechanical classes had no hearing. Yet even property owners had only a semblance of power, for sessions of their representatives could be called and dissolved at will by the English Crown-appointed Governor, and their every act must be approved by an appointed Council before it became law. Nevertheless, this government, undemocratic though it was, could not be entirely blamed for conditions in Jamaica.

What, then, was the root of the trouble? Americans in the South had long answered that the wage system which replaced slavery made competition with the slave-run sugar lands of South America impossible. Bigelow disproved that by incontrovertible figures showing that Jamaica had been insolvent before emancipation in 1834. He could find no indication whatsoever that the misery on the island was related to the legal status or the capabilities of the Negroes. Indeed, the theory that the Negro was inherently inferior to the white man was so repugnant to the Free-Soiler, so completely without foundation as far as he could learn, that he took pleasure in citing the successful operation of small farms by some hundred thousand blacks during the last sixteen years and in praising their wisdom in cultivating small patches of gardens in preference to working longer hours for whites at starvation wages. He concluded that the decadence, first evident in slavery days and increasingly obvious after emancipation, resulted almost entirely from the ruinous economy of a one-crop system and the absentee landlordism which for scores of years had swayed the fortunes of Jamaica.[1]

Three weeks is a short time in which to make accurate examination of even a small island, and when one of those weeks is spent in bed with a fever, the resulting study is apt to be sketchy. Bigelow did his best, however, and his best was good. Articles written on the island and others written at home from his notes appeared at intervals in the

Post between February and May 1850. Within a year they were collected and published in a two-hundred-and-fifty-page book. "To travel in foreign lands and to write a book about them and sell it all within a year is pretty rapid work," Bigelow confided jubilantly to his diary.[2]

His writing was easy, descriptive and touched with humor, yet comments in the American press were only fair. The book aroused little interest, and indeed was sneered at by political opponents like Charles A. Dana, who warned a friend soon to go to Jamaica, "B's book isn't worth a cent as a guide to forming an opinion." Yet more than eighty years later a foremost historian of the island rated Bigelow "an exceptionally well-qualified American observer. . ." who left "a good critical commentary." The liberal London *Examiner* expressed the same view in four long articles in 1851. Bigelow was elated. He wrote Charles Eames about them and copied part of one review into his diary: ". . . the most searching analysis of the present state of Jamaica, and moreover the most sagacious prognostications of the future prospects of the island that have even been published." When the influential *Westminster Review* carried a brief, friendly note about *Jamaica in 1850*, Bigelow thought of inserting the English comment in the *Post*, because he still had almost a hundred copies to dispose of. Bryant admitted that was normal practice, but when he quietly pointed out that he himself had never permitted praise of his poetry to appear in his paper, Bigelow dropped the idea.[3]

While Bigelow was in Jamaica, the slavery controversy flared again as California, asking admission as a free state, forced the Senate to declare itself. Once more a united South prepared to stand firm against the North. Once more fears, threats, recriminations swept the country. Once more and for the last time the old statesman, Senator Henry Clay of Kentucky, proposed a compromise: California should be a free state; in the other lands taken from Mexico, plebiscites, held when the territories applied for statehood, should decide between freedom and slavery; the slave trade, but not slavery, should be prohibited in the District of Columbia; a strict law should be passed providing for the return of fugitive slaves upon the demand of their masters. These measures were the topic of every conversation when Bigelow returned to America. He found that many former friends of freedom, men like Tilden and Horace Greeley, believed them reasonable and advocated their passage; yet he at once joined Bryant in the *Evening Post's* fight against them. He formed the habit of arriving at the office almost as early as Bryant, even gave up smoking because it interfered with concentrated work, and taught himself to write direct, hard-hitting editorials which were all the more stinging because they were so unlike the outbursts typical of other journals. Bigelow would never write of anyone, as Greeley did of Bryant: "You lie, villain! wilfully, wickedly, basely lie!" He would, instead, wither an opponent through ridicule or blast his position with a penetrating array of documented facts.

Bitterness culminated in March when Daniel Webster, idol of the Whig North, first orator of the century, for thirty years a fearless leader in the fight against the extension of slavery, rose in the Senate and pleaded for the compromise, for an end to disrupting talk. The speech stunned the country. Southerners suspected that the compromise must be pro-North; Northerners felt betrayed. Few men sensed Webster's agony when he realized, a decade before most men did, that talk of secession was not all bluff. Few could understand his need to choose, his bitter pain in choosing, between the two loyalties to which his life was dedicated, between Union and Freedom. Barnburners, Free-Soilers, Antislavery Whigs, honestly convinced that both could be theirs, labeled Webster a traitor and made of him an object for scorn and reviling.

As the great debate on the compromises progressed, the *Evening Post* was crowded with arguments against them, heaping ridicule, irony and personal abuse upon their proponents, offering what the editors considered fair-minded objections to their passage. The Fugitive Slave measure they found particularly odious. On May 8 they asked:

> But is it worthwhile for citizens at the north to part with their own liberty for the sake of adding to the facilities of a planter to reclaim a fugitive slave? Is it our duty to allow ourselves to be arrested at the pleasure of any man who pretends to own us as slaves . . . ? Is it absolutely necessary that all should be decided in a hurry, without a jury, and by men unacquainted with judicial proceedings or legal principles, and unaccustomed to judge of the weight of evidence? The rights of a slave-owner are protected by the Constitution but are the rights of a free man nothing? . . .
>
> To these questions our readers naturally answer no; Mr. Webster answers yes. . . .
>
> A measure of this kind is not a measure of peace. If it becomes a law, it will awaken more anger than it will allay; it will breed more dissension than it will appease. A law odious to the community disappoints those in whose favor it is made, and offends all the rest. The extraordinary provisions of this bill will naturally lead to extraordinary methods of evasion, and exasperate the animosity of both parties.

On May 21, while the debate was still raging, Bigelow high-lighted:

Great Meeting in Boston
TREMENDOUS EXCITEMENT
DANIEL WEBSTER
out in favor of
APPLYING THE PROVISO TO ALL THE TERRITORIES!
NO COMPROMISE IN MASSACHUSETTS!!

Then he copied, with tiny credits at the end, an article from *Niles'*
Register of December 11, 1819, and rejoiced at the fury of Whig
papers which thought the resuscitation of Webster's great speech on
freedom in the territories a confusing and contemptible ruse. Privately he wrote to Charles Sumner: "I am advised that Webster under
the interest of the milling interest . . . is abandoning his opposition to
the extension of slavery, on the ground that the manufacturers of New
England will suffer by the restriction of slavery and their interests be
promoted by its extension. This may be calumnious but the reason is
a good one I think, for such as are unscrupulous enough to be governed by and to use it." [4] For that reason he fought Webster unceas-
ingly, sarcastically congratulated him upon landing a job as Secretary
of State under Millard Fillmore, President after Zachary Taylor died
in July, applauded the election of Horace Mann to the Senate as a
slap at Webster, and never missed an opportunity to kick the fallen
idol.[5] Where editorials left off, Bigelow's "John Brown" began. Webster was his favorite target, Webster's love of liquor his favorite
theme, and whenever Webster made a speech, John Brown did his
small bit to debunk it, as, for example, in his column on December 28,
1850:

> Webster has been on to dine with the New England Society,
> and I perceive, by your paper, has been making one of his evan-
> gelical speeches again. The moment I read the report of it, I knew
> the old sinner had been cutting up; for it is his way, whenever he
> has been giving his propensities an airing, to go somewhere and
> make a pious speech. In the short extract which you give from
> his exordium, of about twenty lines, I find the name of God used
> six times. . . .

John Brown then explained the reason for Webster's speech. At
Jenny Lind's concert in Washington:

> . . . Webster began to accompany her with his voice, keeping
> time with his head. . . . He was soon observed by Jenny, who

seemed to be flattered at having such distinguished assistance at her concert, and recognized her obligations by a bow, as she supposed, in response to the bows of the Secretary. The Secretary did not observe her obeisance, however, at first, but kept on singing louder and louder, and marking the time by bowing lower and lower, while the Nightingale, oppressed by the Secretary's condescension, bowed and bowed again. Thus they went on bobbing their heads towards each other, like two Mandarins in a grocery window. . . .

When Mr. Webster awoke the next morning and learned from his wife what an exhibition he had made of himself the night before, he said: "This will be all over Washington in a few days, so I must go somewhere and make an evangelical speech."

Senator Seward received more considerate treatment from the *Post* after he opposed the compromise measures in March in his speech on higher justice, but he was still suspect. Bigelow decided that Seward was up to something when he subscribed to the *Post* in December 1850, shortly after John Brown had described him as "the most self-complacent man who has crossed the river this season" whose boast it was that he controlled the House of Representatives. Bigelow jotted in his diary: "*Timeo danaos et dona ferentes.* Seward has just subscribed for the daily *Post* and from indications it is apparent he is trying to see whether the *Post* can in any way be secured as an ally of his." [6] He never ascribed noble motives to Seward. Yet Seward's interest might well be a portent, for that Whig, Bigelow believed, would never be on a losing side.

When the compromise bills became law, abolitionists and moderates earnestly talked of starting a new party through the union of all antislavery men regardless of their former political ties. Charles Sumner, Massachusetts Free-Soiler, urged it. Frederick A. Conkling, antislavery Whig, came to Bigelow with such a scheme, but in 1850 Bigelow counseled against it. Let the Hunkers of both parties carry the odium of violating party allegiance, he advised. In their fight to extend slavery they were rapidly drawing together, as the recent Union meeting at Castle Garden of proslavery Whigs and proslavery Democrats exemplified. In time they would form a coalition which perforce would leave antislavery men, without overt action, aligned. Behind Bigelow's reluctance to foster a third party was a deep-seated fear that any party built upon one issue alone could not long survive. If the Free-Soilers, Barnburners, Antislavery Whigs, Know-Nothings, and abolitionists joined to fight slavery, what would become of them when the question of tariffs arose or of internal improvements? [7]

Charles Sumner said that those were problems for the future; the compelling need of the moment was to stop the spread of slavery. Nevertheless, he and Bigelow became close political friends. Sumner's election in 1851 as Free-Soil Senator from Massachusetts was cause for sincere private congratulations from Bigelow as well as public rejoicing in the *Post*, for the new Senator was a brilliant spokesman, an erudite, fluent, outspoken advocate. Years later, thinking of Sumner, Bigelow concluded that in spite of the man's dogmatism, fanaticism, and emotional instability, ". . . during his long term of public service, no man had a more single eye for the interests of the State or spent more hours in qualifying to serve it effectively." In 1851 he was very aware, however, that Sumner, like all men, had the failings of his virtues:

He will be misled by designing men and his approbativeness and self-esteem will prevent sensible and honest men having the control over him which he requires. He will be led by his weaknesses and those mostly will be taken advantage of by bad men. I fear that Seward will appropriate him and yet after reading the *Evening Post* for two years he ought to know better.[8]

So Bigelow watched Seward with suspicion, and cultivated Sumner. The Senator from Massachusetts, aware of the value of the *Post's* support, reciprocated with a stream of hectic notes to Bigelow, suggesting articles, calling some speech or editorial to his attention, imploring: "You must stick!" "For God's sake stand firm!" Not that Bryant or Bigelow needed such admonition, but Sumner always wrote that way. At first one was impressed with his crusading zeal; after a time one skipped the phrases and looked for the meat in the letter. Usually there was a valuable idea for an editorial or for "John Brown" or for "Friar Lubin," another mythical character created by Bigelow in 1851 to use literary and historical material which "John Brown the Ferryman" would be unable to understand.[9]

Friar Lubin told how Virginia was colonized by John Smith, a fugitive slave, and mused upon the strangeness that Virginia, which had given five Presidents to the nation, yet "should be so intolerant now towards a class to which she owes her political precedence among the American colonies."[10] On the birthdays of Washington and Jefferson he presented lists of their antislavery utterances and on other occasions printed the words of other founding fathers to show that there was no precedent for current Southern belief in the necessity for slavery or in a God-given right to hold slaves. Nor did he spare Webster. Virulent attacks against the Secretary of State continually appeared in the *Post*, one outrageous invention of Bigelow's being a letter purportedly from Webster to his childhood nurse thanking her for the bottle she held to his infant lips and sending her fifty dollars "for as yours is the first debt I ever contracted, so it will be the first I ever paid." [11]

Throughout 1851 Bigelow's special columns, news columns, and editorials were primarily attacks upon the opposition. As independent Democrats, he and Bryant agreed with the ex-Whig Free-Soiler, Charles Sumner, that the time for constructive action had not yet come. The Presidency in 1852 was sure to go to a candidate unsatisfactory to them whether he be Whig or Democrat. Their part, therefore, was to maintain principles and look to 1856 as the turning point.[12] Precisely what would happen then and what stand the *Post* would take no one could predict, but the basis upon which its editors would make their decisions was already clear. Bryant put that into words on the fiftieth anniversary of the paper on November 24, 1851:

> . . . the *Evening Post* will continue to battle for human rights in preference to human sovereignties; for the welfare and improvement of the multitude, rather than for exclusive privileges to classes and tribes; for freedom of industry and thought, regardless alike of the frowns and blandishments of power and wealth.

Politically speaking, 1852 and 1853 were relatively calm. People were so bored by talk of slavery, so weary of old, old repetitions, that journals had to give them other fare. Bigelow touched on other subjects important to a mid-century liberal, writing editorials exposing canal frauds, opposing capital punishment, objecting to Congressional appropriations for railroads, and advocating a privately owned transcontinental line, warning against indiscriminate charity, urging international copyright laws, favoring the employment of women at equal pay for equal work.[13] Moreover, the *Post* offered a wider range of literary selections: stories by Dickens and Hawthorne, translations of German tales, biographies of Joseph Story, Fenimore Cooper, Franklin Pierce. Its book reviews, Bigelow's special department, became even more of a feature. In addition, Bigelow found time to develop a literary controversy which he had started in 1851.

Presumably Bryant relayed to him Henry Hallam's remark about the differences in verbatim letters of George Washington appearing both in Jared Sparks's twelve-volume edition of Washington's writings, published between 1834 and 1837, and in *The Life and Correspondence of Joseph Reed*, edited by William Reed.[14] Bigelow investigated and to his amazement soon collated a hundred instances where the eminent historian, Jared Sparks, President of Harvard College, had changed or omitted words. Some of these Bigelow printed on February 12 under the pseudonym of "Friar Lubin." He showed how "old Put" became "General Putnam," how "our rascally privateersmen" lost the adjective, how "he has wrote" turned into "he has written," and so on. "I found that he had not only attempted to correct the probable oversights and blunders of George Washington, but he had undertaken to improve his style and chasten his language; nay, he had in some instances gone so far as to change his meaning, and to make him the author of sentiments precisely the opposite of what he intended to write."

Sparks was ill at the time, but a friend replied angrily for him in the Cambridge *Chronicle*, labeling the unknown Lubin "my assailant." Lubin felt called upon to defend himself. Said he in the *Post* on March 1:

> I stated facts merely, facts which no one will dispute; I gave a list of changes which the writings of Washington had undergone in the hands of his editor; these changes, the writer says, were proper and necessary. Very well, if so, what harm is done? It may have been inferred that I thought differently, but it will not be pretended that I offered any argument to make others think so. . . .

He was ready to agree with Sparks that Washington would not have published grammatical errors, but, he added, "Washington probably would not have published any part of any letter which he had marked 'private.' " Nor did Bigelow let the issue rest there. In June he reported rumors that a new and complete edition of Washington's works was soon to be undertaken, because "the *authority* of Sparks as an editor and historian may be considered as entirely destroyed . . ." by Friar Lubin.[15] Other journals picked up the controversy, for Sparks was at the peak of his reputation and the whole literary world was aroused. On July 1 the *Evening Post* had to make it clear that neither Bryant nor the historian George Bancroft was responsible, as charged, for Friar Lubin. Thereafter the *Post* dropped the subject until Lord Mahon issued a study of Sparks's misquotations in Volume Six of his *History of England*. On January 5, 1852, the *Post* reprinted Mahon's remarks, commenting that his findings were ". . . substantially, if not precisely, the same as those collated by Friar Lubin, and published in this journal, with the addition of some passages which were omitted by Sparks, to which Friar Lubin merely made reference."

This brought three letters to the *Post* from President Sparks in which he defended his alterations of spelling, stated his principles of editorial selection, and honestly described the problems he faced in the variations among drafts, copies, and hard-to-locate originals. Bigelow was not satisfied:

> I do not think Mr. Sparks has changed the position of the question materially, either by his silence or by his letters. I charged and proved, by a collation of some hundred different passages, that he had altered the text of Washington's letters with a view of improving them, and that, in so doing, he had materially changed their meaning. He replies, first, that the letters from which I had quoted, were private, often negligently written, and never intended for publication; that he thought it his duty to revise these carefully for the press, and did it according to his best discretion. Of this I have no doubt. I trust no one is disposed to question Mr. Sparks' conscientiousness as an editor or as a man; his judgment, his discretion, his taste, however, I agree with him in thinking, are not infallible. It may be a good objection against publishing any of Washington's letters, that they were never written for publication, but that is no excuse for publishing as his, those he never wrote.
>
> Washington may have used a naughty expression when he spoke of "our *rascally* privateer-men," more particularly, as most of the class alluded to were New Englanders; but I submit that it was transcending the editorial function to omit the qualifying word which expresses an undeniable truth, and in the writing of which, Washington no doubt experienced great satisfaction.

Later, after a friend of Sparks attempted to defend his changes in spelling, Bigelow burst forth again:

> . . . Should such a doctrine obtain, the next thing we should hear would be that some meddlesome bookwright was correcting the geography of Shakespeare, and adapting Paradise Lost to the present condition of natural science; some Dr. Popkin would be putting the finishing touches to the Aeneid of Virgil, and Dr. Anthon would have to rewrite the history of Livy, by the lights of Niebuhr, for the Harpers. In a few years it would become as difficult to identify the literary as the incorporeal remains of the dead, so wholly would they be a prey to the variable tastes and conceit of bookmakers and publishers.[16]

Bigelow's tone was unnecessarily harsh, yet his purpose, the elevation of accuracy in the ethics of historians and editors, was sound. Once before, in 1849, he had raised the same issue when he criticized Harper's edition of the second volume of Macaulay's *History of England*.

The publishers had called their edition "in every word a faithful and perfect copy of the original," then added that they altered the spelling to conform to Noah Webster. Bigelow had commented: "The question is not which is the best authority for spelling the English language, T. B. Macaulay or Noah Webster — it is whether this is 'Macaulay's History of England,' which they offer to the public in that title. We say it is not. A man's spelling is as essential a part of his style as his grammatical construction. . . ." [17] In 1849 as in 1851–1852 Bigelow served as a forerunner of the scientific historians. Moreover, in all of his own writings he was to act scrupulously by his precept. He might omit parts of letters, but he would indicate the omission; he would suppress letters if in his judgment they were best suppressed, but of his own volition he would not destroy them nor would he knowingly issue an inexact version. It was his belief that the letters of famous men should be preserved most carefully for posterity. Therefore, years later, when Charles Dickens complacently told him that he was burning all but his business correspondence, Bigelow turned on him sharply and retorted: "And you ought to be burned with them." [18] Yet still later he himself helped to suppress and even destroyed many of Tilden's records. He believed that he had no choice, for Tilden had left his executors explicit commands to sift his papers before opening them to the public. At least Bigelow did not mutilate or destroy letters written to Tilden; those he carefully returned to their writers to publish, store, or destroy as they would.

Besides its literary activities in 1852 the *Post* made room once more for a wide coverage of European affairs and looked more into city and state government. It reported canal contract frauds. It told with contempt of a "clique of psalm singing fools" who threw out the novels once permitted in Sing Sing and left the convicts nothing to read but the "dead stock of some theological bookseller." It objected vigorously to extension of government control, on that ground criticized the Maine prohibition law, on that ground objected to government grants for internal improvements. When in February Sumner argued eloquently for gifts of public lands to railroads, the *Post* made no direct attack upon a friend, but privately Bigelow expressed disagreement.[19] Though they saw exactly alike on slavery, never would they agree on other fundamental issues. That was why Bigelow had worked for the reunion of the Democratic party in 1849, why the *Post* continued to call itself a Democratic paper even as it fought the pro-slavery majority in the party, and that was why it supported for the Presidency Franklin Pierce, a "doughface," a Northern man with Southern sympathies. Four years before, the *Post* had crusaded for

Van Buren and Adams; in 1852 it largely ignored the Free-Soil remnant's choice of John P. Hale and George Julian. Hale stood for repeal of the compromise measures of 1850; so did the *Post*. Pierce accepted those measures as final. "The Democratic party of the Union," his platform stated, "will abide by, and adhere to, a faithful execution of the acts known as the compromise measures settled by the last Congress — the act for reclaiming fugitive slaves from service of labour included . . ." [20] Yet the *Evening Post* supported him. The pragmatic editors believed that Hale had no chance of winning, while Pierce did, and once in, he would at least put a stop to the Whigs' grants of public lands.

On September 20, 1852, their editorial expressed the attitude of both editors:

> But we are also aware of the fact . . . that hostility to slavery goes but a short way in making a true democrat, or even a sound economist.
>
> The history of the present Congress alone was enough to destroy all our faith, which was never much, in that democracy which rests upon the anti-slavery sentiment alone. We have not found in that sentiment any protection against the most profligate and lawless schemes of public extravagance. [Subsidies to steamship companies, land grants to railroads, etc.] . . . And how came this wholesale robbery of the national estate to be tolerated? We shall answer our own question. These lands were to the northwest what the steam ship appropriations were to the east, the consideration for betraying the cause of freedom. Members who had been unfaithful to the pledges or the principles upon which they were elected, hoped to propitiate their constituents by bringing home to them title deeds to large tracts of the national domain, which the favored states were to enter into and possess without money and without price.

Yet during the campaign there was little they could honestly say in favor of Pierce. The chief support they gave him lay in their criticism of the Whigs' candidate, General Winfield Scott, another hero of the Mexican War, who, though nominated by the antislavery Seward-Weed forces, accepted as did Pierce the finality of the compromise. Bigelow wrote a series of eleven articles in August and September which he first had "Friar Lubin" insert in the *Post* and then reprinted in inexpensive pamphlet form. These recounted the less happy incidents of Scott's career, particularly controversies in which the military man came off second-best. With them were the Democratic candidate's one speech of which Bigelow wholly approved, his

speech assailing New Hampshire's long-standing Constitutional discrimination against non-Protestants, and two other items which fired
Bigelow's enthusiasm, although they could scarcely be called Democratic propaganda. One was a letter from Benjamin F. Butler upon
the need for a third party in 1852. The other was Sumner's speech
advocating the repeal of the fugitive slave act which Bigelow told
Sumner was "the heaviest blow which has been levelled against the
fugitive slave-bill from the tribune" primarily because it dealt with
issues, not personalities.[21] When the election swept the back-to-normal,
no-controversy Democrat into office, the *Post* could express only mild
satisfaction.

Then Bryant departed for another year in Europe. He could well
afford the trip, for dividends along with subscriptions had more than
doubled in the four years since Bigelow had become a partner, and
though the company wrote off an old debt of Parke Godwin's in
1852, the junior partners each made $6000 during that year and Bryant
even more. Almost 1900 people now bought the daily *Evening Post*,
and over 9000 families took either the semiweekly, appearing on Tues-
days and Fridays, or the Thursday weekly edition, both of them, like
the daily, unwieldy papers of four pages, each covered with 2604
square inches of eyestraining print.[22]

While Bryant was away and the businessmen's truce on the compromise maintained the political calm, Bigelow energetically overhauled
their whole organization, modernized their equipment, moved the office, and established the *Evening Post* and its job-printing office on a
firm basis such as it had never known. He bought a new building and
had the basement floor renovated and a fourth floor added. Then on
the hectic second week end in April, 1853, he moved one block north
from their poor, little place on Liberty and Pine Streets to the four-
story office at 55 Liberty Street on the northwest corner of Liberty
and Nassau. Diagonally opposite was the post office which simplified
mailing out-of-town papers, while from near-by Wall Street the latest
quotations could be brought by messenger in almost no time. The
building itself was as satisfactory as its location. The publications office
was comfortably installed on the first floor; above it were the com-
posing room and five small offices, ample for Bryant, Bigelow, and the
two or three reporters; and the job office occupied the entire new top
floor. Those three floors provided comfort, yet they were far less important than was the well-lighted basement. There, at last, Wm. C.
Bryant & Co. had room for more than the old hand press. Indeed, the
basement had been purposely constructed to hold a four-cylinder,
type-revolving, fast printing press already ordered from Hoe & Co.

Moreover, Captain John Ericsson, the famous inventor, was building expressly for them the first caloric engine to be used in driving a printing press — which was good publicity, though unfortunately the engine proved so erratic that within a year the company shifted to one of the expensive but tested Hoe "lightning" machines. Once Bigelow installed the new machinery in July, '53 — and again he had to attend to all of the details, for Timothy Howe, the business manager, bungled every job he attempted in connection with the expansion — it was possible to print 7000 copies of the *Post* per hour instead of the 750 copies per hour formerly printed. As a result, the paper could go to press an hour later yet be delivered earlier than ever before, which more than compensated for the penetrating noise and the jarring vibrations of the big machines.[23]

The tacit truce between North and South lasted throughout the first half of 1853, though in the North both Whigs and Democrats were splitting into dissident factions. John Brown's pointed gibes did not once appear in the *Post* and diatribes against slavery were rare. Bigelow broke his silence on April 5 only after Southerners, eager for commercial and industrial independence of the North, called a convention to meet in Memphis for the purpose of arranging direct steamship connections between Europe and the South, direct railroad links between the West and the South, and the encouragement of immigration from Europe to the South. Bigelow said that the purpose of the conference was excellent; but, he added:

> . . . the South should remember that the advancement of society depends upon human industry as well as natural position and circumstance. . . . Labor, therefore, free, equal and well-rewarded labor, is the necessary condition of all social developments. . . .
>
> An agricultural state, or a warlike state, may be maintained for a time by a society in which one portion of the population is held in bondage by another; but a commercial and manufacturing state cannot be, simply because the open air is essential to the life of enterprise and industry.

His temperate advice was not welcomed; indeed, the Charleston *Mercury* soon found occasion to excoriate the *Post* in an editorial which must have filled Bigelow with pride:

> . . . what has the *Post* and its party done? True, it has opposed the mad extravagance of the extreme anti-slavery party at the North, and sought to moderate a wild and impracticable fury into a cool-headed, politic and safe hostility. It has restrained and dis-

countenanced that spirit which, because of its very violence, was less dangerous to the South than that policy which, combining political and moral tactics, insidiously avails itself of all opportunities to worm into and destroy her peculiar institutions.[24]

In midsummer the Richmond *Enquirer* and the Washington *Union*, condemning the *Evening Post* even more vigorously than had the *Mercury*, read it out of the ranks of the Democratic party, the immediate issue being Bigelow's reiterated editorial satisfaction over the talk of emancipation in Cuba. But the *Post* had no intention of being ousted from its party. Both its principles and its pocketbook demanded that it remain Democratic. Although its circulation still was minute compared to the popular morning papers, it gave its proprietors a handsome return and in the year between May '52 and May '53 gained almost two thousand new subscribers. These people, not Southern die-hards, were the people whom Bryant and Bigelow intended to satisfy.[25]

In July Bigelow enlarged the size of the daily by four columns. That same month he began the *Post's* biggest scoop of the decade, presentation of pre-publication chapters from Thomas A. Benton's *Thirty Years' View*. Every editor in the country must have envied Bigelow that triumph. Copies of the *Post* became precious as people of every political faith sought to find out what the old Jacksonian Democrat had written of controversial issues and of his contemporaries, particularly of politicians still alive, for Benton was at the height of his fame. Before the last election many Free-Soilers and Barnburners had talked of him as Presidential material because of his courageous stand against Clay's compromise measures, which had cost him his seat in the Senate. Many men throughout the North hoped that he would run for the Presidency in 1856. Therefore what Benton had to say was important, as Bigelow had long since realized. For months he had angled to get the book, working through Charles Sumner and Preston King, but getting nowhere. Finally he had turned directly to Benton, pointing out that if excerpts of the work were to appear in any journal prior to publication, the Democratic *Evening Post* with the same free-soil, antitariff tenets as his should be the organ. His arguments succeeded; in July long passages from *Thirty Years' View* were filling columns on the front page of the *Post*, for which Benton received ten dollars a column, free copies, and a steady stream of publicity on the editorial page, while Bigelow won for his paper and himself an important friend.[26]

After Bryant's return in the fall to his new office and his old desk, which Bigelow had tidied in the mistaken belief that it would please his partner, the *Post* continued to publish literary selections and editorials upon diverse subjects. Not until November 15 did a new, ominous note creep into the paper. On that day the editors charged that plans were under way to block a coming application of Nebraskans to organize as a state. Senators Atchison of Missouri, Bell of Tennessee, and Butler of South Carolina, they added on November 18, were leading the opposition to the admission of any new free state. But before the full story broke, Bigelow once more left the United States, this time going to Haiti to do a task similar to the one he had done in Jamaica four years before.

CHAPTER 8

From Agnostic to Believer

[*1850–1854*]

THE PASSPORT issued to Bigelow in December 1853 carried no hint
of the changes which had taken place in his life since his Jamaican
trip three years before. It stated only that going to Haiti was one John
Bigelow:

AGE	37	MOUTH	*medium*
HEIGHT	6' ¾"	CHIN	*round*
FOREHEAD	*high*	HAIR	*brown*
EYES	*gray*	COMPLEXION	*fair*
NOSE	*Roman*	SHAPE OF FACE	*oval*

That is, it stated in detail that John Bigelow resembled a typical
American of Anglo-Saxon stock.[1] Were passports concerned with
more than physical identification, the sheet might have continued:
MOOD — sober; ATTITUDE OF MIND — inquiring and reflective; RELIGION
— agnostic; MARITAL STATUS — married and a father.

He had been a carefree young man when he sailed in 1850, confident of himself and of his ability to direct his life. Now it would
seem that he had even more reason for self-confidence; his success
was evident in his dividends, in Bryant's attitude, in his growing
friendships with eminent men. Yet now he sailed soberly, and his
manner, though friendly, was touched with reserve.

To account for the change it is necessary to go back to the day he
landed in New York after his voyage to Jamaica.

Bigelow had made friends on the Jamaican trip, as he did everywhere, and he disembarked with two gallons of turtle soup, the gift of
an admiring steward. What could a bachelor do with all that soup?
He sent it to the most attractive girl he knew, Jane Poultney, whom
he had met three months before at a dance.[2] Then he hastened home
to see his family. It was an awkward trip to arrange, because as yet no

railroad ran on the west shore and no boats could cross the ice-choked river north of New York City. Finally he took the train to Poughkeepsie where his brother Ed managed to meet him with a sleigh. Together they skimmed across the river and drove thirty miles through blanketed country, exhilarated at first by the nipping wind but more than ready when they reached the homestead to thaw and relax in the warmth of roaring fires and welcoming kinsfolk.

There was much to talk about: Clay's compromise measures which were creating a stir even in quiet Malden, the trip to Jamaica, local gossip, new ideas and plans. Old Asa Bigelow enjoyed the evening thoroughly and held his own as keenly as the younger man. Nine o'clock was the usual bedtime on the farm, but father and son talked until after eleven, retiring then with a mutual sense of well-being and understanding, for they had had little opportunity to know each other since John at eleven years of age went away to school. The next morning the father arose at his usual hour, but suddenly collapsed and died within twenty-four hours. John Bigelow experienced shock, perhaps, as much as sorrow, yet the sense of loss was inescapable and he was grateful to have a few days at home with his family.[3]

After the funeral he returned to the city, leaving his mother, her memory now completely gone, with the two brothers who had remained in business in Malden. Besides his work to bring him back to New York there was Jane Poultney, clever, versatile Jane Poultney, in his eyes the most beautiful girl in the city — "as near the perfection of womanly beauty as any woman I had ever seen," he recalled forty years later — and certainly, with her vivacious blue eyes and famous Poultney complexion, one of the loveliest. Bubbling with good spirits, never tired no matter how late the hour, this girl of twenty-one completely captivated the serious New Yorker. They had met only the preceding November, but once she accepted his suit, neither saw reason in a long engagement. In June 1850 they went to her old home in Baltimore for the wedding on the eleventh, after Bigelow had supplied himself with a fine new suit, with twelve dollars' worth of shirts, stock, and hose, with a ring selected, properly enough, from the store of Tiffany, Young and Ellis, and with two hundred dollars in cash. For their honeymoon they traveled to Niagara by way of Canada.[4]

Once back in New York they took rooms on Fourth Street and later on Fourteenth Street. But though boarding for a bachelor had been satisfactory, Bigelow now was loathe to continue it. Yet what else could he do? To live beyond or even up to his income would be demoralizing, especially as he still owed the company more than

$9000. Now they must share hopes for the future; later they could indulge them.

Within a year, however, the Bigelows were house hunting. They were expecting a child and had no intention of rearing him in a boardinghouse. Presently they selected a two-story-and-attic house in a pleasant, modest neighborhood, at 288 West Twenty-second Street, opposite the home of Clement C. Moore, professor of Oriental and Greek literatures at the General Theological Seminary, and famed as the author of " 'Twas the Night before Christmas." It cost $5500, more cash than Bigelow had at the time, but he succeeded in purchasing it on the installment plan with the right to pay for it as fast as he desired, and five years later he sold it for more than enough to cover all interest charges, so that in effect he lived rent-free. Soon their first son, Poultney, was born. Then more than ever Bigelow loved to go to his home each evening — the first home he had felt part of since he was eleven — to see what new tricks his baby had learned that day, to help care for him and to get up at night when the child cried, rather than have his wife or the nurse disturbed. Somehow theaters and parties seemed more pleasurable now that he went to them from his own home, escorting his wife. Quiet evenings likewise took on a new charm. No longer were his books piled helter-skelter in a hired room. Here he had space to arrange them properly. Rather, temporarily he had space. As his wife pointed out to him on more than one occasion, a book was one temptation he could not resist; he found them an essential to life, to be taken in large quantities. Almost as soon as he moved into the Twenty-second Street house, he satisfied an old yearning by buying a complete file of *Niles' Weekly Register* and of the *Congressional Globe*.[5]

Early on the morning of August 11, 1852, their second child and first daughter, Grace, was born. For some months the Bigelows lived an almost idyllically happy life. Then death visited them. Little Poultney, nearly two years old in February 1853, was just at the age when a child's every move is a tender joy to parents, when navigating on two feet is accomplishment and happy peril, and the whole house becomes a world to explore. Left alone one day, he clambered on top of a bookcase but lost his balance and fell to the floor screaming. His father rushed upstairs, calmed and petted him and then on the nurse's advice let him go on playing. At that moment the doctor chanced to come in for a routine check-up and thought the boy all right. So indeed he seemed to be. But a few days later he was fretful and a fever developed. All night Bigelow sat by his bed, soothing him, keeping him covered. In the morning the father slept briefly and then went to the office, for Bryant was in Europe in 1853 and the paper had to come out. For three nights Bigelow cared for the boy, for three days the mother and nurse tended him, but they could not save him. During the fourth night Poultney died.

Bigelow was gripped with anguish. He had faced finality before, but there was no reason in this. A little child, his baby son, gone before he had his life. The child had been so loving, held such promise. What sort of a God could permit this death? Bigelow had given little thought to God in recent years. He had been too busy with the realities he saw to bother about the unknowable. He thought little of the tribe of ministers; he had long since rebelled against the vindictive God of his Presbyterian childhood; he had long since stopped puzzling over the three Gods to whom he had prayed daily at his Episcopal school and college; nowadays he rarely even bothered to scoff at such inconsistencies in the Bible as the idea of vegetation and light on the earth before there was a sun.

Yet such was the hold of early training that he still read the Bible. He found abiding truth in some of its pages, the simple story of the best of men, and a powerful imagery that compelled attention. And as he read words familiar since childhood, he sometimes felt at one with that little John who used to read the Bible to his mother and felt a comfortable nearness to his parents and his forebears. If not Word of God, the Bible was for him a book apart; Bigelow could never deny vague feelings that something more than man was in it, even while his intellect derided the idea. His friends had as little faith in the Holy Book as he, or less, which tended to confirm his disbeliefs. Some of them were out-and-out materialists, acknowledging only a code of ethics; others were willing to admit the possibility of a God or, as Bigelow did, to acknowledge hazily that a Divine Being or Providence or Something existed.[6]

For the ordinary routine of life that had served him as a sufficient creed, but to be reconciled to the death of his own dear son he needed more. He knew of the current interest in spiritualism; he himself had attended several séances; though no believer, he had admitted the possibility of communication with spirits. Temporarily that possibility became a hope and he drew some consolation from their doctor's statement that a spirit medium had told him Poultney would be happy in "spirit land." Somehow Bigelow had to deny extinction. It was too contrary to all the influences of his childhood and youth, and too revolting to his self-hood. Lacking a sure faith, he took bleak comfort from his concepts of an impersonal Providence, of a vague form of eternal life and of the moral lessons to be found in all experience. In his diary he wrote out his anguish and love and sorrow, until, purged of emotion, he sought to apply the lesson to his own life:

> I now feel that I needed some dispensation like this to remind me that I was not independent of Providence. I have been so prospered in everything, that I think I was getting to feel too much that I was the master of my own destiny, that others were less successful because they were less deserving and I was too insensible to the sorrows and reverses of others. I sympathized too little. I made my own ambitions and cares of too much importance and attached too little importance to those which occupied the minds and hearts of my fellows. I feel that I am already a somewhat better man. I am in hopes of becoming more tolerant, more patient, more self-accusing and vigilant, especially in the use of my tongue and pen, less heedless of the feelings of others.[7]

A little coffin, a cemetery plot selected, a funeral service performed, $18.50 given to the undertaker — then the duties of everyday life were resumed. But just as the first sharp pain was beginning to ease, his mother died in September. Bigelow thought death for her a happy release, though to him it brought a resurgence of thoughts of his own son.

So the great mysteries of life and death were in the front of his mind when he sailed for Haiti in November 1853. Since he had last left the country his younger sister had died, his parents had died, his son had been born and had died, and now at home with little Grace was his wife who was expecting another child in the spring. Perhaps unconsciously Bigelow was longing for some surer guide than himself. Only thus can be explained what happened on that trip, for a practical man does not turn from agnosticism and occasional attendance at a Unitarian church to devout belief in the Man-God Jesus Christ and in Swedenborg as expounder of His Word merely by chancing upon the *Arcana Coelestia* in an idle moment. A growing sense of his own limitations and of the inadequacy of an impersonal Providence must have prepared the way.

It was merest chance, or Divine Providence, which led him to Swedenborg. The *Clara Windsor* reached Haiti on December 21 precisely according to schedule, landing Bigelow at Port-au-Prince, where he intended to stay several weeks before returning directly to New York. He made his investigations also according to schedule and began at once to collect material for the lively letters to the *Post* which were expected of him, as well as evidence that Southerners in the United States government were using undue influence to force Haiti to recognize the independence of Santo Domingo.[8] He met leading Haitians, was properly presented to Emperor Soulouque, and found the island as excellent an example of Negro administrative capacities as he had anticipated.

A severe epidemic of yellow fever was the only unexpected event. Even that did not particularly trouble Bigelow, though he was sorry to learn that all but two of the crew of the *Clara Windsor* had died from the fever within four days of their arrival. His own health was and remained excellent, thanks largely to the hospitality of a merchant to whom he had a letter of introduction and who had been expecting his arrival. This gentleman, B. P. Hunt, a Harvard man, a classmate of Emerson, met Bigelow's ship and whisked him at once to his home and away from the harbor and the town hotels where fever stalked. There Bigelow maintained headquarters until he had completed his survey; then only did he realize how serious the epidemic was.

For lack of crews no ships were leaving the harbor. Faced with an indefinite wait or an unwanted trip to St. Thomas in hopes of catching a ship there, Bigelow chose the latter, for in two months he had had no word from his family and had no way of knowing how they were or whether his letters had reached New York. But he crossed to St. Thomas only to find that port completely closed by a cholera outbreak. Perforce he settled in the one hotel and waited. He wrote up some of his notes, read again the books he had carried with him, discovered, as he always did everywhere, the town's one bookshop, and started in on its contents. Soon he had exhausted its limited stock and found himself one morning bored to death, reading the Bible as a last resort as he sat in the hotel's huge, empty dining room, empty, that is, except for himself and a Mr. Kjerulff, a Dane similarly held up by the epidemic.

He started methodically with Genesis, but by the time he reached the twelfth chapter, where Abram passed off his wife Sarah as his sister in order to save himself, he put the book down in disgust and proceeded to tell Mr. Kjerulff what he thought of calling such an unmoral man God's chosen one. He expected agreement or possibly a good argument. Instead Kjerulff mildly asked if he had ever read Swedenborg on that particular passage. Bigelow replied that he had once owned a copy of *Conjugial Love* given him by a friend whose ideas were rather peculiar, but he could not recall having read it. Mr. Kjerulff then described something of Swedenborg's doctrine of correspondences which, he said, was set forth in the *Arcana Coelestia*. What he said was quite unintelligible to Bigelow so he asked if Mr. Kjerulff had a copy of the book. Kjerulff had; shortly Bigelow was absorbed in volume one of the *Arcana Coelestia — The Heavenly Arcana contained in the Holy Scriptures or Word of the Lord Unfolded.*

At least, he decided, it would pass the time and he could get some enjoyment finding flaws in the argument. But as he read he found nothing illogical in what he understood, though much of it was completely over his head. This was challenging and he proceeded to read with the utmost attention. At dinnertime, his curiosity fully aroused, he asked Kjerulff for details of Swedenborg's life. The enthusiastic description held his attention and the book Kjerulff gave him, *Documents Concerning Swedenborg*, compiled by Professor George Bush whom Bigelow had long known as a scholarly Christian but never suspected of heresy, he read almost at one sitting. He was intensely interested now. That he, who prided himself on his wide reading and his literary and historical background, had never heard more than the name of such a man amazed him. Indeed, it seems scarcely possible, considering that Emerson delivered his lectures on Swedenborg in 1846, that Professor Bush answered him that same year in a lecture which strongly set forth his full acceptance of Swedenborg's claims, that a New Church in New York City was firmly established, and a number of intellectuals had publicly announced their adherence to Swedenborg. Rather it seems likely that Bigelow had heard scraps of information about the man and his doctrines but that his own indifference was so great that he promptly forgot them. Certainly not until he reached St. Thomas did he experience Swedenborg.

The enigma of the Swede's life now interested him as much as it did the elder Henry James or George Bush or John Clowes or as it would the later psychologists and psychoanalysts. Bigelow was tremendously attracted by the picture of the well-born, well-educated gentleman, devoting years to scientific studies, writing numerous treatises which placed him as one of the eighteenth century's great thinkers, producing inventions which were of direct use to his contemporaries, not limiting himself to one field but studying mechanics, mining, metallurgy, geology, engineering, astronomy, chemistry, and anatomy. Swedenborg's earlier self-esteem and desire for recognition and status were equally sure to interest a man who since boyhood was quick to deprecate self-approbativeness in others and to admit to himself — only to himself — that that was his own chief weakness. Bigelow accepted at face value the statement that Swedenborg turned wholly to a study of religion at the age of fifty-five, but he could not believe that Swedenborg conversed with angels and with God. Yet neither could he disregard the decades of rational scientific investigations and dismiss the man as mad.

He decided to turn back to Swedenborg's writings to see what ideas they held regardless of Swedenborg's claims of divine inspiration. Mr. Kjerulff, whose luggage was all neatly tied up waiting for a ship that did not sail, obligingly hauled out all the pamphlets, essays, and books he had by or about Swedenborg. Nothing interrupted Bigelow's study except daily inquiries about possibilities of transportation. For two weeks he read morning and afternoon. The more he pondered the more he grasped the significance of correspondences, of Swedenborg's conception of the Bible as the actual Word of God delivered in superficial terms understandable by the immediate audience, but carrying, too, spiritual meanings for all times and all places which could be read only by those in a state to comprehend. Bigelow was not satisfied with Swedenborg's explanation of how he arrived at that state, but each day he was more sure that Swedenborg had the key to clear confusions. If not the Revealer of the Word, he was surely the greatest of all interpreters.

Finally the master of a small schooner agreed to take Bigelow and Kjerulff to New Orleans. Hastily they repacked their trunks, keeping Kjerulff's Swedenborgian literature easily available, and went aboard. There Bigelow continued poring over the documents. Before the thirteen-day trip was completed, Bigelow the scoffer, the self-confident rationalist, was on his knees murmuring, "Lord, I believe. Help thou my unbelief."

He took one day off in New Orleans to discuss with the editor of the *Times-Picayune* the state of Southern opinion, and then, traveling up the Mississippi, he resumed the all-consuming quest for faith. Kjerulff left him at Cincinnati, of course taking his books with him, whereupon Bigelow searched a bookstore and came out triumphant with an inexpensive because unwanted copy of Swedenborg's *Divine Love and Wisdom* bound with *Divine Providence*. These he read on the train trip east and arrived in New York eager to share his new faith with his wife. But religious problems affected her as little as they had Bigelow shortly before, nor was Bryant more interested, though he had no objections to increasing announcements in the columns of the *Post* of coming New Church attractions or of lectures on Swedenborg or to reviews of Swedenborgian books. George Bush welcomed his views, however, and so did the pastor of the New Church on East Thirty-fifth Street where Bigelow went to hear Swedenborg's teachings expounded.[9]

Bigelow was satisfied that he had, in his thirty-seventh year, stumbled upon a rational interpretation of man and God and the universe. He no longer found the miraculous birth of Jesus and the miracles He performed obstacles to faith; he was no longer confused by chronological and scientific inaccuracies in the Bible, because he believed that the spiritual meanings of the physical references, as explained by Swedenborg, were understandable, consistent throughout, and universally true. And though he could not accept Swedenborg's claims to conversations with Divinity, he refused to let a doubt about their origin blind him to the validity of the ideas themselves. More than thirty years later, when he was an authority on Swedenborg and an absolute believer in his doctrines, he still wrote cautiously of Swedenborg's visions in *Emanuel Swedenborg Servus Domini*, published in 1888:

> Whether Swedenborg did hear the Saviour's knock and open the door, whether he did hold the commission and receive the instructions he professes to have received, are questions which cannot be determined by the testimony of Swedenborg; for though there was never probably a more truthful man, nor one who lived more exclusively to the honor and glory of God, he was human and therefore liable to illusions; neither can these questions be determined by other witnesses, because from the nature of the case there were and could have been none. . . .
>
> If they [his concepts] seem to be of sufficient importance to justify their alleged divine origin; if they harmonize at all points with the record which all Christians accept as the genuine Work of God; if they make the Word plainer; if they reconcile things in the Word which before seemed inconsistent, and tend to unite those who before were divided in regard to its teachings, then it would be unreasonable to suppose that Swedenborg was the victim of illusions, and did not enjoy the intercourse with our Lord and the angels which he professed and believed he enjoyed.

That passage read in conjunction with the following indicates that in the end Bigelow decided it was "unreasonable to suppose that Swedenborg was the victim of illusions" and was more willing to accept than to reject his teacher's explanation of the source of his authority:

> To those whose education and training have made it necessary for them to have a reason for the faith that is in them; who are too conscientious to profess a belief in statements which they cannot reconcile with their experience or their reason; who think the human intellect is fully competent to measure and appropriate all the truth of which man has need in this life, Swedenborg has brought unspeakable comfort and satisfaction, by letting them see that they were the victims of their own blindness rather than, as they had allowed themselves to suppose, of the obscurity of the Scrip-

tures. Of the already large number of this class who owe to the writings of Swedenborg the restoration of their impaired faith in the Divine authority of the Word, the writer gratefully acknowledges himself to be one.[10]

Primarily Swedenborg gave him belief in the Oneness of a personal God, whose infinite love was as manifest in hell as in heaven, and an explanation of the apparent incongruities in the Bible. Bigelow came to believe not only that all causes are spiritual and that all natural objects have their origins in spiritual truths, but that the Bible was written according to the law of correspondences between material phenomena and their spiritual meanings. Man, however, had forgotten the true meanings of the Biblical words until Swedenborg revealed the road to understanding which others could travel if they would study and reflect and pray.[11]

So deeply was Bigelow influenced by Swedenborg that from 1854 on, from his thirty-seventh to his ninety-fifth year, his life can be understood only by bearing in mind Biblical standards of faith and conduct along with Swedenborg's interpretation of them. Yet though the conversion occurred in a brief period, it was but the sowing of the seed. No immediate revolution occurred in Bigelow's business, friendships, or mental attitudes. For years political affairs and reforms leading to increasing political, social, and economic freedom absorbed most of his time. For thirty years and more, opportunities for self-advancement continually tempted him. Only gradually did he subdue the promptings of his proprium, and indeed, at first only occasionally did he try.

He had the background, the training, the mental capacity, and the emotional stamina, the personal charm, and the aggressive strength that should have enabled him to reach as exalted a worldly position as any one of his contemporaries. He knew the people who could best further ambition. He was to hold positions which could easily be used as steppingstones. Yet he never was wealthy, and he never completely fulfilled the worldly promise of his youth. The explanation lies in his religious convictions, deepening as the years passed and widening the split between his earthly and his spiritual goals. His religion made him unable to lend himself entirely to the necessary compromises inherent in worldly success (even when the desire for it was still in him) and led him increasingly to measure his daily acts in terms of their utility to others, giving credit for whatever was good and useful in his life not to himself but to the God-Spirit acting through an inert physical receptacle, his body.

CHAPTER 9

A New Party;
Campaigning for Frémont

[*1854–1856*]

IN 1850 Bigelow had returned from Jamaica to find the country roused by Clay's compromise measures; in 1854 he returned from Haiti to a nation erupting in a stream of invective and hatred and searing bitterness, its two great political parties rent roughly in twain and the northern part of each torn and torn again by insistent, conflicting demands. He had left before Bryant even penned on December 1, 1853 his dark prognostication: "We shall have a battle for the rights of the settlers of Nebraska at the next session of Congress." Now in March that battle was in full swing. Bigelow's friends lost no time in describing to him what had happened.

In January Senator Stephen A. Douglas had proposed organizing the territory of Nebraska and repealing the Missouri Compromise. That is, Douglas had proposed removal of the lone surety of freedom north of 36°30′, giving slavery, after a thirty-four-year ban, at least a chance to expand. Apparently Douglas trusted to the magic of popular sovereignty, the businessmen's fear of dissension, and the American dream of a railroad to swing the North. He badly miscalculated. Within forty-eight hours, newspapers throughout the North had sent their thousands of readers a call to resist. Within a week, masses of citizens — even conservative citizens — had crowded to gigantic meetings to make their protests known. Merchants, lawyers, ministers, farmers, circulated petitions by the hundreds and deluged their senators with angry letters. Meanwhile in the Senate the bill was flayed by Salmon P. Chase of Ohio, Charles Sumner of Massachusetts, Sam Houston of Texas, and William H. Seward of New York. But Southern Senators found it good, the Administration supported it, and Douglas fought for it. It passed the Senate at five o'clock on the morning of March 4.[1]

All of that Bigelow had missed. Now at the moment of his return the Nebraska bill was before the House of Representatives. The *Evening Post* with other Northern newspapers was in the thick of the battle, straining its political alliances to support men of all parties who opposed the bill. Without wasting a moment Bigelow set to work. He shared with Bryant the stint of daily editorials denouncing the bill, followed day-by-day opinions in every state, revived "John Brown the Ferryman" to relay his findings. In April he congratulated the nation upon the Emigrant Aid Society which Massachusetts citizens were establishing to help antislavery men, regardless of Congress, insure freedom in Kansas. Later when the hated bill became law, he pinned his hope to the Emigrant Aid Societies which by then were being organized throughout the North. The only immediate practical endeavor, he believed, the one hope for freedom, lay in the settlement of Kansas by Northerners. So he joined several like-minded Whig and Democratic New Yorkers who met regularly at Edwin D. Morgan's home on Lafayette Place to act as a steering committee for the dissemination of information about Kansas and for the collection of money to help free men migrate there.[2] In the *Evening Post* he ran descriptions of the territory, letters from settlers praising its fertile soil, accounts of the various Emigrant Aid organizations, and appeals for funds. At the same time, he and Bryant repudiated President Pierce. They had supported him for two years, but they could not stomach his approval of the Kansas-Nebraska bill.

Thousands of citizens, Democrats, Whigs, Free-Soilers, abolitionists, nativists, were equally outraged. Already the man-on-the-street was beginning to hear sporadic talk of a new party. On May 23, the day after the Kansas-Nebraska bill passed the House by the close vote of 113 to 110, thirty determined Congressmen endorsed a new party, a "Republican party." Two days later when the House bill reached the Senate, Salmon P. Chase, longtime champion of the Free-Soilers, solemnly declared that passage of the bill would give rise to new political alignments. His was no idle threat. Senators Truman Smith and Ben Wade were openly advocating a third party. Preston King was urging a Benton-Seward ticket in '56, with Seward promised the top place in '60 in order to divide honors between anti-Nebraska Democrats and anti-Nebraska Whigs. The *Evening Post* reported the hope of an "old subscriber" — surely Bigelow's close friend King — that Thomas Hart Benton would lead a "personal party." In itself that editorial was unimportant; yet it had significance as the editors' first word, and among the earliest of printed words, in a campaign to canalize the rising flood of dissent.[3]

Meanwhile other states moved more rapidly than New York. In June the Whigs of Vermont demanded a fusion antislavery party. On July 6 indignant Michigan citizens met at Jackson and formally organized the first state Republican party. One week later fusion anti-Nebraska parties existed in Vermont, Ohio, and Indiana. The next week Massachusetts Free-Soilers adopted the title "Republican," though as yet the Whigs and Democrats there remained distinct and powerful groups. By the end of July, only two months after the Kansas-Nebraska bill became law, seven states had protest parties and in August Maine became the eighth. New York, however, was not of their number. For one thing, in that state business interests were closely tied to the South. For another, anti-Nebraska leaders of each of the strongly entrenched old parties were ready to enlist all men under their banner, but few of them wanted to raise a new one. True, Horace Greeley tried to lead to the inevitable by calling in June for a New York Republican party, just as A. N. Cole, editor of the *Genesee Valley Free Press*, had on May 16; but there was little response.[4]

The tactics of Bryant and Bigelow were more astute if less heroic. Throughout the summer their editorials and news columns were strongly anti-Nebraska in sentiment. But their editorials held firm to party allegiance, carefully avoiding the alienation of readers, while their news columns carried a barrage of small items about a third party shrewdly calculated through multiple suggestion to make their impression. One correspondent wrote that a group very like the Free-Soilers of 1848 would prevail in the next election. Another called for Benton as President and Seward as Vice-President. Still another suggested as leader of a new party Sam Houston, one-time Governor of Tennessee, hero of the Texan War for Independence, President of the Republic of Texas, for the last eight years U. S. Senator from Texas and one of the two Southern senators to oppose repeal of the Missouri Compromise. Bigelow privately thought him well worth watching. He helped to plan Houston's trip to the north in June and arranged for his speech in New York City. But editorially he, like Bryant, was careful not to commit himself.[5] Though Bigelow had been an avowed fusionist for some months and Bryant was already half-committed to the new party, they were convinced that their cause and their purse alike forbade their announcement of a new alliance until they were sure of carrying into the Republican party their readers, the intellectual Jacksonian Democrats.

Meanwhile they were frank to admit their dilemma, which they knew their readers shared. They believed in the principles of the

Democratic party. They did not want to join a short-lived party formed to oppose just one feature of American political conditions. Yet they objected to perennial truckling to the South. And when the New York anti-Nebraska convention registered opposition to the Kansas-Nebraska Act, but decided not to disturb existing parties, and when the Barnburner convention labeled the Nebraska Act "inexpedient and inadvisable," yet lamely recommended acceptance of it, Bigelow was ready for a clean break. Fusionism was sweeping the country, the *Post* clarioned; now let it come to New York.[6]

In a sense it did, when the New York Whigs, meeting late in September, roundly condemned the Nebraska Act, denounced Douglas's theory of popular sovereignty as "too flimsy to mislead any but those anxious to be deluded and eager to be led astray," wrote a platform in the strongest anti-Nebraska terms, and, though Seward and Weed were still unwilling to forgo the name "Whig," applauded Roscoe Conkling when he spoke of their convention as belonging to the "Republican party," which resulted in the endorsement of the Whig candidate by anti-Nebraskans, Free Democrats, and temperance men. But it was Whig-dominated fusion, which Bigelow and Bryant feared. So they remained neutral in the state campaign, and the *Tribune* and the *Times,* their shift an easier one because it was evident that Whigs would control the fusion party in New York and probably throughout the North, had the honor of preceding the *Evening Post* into the Republican party.

Their sympathies were obviously with the fusionists, against the Democrats, and against the Know-Nothings — the secret, anti-Catholic, anti-immigrant Native American party. Ten years before, the Know-Nothings had risen to sudden power in New York City, elected a mayor, then dropped into oblivion. Now they were powerful once more, spreading like wildfire across the land, feeding on men's love of mystery and their need, in uncertainty, for a scapegoat. New York alone had approximately 65,000 Know-Nothings in 1854. Even fairminded citizens who had no love for racial or religious discrimination were joining the party in hopes of using it to force Whigs and Democrats to stop temporizing on slavery. But not the editors of the *Post*. The vital issue was freedom, they said; not religion or place of birth — freedom of belief, of speech, of action for opponents as well as partisans. In 1852 Bigelow had devoted an entire campaign pamphlet to condemnation of General Scott's relations with the Know-Nothings in 1844. Now in 1854 the *Post* took its stand against them, in a noteworthy editorial on August 18:

. . . There is, moreover, not a little danger in widening the space between our native and our adopted citizens, and in giving the latter a distinct and isolated character under the denominations of Irishmen, Germans, Catholics, etc. No such distinction should be recognized. They are all, in the regard of our laws and constitutions, Americans, and any attempt to aggravate the natural jealousy and enmity of race should be frowned down, from whatever quarter it may come. Especially should the sectarian element in our politics be discountenanced. . . .

The formal break of the *Post* with its old party came only at the end of 1855 over the question of organizing the House of Representatives. By that time Free-Soilers, Democrats, Whigs, Know-Nothings, Republicans, and factions within factions caused such general confusion that one fact alone was certain — the Speaker would have to be elected by some combination of parties. Balloting commenced on December 3, but no one received a majority. A month passed; the deadlock continued. Election of the Speaker, usually a routine matter, became the battleground of slavery and antislavery men not only in Congress but throughout the country in every journal, tavern, and club. For two months Bryant and Bigelow poured out daily editorials on the importance of the issue. If an antislavery man, regardless of his party label, became Speaker, the "right" men would be appointed to committees, rules would be interpreted favorably, and the whole country would be stirred by proof that freedom in the territories would prevail. Finally the contest narrowed to two men, Nathaniel P. Banks of Massachusetts, alternately labeled coalition Democrat, Know-Nothing, and Republican, and Administration-supported William A. Richardson. In their support of the former the editors of the *Post* at last openly declared themselves Republicans. And after the one hundred and thirty-third ballot, on February 2, 1856, Banks was elected Speaker. Republicans were jubilant. They had won their first national recognition. Now, with the House favorably organized, they could turn to the major issue, the coming campaign.

The immediate necessity was to select a candidate sufficiently innocuous not to antagonize any of the heterogeneous groups which found themselves drawing together, a man new to politics yet known to the country, whose antecedents would alarm neither Whig nor Democrat; who was unsmirched by abolitionism or nativism, yet was acceptable to proponents of both; who was opposed to the extension of slavery, yet was not hated in the South. The process of finding such a man and of deciding which special interests should shape the platform already had brought political jockeying to the fore, giving rise to a cry of "cheap politics" among political illiterates who did not know that combination and compromise were their only means of putting a political ideal into practice. The leaders of the new party, however, were well read in politics. Governor Chase of Ohio, outspoken leader of the Free-Soil elements, had already engineered a call for a national meeting in February of all anti-Nebraskans — his purpose being to control the new machine. For his part, Seward of New York was hoping that he could prove the deciding element in the new party. So also, of course, hoped the old Jacksonian Democrats led by Francis P. Blair, Sr., and the Native Americans.

The "heirs of Jackson" concentrated on picking the candidate. Blair early realized that Chase and Seward would stalemate each other, that Houston, once a possible candidate, had proved too noncommittal on Kansas and too friendly to the Know-Nothings; so he looked for an acceptable man whom his group could control. As far back as July 17, 1855, the *Evening Post* had hinted that an unknown was being considered. A few men in Philadelphia, another group assembled by Blair in December, talked of the youthful John Charles Frémont, whose daring explorations in the West had caught the popular fancy. Bigelow knew the direction of Blair's thought, but at the time he was too absorbed in the essential first step of electing Nathaniel Banks Speaker of the House to take part in planning next moves.[7]

Once the House was organized, however, Banks himself came to New York, saw Bigelow, and discussed with him how best to use their recent victory. In less than three weeks the Republicans would convene at Pittsburgh, and though their nominating convention would not come until later, insiders should be agreed upon a Presidential candidate. Banks, who had won Blair to Frémont, now urged Bigelow to back the explorer. As Banks knew, Bigelow had thought enough of Frémont to give him favorable publicity in the *Post* on January 28 and 30. But, Bigelow now said, he had not yet met the explorer; and until he did meet him, he would not commit himself. By noon the following day that obstacle had been removed; Bigelow had talked with Frémont at the Metropolitan Hotel and had been favorably impressed.[8] A few days later, after ascertaining that Thomas Benton, Frémont's father-in-law, did not intend to oppose the candidacy (though in fact he later did) Bigelow and Blair went to the new Frémont home on Ninth Street to pledge their support.

Bigelow's first task was to persuade Bryant to endorse Frémont so that the *Evening Post* could become an effective campaign instrument. Next he invited a few men to his home one evening, ostensibly to meet Mr. Blair. Among his guests were Tilden, who still called himself a

Democrat, Edwin D. Morgan, with whom Bigelow had worked in the Emigrants Aid Society and who was soon to be Chairman of the Republican National Committee, Edward Miller and some others. Before they departed, all but Tilden had agreed to work for Frémont. In like manner Bigelow was to work for Frémont, through his friends and through his paper, from February to November.[9]

When the first Republican National Convention met in Pittsburgh on February 22, the "heirs of Jackson" took the lead. Francis P. Blair, Sr., was made permanent chairman. E. D. Morgan, an ex-Whig, influential among the Americans and privately committed to Frémont after the meeting in Bigelow's home, became Chairman of the National Committee. Before adjournment, arrangements were completed for a nominating convention to meet in Philadelphia on June 17, Bunker Hill Day, not four months off. Frémont adherents began to work in earnest. On February 26, Bigelow wrote to Salmon P. Chase pertinently, though with elaborate circumspection:

> . . . If the election goes to the House we shall probably lose the President but it will be enough of a victory to have defeated the pro-Slavery party with the people in a fair fight as we unquestionably can do if anything like the same discretion and singleness of purpose are exhibited by the Republican nominating convention which shall meet in June as were exhibited by that which has just adjourned at Pittsburg. All I ask for is, that the delegates to the former convention may keep before their mind the great and single end *success for freedom*, in the selection of their candidate without regard to personal relations or preferences of any kind. If they do and I think that was a distinguishing feature of the Pittsburg deliberations, we shall have a candidate — who he will be I cannot pretend to guess but I am sure Providence will provide us with one — who will achieve the emancipation of the country from the dominion of the Slaveocracy, if he is not elected President.
>
> I do not learn that much was said at Pittsburg about candidates, nor is there much talk here upon the subject. Your name is mentioned of course as one of the few from whom a selection is to be made. Fremont also is talked especially by the Old Whigs who like him naturally, better than any man who is or has been identified with old party controversies. Blairs name has also been mentioned with favor especially by some of the old Van Buren party here and his running capacities canvassed, but no one seems quite prepared to say either is exactly the man for the emergency, or of either which, until events develop themselves a little farther in Congress. The Kansas question I fear is getting into a bad shape;

that the Free State men and their Eastern Champions are getting
into an insurrectionary attitude from which they cannot escape
without a collision with the general government of such a nature
that the people of the states will be drawn to the support of the
government. That is what the President is playing for with all his
might and it becomes you and those who guide the party to keep
your eye open upon this matter. For my own part of course I
would prefer to have a personal friend nominated for the Presidency rather than a stranger but I am prepared to support with all
my might any man who is nominated fair & square in opposition
to the nationalization of slavery. I shall be glad to hear from you
always and especially at a time when I feel a professional need of
the best advice.[10]

Shortly thereafter Bigelow started a biography of Frémont. On
May 18, before any other New York City newspaper had singled out
the explorer, he began publishing in the *Post* a chapter a week from
his forthcoming biography. Nor did he permit the pressure of daily
editing, of letters and conversations to persuade the reluctant and to
counsel with the convinced, interrupt his Saturday biography. He did
not spend a day away from New York until June, and then he left
only for a few days to serve as delegate from the fifth district of
New York to the Republican nominating convention held in Philadelphia.

There, grim and bloody Kansas was the theme. Every citizen in the
country knew that under a fraudulent, proslavery Constitution, a
farcical election had set up a territorial government. They knew, also,
that the Northern settlers had in turn written their own factional Constitution forbidding slavery, under it had elected Reeder — ex-Governor of Kansas who turned against President Pierce — as their delegate
to Congress, and in February 1856 had asked for admission as a free
state. They knew that from North and South alike, advice, encouragement, money, and weapons had flowed to the men of Kansas. Fresh
in their memories were Charles Sumner's philippic, "The Crime against
Kansas," the vicious thrashing it earned him on the floor of the United
States Senate, and the renewed outbreaks in Kansas: Lawrence burned,
Osawatomie sacked, settlers killed, the antislavery Topeka legislature
dispersed by United States troops.

Then it was that the five hundred and sixty-five Republican delegates,
and hundreds of well-wishers from every free state and from Delaware,
Maryland and Kentucky, met in Philadelphia. The moment boded
well. National Hall shook with the cheers of the immense throng which
assembled on Monday evening, June 16, to hear General Pomeroy and

Judge Conway demand action in the name of Kansas and to listen to John A. Wills of California announce the theme of the party: "Tolerate slavery where it is, as many a nuisance has to be tolerated; but do not give it power to control, to govern, to wreck the great experiment in freedom on the continent of America." [11]

Shortly before noon on the following morning the delegates met at Musical Fund Hall for their first session. As politicians, they knew they were no consultative body, knew that their decisions had already been made, that to form a national organization numbers of compromises had been necessary. As practical men they accepted that necessity; as purposeful men they welcomed it as the means by which they could accomplish their primary aim, the exclusion of slavery from the territories. It was soon evident that the Seward Whigs had written the platform, and written it carefully, for it opposed the repeal of the Missouri Compromise, opposed the extension of slavery, condemned the atrocities in Kansas, demanded its admission as a free state, and denied that Congress had the right to establish slavery in the territories so emphatically that a plank favoring the old Whig policy of government-fostered public improvements passed without objection.

Balancing the Whiggish platform was the nomination of the Jacksonian Democrats' candidate for the Presidency — a foregone conclusion thanks to the preparatory strategy of Banks, Blair, Bigelow, and Morgan. On Wednesday morning, June 18, after Seward, Chase, and McLean withdrew from the contest, releasing their pledged delegates, an informal ballot overwhelmingly endorsed Frémont. The first formal ballot gave him all but thirty-seven votes, whereupon the nomination was made unanimous by acclamation. Then came three cheers for Frémont, then three more and more. Suddenly a flag appeared upon the platform: "For President, John C. Frémont." Delegates, springing upon settees, waved their hats and shouted in unprecedented enthusiasm. The next morning nominations for the Vice-Presidency were in order. Bigelow had labored to secure that office for Charles Sumner, thinking it highly appropriate that he should preside where he had been so brutally treated. But the Massachusetts delegation withdrew Sumner's name, and Senator William L. Dayton, ex-Whig from New Jersey, was nominated unanimously after an informal ballot gave him 259 votes to 110 for the West's choice — Abraham Lincoln, ex-Whig from Illinois. [12]

With the cheers of "Free Speech, Free Soil, and Freemont" ringing in his ears — a handy slogan though it put a false stress on the first syllable of the candidate's name — Bigelow hastened home to divide his time between his newspaper office and campaign headquarters at

34 Broadway, where E. D. Morgan, F. P. Blair, Bigelow, Isaac Sherman, Col. Charles James, and Thurlow Weed steered Republican fortunes. They organized meetings, set up a speakers' bureau, collected funds, established a center for the collection of statistics and gossip and for the preparation of releases. Bigelow's first job was to enlarge his articles about the nominee and publish as soon as possible a complete, interesting, and inexpensive biography. Mrs. Frémont gave him invaluable help by undertaking in those hot July days to write the opening chapters about her husband's ancestry and childhood. Frémont supplied reports of his trips, and as Bigelow organized the material, many a conference between the two was fitted into odd moments. On his way to the opera one evening Bigelow dropped in to hear Mrs. Frémont's opening pages, and was delighted.[18] But the book was taking too much time. Other biographies of Frémont were on the market before Bigelow's book even reached the publisher. His own paper was carrying advertisements like the following, which flooded the press of the country:

Ready Thursday — July 17
SMUCKER'S LIFE OF FRÉMONT
WHY IT IS THE BEST

. . .

Thousands of Agents wanted
. . .   Upham's   . . .
Illustrated Life
of
Frémont
The Authorized and Best Memoir

. . .

You will "get the best" if you wait for
Bigelow's Life of Frémont
AUTHORIZED LIFE AND PUBLIC SERVICES
of John Charles Frémont

That last advertisement was weak. Each day it seemed less convincing. Horton's biography of Buchanan, the Democratic candidate, was issued on July 19. That same day Upham advertised that 30,000 copies of his life of Frémont were already printed, while Bigelow asked the public to be patient and "wait for Bigelow's *Life of Frémont*." Two days later Smucker needed "thousands of agents" to sell his book; Upham wanted "a hundred thousand" agents; still the public was to be patient and "wait for Bigelow's *Life of Frémont*." Mrs. Frémont never knew much about patience. Neither did Bigelow in those days.

On July 31 he ran a new advertisement, one third of a column long, assuring the public that his book would be ready "soon" and stating exactly what in it was not available elsewhere. To every editor who copied that advertisement he offered a free copy of the book. On August 2 the whole first page of the *Post* was devoted to excerpts from it, and two days later the *Post* gave columns to another excerpt, this one copied, with credits, from the morning *Times!* Finally on August 6 Derby and Jackson began distribution.

New advertisements appeared, high-lighting the *New York Independent's* review: ". . . fullest, most complete account . . . and by its plain and irrefragable facts forestalls and silences the whole immense brood of malignant slanders . . ."; and the Washington *National Era's* statement: ". . . prepared with excellent judgment by an intimate friend of Frémont's." [14] Before long some 40,000 copies of Bigelow's book were sold; a best-seller, it replaced the family album on half the living-room tables in the United States, according to one partisan reporter. (Yet for all its popularity at one dollar a copy, Bigelow made nothing on it. He put away the notes given him by the publishers and forgot to present them until some time after the company had quietly died.) [15]

His *Memoir of the Life and Public Services of John Charles Frémont* had to compete with three other biographies of the Republican candidate which were already in circulation, Bartlett's, Smucker's, and Upham's. Bartlett's thirty-two page pamphlet was written at Horace Greeley's command and was sold through the *Tribune* office for twenty-five cents a copy. Frankly admitting that his only excuse for writing it was to help put Frémont in the White House, the author derided other biographers for saying they were motivated by a pure desire to tell of Colonel Frémont without reference to the coming election, and then proceeded to help his candidate by announcing his amazing similarity to Washington, both of whose lives reflected "that calm steadfastness . . . that strength of will. . . ." [16] Samuel Smucker went even further; he not only found that Frémont and Washington had much in common but remarked his hero's resemblance to Jackson as well. One chapter of this biography was Smucker's writing, the others were excerpts from Frémont's reports, and the whole did not carry the story to 1856. [17] Competing most with Bigelow's book was Upham's, a fair, impartial, lasting record, the author said. Here were detailed the brilliant, successful episodes in Frémont's life; incidents which might need explaining were slurred over or ignored. About the court-martial, in which Frémont had been convicted of insubordination in California, Upham noted only that as Frémont sent a message "to the dying pillow of the principal prosecutor, of forgiveness, Christian sympathy and good will, it would ill become these pages to renew the controversy. . . ." [18]

Not so Bigelow. His book was hastily written and had all the faults of haste. Yet he not only mentioned the court-martial but gave the record of the entire proceedings, an astute inclusion, as Thurlow Weed, newspaperman and political boss, was quick to realize.[19] Anyone owning Bigelow's book could look to the record and check against it the exaggerated statements the opposition was making. And anyone in his senses would know that a campaign biographer would include nothing to the discredit of his hero, so that Bigelow's readers might well believe it was Frémont who carried the honors of that court-martial. In like manner Bigelow stated the entire circumstances of the two challenges to duels which Frémont sent, the one in California, the other in the Senate of the United States. Charles A. Dana, then managing editor of the *Tribune*, who had agreed to read proof, wired the publisher to stop the press when he reached that section, and hastened to Bigelow to implore him not to lose the Quaker vote by writing of duels. Bigelow's reply, that the sin of omission would cost more votes than it might gain, sent Dana off in high dudgeon, predicting that Bigelow would lose them the election and swearing to go to Europe and have no more to do with the campaign.[20] But he did not go, and Bigelow put in all the facts, though he undoubtedly added coloring. That Frémont was slow to take offense or to suspect evil motives, that he never appealed to the code of honor to avenge personal wrongs but only to champion the rights of others, was obvious propaganda.

Yet Bigelow always made it clear where documented fact ended and his interpretation began. His intention, he said in his preface, was to give sources for all his statements so that guided by them the reader could "adjust for the partialities of political or personal friendship." And he succeeded as fully as he could have wished. His material was sufficiently documented to satisfy the most particular critic, while his tone was nicely calculated to win the average reader's vote for Frémont. In the last chapter he presented a careful analysis of the explorer's character and accomplishments, which, though not critical, did avoid stupid generalizations likening his subject to heroes of the past. Many years later Frémont's ablest biographer, in a fair, thorough estimate, was to credit the pathfinder with strengths very similar to those Bigelow remarked, though he was also to include weaknesses which Bigelow carefully and understandably omitted.[21]

Once the book was published, Bigelow could help more in other

CHAPTER 10

Through Panic to Profits

[*1857–1858*]

BRYANT departed for Europe in May 1857 after a hard winter during which he and Bigelow had ceaselessly denounced Fernando Wood in New York, the President and his weak cabinet in Washington, General Walker's filibuster in Nicaragua, and the tragedy of the year, "a conspiracy . . . of the most treasonable character" — the Dred Scott decision of the Supreme Court.[1] Now for the third long period the *Evening Post* was left in Bigelow's capable hands.

Fortunately running the paper was temporarily a routine task, for Bigelow was absorbed in his own affairs. He had purchased a country home the preceding summer in Buttermilk Falls — later called Highland Falls — a Hudson River village perched on the high cliffs two miles south of the fashionable summer resort at West Point. The house was close enough to the road and the town so that even in winter it would not be isolated, back enough to give some privacy which could be made complete by judicious planting of shrubbery, and only a five-minute drive from the dock of the New York steamer on which Bigelow would commute. Careful though Bigelow had been to check such practical matters, what had determined the sale was the clear air, the wide lawn sweeping to the cliffs' edge, the sight of the long-loved river below and the rolling foothills of the Catskills in the distance. Bigelow wanted this for his children, for sturdy four-year-old Grace, for two-year-old John, Jr., and for the baby, a second Poultney. He wanted them to know the fresh reality of space; he wanted, too, to regain for himself something he had missed since at eighteen he had made New York his home. He had bought the house on the spot, closing the deal with the customary one dollar token payment before returning to New York to arrange a first mortgage of $2990 and a down payment of $510 on the $10,000 place.[2]

In December, after the election, he had purchased an adjacent farm to get a full twelve-acre estate. Next he had placed his city home on the market and soon disposed of it at a handsome profit. In the spring he had engaged Calvert Vaux, the brilliant young English architect who, with Frederick Law Olmsted, was shortly to be awarded the contract for planning Central Park, to make alterations and additions to the low-ceilinged farmhouse. He hired workmen to plant fruit trees, plow the fields, and fix the roads. Finally in May, shortly after Bryant sailed, the Bigelows' moving day arrived. It took nine wagons to transport their possessions; nine trunks filled with clothing, linens, yard goods; bureaus precariously packed with clothes, pictures, and jellies; all of their furniture and carpeting; barrels of china, boxes of blankets and music, and the inevitable last-minute box of temper-trying odds and ends — in this case, stray bits of clothing, a hammer, a saw, a gravy boat, and a nursery clock.

There were also ten large crates of books, which were Bigelow's most prized possessions. Aside from law books, dictionaries, and a mass of pamphlets, he now owned almost fifteen hundred titles, making considerably more than twice that many volumes (a much larger library than that of Washington College where he had studied for almost three years). Among them were a few religious works — Bibles, all of Swedenborg's writings which were available in translation, Theodore Parker's sermons, two books on spiritualism. He had some science textbooks, probably acquired at college, and he had a smattering of poetry, chiefly Roman poets and his famous British and American contemporaries. But there were large gaps in this field, for poetry never appealed to Bigelow as did a well-presented argument; significantly, no writings of Poe or Whitman, both of whom he had met, were among those listed in the worn leather notebook he usually carried in his pocket these days. He liked novels, however, and though Fielding's were the only eighteenth-century tales on his shelves, almost every important novel and short story of the nineteenth century was there.

The bulk of his library consisted of history, biography, and the writings and speeches of famous men. The greatest of the Greek and most of the Roman prose writers were his as well as the best histories of ancient times — Grote and Heeren on Greece, Gibbon and Arnold on Rome, and so on. Modern European history was more sketchily covered; he did not, for example, own Motley's *Rise of the Dutch Republic*, but his volumes on America were almost all-inclusive. He owned the writings of Washington, Franklin, Jefferson, Paine, Adams, Clay, Webster, and numbers of lesser Americans. He had four volumes of Richard Hildreth's *History of the United States of America*, a work he would have considered excellent had he, like Hildreth, identified

Jefferson with Antichrist.[3] He owned the six volumes which Bancroft had published in his classic history and he had also several lesser one-volume histories of the United States, including William Grimshaw's textbook, specialized histories of states or periods such as the first volume of John Brodhead's *History of the State of New York*, Jabez Hammond's three-volume *History of Political Parties in the State of New York*, and Jay's *History of the Mexican War*. Strangely enough, he did not have Prescott's *History of the Conquest of Mexico*, unless he meant that by a book he listed as "Mexico —." His was no library built to impress. It was the record of Bigelow's own intellectual life, of his early wide interest in all past times, his increasing concern with his own country and with sources which would explain its present institutions, and his constant delight in a well-phrased idea.

Fortunately Bigelow had no cause to worry about the expense of opening "The Squirrels" — the name they gave to their home, to Nathaniel P. Willis's mock dismay — because each year he earned a larger income than he had anticipated. In 1850 he made over $4000; in 1856 his share was $9448.86. By then, eight years after he had joined the *Post*, he had repaid the $15,000 he had borrowed for his shares, and he had a credit of almost $2000 on the company's books. Obviously the confidence he had expressed in himself was well-founded, for Bryant was no businessman and not all of the credit for the new office, the new equipment, and the mounting profits belonged to the stirring times which made more people anxious for the latest news.

Part of it resulted from the business Bigelow had brought to the job office; part of it resulted from his insistence upon a new business manager. Three years before, in '54, after Timothy Howe had repeatedly failed to measure up to his responsibilities, Bigelow asked for a partners' meeting in Bryant's office. Bluntly he announced that the present arrangement could not continue; either Howe would have to buy him out or sell out to him. Howe stammered a bit, looked at Bryant, who would not raise his eyes from the papers on his desk, then, with lips whitening, said: "Very well. I see that Mr. Bryant is with you in the matter and I will go." Shortly thereafter Isaac Henderson, who as head of the job office had showed a talent for detail and for getting full value out of every penny, bought Howe's shares, cheerfully paying $17,000 and 6 per cent of the dividends for the next five years, a decidedly larger sum than Bigelow had paid just five years before. At the same time the partnership was reorganized, Bryant selling some of his holdings so that each partner held a full third of the company.

Later, it is true, when Bigelow was no longer a partner, Henderson's

love of money took him across the dividing line between sharp business and dishonesty. As Naval Agent in New York during the Civil
War he was charged with accepting commissions on government contracts which he let, and escaped conviction only on a technicality. At
the time his partner Bryant and his ex-partner Bigelow stood by him,
because, though they themselves were men of unquestioned integrity,
they knew that Henderson's crime was, in fact, almost customary, that
if he were convicted almost every man in the country holding a
similar position should be similarly convicted, and that he would never
have been prosecuted had not Thurlow Weed wanted to hit back at
the *Post* for Bryant's ceaseless condemnation of Weed's morals. Still
later, Henderson was involved in other irregularities, but so long as
Bigelow was connected with the company, the man was a decided
asset.[4]

Financially, therefore, Bigelow had no problems early in '57, though
he now had to hire a farmer as well as a nurse and cook, and he had
constant driblets going out for tools, plants, seeds, new sheds, an icehouse, work animals. In fact, he had few serious problems of any sort
during the first half of the year. Each day he took the river boat, the
Mary Powell, for a two-hour sail to the city. At first he spent those
hours in luxurious enjoyment of the cool breezes and the eye-delight-
ing view. Then he became acquainted with fellow commuters and
looked forward to joking with them and picking up stray bits of
news. In July, however, business conditions forced him into new
studies and his work piled up alarmingly, until he arranged for undisturbed use of a standing desk in the ship's baggage room, where each
morning he turned out an editorial or a book review.[5]

Occasional murmurs of scarce money had gone unheeded throughout the spring, but by July it was obvious that specie was hiding, an
ominous sign. Yet the country was unquestionably prosperous. Customs revenue for the year ending June 30, 1857, surpassed $64,000,000.
The national debt was a mere $29,000,000 — $40,000,000 less than it had
been only four years before. Railroads were doing unprecedented
business, their cars clacking over 25,000 miles of track as compared to
the 8600 miles which had existed in 1851. Farmers this year were raising bumper crops. Men were starting new businesses, or expanding old
ones, with ample support from the state banks, which had more than
doubled in number since 1850 until now there were over 1400 of them.
Prosperity was evident in the elaborate mansions, the luxurious trains
fitted with sleeping compartments and swivel chairs, the vastly increased pleasure traveling, the millions of dollars spent on unessentials,
on silks, laces, jewels.[6]

At that point the Erie Railroad, in constant financial trouble even in these boom years, elected a new president, Charles Moran. His task (which proved hopeless; two years later he was succeeded by the notorious cattle-trader, steamboat and railroad magnate, Daniel Drew) was to put the Erie in shape. For this he was to be paid the unheard-of salary of $25,000 a year. Bigelow wrote an editorial on July 23 congratulating the Erie. As a lifelong believer in free enterprise and in the rightness of a society that gave full monetary reward to those men whose abilities were most in demand, he had reason to commend the railroad; and, because he also believed that society had the right to demand good service from the able, he urged other companies to put an end to their current practice of hiring low-salaried presidents, who notoriously acted as ex-officio stockjobbers, playing the market with their inside knowledge to their own profit and their company's loss. Pay a man well for his services, he pleaded, and pass a law forbidding officers to own stock in the company they serve.

So far as Bigelow could see, such speculation was causing much of the business uncertainty so obvious in July. On August 3 he penned an editorial on "A Growing Evil," telling of $22,000,000 worth of stock traded in the last two weeks. The situation was becoming impossible; merchants, professional men, literary men, even the clergy, were playing the stock market. They were unsettling the commercial credit of the land and were ruining real business. Bigelow said 7 per cent was enough return on capital for anyone; this gambling to get something for nothing was as unsound economically as it was morally. Obviously companies were as guilty as private citizens. Bigelow asserted that the Michigan Southern Railroad stock was secretly overissued, to the hurt of the stockholders; this he reiterated on August 11 after the company denied the charge.

On August 12, the morning *Journal of Commerce* arraigned him for careless, incendiary writing:

> If the *Post* really thinks that the stock of the Michigan Southern *is* worthless and the immense capital expended in its construction is totally sunk, has it a special mission to denounce those who try to sell it *at something over its value? Cannot buyers be left to exercise, for a brief space, their own right of judgment, without having the danger of making a bad bargain rung daily into their ears?* [7]

Bigelow read that editorial and reached for paper Shortly after noon the *Post* went to press with his long essay on man's responsibility for man, on a citizen's responsibility when he sees a robber sneak into a neighbor's house. He concluded:

In our capacity as journalists we recognize the same code of ethics that we endeavor to preserve as individuals, and if there is any one duty which we regard as more obligatory than another upon the conductor of a public press, it is to publish whatever intelligence we possess, calculated to protect innocent parties from fraud and imposition.

Later the Michigan Southern admitted the issue of several hundred thousand dollars' worth of stock, not to sell but to pledge as security with the banks in order to borrow funds, the use of which the company confidently expected would improve the road and provide future profit beyond what would be needed to retire the stock. Here for Bigelow was proof of the growing propensity to gamble. That a reputable company could thus secretly jeopardize the investments of its stockholders on the chance of future gain, that the banks not only tolerated but connived at it, showed the demoralized state of the country. Not content with the share of the gifts of Providence to which honest industry would entitle them, this company and most others, he charged, were seeking other men's shares without offering any equivalent for them.[8] On August 18 he pointed his moral by showing the loss of a half-million dollars the company sustained when it had to sell the secretly issued stock at a loss to cover its pledges to the banks, consequent to the drop in the market once the watering became known. Proper ethics, Bigelow believed, undisturbed that he had helped make known the watering, would take a company to the open market when it needed funds, and, if there unable to borrow, it should give up efforts to increase capital.

Nevertheless the plea of the *Journal of Commerce* not to destroy business confidence had some justification. The current revolt in India affected international exchanges, the New York stock market had been falling all year, bank deposits, lowered by the usual spring buying, were sure to sink further in the autumn. Yet total loans and discounts steadily increased until they amounted to $122,000,000 by August 8. The inevitable happened when the New York branch of the great Ohio Life Insurance and Trust Company, holder of a half-million dollars of country bankers' deposits which it had lent to unsound railroad companies, was unable to meet the seasonal withdrawal of balances. On August 24 it was forced to suspend, and the crisis was on.

Within two weeks the frantic banks of New York had contracted their loans by $7,000,000 in an effort to avoid the fate of the Ohio Trust Company, and fifty-nine businesses in New York were driven to the wall, thirty-three of them in the city itself. The stock market broke. Failures mounted as men sought in vain for specie to cover their marginal purchases. In every business center the list of bankrupts lengthened. On September 24 the Fond du Lac and the Delaware, Lackawanna, and Western railroads failed. The next day the Bank of Pennsylvania closed, and all the banks of Pennsylvania agreed to suspend payments on notes. Not since 1837 had America experienced such a panic — and never until 1893 would so large an amount of capital be involved.[9]

"Business of all kinds is more completely suspended than it would have been two months ago if a hostile fleet had anchored in our harbor, or if a pestilence were sweeping the land," Bigelow wrote.[10] Four questions demanded answers: What caused the panic? What could stop it? How could its repetition be averted? By what standards should men guide their conduct during it? Bigelow tackled the last question on September 29:

> . . . The wise man begins to realize his weakness; he is ashamed of his harsh judgments of others, and his too flattering judgments of his own wisdom and goodness. . . . The curtain of selfishness which bounded his vision seems to be suddenly drawn aside. . . . Who knows how many it will teach to think moderately of their own achievements, and judge leniently the shortcomings of the less successful? . . . What, after all, is the loss about which we make so much ado? The money or the property for the want of which so many fail, is not lost. . . . The wealth of the country is merely changing hands.
>
> The unexampled prosperity of this country, and the prompt reward which every specie of intelligent industry commands here, have made Americans the most conceited and self-reliant people upon the face of the earth. . . . We have been growing, as a nation, grasping, arrogant, quarrelsome, indifferent to international obligations, and tolerant of private as well as public fraud. . . . All our past follies are coming to light; the great men of the Exchange, to whom we bowed with a selfish idolatry, are proving to be but wooden images.

On October 9 he returned to the subject, writing:

> When the calamity is so universal, when property of undisputed value ceases to pay debts, it is no dishonor to any man to surrender his property to his creditors. But what they have to look to is, that in their anxiety to preserve their property and their credit, they do nothing which they or their children will have reason hereafter to regret; that they do not neglect that forbearance and consideration for others, of which all now stand in so much need; that in these hours of general misfortune they yield to

no selfish impulses; that they close their hands and hearts to no just appeal, nor, in following too faithfully the instinct of self-preservation, do anything calculated to alienate tried friends, whose respect and good offices are better worth retaining than all the property which it is possible to gain or lose. No amount of wealth is worth securing at the expense of our self-respect, or by the sacrifice of a single generous impulse.

Experts tried to account for the crisis, and Bigelow with them, though he had little to guide him beyond a general acquaintance with Manchester dogma and a conviction, springing from Bentham, reinforced in new accents by Swedenborg, that life must be useful. As did other editors in October, he blamed the speculation in stocks, the exorbitant railroad expansion, and the wild extravagance of material-minded Americans. But the variety of current explanations merely confirmed the general bewilderment. Then came a run on the Park Bank, failure of the Bowery Bank, runs on seven other city banks, suspension of payment in eighteen of New York City's fifty-six banks. Finally, on October 13, after Wall Street was jammed with thousands of people madly trying to get their money, the other banks agreed to close as a protective measure, though their specie reserves were adequate.[11]

"Credit no longer exists, and business is entirely at a standstill," the *Evening Post* announced on October 14. Five days later fourteen railroads had gone under. Before the crisis was past four hundred companies in New York and Brooklyn alone went bankrupt, and thirty to forty thousand New Yorkers were out of work. A cry arose for legislative action, for a special session to save the state. Bigelow uncompromisingly opposed it, asserting that "all legislation in a panic is apt to be crude and unfortunate," and when his view prevailed, men like Preston King praised him for his leadership.[12] Yet desperate mobs were parading through the city. One horde even dragged a cannon through the fashionable streets. Five thousand hungry men gathered at Tompkins Square on November 5 and marching first to the Mayor and then through Wall Street, threateningly demanded a "right to a living." Day by day their situation grew worse.

Then Fernando Wood, Mayor of New York whom the *Evening Post* constantly attacked for underhand, corrupt practices, proposed employing the poverty-stricken in the new Central Park and the purchase of fifty thousand barrels of flour to be sold to them at cost. The panic had cost the innocent poor their employment, he reasoned; for them the coming winter would be one of crime-inducing calamity unless the city looked after its own and endorsed these arrangements of the Mayor's.[13] The plan went through, despite the indignant opposition of the *Post*. Bigelow did not believe that people were in actual want, though it was a fact that thousands of them were. He did believe that the whole scheme was concocted to strengthen Wood's corrupt machine, which in part it undoubtedly was.

Yet aside from the possible sufferings of some individuals at the moment and the probable profits Wood expected through the project, Bigelow saw a deeper problem. Was government to exercise an all-embracing control? Bigelow believed that no good could possibly come from favoring any one class. This scheme of Wood's would create a pauper class of the sort that would never grow smaller, a class that throughout all time had tyrannized government and sent it to bankruptcy or revolution. If times were bad, and they were, government should retrench, should live within its income, while private citizens should help their less fortunate brothers first by learning the facts, as in this instance Bigelow, S. B. Ruggles, Peter Cooper and others did by asking H. W. Bellows, D.D., to give a series of lectures upon "The Treatment of Social Diseases Related to Pauperism and Crime," and then by opening their purses.[14] Certainly, Bigelow believed, government should not seek funds for public improvements with the argument that unless the poor were put to work there would be violence. Such a doctrine was not only foolish, it was dangerous. Wood was saying, wrote Bigelow: ". . . Buy up our criminals; hire them to respect the laws, or they will rob you. 'Honest men, toil, economize, deny yourselves and your families, that your earnings may be sufficient to pay the scoundrels of the metropolis not to plunder your house, not to knock you down in the streets for your watches, not to seek your storehouse or your barns.' " [15]

Fortunately the depression was of short duration. The business of the country was sound, and as specie started pouring back to the banks, business houses reopened and jobs gradually were available. From a low of $8,000,000 in October, the banks held $28,000,000 in specie before the end of the year. Bigelow had reason to write on December 7 that New York banks at last held sufficient sums to make a full shift to specie payments without the shock of contractions, and he proclaimed:

> Today is New York's opportunity. Will she use it? The position which New Yorkers felt sure their city was to occupy at some distant day, that of being the banker of the world, the depository of the world's currency, the great center of the world's commerce, the agents at whose counters all the exchanges and credits for the world's business are to be adjusted and settled —

this position is offered her today, if she will assume it. She has to take but one firm step to gain it. *She must reform her currency*. If she would be the world's banker, she must deal in the world's only currency; in that money which alone passes current all over the commercial world — gold and silver.

Already the New Orleans banks had reopened; on December 12 New York banks resumed, and two days later Boston banks followed suit.

The outlook brightened throughout the nation, though to neighborhoods like the Five Points section of New York the winter brought frightful suffering. Most people, however, like Bigelow unable to comprehend the miseries of city-bred poor, looked forward to the holidays with lighter spirit and more hope for the future. Greeley and some other editors urged young men to go West, to return to the farms for a sure livelihood. But not Bigelow. He was convinced that America's future lay in large-scale production. In a prophetic editorial on December 31, 1857, he urged the youth of the city not to succumb to the fallacious reasoning of those who advised a return to the past:

. . . Why this advice? Do we lack a full supply of agricultural products? Have we a large surplus of manufactured articles? Our tables of exports and imports show a yearly export of agricultural products of over two hundred millions value, and an import of nearly the same amount of foreign manufactures. Our export of manufactured articles is not much beyond a tenth of our imports.

How preposterous, in presence of this state of facts, to urge men to go from city to country occupations. . . . Farming as a profitable pursuit for obvious reasons, is overdone in this country. . . . It is likely to be more so in the future. Every year will find the small farmer engaged in a more stringent competition with the capitalist, whose money and machinery have not, until lately, found profitable employment in the cultivation of the soil. Lately he has begun to take to himself whole townships of land, and to grow his wheat and corn on thousand acre fields, and to count his herds by myriads. Every year improved machinery adds to the concentration of power in the great farmer, and reduces the cost of production. He is just beginning to use steam to work for him; and it is not extravagant to expect that he will soon make it plough, reap and thresh, and perhaps carry his harvest to market, on his own hook.

He did, to be sure, urge men to move West, to the great plain extending from Quebec to New Orleans, from the Appalachians to the

Rockies, if they wanted to live where the great opportunities lay. But once there, they should enter business, not farming:

> Raw materials for manufactures and cheap food everywhere abound. . . . The great industrial development of the next ten years, and of many succeeding decades, is likely to find its chief theatres at the best commercial towns of this plain. In a constantly-increasing ratio our youth should, and they probably will, direct their energies to the prosecution of the useful and ornamental arts which flourish best in commercial cities. In this field of industry the greatest success may be anticipated. Our farming population has already scattered itself — in most places very sparsely — over nearly all of the plain worthy of cultivation. . . . Hereafter we may expect to witness an increasing disposition to bring our society into a more compact form.

Meanwhile he continued to study the weaknesses in the credit structure which could so badly dislocate business. No more than any of his contemporaries did he place the blame squarely on the call loan market, but he was among the editors who pointed out some of the evils later cured. Dispersal of coin was the fundamental evil, he believed. Money, he said, was merely to cancel indebtedness; when there was not enough specie on hand to perform this service, business was bound to suffer. Therefore he advocated collection of coin in New York, the center where indebtedness was finally canceled. This would require not a bigger bank but a new type of bank, not a bank which depended upon its loans to make its profits, but a bullion bank which would hold money, make profits on service charges, and act as a panic preventive.[16]

There was more than the improvement in business to please a Republican editor at the turn of the year. There was the defeat of Fernando Wood and the election of the Republican, Daniel Tiemann, as New York's Mayor. There was the collapse of General William Walker's filibuster in Nicaragua. Early in November Bigelow had attacked Walker's third expedition as vehemently as he had the earlier ones and had correctly charged the E. D. Morgan and the Vanderbilt steamship interests with working with the administration to help the filibusterers. Now Captain Paulding of the U. S. Navy gave the North a Christmas present of the capture and the ignominious return of the would-be conqueror.

An even greater cause for satisfaction was the situation in Kansas. It was good to chronicle that Robert J. Walker, the fourth Governor sent to Kansas, had come over to the side of justice as Reeder had done in '54 and as Shannon had in '56. Walker, the stooped, emaciated little ex-senator from Mississippi who had been Secretary of the Treasury under Polk, accepted the governorship only after receiving assurances from Buchanan that a new Constitution should be drawn up and submitted to the people for a fair vote. But the delegates who assembled at Lecompton in September, proslavery delegates, wrote into the Constitution a clause upholding the right of an owner to his slave property and its increase, and provided for a popular vote "for the Constitution with slavery" or "for the Constitution without slavery." In other words, the rights of slaveowners already in Kansas were forever protected; at the most, Kansans could merely keep more slaveowners from entering. Walker refused to countenance such a blatant fraud, insisted that the Constitution must be submitted for acceptance or rejection as a whole, and expected Buchanan to back him up. Buchanan did not, and Walker resigned. Moreover, Stephen A. Douglas objected to foistering any Constitution upon an unwilling people, formally broke with the administration on December 22, and prepared to campaign for popular sovereignty in Kansas.

Bigelow, N. P. Banks, and Parke Godwin spent an evening with him discussing the whole Kansas problem when he came to New York at the end of December. They were delighted to have Douglas in their camp, even though his reasons for opposing Buchanan were not theirs. Bigelow wrote Bryant of that and other matters in a long letter on December 28:

> . . . In regard to public events, we have most reason to congratulate ourselves upon the defeat of Wood, the defection of Governor Walker and the open rebellion of Douglass. The upshot of the whole is that Buchanan's administration is already weaker at the beginning of his first Congress than Pierce's was at the close of its first session. Douglass I am satisfied is in earnest. I met him this evening in Bank's room at the St. Nicholas when I was calling (Godwin was with me by the way and is very well family included) and he talked without the least reserve about his plans. Banks says he is not deluded as some of his followers are with the idea that there is a halfway house between their support of the administration and Republicanism. Douglass does not disguise his conviction that he can never be forgiven by the South if he were ever so much disposed to ask forgiveness and I thought I could perceive in the way he talked abundant evidence of an old hostility rankling in his bosom of which this outbreak about the LeCompton Constitution was as but the flash of the priming to the discharge. The great significance of this movement is that it gives to Republican sentiment of the Northwest a competent exponent in the country, what it never had before. He is disposed I think to go as far as the farthest now for freedom in Kansas

though he does not mean to permit his enemies to make up a slavery issue with him at least until he has beaten them which he confidently expects to do by preventing their coming to a vote on the LeCompton Constitution before next summer by which time he expects to secure a party in Congress large enough to defeat the south or to adjourn without action. Meantime he is destined to be greatly aided I fancy by the unexpected and to the administration, most unwelcome capture and return of Genl Walker from Nicaragua.

With Wood out of office, business recovering, the filibusterers' failures, and the Kansas prospects bright, Bigelow looked forward to relative ease. In January he spent three weeks in Washington watching Government in action, a trip he had once tried and failed to persuade Bryant to take, because Bryant thought he could see more clearly from his paper-cluttered desk. Bigelow came back to New York completely disgusted with Buchanan, writing to his partner:

> The President commands no personal respect and less respect for his abilities is felt even by his own partisans than was felt for Mr. Pierce at any time by his opponents. Also his papers are feeble and are written with so little regard for truth and logical justice that his best friends cease to defend him in private.[17]

During the winter no one interest absorbed the public, as the range of Bigelow's editorials showed. He wrote of the weather, a most unusually warm winter; people were already worrying about next summer's ice-supply. He told of the remarkable religious revival which seemed to have no special reason for being but nevertheless swept throughout the country. Church after church started daily noontime services and found their pews full. The clergy of New York, deeming it an excellent opportunity to revert to a stricter Sabbath, campaigned to stop all businesses on Sundays and to bring still more people to the churches. Bigelow's religion was not of an institutional nature, and though he believed that man should reserve one day a week for communion with his Maker, he doubted the wisdom of outer compulsion. So he commented:

> A man may violate the Sabbath as grossly while chanting the litany, with his mind on the stock market, as if he were driving fast horses on the Bloomingdale road. . . . Indeed, it may well be doubted whether the observance of the Sabbath as a conventional formality is not prejudicial rather than beneficial to good morals, as it adds hypocrisy to the original offense. . . .[18]

Throughout the winter he followed the fortunes of Kansas, pleased with Douglas's efforts, although never one of the many who felt that he now deserved the grateful support of the Republicans. Men like Greeley hoped to see Douglas returned to the Senate in the fall, but Bigelow found Douglas's late course not enough. If he came entirely into the Republican fold, he should get their support. Otherwise Bigelow would, and did, uphold the candidacy of Abraham Lincoln, whom Republican leaders in Illinois seemed to think a good man.[19] Bigelow was never to change the opinion of Douglas which he had recorded in his diary in 1851: "D. is a shameless unscrupulous fellow of great energy and more than ordinary talent perhaps though of moderate culture and refinement. He will never be President for he shows himself too greedy for it." [20]

The strong, steady policy of the *Post* was rewarded. Bigelow, who had pridefully written Bryant at the peak of the crisis: "In fact everyone pretty much except WCBryant and Co. has stopped or are going on under indulgences," had still more reason for pride when the annual balance sheet was drawn up in May 1858. Never before had the *Evening Post* been so well off; profits topped $34,000, the subscription list was over twelve thousand, more advertisements were offered than could be handled, and in June Bigelow started a 2 P.M. edition. With his income over $11,000, his expenditures not more than $5000, Bigelow for the first time in his life looked for a good investment. That was hard to find in 1858, though he finally put about $5000 in the Panama Transit Co. He wrote to Bryant of the

> . . . unusual dullness and inactivity . . . arising from the general distrust. . . . The characters of our presidents of late years is but a reflection of the national morals. Buchanan is a far better representative of the American people I fear than Washington would be. . . . the fact is, I have been trying to place a little money lately and could find nothing that was not subject to some sort of chronic roguery which spoiled it as an investment for any man who had not the leisure & taste to sit and watch it all the time. I never before knew what a bother it was to have more money than I wanted to spend.[21]

Once more in Paris, this time in a comfortable pension, the family settled into routine. Bigelow began studying the life of Fénelon, the late seventeenth-century bishop whose mystic search for a personal relation with God strongly attracted him. Then he delved into the whole period of Louis XIV, especially studying the religious and philosophical ideas of the age. He pondered and sorted, accepted some and rejected others, steadily turning more towards the quietists. By now daily reading of the Bible, a chapter of the Old and one of the New Testament, was more than habit. In spite of or perhaps because of the successful years of newspaper work, the clash of men in satisfying their material wants seemed of slight importance to him beside a search for basic principles to relate the finite to the infinite.

Such reading and such thoughts, however, were for the few quiet hours. Bigelow had come to see Europe, and he set a strenuous pace. Hardly a day passed that he did not see some new sight — now to the Sorbonne to hear Laboulaye lecture, and dull he was, too; off to Meaux to see where Bossuet had lived; to the galleries with Mrs. Bigelow or with her to the Théâtre Française or to a concert, where he was apt to doze, and always and everywhere to the bookstalls.

Charles Sumner was spending the summer in France, still recuperating from the infamous attack made upon him in the Senate three years before, and the two friends were frequently together, alternating critical literary conversations with discussions of the United States political scene. Seward also was in Paris, enjoying the last vacation he hoped to have before he would be President of the United States. Often he and Bigelow drove or dined together and before long their political friendship was cemented. Seward hoped to line up the *Post* on his side, while Bigelow, though not at all blind to the qualities in Seward which once antagonized him, appreciated his political astuteness, his usefulness to the Republican party, and his power. He was willing to accept Seward as their next candidate and to work for his election because Seward, he believed, was the one man sure to carry the country.

He was with Seward shortly after news of John Brown's raid on Harper's Ferry reached Paris, and he quite approved Seward's pragmatic view. The Senator, he wrote Bryant, "is not disturbed in the least about the Harper's Ferry incident. He says it must prove fatal to Douglass and whether they hang Brown or imprison him for life — & they have no other alternatives — it must react against them." Bigelow's own views were similar:

Whether they hang Brown or prison him for life it seems to me that a great reaction will be inevitable. Either event will be calculated to make discussion of the merits of his cause & condition, and discussion is the last thing that the subject can bear. If they hang him there will be a monument erected to his memory at Harper's Ferry within six years to which I will subscribe for the good he will do the cause of Republicanism, much as I disapprove of his conduct & deplore its immediate consequence. If they commute his sentence they will find his residence in the Richmond jail the most formidable Evangel of Abolitionism that has yet been heard from.[4]

In July Bigelow took his family to Switzerland, where one evening at a hotel in Berne he found himself sharing amusement with another gentleman, like him vainly trying to secure potatoes in the off season at the behest of a dauntless wife. The next day both families chanced to meet again in Thun, where Bigelow discovered that his fellow potato seeker, a robust man with black curling hair and a florid complexion, was William H. Russell, famous war correspondent of the London *Times*. The two men struck up a friendship which was to last through the years; Russell would see that Bigelow met literary men in England; Bigelow would help Russell meet the "right" people when he came to America to cover the War between the States. Each was to supply the other with information useful in his work and to share the other's joys and sorrows.

For almost a month Bigelow left his family in Switzerland while he toured Northern Italy and Austria. In that time he learned how much he disliked traveling without his family. Never again until all of his children were grown up was he to leave them for so long a time. After returning to Paris in the fall, he circulated more than ever in European society in an effort to understand French politics, Napoleon's character, and the nature of French imperialism. His articles on the latter were, according to Bryant, eagerly read and much talked of by *Evening Post* subscribers. His political articles, his travel sketches, and his literary essays on Buffon, Montesquieu and others so impressed Evert Duyckinck that he declared them "worthy of preservation in a more accessible form." [5] Bigelow made it his business to get acquainted with French journalists and with Americans long resident in France in order to study the viewpoints and problems of French liberals. He met Richard Cobden, who was in Paris negotiating a commercial treaty with France, and won his lasting friendship. Bigelow prized that, because the Englishman's political and economic philosophy exactly matched his, while the persistence, vigor and wisdom he displayed and his usefulness to his countrymen commanded Bigelow's respect. For some years thereafter Cobden's views expressed in occasional meetings and more frequent messages were to influence Bigelow's actions, while Bigelow, in turn, was often to supply information helpful to Cobden.

Another man whom he met that winter was Sainte-Beuve, then at the height of his literary fame. Thinking of the feather it would be if the *Post* could secure him as a correspondent, Bigelow offered him twenty-five dollars for a letter, overrode the Frenchman's reluctance, and finally was able to mail to Bryant a long essay by the critic upon Bérenger. Though no more letters were written — Sainte-Beuve finding the work too onerous even though Bigelow offered to raise the fee to thirty dollars a letter, while Bryant properly realized that only a few people in America would read his essays — nevertheless the impression made by that one letter was sufficient for Parke Godwin to recall it almost fifty years later as the literary high light of the *Post*.[6]

January 26, 1860, was a memorable day for the Bigelows, for they had been invited to a ball at the palace and were to be presented to the Emperor. They admired each other's costume, had a cab call for them at 8 P.M. and drove off with a flourish, so impressed with the occasion that, as Bigelow noted in his journal, he forgot to hire a valet and when they reached the palace he had to open the carriage door "and paddle into the palace unheralded and unsung by flunkey or tiger." However, the evening was a complete success. They were presented; they saw all there was to be seen. When told there was no more space in the ballroom, Mrs. Bigelow plunged in anyway, and her husband stood until his legs were exhausted, but he did not miss a thing. This was the high point of their sojourn in France, and a few days later, after Mrs. Bigelow had completed sittings for her portrait, the family crossed the channel.

The trip was rough. Except for the baby girl born in Paris they were all seasick and all thankful when at last they reached the comfort of their quarters on Pall Mall on February 2, 1860. For several days they were typical tourists. Mrs. Bigelow took her husband to see the shops their first afternoon in London, they called at the Legation, they called at the bank, they visited Westminster and took the children to the zoo. They visited a good English dentist, also, and indulged in a round of head colds and fevers.

Then through their few acquaintances they met numbers of people. William H. Russell introduced William G. Romaine, Secretary of the Admiralty, and John T. Delane, the conservative editor of *The Times*, Palmerston's friend, an able, quick-witted man whose love of accuracy impressed Bigelow. Through letters from Cobden, who was still in Paris, they met William Hargreaves, a gentle, unassuming man of whom Cobden was very fond, and whose friendship was to mean much to Bigelow. The Hargreaves in turn invited them to meet their relatives, the Lemur Paultons, who belonged to the Cobden circle, as well as John Bright, the greatest liberal orator of his century and co-founder with Cobden of the Anti-Corn Law League, and his brother-in-law Samuel Lucas, editor of the liberal *Star*. Bigelow was delighted. "They can't budge me 'til the last of May nohow," he said in mid-February upon reading Julia Bryant's letter about the under-staffed *Post*. These English liberals were vibrantly alive and their interests were his. Bright he liked from their first meeting; an eminently practical man, he found him, though dogmatic and apt to be intolerant, and definitely less wise and useful than Cobden. More briefly Bright noted in his diary: "*25th:* Evening to dinner with Hargreaves. Met Mr. & Mrs. Bigelow, New York. He is a partner with the poet Bryant in the *New York Evening Post*, and is a pleasant and intelligent man." [7] Soon William M. Thackeray and William H. Russell called to tell him of his election to the Garrick Club for three months, where he met Dickens, Millais, Trollope, and Reade. Yet with all the activity, the rounds of dinners and breakfasts to which Bigelow was invited, he still reserved time for the bookstores and was pleased indeed when he bought for half a guinea a copy of Molinos's *Spiritual Guide* which Charles Wesley once had owned. He found hours, too, to compile data on Fénelon in the British Museum for a biography he was contemplating.

Pleasant and full though life was, before long Bigelow began to look homeward. He wrote to Bryant on March 20:

> I am getting homesick. After all there is nothing which compensates for the want of manhood which an American notices at every step in Europe and in every circle. We have no class so servile so destitute of true manhood as the least servile class of Queen Victoria's subjects. I am rapidly settling down to the conviction that in spite of the elevation of John Brown and Fernando Wood and James Buchanan our country in its worst state is at least half a century in advance of any European State in Civilization.

Obviously Bigelow was a sufficiently typical American to take umbrage at inherited authority. Obviously, too, he was typical of white Americans who completely forgot the existence of Negro Americans when talking of their free young land. More to the point, what he was homesick for was the coming election. Preston King was urging him to come home. Seward, who frankly intended to have the nomination this time, wanted Bigelow at the convention. Blair, Bigelow's comrade in '56, wrote of his hopes that Edward Bates of Missouri would be nominated, but Bigelow could not go along with him.

As he wrote Bryant, the Blairs were so blinded by their Pacific rail-road scheme and plans for the colonization of Negroes abroad, which Bigelow did not consider feasible, that Bates seemed their man.

What I apprehended, I see now threatens the Republicans. In throwing or trying to throw Seward overboard for the sake of getting a better man, you will have an old Clay Whig from Missouri put upon you who has been two years or more the candidate of Erastus Brooks and Gov. Hunt, who is not only not a Republican but who is just forward because he is not a Republican and whom the Tribune recommends because he can get some votes that a strait-out Republican cannot get.

As in '56 Bryant knew better whom he did not want and most of all, he intimated, he did not want Seward. Bigelow answered that statement in the same lengthy letter in as strong and vigorous expression of his attitude toward the new party as he ever wrote:

There is no possibility of nominating Fessendon or Chase or Banks or any such man within the range of my vision. Circumstances, his enemies, the Devil if you please have made Seward the Representative man of the Republican party. The triumph of no other man in the country not even Preston King who however would not permit his name to be used under any circumstances while Seward was within reach of a candidacy would be so emphatic a declaration in favor of free labor. True he might be feeble or corrupt in his administration. But in his election the victory is accomplished. That can never be undone. It has decided finally and conclusively on which side of the Potomac the power of the nation lies and from that moment the demagogues, the time-servers, the office seekers throughout the land and they are the most active politicians are on the side of freedom. The sensible and patriotic men of the South who are now speechless, will have their tongues loosed and in two or three years a man would rather be called a Garrison abolitionist than a Virginia democrat.

Looking ahead to the future, he added:

You apprehend that with Seward for President, the democratic Repub. will all be forced into opposition, within a twelve month. Not so soon as that I think, but I anticipate no different, except a worse fate from Bates or any other old Whig. I know full well that the democratic party must rule the nation, and if the Republicans do not pursue a genuine democratic policy they must sooner or later go to the wall and if, to settle the great issue between freedom and slavery now it is necessary to take a man of exceptional views on other subjects and if in consequence of his entertaining those views, he is afterward turned out, why should we complain. I never supposed when we entered into the Republican organization that the old distinctions in principle between the whigs and the democrats which are older than Christianity and will endure as long as sin, were to be obliterated or that the men who compose it now will continue to be its constituents after the negro question from which it draws its breath of life is thrust out of federal politics — which if the issue is fairly presented in the next election will take place before we shall have occasion to make another choice, I have not a shadow of doubt. I mean that it will be sent to the States where it belongs. Should Mr. Seward or any other President fail to meet the expectancy of the country and he will fail, without he adopts a substantially democratic policy, the fact that he will readily be turned out, is rather in his favor. All I ask of him or of any candidate now, is to give us an issue in the canvas which if we are successful will be conclusive. Resolutions are not so good as an incarnation of the anti propandist policy and I know of no person whose name if successful would so effectually symbolize the triumph of our cause. Besides if you get Bates you will not even get resolutions. That is sufficiently manifest from the course of the *Tribune*. If the majority cannot be made up for a strait out Republican, it certainly can not for strait-out Republican doctrines. Hence you see that the Bates men have put his nomination expressly upon ground which is as fatal to Chase and any other genuine Republican as to Mr. Seward and our only alternative I am persuaded is Bates or Seward. I confess I prefer Seward a thousand times. I have not much respect for any man who could be a devot to Henry Clay I do not believe in placing at the head of our army an officer who refuses to inscribe his name on the muster roll. I do not believe in disranking men who have fought in every field since the campaign commenced for the sake of advancing one who has never left the baggage wagons and who in no way represents any question or principle at present in controversy & who would be as like to choose Erastus Brooks for his postmaster general as any man in the nation outside of Missouri.

But the main objection to Bates is that if successful, and he would not be, he would settle nothing. The Slavery interest would rally immediately and the fight would be renewed, northern merchants & journals would be menaced. Bates would find the associations both in respect to men & doctrines into which he would be thrown in the Republican ranks when the fight was renewed, uncongenial and the end would be that the old Whig party of which in his person you would have effected the resurrection, would sink back into its grave after a second time betraying the cause of freedom and strengthening the conviction already so formidable

that the South only can furnish the statesmanship and slavery
furnish the policy which can govern the country.

Now if you see any way to prevent such a catastrophe except
by the nomination of Seward, you see a great deal farther than I
can. My own conviction is however, that Seward will be nominated. I do not see how any other person can be, and if not
nominated I do not see how any other person who [can be nom-
inated] can be elected for he has a very strong party of followers
who would resent the nomination of a Clay Whig, the worst kind
of Whig known, and one of a class with which for years Seward
has had a relentless enmity.[8]

If Bigelow and Bryant no longer saw eye to eye, Bigelow was the
one who had changed. Once both of them had hoped to curb slavery
through the new party while maintaining their democratic ideal of
government. Bryant still clung to that hope, but Bigelow, convinced
that now or never would the issue of slavery reach a happy termination, was temporarily willing to submerge all else.

The pull to return home was strong; yet stronger was the desire to
see more of Britain, for another trip abroad might never materialize.
While he was weighing the chances of the various Republican leaders,
he visited his tailor and watched the making of a court costume. He
and his wife were going to the Queen's drawing room, this time with
the proper footmen. They were prepared to enjoy every aspect of
the occasion, except having to go with the United States Minister to
Great Britain and be presented by him, for the Minister was the dignified, strikingly handsome George Mifflin Dallas, a protectionist, a
conservative, and in Bigelow's view, the traitor who accepted the
Democratic nomination as Vice-President in 1844 after Silas Wright
had the decency to refuse it. The Dallases were formally cordial and
quite approved the Bigelows' attire for the evening. Had they known
that Bigelow's cocked hat, black silk stockings and buckles were bor-
rowed, they might have looked askance, Bigelow believed. However,
even Mrs. Dallas, he noted in his diary, "with her old dryed apple
complexion and haggish features" admitted that Mrs. Bigelow looked
very pretty though she had not gone to the recommended court dress-
maker. Bigelow himself thought that his wife had never looked worse
than she did with the new-fangled "rats" puffing her hair out at the
sides. Next to Mrs. Dallas she was, of course, charming, but Bigelow
never could find anything pleasant to say about the Dallases.

Four years before he had made capital of Frémont's manly dislike
for society affairs and *élite* gatherings. But not a detail of this affair
missed his diary. He recorded what he said, whom he saw, what he

thought, a sketch of exactly where each one stood, and sent a long account home to the *Post*. Victoria may have been a short woman with a dumpy figure, a florid complexion and protruding eyes — "She peels her teeth to the very top of her gums when she laughs which is not becoming at all as her front teeth are too prominent to bear such exposure" — nevertheless, she was Victoria, and the Bigelows had been presented to her.

A week later they were in Scotland. They had few acquaintances there and made little use of the letters which friends had supplied. They saw most of the places most tourists visited, heard some excellent sermons, and Bigelow rather enjoyed the time away from friends for reading more of Molinos and reflecting upon the wisdom of Providence, expressing himself in such words as: "I have often said that the three last who have been unquestionably the least creditable American Presidents . . . have done more for the progress of enlightened opinion upon the subject of slavery than any of their predecessors." [9] The outstanding event of the trip to Scotland was attending the inauguration of William E. Gladstone as Rector of the University of Edinburgh. Bigelow made it the subject of a delightful communication to the *Post*, written in the easy, conversational style of which he had made himself the master. His description of the new Rector was a vivid one, yet more interesting, perhaps, was his impression of Gladstone's abilities:

. . . He seemed to labor with his *piece de resistance*, and failed to satisfy his audience that he had anything to say about universities in general worth the time and trouble he was taking to say it. Nor do I think he removed that doubt altogether, though in print it may appear differently. The impression left upon my mind by the whole performance was that he was not inspired properly by the occasion; that he wrote about universities because it seemed to be the most obvious topic for a man going to address a university audience, and without having anything special to communicate; he trusted, as he has learned that he may safely do, to his skill in handling commonplaces, and, if I may use the expression in no offensive sense, bastard generalization, for his success. Of course, with his other cares and employments, he could not be expected to make the same preparation for this occasion that he would have done if he had his mark in the world yet to make; but I think it will be found that Mr. Gladstone's power, like the late Daniel Webster's, consists more in his skill in using material than in his ability to provide it; that he is a manufacturer rather than a producer, and his wonderful faculty of clothing and adorning an idea or doctrine that is put into his hands has tempted him to the publication of a great deal of learned nonsense, which would never have seen the light if he had anything like the same capacity for discovering truths that he has for propagating them when discovered. . . .[10]

On the whole Scotland did not charm the Bigelows and they were glad to return to England. May, the month they had planned to sail for home, was almost upon them. Whether to leave at once in order to attend the Republican convention on May 16 was the problem, for although Bigelow had declined to be a delegate, Seward was counting on his presence. Fortunately, just as Bigelow was facing a choice of the Queen's Ball on May 15 and her birthday reception on May 18 or the Republican convention, a letter from Preston King bore tidings that Seward was positive of the nomination and that Bigelow need not hurry home. So there were four more weeks in England, four short weeks for parties and last visits with their many friends. Among them was Mr. Thackeray, the author, to use the formal title Bigelow by now conferred upon even his close friends, whom he saw frequently at the Garrick Club and at Russell's home and who, he noted, ate and drank with remarkable freedom; in fact, one evening "he said he was tipsy, and talked a little to verify his diagnosis." The novelist was absorbed in the *Cornhill Magazine*, his latest venture, which he said already had 95,000 buyers. When Mrs. Bigelow told him that she most enjoyed a story about a school for girls in the second issue, she became a great favorite. "Did you?" shrieked Thackeray, jumping up and seizing both her hands. "Did you? My daughter Emmie wrote that." In describing the incident Bigelow added: "I doubt if Thackeray ever received a compliment for anything he wrote himself that gave him the pleasure he got from this involuntary tribute to the maiden effort of Miss Emmie." [11]

Through Thackeray the Bigelows met Laurence Oliphant, "the eccentric though gifted husband of an eccentric wife," who once made the vast mistake of wanting to buy a wig as elegant as Mr. Bigelow's. Dr. Peter Roget, eighty years old now, who had retired from medicine twenty years before to devote himself to his *Thesaurus of English Words and Phrases*, published in 1852, made a point of taking Bigelow to the Royal Society, where he met, among others, short, concentrated Michael Faraday, and Charles Babbage, inventor of the adding machine. More dear to Bigelow, however, were his liberal friends, William Hargreaves, Cobden, Bright, and Lucas. Friendship with them had given him a truer view of liberal English attitudes and some understanding of British relations with the continent. Of more importance, he learned as he never could have within the United States what Europeans thought of his country and what sources they used in forming opinions. He carried to America with him an intimate knowledge of the attitudes of the major parties in France and England toward their own domestic issues and toward American problems, and he knew many of the men who steered those parties. Yet he little guessed that his vacation had prepared him for his greatest service to his country.

Mr. and Mrs. John Bigelow, their four children and two servants, reached New York on June 11, 1860. From eighteen months of travel they went directly to "The Squirrels," all of them delighted to be home. The elder children had their old toys out before two hours had passed and made happy bedlam in the place while their parents went over the grounds, noting the wise care of Kolish in their absence, the evergreen trees just where Bigelow had written him to put them, the strawberry plants strong and fruitful, the icehouse full. Bigelow looked at his home with the sharp eyes of affection. Presently a bill went out to the tenant of the past summer. The long, carefully itemized list of the missing or damaged articles, neatly recorded room by room, ranged from chairs and a dozen cut-glass decanters to a rosebush, a cake pan, a kitchen knife and even a tooth-brush holder.[12] The seventy-one dollars were not important; what mattered was Bigelow's desire to find everything on his estate exactly as he had left it.

Turning Points

[*1860–1861*]

B RYANT was pleased to have Bigelow back. He wrote to Charles A. Dana that he expected more leisure now that his partner was home.[1] But Bigelow was less satisfied, for it was a bitter disappointment to him not to be campaigning for Seward even though he still considered him a self-seeker with unsound Whig economic theories. He made it quite clear to all of his friends that had he been home for the convention, he at least would have been loyal to Seward, the Republican who above all others had a national reputation and tested capacities, the one man whom they could trust to doom the nationalization of slavery. However, he had not been home, and had he been, the outcome would have been no different. Abraham Lincoln was the Republican candidate to whom the *Post* and its editors were pledged.

Bigelow wryly admitted that Lincoln was the perfect candidate in that he was painfully representative of the average of American intelligence and therefore should, according to Bigelow's own political philosophy, stand a good chance of winning. He had never seen Lincoln and knew little about him, though he had written editorials on his behalf in 1858 when Lincoln ran for the Senate. Those editorials had been favorable simply because Bigelow was a party man and Republican leaders in Illinois wanted Lincoln. In 1860 Bigelow could find no better reason for supporting him for the Presidency. It was true that Bryant, the urbane man of letters, spoke with respect of the Cooper Union Address which Lincoln had made while Bigelow was abroad, and after reading the speech Bigelow agreed that the man undoubtedly had talent. But the ridiculous figure he cut, according to all accounts, his lack of background and the bawdy stories he told apparently without any awareness of the significance of the times or of his position, scarcely seemed to justify his selection for the Presidency. However, Bigelow comforted himself, the candidate was probably unimportant; in the success of the party the stranglehold of slavery would be broken.

The campaign started late and moved quietly, in strange contrast to the last one. Newspapers again reduced their rates in order to reach a larger audience, the *Evening Post* offering its semiweekly for fifty cents for three months and its weekly for a quarter, yet little in their contents suggested that there was urgent need for a larger circulation. Bryant and Bigelow found time and space to devote to European affairs and to domestic activities quite unrelated to the election. They did write frequent mocking or scathing editorials about the other candidates, but they had almost nothing to say of their own man. They tended to ignore John Bell of the Constitutional Party and Houston, nominated by Southern Know-Nothings, because those two men would be supported almost entirely by minorities in the South where Lincoln could expect few votes. His real opponents would be John C. Breckinridge, candidate of the Southern Democrats, and Stephen A. Douglas, candidate of the Northern or "squatter-sovereignty" Democrats. Of the two of them, the editors of the *Post* said, Douglas presented the greater threat. Consequently they treated Breckinridge rather gently, writing: "He is not brilliant in intellect, nor of much importance as a statesman; but he bears a good name, has many popular qualities, and is open to none of the objections that have grown out of the past disputes of the party." [2] For Douglas they had only scorn:

> With no genuine earnestness of conviction, and under the simple pressure of circumstances, the Douglasites are attempting from policy what the freesoilers did from principle. They are arraying themselves between the two great parties of the nation, and the inevitable consequence would seem to be that they must fall between the two. The slavery question is one that cannot be shirked; no shallow pretext of non-intervention can hide its national aspects; either the civilization of the North or the civilization of the South must give tone to our societies; and the energies of the general government must be directed to the perpetuity of the one or the other.[3]

The reason for the seeming unconcern in Northern Republican journals, the *Post* exclaimed, was not lack of interest but certainty of success arising from the disintegration of the Whig and Democratic parties. Bigelow wrote to Sumner: "The task of electing Lincoln does not promise to be a very severe one, though on that very account the difficulty of keeping the issues right . . . is increased." [4] He pressed that point in an editorial appearing on July 26:

> . . In the present confused state of the campaign the Republicans have scarcely enough to do to keep them warm, even in the dog days. They are drawn up in battle array, are well sup-

plied with ammunition, have an intense eagerness to engage the enemy, but they see that enemy in the most extraordinary state of disorder and demoralization. Some of them are scattering, far and wide over the plain, others are skulking behind bushes and trees, and the whole are thoroughly distracted by the rival commands of four different generals. . . . How are the poor fellows to do anything in such a medley; and above all, how can the Lincoln bowmen be expected to display their fine shooting on such a mob of mere stragglers? What we want to call forth our energies is an organized, trained and well-appointed foe — not a flock of sheep. . . . The issue which has arisen between our northern and southern social systems as to the future possession and peopling of the territories is one that has to be fought out, sooner or later; it may be postponed, but it cannot be evaded. We say, let it be fought out now. Let all the pro-slavery candidates whose running only serves to confound the issues, withdraw, with the exception of one, and let him have a fair and square fight with Lincoln. Victory must then ensue to one or the other, and that victory will be definitive for all time to come.

Deep if quiet satisfaction in the sure knowledge that the victory would be theirs pervaded Bigelow's private letters these days. He wrote to his friend William Hargreaves in England on July 30, describing Lincoln and the prospects of the party:

I have been engaged more than ten years in a contest which has hitherto been but one uninterrupted succession of defeats, the result mainly of selfishness cowardice & treachery, but we have been gaining strength every day & now no one is reckless enough to deny that the day of our triumph is at hand. . . .

In regard to American politics I have already expressed my confidence in the success of the Republican ticket this fall. Our adversaries are divided irrevocably while our people are all compact. In this state there was great disappointment felt by the friends of Mr. Seward that he was not nominated but there was nothing either in the antecedents of his successful rival or in the manner of his selection calculated to render Mr. S's friends indifferent to his success. Even if the fact were otherwise, they will be obliged to exert themselves to secure the election of a Republican legislature in order to secure the return of Mr. Seward to the United States Senate which is now deemed desirable, and as the state and federal elections take place the same day, it is impossible to labor efficiently for one ticket without favoring the other.

Mr. Lincoln whom we have nominated for the Presidency is not precisely the sort of man who would be regarded as entirely *a la mode* at your splendid European courts, nor indeed is his general style and appearance beyond the reach of criticism in our Atlantic drawing rooms. He is essentially a Western man; he has passed most of his life beyond the Alleghanies, and owes few of the honors which his countrymen have conferred upon him, to the advantages of early education or of cultivated and refined associations. He is essentially a self made man and of a type to which Europe is as much a stranger as it is to the Mastodon. With great simplicity of manners and perhaps ignorance of the trans Atlantic world, he has a clear and eminently logical mind, a nice sense of truth and justice & a capacity of statement which extorted from Mr. Bryant the declaration that the address he delivered in this city last winter was the best political speech he ever heard in his life. I anticipate great advantages to the country from his election and by reflection I think that his administration will serve the cause of popular sovereignty throughout the world for I have no doubt that he will give it credit.

In the fall, at last, campaign news took full precedence. Then the editors of the *Post* had room for nothing else. They lauded their platform; they lauded their candidates; they praised Seward for the speech at Detroit, in which he said: ". . . slavery is and must be only a purely local, temporary and exceptional institution, confined within the slave states where it already exists; while freedom is the general, normal, enduring and permanent condition of society within the jurisdiction and under the authority of the constitution of the United States." They charged Buchanan with fostering secession sentiment, though they had so little fear of it that they met talk of secession with "the following choice lines of Mother Goose. 'Says Aaron to Moses, let us cut off our noses; Says Moses to Aaron it's the fashion to wear 'em.' We are with Moses and the fashion, and that is to hold on to the Union 'now and forever.'" More seriously they attempted to show the benefits which every section of the country would derive from a Republican administration.[5]

As the campaign reached its climax, Democrats tasted the bitterness of the coming defeat, helpless before the catastrophe they saw approaching. Republicans waited in happy expectancy, most of them confident that by their victory the major American problem of the nineteenth century would be solved. So deep was the cleavage in thinking that friendships built slowly through the years split in a trice. Bigelow escaped that trial no more than others. John O'Sullivan, his friend and associate for many years, but a Buchanan Democrat and lately Minister to Portugal, closed their friendship forever with the declaration that slavery was a blessing to the Negroes who in all conscience should erect a monument to their greatest benefactor, the first slave-trader.[6]

Yet Bigelow never lost Tilden's friendship, regardless of the political differences which led Tilden in this year of decision to remain a Democrat, to place preservation of the Union above all else, to work for the election of Bell through the establishment of a fusion New York Constitutional Union party composed of all anti-Republicans. The *Evening Post* sardonically described the one tremendous rally of the fusion party, which was held in Cooper Institute on October 8, as so uncontrollable a mob that Samuel Tilden was unable to deliver his speech. The *Post's* readers, Bigelow challenged, were interested in Tilden's views even if his fellow Unionists were not; and he offered unlimited space for the unheard words. Privately Bigelow urged him to put them in the form of a brief letter as most apt to get and hold attention. Some days later Bigelow received a typical, detailed, carefully stated argument of his friend's position presented in a letter formally addressed to Judge William Kent. This Bigelow published on October 30, promising a considered answer in exactly one week; in other words, blithely promising the electoral results as his reply.[7]

Several days before the election Bryant, Bigelow, Hiram Barney, Collector of the Port and erstwhile staff member of the *Post* (who, some years before, had chaffed Bigelow out of the habit of swearing), William Osborn, President of the Illinois Central Railroad, and John A. C. Gray, a Park Commissioner, were idly chatting in the office of the *Post* after the last edition had gone to press. Tilden called to see Bigelow and was asked to join the cheerful Republicans. The lawyer sat frowning and silent while the others, scoffing at the threats of disunion coming from the South, derisively labeled it the shout of spoiled children who had found the cry effective enough in the past. Suddenly Tilden rose to leave, turned and said slowly and deliberately: "I would not have the responsibility of William Cullen Bryant and John Bigelow for all the wealth in the sub-treasury. If you have your way, civil war will divide this country, and you will see blood running like water in the streets of this city." Bigelow was amazed at the intensity of his friend's emotion; Tilden must be in worse physical condition than he had thought if he could be troubled by such ridiculous bogies. Quietly he asked Andrew H. Green, Tilden's assistant who came in just after Tilden left, to follow him and make sure that he reached home safely.[8] Thereafter for almost a decade he scarcely saw Tilden, yet it was space rather than opinion that separated them. Though utterly unlike in person, in capacity, in ambition, each had sufficient respect for the other's integrity to preserve their friendship.

On November 6 Lincoln was elected. Four days later Bigelow triumphantly wrote to Hargreaves: "A more important, bloodless revolution, it seems to us, has never been accomplished, for four years more of a pro-slavery administration would have been almost more than our Constitution could have withstood." The discontented mutterings from the South were understandable, he continued; they were good politics, "a faint hope of frightening Lincoln into modification of Republican policy and the concession of a Cabinet minister to the Fire-Eaters. Something which none but lunatics would dream of at present. There is nothing in our history so creditable to us as a nation in my judgment, not even our rebellion and revolution in '76 as this through which we have passed during the past ten years and which passed its crisis on the 6th inst." Apparently the critical days were over. For seventy-one years America had striven for democracy while burdened with the fifth clause of the Constitution with its aristocratic conception of the political power ownership of men should confer. Now that aristocratic power would be broken. Eventually each free man would receive one vote regardless of his possessions, and America could go forward under a truly democratic Constitution to a larger conception of a democratic way of life.[9]

For several days the country did seem quiet, but presently nerve-wracking rumors were circulating. The South might not acquiesce in the results of the election. Yet it could not secede; widespread opinion in the North agreed with the *Evening Post* when it asserted on November 12 that secession was not only a legal absurdity but that it was impossible to achieve in fact. On December 14 the *Post* again denied the possibility of secession. The editorial ended on a somber note:

> In short, there are but two ways in which the people of South Carolina can release themselves from their obligation of obedience to the United States government, which in the exercise of their sovereignty they have helped to establish. One is, possibly, by amendment in the way provided by the United States constitution, and the other is, possibly, by revolution, the right to which always exists when governmental grievances become intolerable and otherwise irremediable.

Yet the editors of the *Post* did not expect revolution. "Devils are apt to rend the bodies from which they are expelled," Bigelow wrote Hargreaves comfortably, as late as December 12, "and the devil of slavery is no exception to the race. But we shall go through the trial triumphantly, I am confident." The danger lay not in secession, he explained, but in the possibility that the untutored Negroes, excited by the election of Lincoln, would rise against their masters. In itself that was an argument against disunion, for the South would need Northern assistance to quell the uprisings: "the Republican party will have to be charged with putting down the servile insurrections, a task for which I must say I have no stomach though I would rather do it than see white people outraged."

Yet on December 20 South Carolina did secede by a unanimous vote of the delegates assembled to plan the state's future. Northerners were sunk in gloom and indecision. Business was near a standstill as bankers wondered whether loans to Southerners would be repaid and merchants feared cancellation of outstanding debts. Faced by a possible dissolution of the Union, vast numbers of Americans knew deep emotional distress. Some said with the *Tribune:* Let the South go in peace. Others with the *Evening Post* held that the Union must be preserved however fearful the cost. Still others wanted to make concessions to save the Union, as Tilden did, as Webster had ten years before. Many others, and Bigelow among them, thought the uproar would abate once Lincoln was inaugurated and Southerners realized how fallacious were their conceptions of his program. At the end of the year Bigelow was still sure that the issue of slavery in the territories, to which he had devoted his best energies for twelve years, was a thing of the past. He was more fearful of the business picture. It was all too probable that the country was in for a worse financial convulsion than it had experienced in '57, and he feared Whig Republican methods of coping with it.

This winter of 1860–1861 was a turning point in Bigelow's life as well as in his country's. He had left the law twelve years before in order, through journalism, to help curb the power of slaveowners. Now that seemed practically accomplished. He was forty-three years old, and he could reasonably expect to do his best work in the next twenty years. Should it be in journalism? Was it his ambition to have as his memorial thirty or forty years of newspaper writing, of influencing contemporary opinion upon immediate issues? It was at this point that Parke Godwin, who had earned about fifty dollars a week on the *Post* while Bigelow was in Europe, asked Bigelow to write to Salmon P. Chase, the incoming Secretary of the Treasury, to appoint Godwin to the Custom House where he would at least have a steady position, a sure income, and work which would not be too arduous for his delicate health. Bigelow thought such a routine task a waste of ability. "Godwin," he said suddenly, "buy out my interest in the *Evening Post* and come in here and make your fortune." Godwin was dumbfounded; Bigelow later said that he was equally amazed, for he had not thought of the idea until ten minutes before proposing it. The two parted,

Godwin to sound out the other partners as to their willingness, Bigelow to think over terms. Within several days the sudden decision was put into effect, followed by announcements but preceded by consultation with no one, not even with Mrs. Bigelow.[10]

From a worldly view the sale was not sensible. Bigelow was making almost $25,000 a year and at the rate the paper was forging ahead he could double that in five years and then sell his interest for twice what it was worth in 1861. Yet from a worldly view Bigelow certainly was not a bad bargainer. At thirty-one years of age he had joined the *Post* with nothing but his abilities and his credit for capital. Since then he had increased his holdings to a full third of the company, the net income of which had grown from $15,708.31 in 1850 to $68,774.23 ten years later. As he noted in his journal:

> I have had two trips to the West Indies occupying together 5 or six months and 19 mos. in Europe, a good respectable living the whole time, laid up some thirty or forty thousand dollars and sold my interest to Godwin for $112,060.43. . . . Besides this the firm owes me $18,000 which with the other makes over $130,000. This, in a merely pecuniary point of view, is a tolerably satisfactory twelve years' work. In other respects I have no reason to be discontented with my success when I began the paper was at war with the federal, city, and state administrations on the slavery question and was odious to the commercial community from which it drew its breath. Without changing its principles, and without faltering in its course, it has lived to witness the triumph of its principles in the election of a Federal President, and the banner under which it has fought floating over the Capitol of every non-slave holding state in the country.[11]

For a newspaperman he had prospered amazingly. George Bancroft found the rumor of it so impressive that he stopped him on the street one day to make sure it was accurate.

Bigelow could afford to retire. He had enough money — "that power which is *power*" — to care for his family on a scale which from choice was modest. If ever he was to give up journalism, this January 1861 seemed the logical time, when one issue was settled (assuredly the current insurrection would end "without serious alienation and without serious bloodshed") and before new ones could arise. And he wished to leave journalism. He wished to write a biography of Archbishop Fénelon and had wished to ever since, during his vacation in Europe, he stumbled upon Bausset's biography of the great Catholic. In Paris and in London he had spent hours collecting materials for a study of the relations between Church and State which he intended to present through a life of Fénelon. But since his return to the United States, he had been forced to put it aside. For that reason he refused Thurlow Weed's sudden proposal that together they buy the *World* and make it the administration organ, Bigelow putting up most of the cash, Weed providing direct connection with the White House. The picture was one of scoop following scoop, but Bigelow was not interested. He began indexing his diaries relating to Fénelon and reading the books he had collected on the period.[12]

He did not lose Weed's friendship, however. A few days later Weed's *Evening Journal* remarked:

> We do no injustice to the other distinguished and gifted editors of the *Evening Post* when we say that this excellent Journal owes its success and its high character to the industry, taste and talents of Mr. Bigelow, who has been its presiding genius. While imparting daily interest to his paper, in his discriminating selections and effective editorials, Mr. Bigelow's personal, political and social virtues won troops of patrons and friends for the *Post*.

Bigelow carefully cut out the item and pasted it in his journal with a sensible comment to the effect that it looked as if Weed was still angling for him.

The early months of 1861 saw him at "The Squirrels," busy as a literary country-gentleman with many political friends. He enlarged his house — another son, Ernest, his fifth living child, was born in January — and built a study where he crammed many of the books gathered over the years. There he worked part of each day on his life of Fénelon. Outside he directed the laying of a new road according to sketches he had made several years before, started a pear and apple orchard, set out hundreds of evergreen seedlings and some juniper and larch, and searched the woods for strong young maples to be transplanted. In his retirement he followed with a cheerful eye the course of public events, writing Hargreaves on February 21:

> As the time for the new government to go into effect approaches, the horizon begins to clear up. The elections in the border states are all favorable to union and this sentiment gains strength in the Southern States hourly. The President elect passed through the city yesterday on his way to Washington. His reception was very enthusiastic though his forensic performances have not raised the standard of American oratory materially. There is a combination forming to drive Seward out of his Cabinet but it will hardly succeed. Lincoln does not yet begin to apprehend the difficulties of his position, nor the extent to

which in consequence of his ignorance of the world, he will be dependent upon other Statesmen. When he reaches Washg he will be likely to get his eyes opened and then he will see that he cannot get along without Seward for the present.

But he was less philosophic than he indicated to Hargreaves when he contemplated the determined efforts of the Chase-Blair wing of the party to drive Seward from the cabinet. He wrote and had Bryant print in the *Post* a slashing condemnation of the tactics of Seward's enemies at the Peace Conference in session in Washington. "The attempt to expel Mr. Seward from the Cabinet . . . shows either a deliberate purpose to disorganize and break up the party, or simply the selfishness of men who do not know the consequences of succeeding in what they attempt." Should it succeed:

> It would show that we are a hopeless prey to faction; that there was neither dignity, forecast or wisdom in our political organizations, and that neither the character or the honor of a patriot was safe in their hands. The best that can be said for the parties engaged in this combination is that they know not what they do. They have never realized the difficulties — I may say the dangers — of the incoming government.[13]

Support through the columns of the old Democratic *Evening Post* was welcomed by the ex-Whig, and though it cost Bigelow the friendship of the more radical Republicans, it brought Weed and Seward closer to him. Later Weed told him that "when the fight was raging so strong against Seward for the Cabinet, Seward resigned or rather handed the President a letter withdrawing his acceptance. The President asked a few days to see what he could do, Mr. S. in the meantime to keep his step a secret, and finally the day before the inauguration was delivered the President said he could not get on without his help & begged him to hold on: S[eward] took till the next day to consider & then accepted, on which occasion the President gave him to understand that whatever others might say or do, they two would not disagree but were friends." [14] Preston King added to the picture of pre-inauguration politics when he visited Bigelow early in May. In his journal Bigelow summarized King's views:

> He thinks Lincoln weak and unequal not only to the present crisis but to the position he holds at any time. He says he spoke about the carriage presented by Dennison to Mrs. Lincoln to the President. He also told Cameron he had better not insist upon the Treasury. He says he was requested to ascertain whether Seward

would decline the Secry of Statesship if offd. Hamlin made the request on behalf of Lincoln. He spoke a little with Seward but soon saw that it would not do for him to go farther. So he told Hamlin that the President had best ask Seward directly, that it was not a mediation that he could undertake exactly — This King stated not in words but in substance with a suggestive laugh. In about a fortnight Seward came to him with a peculiarly important air to say that the Prest. wanted him to be Premier and in view of the peculiar situation of the country which was ascribed mainly to him & so on. He says S. has a very controlling influence with the Prest. apparently and is very much disposed to do and be responsible for everything done himself. I knew the fact before but I never knew King to admit it to anyone so fully before.[15]

In February when Seward was fighting for his Cabinet position and in March when Lincoln was feeling his way in his new position, Bigelow was content with his retired life. But his wife objected to isolation in the country when the cheer and society of the city could be theirs if they wished. So, to surprise her, Bigelow bought a house at 69 East Twenty-third Street one Friday in March, paid $20,000 in cash for it at an auction, and tried to persuade himself that he wanted to winter in the city. The following Monday when his wife inspected his purchase, he saw for the first time the inadequate closets, the dark rooms, and worst of all the absence of fireplaces in the bedrooms which would necessitate dependence upon unhealthy central heating. There must be something in superstition, he reflected ruefully during the following years as he tried to sell the place; certainly that Friday March 8 had been a bad day for a new undertaking. Yet at least he could remain in the country, as he wished, reading about Fénelon, working outdoors, enjoying his children, helping friends to get political appointments, seeing that William H. Russell, sent by the London *Times* to cover American affairs, met Seward, Sumner, King, and the Blairs.[16]

That tranquil life lasted less than three months. Just before dawn on April 12 a shell burst above Fort Sumter, the one fort in Charleston Harbor held by the Federals. For thirty-four hours one hundred and twenty-eight grim defenders hung on while batteries on three sides of them hurled a fury of shells. At last, their fort battered and in flames, their supplies nearly exhausted, they surrendered and with a last salute to their bullet-ripped flag marched down to their boats. Wires screamed the news across the land. The horror of civil war burst upon the nation, smashing all the dreams and ambitions of a peacetime world. War between brothers, between men whose fathers had fought side by side, whose grandfathers had given themselves to create the Union, split the country into two gigantic camps. The shock of it, the tragedy of their stupid blindness, hit masses of Northerners who like Bigelow had never doubted that Americans could solve their problems by a ballot and peaceful negotiation. Few were the men who did not re-examine their personal ambitions and the interests and cares of everyday life. Unless this noble experiment, this government of the people, this union one and inseparable was preserved, there seemed little value to a man or his posterity in the richness of his personal life. Bigelow's dream of a career of quiet writing faded.

He served as one of the secretaries at the Union Square mass meeting of one hundred thousand New Yorkers assembled on Saturday afternoon, April 20, in response to the call: "All good citizens who prize liberty with order, over usurpation and anarchy, are invited to assemble in mass convention, to give expression to the views of the city of New York in the present emergency." He wrote to his old friends Senator Preston King and E. D. Morgan, now Governor of New York, offering himself in this time of disaster for any task in which he might prove useful. The Governor responded with a request that Bigelow represent him at the Cleveland Governors' Conference called to consider the crisis. Bigelow accepted, went that same day to Albany for instructions, and left by night train for Ohio. There he met with Governor William Dennison of Ohio, the Governors of Wisconsin and Michigan, Major-General McClellan, commander of the army in Ohio, and several other men to discuss what action Northern border states should take in case they were attacked, what defenses they should prepare and how far they should go without authorization from the Federal Government which to date had offered neither suggestions that the states take care of themselves nor an integrated plan for national defense. Governor Dennison's call for an aggressive war met unanimous agreement after he presented proof that the Governor of Kentucky had sold quantities of United States Army material to the Governor of Louisiana. The conferees resolved to send commissioners to Washington to urge their views upon the President and to stress the crying need for immediate action. Bigelow was asked to be one of them, but he declined; it was his place to report to Governor Morgan and let him decide next steps. So he returned to Albany, reported, received thanks for his services, gossiped a bit with Weed who had just come from Washington, and took the train for home after making it clear that he was not interested in an office for the sake of having an office, but he was interested in doing a job.[17]

The taste of action after several months of retirement gave zest to life. When Bigelow heard that the Paris consulate was open, his whole attention focused upon it. James Bowen, the Commissioner of Immigration, told him on the cars one day in June that he had suggested Bigelow to Weed as the man for the Paris post and that Weed had replied that he and Seward wanted him there but had to consider the claims of Raymond of the *Times*. Bigelow listened and cannily said nothing. He determined on the spot to wait for an offer before he spoke his mind. Two weeks later, Preston King, while visiting at "The Squirrels," reported in an off-hand way that Weed thought it high time Bigelow turned up in Washington. That was enough for Bigelow, who by mid-June wanted nothing so much as the consulate and had been pleased the day before when the *Herald* said that the position was at Weed's disposal and he intended it for Bigelow. That Weed wanted his power clearly understood mattered little; Bigelow took the train for Washington.[18]

There he saw General Banks, his fellow campaigner of '56, and with him visited General McDowell, who promptly offered Bigelow a position on his staff, an offer tempting to vanity but obviously not the place for a man in his forties who lacked military skill. The next day another job, the one he had come for, was tentatively offered. Bigelow recorded the event in his diary on July 3:

> . . . Weed asked me how I would like the Paris consulate. I asked what he meant and he said S was going to ask me to accept the Paris consulship that it was a place of which he had the control — that he had intended it for Raymond but the *Times* had behaved so it was impossible. [The *Times* had bitterly attacked Lincoln.] . . . Motley and myself are the only persons on his string. If I decline it, it may go to him. I told him I was free to confess that there was scarcely any office in the Prest's gift that had as much temptation to me as this Con & that if I could bring my mind to accept any office I would accept that with great pleasure and satisfaction.

Yet though he stayed in Washington until July 12, he heard nothing more of the consulate. He met President Lincoln and was not impressed. He accepted indifferently the coolness of the Blairs and Chase, the result of his vigorous letter to the *Post* defending Seward's conciliatory program and proclaiming the nation's need of him as Secretary of State. He breakfasted and dined and drove with Seward. But no one except Weed mentioned a niche for him. Disgruntled, yet aware that

a whole list of officers had to be settled, he went home to sink patriotism in "philosophy, homeopathy, buttermilk and domestic joys," as
William Russell happily phrased it.[19]

To Hargreaves he sent a long description of conditions as he saw
them at the end of July, a description worth quoting in full, for it was
the letter of a trained observer trying to make the domestic picture
of a nation at war clear to a foreigner. He began by saying that the
pressure upon General Scott to engage the Confederates in battle came
less from the belligerency of press and people, than:

> . . . from a well grounded distrust of the President and Cab-
> inet. I say well grounded because all were unaccustomed to ad-
> ministrative duties under the federal govt when they went to
> Washington, they were all aspirants & therefore rival candidates
> for the Presidency; they are not harmonious in their councils,
> neither do they treat each other in public with the respect which
> inspires confidence. At the formation of the cabinet there was a
> division of sentiment in regard to the proper mode of prosecuting
> the war which had a political origin. One section recommending,
> wisely as I think a slow & bloodless reconquest the other a speedy
> though bloody one. The former were suspected by the latter of
> lukewarmness to use no stronger terms on the political issues
> which had been decided by the election of Lincoln. These sus-
> picions gathered strength from the fact that General Scott to
> whom the conduct of the war was committed had never been a
> Republican, was a Virginian and had been the great exemplar of
> the officers whose talents & culture gave body to this treasonable
> movement. The President was destitute of experience and withal
> lacks superiority of every kind except inches, though a very
> well disposed person and good enough president for ordinary
> times. He did not realize the emergency in which he was placed
> on his inauguration, nor does he now, in my opinion, he does
> not know the importance of having a united Cabinet and a fixed
> policy in times like these, neither does he know how to ensure
> such unity if he did desire it. He does not profess to have any
> knowledge or will of his own, but his policy from day to day is
> merely the resultant force of the contending members of the
> cabinet. Is it strange that such a want of confidence on the part
> of the Executive as this state of things reveals, should be shared
> by the press and Congressmen and others near enough to be wit-
> nesses of it, and that they should have been willing to assert
> their own judgments & preferences in regard to the war with some
> — with *considerable* earnestness, in order to countervail the in-
> fluences which they supposed were working to the disadvan-

tage of the North? Had we a President with anything sovereign or commanding in his character; a man who seemed at all to comprehend the situation and the immensity of interests at stake upon his management, there would not have been the least disposition to meddle with his prerogative. I never saw anything so wonderful as the discipline of our people and their prompt response to any public consideration addressed to them. A telegraphic dispatch will make the nation rise up and sit down just as promptly & as inevitably as the motion of the planets will heave the bosom of the sea. The public reasons as logically and acts as consistently in all these trials as any member of the government if not more so. Now, our difficulty is precisely what it has been, the want of some central mind to take the lead & control things. If the times do not produce such a man constitutionally, he will be produced unconstitutionally. At present there is no expectation I believe of a forward movement on our part before the last of September. The Cabinet will not be changed probably, but I hope and rather expect that the late reverses will scare the members into greater unity. Unless they can unitedly support their own govt. they cannot expect it will be supported by the people. Unhappily there is no military genius whatever in the Prest or his advisers McLellan who has been ordered to the command of the army of the Potomac has superior military talents & what is of almost as much value now, the prestige of military success. He may be equal to the emergency but my impression is that the sea's destined to be the field of operations now. The Navy Dept is making very extensive preparations and we shall have a very large fleet of moderate sized vessels of war and gunboats afloat in less than ninety days. From its operations I anticipate some results which will raise the courage & hopes of this nation. Yours very sincerely and in extreme haste . . .[20]

There was nothing in this letter about a possible trip to Europe, for Bigelow had heard no more of the Paris consulate. On August 14, however, the mail brought the New York newspapers of the day before, each with an announcement of his appointment as consul in Paris, and a congratulatory letter from Senator Preston King. Not until nightfall did Bigelow receive official word and then it came in the form of a cryptic telegram:

MR. MOTLEY GOES OUT ON THE EUROPA, FROM BOSTON, AUGUST 21. CAN YOU GO AT THE SAME TIME. F. W. SEWARD.[21]

CHAPTER 13

Consul in Paris: The First Months

[*1861*]

BIGELOW had often used the columns of the *Evening Post* to mock at the consular and diplomatic corps. "If most of them talk abroad as they do at home," he had written in 1853, "the fewer languages at their command the better." [1] It would have suited him had the whole system of representation abroad been abolished and replaced by the appointment of special commissioners to look after United States interests only when specific needs arose. In 1861, however, he did not stop to argue the merits of resident ministers versus special agents. It was enough for him that the United States had not been so desperately in need of Europe's friendship since Benjamin Franklin saved his country by his diplomacy in France. The Republic might be doomed if Britain and France kept the sea-lanes open to commerce and supplied the South with the tools of war. It would be doomed if they allied their mighty forces with those of the Confederacy.

Already the South had three accredited agents abroad working to gain such help. The leader was William L. Yancey, a high-principled, outspoken Alabaman, a veritable gadfly of petty politics, whom Woodrow Wilson later called "the fiery soul of secession." Yancey, men whispered, received his appointment because it relieved Jefferson Davis to have a possible rival for the permanent Presidency of the Confederacy a full three thousand miles away. With the Alabaman were two second-rate men in their sixties, Judge Pierre A. Rost and Ambrose Dudley Mann. Rost, a Frenchman by birth, was a Louisianan by adoption whose broken French and airy "*Tout va bien*" in response to all inquiries on the progress of the war eventually earned him more ridicule than respect in Paris, while credulous, obtuse Ambrose Dudley Mann was little more than a figurehead who had served without special distinction as a United States representative in the German States, in Hungary, in Switzerland, and as Assistant Secretary of State under

President Pierce.[2] The three men left for Europe in April with instructions to seek help in breaking the Northern blockade and recognition of the Confederate Government. They were to talk their free trade doctrine, which even Napoleon was beginning to embrace, and mention the magic word "cotton," because it was to the South, not to the North, that much French and still more British industry looked for raw goods and for markets. True, Europeans hated the "peculiar institution" of the South, but Lincoln's Government had as yet done nothing to suggest that a Federal victory would affect slavery in the old Southern states.

Bigelow knew that, relatively speaking, Union representatives had almost no economic arguments to offer. Charles Francis Adams, stiff, able, impeccably correct, appointed Minister to Great Britain in April, had come into the Republican party through the ranks of the Free-Soilers, but prior to that he had been a Whig. Hence he could be accounted friend to the tariff and American manufacturing. Likewise William L. Dayton, Republican Vice-Presidential candidate in '56, now Minister to France, was an avowed high tariff man. All of Lincoln's early appointees to diplomatic posts were erstwhile Whigs: Cassius Clay to Russia; James Watson Webb to Turkey; Thomas Corwin to Mexico; and George P. Marsh to Sardinia. Not one came from the ranks of the old-time Democrats.

Bigelow realized that as consul in Paris he would work directly under William Dayton, a prospect over which he was not enthusiastic. Dayton was a lawyer ten years Bigelow's senior, a successful New Jersey politician and a well-meaning man of limited ability. In a political sense he deserved the appointment because he had been Frémont's running mate and had done his best, though it was not enough, to carry his state for the Republicans in 1856. During that campaign he had been asked by Bigelow to make some speeches which he reluctantly consented to do, provided Frémont, Bigelow, and the other managers considered it absolutely necessary. However, he had added, "Whatever may be the precedent set by others, I shall certainly not go about — stumping the country." [3] The sentiment was more indicative of the man than perhaps Bigelow suspected. Appearances were important to Dayton; primarily in appearances, in courtly manner and dignified bearing, he was to fulfill the role of Minister.

Nevertheless, Dayton himself realized that this was a time for more than gestures. He wrote to Seward from Paris on May 27:

> If a gentleman accustomed to the use of the pen, and especially if he had some acquaintance with the leading men connected with the European press, could be sent over here in the possession,

nominally, of a *good* Consulate (the duties of which could be performed by clerks) while his attention could be really directed to the press, it might be of great use in giving a right direction to public sentiment. It is a duty which a public Minister could not, *with propriety*, perform, if he would.[4]

When Bigelow went to Washington to learn precisely what would be expected of him as consul, Seward repeated that idea, stating emphatically that Bigelow was not being sent to care for routine consular duties. Obviously he would attend to them, but the purpose of his going to France was to create a favorable French press, to counteract Southern diplomacy, and to keep France from intervening in American affairs.[5]

No one in America was better prepared than Bigelow for just such a mission, nor did anyone know better than he the difficulties he would face, though even he underestimated the peril of the days ahead. On his European trip he had been impressed by the avowed pro-Southern sentiments of Buchanan's diplomatic corps as well as by the swarms of Southern tourists he met everywhere who consciously or unconsciously served as agents for Southern views. Moreover, he knew how great were the obstacles to the expression of any republican views in the French press. Censorship was a Damoclean sword; the Government had the right to serve warning if any article was "excessive, dangerous, or disagreeable" and upon the third such warning to suspend the publication of a newspaper for three months.[6] Though infrequently used, the fear of such action effectively curbed the press. And since Napoleon III could offer his subjects no better lesson on the impracticability of democracy than the collapse of the United States, Bigelow could expect articles upon the importance of preserving the Union to be rated, at the very least, as "disagreeable." On the other hand, he knew personally many Frenchmen who were fretting under the Empire, whose lives were dedicated to republican doctrines, and who of necessity had become adept wielders of innuendo in order to by-pass a hostile government. He knew, too, as who did not, the mercenary reputation of the average French journalist. Give him money and his principles were yours. Bigelow had faith that through his former business relations with journalists whom he had engaged to correspond with the *Post* and through his friendship with French liberals he had a sufficient entry to be useful to his country.

Regretfully he put Fénelon aside, though he did pack up for shipment to France all the books and documents pertinent to his project; surely there would be some free hours in the day of a consul. Hastily he closed his house, put his financial affairs in order, helped Mrs.

Bigelow gather all the necessities for themselves and their five children, and with his family sailed on August 30.

On shipboard he spent hours each day studying French, for though he read it fairly easily and could make himself understood in it, the job he was facing demanded idiomatic fluency. Not all of his thoughts were on his coming duties, however; he never could and never wanted to forget the country gentleman he had begun to be. When the S.S. *Persia* docked on September 8, he had a long letter to mail to Kolish, his gardener: fatten the oxen, try to get nine cents a pound for them, send an inventory of the chickens, turkeys, pigeons; forward all mail; and above all send a detailed monthly account of what happened at "The Squirrels." It was a hearty letter from one countryman to another, but as the months turned into years a pathetic monotony crept into Bigelow's notes; the tone varied from entreaty to reproach to demand, but the topic was always the same: "Send a report." . . . "Why don't you write?" . . . "I must demand." [7]

While he was still on shipboard he faced his first official problem. A kindly woman, fond of other people's business, chose to offer his assistance to a lady who was worried lest her husband fail to meet the ship and she have no escort to London. She explained that Mr. Bigelow would be delighted to be of service to a compatriot. The consul, however, felt the antithesis of delight when he heard that he might have the pleasure of escorting Mrs. James Bulloch, should her husband, the purchasing agent of the Confederate States, be too hard at work to meet her. Fortunately for Bigelow, Mr. Bulloch was waiting at the pier. But the news he brought his wife, news which spread rapidly through the ship's company, was alarming: England and France, he said, were openly sympathetic to the South; it was only a matter of time before Napoleon would break the blockade. [8]

Rather fearfully Bigelow hastened to London. He knew that in May Yancey and Rost had been informally received by Lord John Russell, Secretary of State for Foreign Affairs, and he presumed that it had been their arguments which persuaded Britain and France to grant belligerent status to the Confederacy. During the summer Rost had crossed to Paris, where the talented, delightful, corrupt Duc de Morny, Napoleon's half brother, and Edouard Thouvenel, the serious Minister for Foreign Affairs, had shown him marked cordiality. [9] More than that Bigelow did not know, until he reached London and there learned the rumor that Bulloch had already spent $700,000 contracting for ships from English yards. He looked for his friends the Hargreaves, Cobden, Bright, but all were out of town. Only Samuel Lucas, Bright's brother-in-law and an early member if not the founder of the London Emancipation Committee, was there, and he was depressing. His newspaper, the *Star*, called "un-English" by conservatives, but with many enthusiastic adherents among the 10,000 subscribers to the morning or evening editions, was staunchly pro-North.[10] Yet privately Lucas gloomed over the prospects; he thought as Greeley did that the best course would be to let the South go, though he at least was not publishing that view. Bigelow discussed with him the new Morrill tariff, first sop to Whig Republican protectionists. Why not, suggested Bigelow to Lucas as one free trader to another, write an editorial explaining that British indifference to the Northern cause was largely owing to preference for the South's low tariff policy? It certainly would be read in America — Bigelow would see that it was published there — and it might possibly influence Congress.

Bigelow's own work seemed well under way by the time he went to dine with Charles Francis Adams. At the legation he expected to find tremendous alertness and energy. Instead he found John Lothrop Motley, United States Minister to Austria, still in London, displaying his new rank among his noble friends. Adams found him amusing, as an Adams could; so too did Bigelow, but he was irked as well. Then it came out that Adams, who had been in London since May, did not know Lucas — Samuel Lucas, the editor of "the only organ of the only biggish English party in favor of the North." Bigelow was shocked. As a newspaperman he expected everyone to sense immediately the importance of good press relations, and, too much of a novice to understand the slow motions of diplomacy or the multiple problems confronting Adams, he felt his respect for Seward's appointments diminishing.[11]

Depression resulting from the apparent idleness of Union representatives was mingled with anger at English hostility to the North. Using Hargreaves as a safety valve, Bigelow poured out his feelings: Europe need not expect the United States to beg for favor; if the Union could not get along without foreign help, it deserved to go to pieces. But that would not happen, he asserted grimly. Moreover, if Britain's leaders persisted until they brought war between their land and the United States, there would be just one result — revolution in Britain. The people would rise against an outworn aristocracy that ordered them to fight on behalf of cotton and slavery. And they would be right, Bigelow thought, though fundamentally he was anything but a believer in revolutionary remedies.[12]

The wall of red tape, indecision, and blindness was frustrating to a man keyed to the urgency of the moment. No parades for him; he must hurry to Paris, Mann had just arranged with Reuters to have

Confederate news items sent throughout Europe; Dayton was writing Seward that the South controlled the entire French press and was writing Bigelow to come over at once. So, after only four days in London, the Bigelows crossed the channel. By September 14, they were settled on the Rue de Rivoli, where, incidentally, they might have been settled the day before, but that was a Friday and Bigelow was still cautious about Friday beginnings.[13]

Conditions were utterly disagreeable at first. Bigelow had come to act and instead found himself thwarted at every turn. His French was not yet adequate and he was as disappointed as Dayton when he could not serve as interpreter in consultations with Thouvenel, the Minister for Foreign Affairs. Dayton had to hire an interpreter — he had no thought of learning French — while Bigelow studied to acquire command of the language, reading French books, taking lessons, occasionally keeping his diary in broken French. He tried to get on with his consular tasks but found his office too crowded and dismal to permit work. Moreover, a recent change in city ordinances forbade long leases in the neighborhood where the American consulate chanced to be. Bigelow had, therefore, the choice of renewing the lease each year with the annual prospect of a forced removal or of taking the time to move at once to another section. In order to have a permanent establishment he decided to re-locate, which he did at his own expense, since the budget did not provide for moving costs. "But," he wryly observed later, "this was not a very serious matter for all the furniture of the consulate consisted of a bookcase, a desk worth perhaps $3.00 and a chest filled with old papers and books. I had to borrow the chair on which I sat and the table upon which I wrote my dispatch announcing my arrival at my post. I then had to furnish the consulate, also at my own expense. I have to warm the rooms and light them when necessary, at an expense of about $50 a year. I have also the expense for cleaning and taking care of the office." [14]

Fortunately Bigelow had a private income to use in improving the office. The first sight of the dingy, cramped rooms might easily have deepened into contempt for governmental parsimony or into a poverty of effort consistent with the surroundings. His income would not permit luxury, nor did he wish it, but he could afford a satisfactory office at 47 Champs-Élysées of three small rooms, adequately furnished except for archival equipment. Boxes of records tumbled crazily about the office when he arrived and continued to pile higher during his stay for want of room and facilities to care for them. In fact, one or two trunks of government records which he heard were stored somewhere in Paris never were located.[15]

It took time to get acquainted with his routine duties. Lightly Seward had blanked out the ordinary business of a consul in describing why he wanted Bigelow in Paris, but that was no comfort when immediate tasks called for legal knowledge unused these past twelve years. There were wills to draw, estates to settle, marriages to be arranged, destitute Americans to be cared for, and constant demands for advice about business and travel to be handled. Then there were personal calls, letters from exporters, letters from importers, all to be cared for by Bigelow and two assistants, all of them time-consuming and none of them related to his reason for being in Paris. The hardest burden was the coldness surrounding him. The only government people whose devotion to the Northern cause he never doubted were Dayton, Henry S. Sanford, the competent United States Minister to Belgium, and the voluble colored porter at the Paris consulate, David Fuller. Parisian papers were unfriendly. He had expected the liberal press to favor the North, if for no other reason than that the government was notoriously pro-South, but even the liberals were gloomy in the fall of '61, for the war in America threatened to hurt French business. In September the leading Orleanist paper, *Le Journal des Débats,* Northern in sympathy though it was, definitely came out for peaceful separation of the North and South.[16]

The first gleam of hope came on October 5 when *La Presse,* a liberal Paris paper, carried an article by a M. Juif favorable to the North, and *Le Journal des Débats* had an equally friendly article by Edouard Laboulaye, member of the Institute, professor at the College of France, lecturer on American constitutional history, and, now in his fiftieth year, a long-standing friend of republican institutions. At once Bigelow sent an appreciative note to each man and expressed his hope of an early meeting. Laboulaye, who was then at his country home, replied that he would call as soon as he returned to Paris. This he did on October 20, and from then on, without thought of financial reward, he wrote frequently on behalf of the North. Juif called on Bigelow as soon as he received his note. He had practised law in New York for nine years and was delighted to meet a fellow member of the bar. Together they reviewed the latest news from America and the attitude of France. When Juif departed, he left a lighter atmosphere behind him, for he had promised to devote his column in *La Presse* to anti-Confederate articles. Bigelow's alertness to see an opening and pounce on it without a moment's hesitation had carried Northern propaganda over the first great hurdle. As soon as one publication began a series of articles friendly to his cause, it was relatively easy for him to persuade others to follow suit. By October 15, he could write Bryant that whereas three weeks before not two journals in all France were friendly, now the tone of the press was improving. A stream of letters to Seward showed that the Paris consul was doing all possible to cement good relations, nor was it long before Seward was congratulating him "on the new work so well begun." Seward, who in the spring had toyed with the idea of a foreign war in order to reunite the states, now wrote: "The only anxiety that remains, results from the fears of European intervention." [17]

Then came the *Trent* affair: on November 9 the English ship was stopped by an American war vessel and two recently appointed Confederate commissioners, James M. Mason and John Slidell, were removed before the *Trent* was permitted to continue its trip. When that news reached France on November 27, unanimous opinion roundly condemned the North and demanded, regardless of the means, that the rights of neutrals be guaranteed. Some papers commented, not uncheerfully, on the probabilities of war between Britain and the United States. From a French point of view there could be little objection to such a war, for France could then control trade with the Confederacy, sell its own wares, and get plentiful cotton supplies. Dayton was told by the cautious Foreign Minister that France would probably remain neutral in the event of an Anglo–American war, though its sympathy would be with Britain, while Lord Cowley, the British Ambassador to France, reported his belief that France would back Britain to the limit.[18]

Meanwhile, in England, all the latent animosity against the Yankee upstarts, all the deep-seated fears that across the ocean was building a state which one day might challenge Britain's sea empire, rose to the surface. So ominous were the press, the Ministers, the public, that before long Adams wrote Motley: "My dear Sir — I am here quietly waiting the development of events over which I have no control, and in which I had no participation. . . ."; and resignedly announced to Seward:

> My present expectation is that by the middle of January at furthest diplomatic relations will have been sundered between the two countries without any act of mine. I am therefore endeavoring to complete all the ordinary business of the legation in advance of the moment when the proper instructions will arrive in regard to the final disposition of its affairs as well as to the course I am myself to pursue.[19]

Except for its own agents the Union seemed not to have a dozen friends in all Europe. Almost everyone was convinced that the seizure had been authorized, that now was the time, once and for all, to rid the world of a brash democracy. In Paris, Bigelow's journalist friends lost faith or dared not talk. Dismayed, he called upon the eminent Louis Antoine Garnier-Pagès, one of the few Republicans in the Chamber of Deputies, whom he had first met in 1859 and who, as an elder statesman and friend of the Union, would take a temperate view if any Frenchman would. Garnier-Pagès met Bigelow gravely, stating that disruption of the Union now seemed inevitable, for England must intervene. For twenty minutes Bigelow argued the merits of the case, saying all that he could to place the incident in perspective. At the close his host suggested: "Why don't you sit down and write out just what you have said to me, and publish it over your own signature tomorrow morning? It would have a very reassuring effect and would afford as substantial comfort to others as it has afforded to myself." [20]

Such unauthorized action on the part of a government official was prohibited, but Bigelow was determined to have his argument appear in print. At least he could put it in the form of a letter, even though another must sign it. General Winfield Scott, recently General in Chief of the United States Army, and only just arrived in Paris on an unofficial mission for the government, was the most illustrious American in France and the one whose name would most impress Europeans. As Bigelow walked away from the Garnier-Pagès home, he decided that Scott was the man to sign the letter, in spite of a private opinion, expressed years before but never changed, that the general was little more than a pompous, gouty old man, "a broth of a statesman. He should live in a country where they estimate greatness in men altogether by the square inches." [21] So he hastened to Thurlow Weed, who with General Scott and Archbishop Hughes had been sent by Seward to propagandize for the North. Rapidly he outlined his plan. Immediately Weed endorsed it and went off to consult with Dayton and Hughes. With their approval, he then set out to tackle the General. Weed's was a delicate task, for in the best of tempers Scott in his pride might refuse to father another's composition, and just now his temper was frayed by a swollen right arm. Bigelow, meanwhile, worked on the letter. Within three hours it was written. The old General, obviously delighted with its tone and contents, signed it. The next morning, December 3, all the Paris papers carried the translation sent them by Bigelow, and copies mailed by Bigelow were en route to London, while Weed himself took others to London to ensure its publication. [22]

The letter proved that the act could not have been committed by order of the government, emphasized the importance of British friendship to the United States, and calmly reviewed the circumstances of the seizure, insofar as they were known. Bigelow pointed out:

> . . . Nor is there anything, I venture to affirm, in the seizure of these rebel emissaries which ought to receive an unfriendly construction from England. Her statesmen will not question the legal right of an American vessel of war to search any commercial vessel suspected of transporting contraband of war; that right has never been surrendered by England; it was even guaranteed to her by the Treaty of Paris; and British guns frowning down upon nearly every strait and inland sea upon the globe, are conclusive evidence that she regards this right as one the efficiency of which may be not yet entirely exhausted.
>
> Of course there is much that is irritating and vexatious in the exercise of this right, under the most favorable circumstances; and it is to be hoped that the day is not distant when the maritime states of the world will agree in placing neutral commerce beyond the reach of such vexations. The United States Government has been striving to this end for more than fifty years; to this end early in the present century, and in its infancy as a nation, it embarked in a war with the greatest naval power in the world; and it is even now a persistent suitor at every maritime court in Europe for a more liberal recognition of the rights of neutral commerce than any other great maritime nations have yet been disposed to make.
>
> But till those rights are secured by proper international guaranties upon a comprehensive and enduring basis, of course England cannot complain of an act for which, in all its material bearings, her own naval history affords such numerous precedents. . . .
>
> If under these circumstances England should deem it her duty, in the interest of civilization, to insist upon the restoration of the men taken from under the protection of her flag, it will be from a conviction, without doubt, that the law of nations in regard to the rights of neutrals, which she has taken a leading part in establishing, requires revision. . . .
>
> On the other hand, should England be unprepared to make a corresponding sacrifice; should she feel that she could not yet afford to surrender the advantages which the present maritime code gives to a dominant naval power, of course she will not put herself in a false position by asking us to do it. In either case, therefore, I do not see how the friendly relations of the two governments are in any immediate danger of being disturbed.[23]

Reprinted throughout Britain and Europe, the subject of editorial comment and of general discussion, this "most successful single bit of propaganda in the whole war" was a striking illustration of Bigelow's resourcefulness in an emergency and of his capacity for quick and effective decision.[24] It carried conviction to sober-minded men that the seizure was not made upon government order, disposed many Europeans to await news of the United States government's attitude before taking drastic steps, and raised some doubts as to England's right to object. Cobden's view was typical of that of many liberals. He wrote Sumner in praise of the letter, "worthy of the reknowned sagacity of its author," and urged that the United States act upon its suggestion: deliver up Mason and Slidell provided Britain would agree at long last to outlaw any seizure of private property at sea. Even John Lothrop Motley pronounced it "admirable." When "Scott's" letter was published in America on December 19, Sumner was at once convinced that Bigelow was the author; he could think of no other American in Paris capable of writing it. So, too, thought Bryant and Godwin in New York. Weed later remarked: "The able, well-timed appeal to the judgment, reason and good sense of both countries . . . reflects equally upon the ability of Mr. Bigelow and the patriotism of General Scott." Meanwhile, in America, the first delirious joy in the capture gave way to Seward's hardheaded attitude, and the Confederates were freed to resume their voyage.[25]

The excitement of the *Trent* affair was hardly over when news reached Europe of the stone-filled ships sunk by Northerners in Charleston Harbor. Southern agents, led by John Slidell, who had just reached Paris, told of the wanton destruction of the great port. The English and the French press elaborated complaints of the barbarous treatment accorded to a natural harbor important to the world's commerce. Weed, again in Paris, again planned with Bigelow to spike Confederate propaganda. To the London *Daily News* went a clear explanation from Weed. To the London *Morning Post* and to *Le Moniteur*, the official government organ of France, went rumor-ending letters from Bigelow proving that no permanent damage had been done, that the ships closed only one entrance to the harbor and were, moreover, in shallow water from which they could easily be raised after the war.[26]

"You did not make a mistake in your consul to Paris," Weed wrote to Seward. "Mr. Bigelow has capacity and fitness for higher duties. I hope you will give him permission to be absent, in his discretion, during the pendency of our troubles. He may be wanted elsewhere and ought not to be restricted to ten days," which was the wartime length of leaves of absence lest citizens at home clamor against the idle lives led by their representatives abroad. The following April, it so happened, Bigelow received formal permission to leave his office at any time for one month provided he informed the State Department and left someone in charge of his office.[27]

Though soothing successive waves of indignation over particular incidents was important, the basic task was to create an atmosphere wherein willingness to listen before passing judgment would eliminate the danger of angry rupture over any minor event. Bigelow was convinced that his efforts to establish such an attitude in France could not be successful so long as American news was relayed to the Continent through England. By the time the aristocratic English press had put its mark upon American news, the damage was done. Bigelow wrote Seward on January 27:

> When I give an editor a document I can give him at the same time the light by which it is to be read and interpreted. When he receives it through an English Journal first, he takes the English view without hesitation, in some instances with satisfaction as it is a way of punishing us for treating him as a secondary influence. This too is the only means I have of placing the press under obligation to me and of establishing claims upon their courtesy.
> . . . I venture to suggest that documents of interest abroad which are likely to be given to the public before they could reach Europe and return, be sent me in manuscript or in early proof: if in print, fifteen or twenty copies, for I would like to supply the leading journals not only here but the correspondents of the leading journals in Belgium and in Germany, several of whom have already expressed to me a desire to be turned to account in this way. With facilities of this sort I can win the confidence of every influential journalist here, the fruit of which I am sure would soon be apparent in my correspondence.[28]

Added to Bigelow's difficulties was the fact that he did not receive American news even as soon as others in France. Vandenbrook Bros., the French bankers, always had word from Peabody & Co. one ship ahead of the regular sources. But what could Bigelow do about it? Eventually he learned that the American consul at Queenstown sent all dispatches from America direct to the legations at Vienna and Madrid. So he asked for the same service to Paris. If the government would not pay for it, he personally would; it was worth it to him to get the news before it was doctored. Yet after a month's trial he called it off. Deliveries from the Paris telegraph office were so slow and wire-tapping by the French government was so consistent that Bigelow gained no advantage.[29]

Obviously the Federal blockade had much to do with the unfavorable attitude in the English press. Similarly in France the blockade, quite as much if not more than the biased news accounts from England, heightened anti-Union sentiment. Idealists in Europe might speak for the North in its battle for the downtrodden, but the pound and the franc talked louder. Bigelow wrote home:

This war has deranged the financial calculations of the governments and bankers of Europe to a greater degree than all of the wars or revolutions that have preceded it in Europe. The Statesmen are at their wits end to know what to do. Sources of revenue are dried up upon which all their calculations have been heretofore based with the greatest confidence. The capital of many states is insufficiently employed; hundreds of thousands of people are becoming a charge upon the governments for their daily bread, and the heavens seem charged with some terrible convulsion from which they think nothing can save them but raising our blockade.

Now more than ever before, as it seems to me, does it become the American statesman, to regard the European situation as a part of the situation with which he has to deal at home and to feel it his duty to provide for both in providing for either. This leads me to ask you whether the Blockade has not answered its purpose as fully as it ever can, and if there is any more speedy way of cutting the throat of Secession than by raising it, upon condition that the Maritime States of Europe will agree that it shall be the last time such a mode of warfare is to be resorted to. Such a proposal from our govt. would remove all pretext for recognizing the South; it would win for our govt. the esteem & gratitude of the continent and if refused by England would isolate her, for France could not refuse to accept such an offer, & would not if she could. It would put an end to all sympathy with the South on this side the Atlantic, it would bring upon the Confederates the animosity now felt towards us.[30]

No words which Seward or Dayton or Bigelow could utter were so eloquent as were the thousands of unemployed in the factories of France. In that country, quite as much as in England, lack of cotton meant hardship, for, though France had only one fourth as many spindles as England, the French industry had not been overexpanded in recent years nor did it have proportionately as large reserves of raw cotton on hand. Sentiment favoring the Confederacy was sure to continue, therefore, so long as the Union blockade appeared to hold up the vital supply of cotton, and apparently that would continue until the North broke the rebellion. ". . . but to me," Bigelow wrote, "looking from this distance, the advance of the army does not seem to be much more rapid than the original colonization of the country, Congress does not seem to have confidence in the commander-in Chief and apparently not without reason; the Cabinet seem quarrelsome and feeble and the public credit is rapidly exhausting itself." [31]

Bigelow wrote to other American and English friends of the advantages to all nations for all time in an international outlawing of blockades. It would be a notable advance in maritime law; it would end the chief sore spot between France, England, and the United States, and would spoil Confederate expectations of European assistance. He was convinced, as Cobden was, though Bright did not agree, that raising the blockade would not hurt the Northern war effort, because he believed that even without it the South could ship little cotton. He asserted that too much Confederate energy was consumed by the war for it to maintain cotton production levels, and that its credit system was inadequate to manage exchanges. Therefore, he reasoned, if there were no blockade to distort European vision, Britain and France would realize that the pinch their industrial communities already felt was the result of the perversity of the South in fighting to extend slavery. Similarly, in the fast-approaching time of a true cotton famine, when mills would stand idle and whole towns would go hungry, they would know that a victorious North could most quickly relieve their distress. Even in the South, when Confederates realized the harm they were doing to themselves, "it would awaken a strong industrial and commercial reactionary interest" which would help to break the spirit of the rebellion. [32]

Few Americans in Europe during the winter of 1861–1862 could foresee that the blockade was to prove one of the most effective weapons of the North. What they did see was the dangerous possibility of British and French retaliation for the blockade by recognition of the Confederacy. They knew that the odds against the restoration of the Union would be enormous if European munitions, ships, and armed forces helped the South. Statesmen at home, however, seeing more clearly the importance of maintaining and strengthening the blockade, wisely frowned upon Bigelow's efforts to change their policy.

Fortunately for the Union, Southern miscalculations unwittingly helped the North to preserve both the blockade and peace in Europe. Cotton was king, the South arrogantly proclaimed in 1861. What need for Southerners to curry Europe's favor? Sheer economic necessity would force England and France to recognize and assist them if they permitted their cotton to go only where their flag was recognized. [33] Therefore one Southern state after another slapped on what amounted to a cotton embargo, which in 1861, far more than the North's ineffective paper blockade, kept cotton from Europe. The Confederate government ordered its commissioners to make the economic realities clear to Ministers and sent purchasing agents to buy essential ships and munitions with what credits the South had abroad. Hired press representatives were unnecessary to such strategy; Southerners like Paul du Bellet living in France did their best in a private capacity to influence public opinion, but it was completely upon cotton that the South counted to force Europe to its knees. To this end the commissioners worked, Rost with most effect in France. They had reported to their government in May, after Rost saw the Duc de Morny, that "the French government would always be ready to receive unofficially and give due consideration to any suggestions we might deem it proper to make provided strict secrecy were maintained; and in the meantime, so long as we produced cotton for sale, France and England would see that their vessels reached the ports where it was to be had." By October they were convinced by the manner of the French Minister for Foreign Affairs that "the French government entertained profound sympathy for the cause of the South, and expected that events would transpire, within no distant period, which would cause it to recognize the Confederate States." [34]

But all Northern agents were not as "the stout and apoplectic William Dayton . . . moving in a vacuum in France." Throughout the fall Bigelow knew the tenor of Southern communications to French Ministers. So, too, did Seward. The two men responded to the Confederate emphasis upon cotton almost at the same time and in highly typical ways. Seward in Washington blandly replied to the French Minister who requested the lifting of the blockade that the North might place an embargo on wheat corresponding to the Southern embargo on cotton. Bigelow in Paris wrote to Seward and Bryant that the North held the whip hand, expressing as fervent a belief in a guiding destiny as ever his friend George Bancroft did. Bigelow pointed out that France had just had its poorest grain harvest in thirty years. Prices were high; people were in need. If their government chose to maintain peaceful and amicable relations with the United States, Frenchmen could buy all the wheat they wanted from the North. He believed that had it not been for grain, cotton might indeed have won the diplomatic war. "But Providence wills it otherwise. It sent us an abundant crop in 1860 and a short crop in Europe and the Southern states, that we might establish the Republican party in Washington, which we could never have done if the prosperity of the country had not silenced the croakings in Wall Street." [35]

So cotton was not immediately decisive. The first Southern plan was a failure; friendship in high quarters was theirs, but recognition was just a hope, for their reasoning had been accurate, but their timing had been poor. Cotton surpluses from the bumper crop of 1860, stored in Europe's warehouses, tided manufacturers over 1861. There had been some grumbling, some hardship, but it resulted chiefly from speculation in cotton prices; the famine itself would not exist until later in 1862. Therefore, in the fall of '61 the Confederacy reorganized its Foreign Department. Yancey resigned and, after his successor arrived, returned home to become a Confederate senator. Rost was given charge of the less important interests of the Confederacy in Spain, and Mann of their interests in Belgium. Two new commissioners, James Mason and John Slidell — those who had been sent on the *Trent* to direct activities in Britain and France respectively — together with A. Dudley Mann, were instructed to form a general clearinghouse for all Confederate projects in Europe.

By February, 1862, after the *Trent* affair belonged to the past, Mason and Slidell were at their posts, and the second stage in the battle for Europe commenced.[36]

CHAPTER 14

Extra-consular Duties

[*1862*]

Two AMERICANS now engaged in a strange contest upon the shifting stage of French imperial policy. One of them was John Bigelow, at forty-four a high-strung, intense, quick-moving Yankee, a long, lean, handsome man of unshakable integrity who made friends easily and had a shrewd grasp of European and American politics. The other was seventy-year-old John Slidell, recently Louisiana's unscrupulous United States senator. Originally a New Yorker, Slidell had fled to Louisiana in 1819 after a duel over a girl. There he turned more Southern than a Southerner, studied law, and entered politics. By methods condemned by decent citizens throughout the land, he became successively political boss of New Orleans, of Louisiana; and after he helped to engineer Buchanan's election to the Presidency, a power even in national affairs. He was a strong, ruthless figure, steely-eyed and suavely mannered, to whom means mattered little so long as his ends were achieved, and his ends now were the establishment of states' rights and the Confederacy.[1]

The strangest aspect of the three-year contest between Bigelow and Slidell were that they never met, that they felt nothing but unalloyed contempt for each other, and that only occasionally did either know exactly what the other was planning. Yet time and again they succeeded in checking each other's projects. Time and again a sudden shift in Napoleon's attitude towards the combatants in America could be traced, in part, to the successful maneuver of one or the other of them. Both men were able, resourceful, quick-witted; eminently suited to their tasks. Slidell was daring and brilliant in large schemes; Bigelow was doggedly persistent in turning little situations to advantage. Slidell pointed his efforts straight towards his ultimate goal of recognition of the South and the breaking of the blockade; Bigelow worked obliquely, piling up many lesser victories to the end of dissuading the

French from helping the Confederacy. Their contrasting methods resulted largely from the resources at their command. As the representative of the Confederate States, Slidell had access to the Ministers of France and eventually to Napoleon himself. His way was made easy by their sympathy for his cause and their expectation that the North would lose the war. He himself observed when he first reached Paris "a degree of prejudice amounting to bitterness against our Northern foes." [2] And he had the solid reality of cotton behind him. Bigelow, as a mere consul, as a Unionist, as an official of a protective-tariff country, had none of those advantages. However, he could point to the formidable wealth and strength of the North, which in the final analysis was to make possible his success; he had the sympathy of republican and monarchist groups in France, and he found articulate friends among literary men and journalists.

When Slidell reached Paris, less than five months after Bigelow, he was disturbed by the prevailing belief that the Confederate embargo on cotton, rather than the Northern blockade, caused the 75 per cent cut in cotton exports in 1861. Even *La Revue des Deux Mondes*, the most respected fortnightly in Europe, gave credence to that theory. Though once it had argued for peaceful separation of the United States and though it had shown the North no mercy in the *Trent* affair, since then it had shifted its emphasis. Late in '61 it registered approval of the North's war aims in an article written, it so happened, by Bigelow's new friend, Auguste Laugel, the companion of the Duc d'Aumale. In January, 1862, it protested criticisms leveled against the Northern blockade, maintaining that with or without the blockade the export of cotton would be vastly curtailed so long as the war, provoked by the South, continued. Slidell knew nothing of Bigelow's cleverly placed insinuations concerning the Confederates' embargo and their productive capacity, but he realized that the Union was fast gaining control of the Paris press. That alarmed him, because he knew that the newspapers of all France took their news and views from the capital. [3]

Hardly giving himself time to get settled, he hastened to Edouard Thouvenel, the Foreign Minister, whom he found pleasant but noncommittal. He had long talks with Achille Fould, Minister of Finance, Pierre Baroche, President of the Council of States, and the Duc de Persigny, Minister of the Interior, all of whom most cordially expressed their hopes that his mission would be successful. And he established friendly relations with La Gueronnière, the proprietor of *La Patrie*, with Felix Aucaigne, its editor, and with Cassignac of *Le Pays*. Suddenly those two papers and Persigny's *Constitutionnel*, which composed the semiofficial press, veered from strict neutrality to advocating recognition of the Confederacy. With just pride Slidell reported to his Government this result of his first two weeks in France, and at the same time he asked for funds with which to bring greater influence to bear upon the French press. Presently he had evidence of friendship from two other Ministers, Count Florian Walewski, Minister of State, and Eugène Rouher, Minister of Commerce, and from many disgruntled French businessmen. He had good reason to expect France to give early assistance to the Confederacy.[4]

It was Bigelow's turn to be disturbed when reports of Slidell's activities reached him. Some of them, like the tale that the Emperor received Slidell on February 16, were exaggerated or completely false, yet many of them were accurate summaries of actual conversations. Happily for U. S. diplomacy, General Grant captured Fort Donelson in February; the arrival of that news early in March blasted the Confederate strategy of winning French help in one brilliant spurt. In the face of the Northern victory Napoleon retreated into hesitancy, Slidell, despairing of direct assistance from France alone, shifted his maneuvers to seek joint Anglo-French action, while Bigelow knew that his worries could be set aside for the time being. But not his work. That had always to be continued, because his job was to achieve a cumulative effect through a series of little acts, seeing amiable friends of the liberal press, suggesting articles and finding pertinent material to lighten journalistic tasks, urging upon Seward a cut in wine duties to strengthen the momentary French disposition to be friendly. He was never to agree with Dayton or with Cassius M. Clay, Minister to Russia, who wrote Dayton at this time:

> I am glad that my confidence in the French Emperor has not been misplaced. His speech in favor of neutrality before the Chambers settled that question. . . . So, my dear friend, we were right at the Paris breakfast in setting 'our life upon a cast' — the die has turned up for us! England, all now see, was the enemy of our Republic."[5]

The minor victory on the battlefield at home did not end the danger of a British or French declaration of war upon the United States. At the most it but postponed that grim possibility. So Bigelow pondered how best his country could prepare for the calamity of a foreign war added to the civil war. The answer seemed to him to be a better railroad system so that troops could reach whatever area of the land Europeans might threaten. Seven years before, when Congress was considering proposals for a transcontinental railroad, he had opposed government grants of money or credit to railroad interests. He had written then:

> In granting a right of way and bounty lands, the general government grants first what is indispensable, second, what it only can grant, and thirdly it promotes an improvement which increases the value of its own property proportionately; but when money or credit is given, at once the government enters into competition with private enterprise, departs from its appropriate sphere of duty, abandons the strict letter of the Constitution, lays the foundation for lawless speculations in public property, extends political corruption, and prepares the swift road to national bankruptcy. . . . Either the credit clause should be taken out, or, if the government are to build it, the government should own it [the railroad].[6]

As a strict-construction Democrat, he at that time had preferred removal of the credit clause to government ownership. Yet he was no rigid dogmatist who would sacrifice practical good to a theory. Since penning that editorial he had seen for himself the revolutionary and beneficial effects of government-controlled railroads upon the French national economy, and he was ready to reshape an old principle in order to ensure benefit to his country.

So he wrote to Seward, enclosing an analysis of French railroads by Nelson M. Beckwith, an American resident of Paris, that ". . . a comprehensive and remunerative system of railroads is next to a free government, the great necessity of our country." Nothing could be more important than to start at once to improve the railroads of America. In fact, he believed that had they been good, the rebellion would not have started or at least would have been more easily suppressed. He continued: "Has not the time to inaugurate such a system arrived, when the want is felt, when the country is not nice in weighing and measuring the power confided to the executive and when the capital of the country is more than usually indifferent to changes and innovations affecting its employment, provided they look to the greater security and integrity of the Union? It is in such times of political and financial trial, that nations receive their great social and industrial impulses." Because he thought war with Britain imminent, he urged the immediate construction of a transcontinental railroad as the one sure way of protecting California. Moreover, he suggested that later, after the rebellion was over, the Southern railroads should be confiscated for use as the nucleus of a nation-wide, government-run network of the highest efficiency. America would have to improve its roads, he predicted, because its exports were going to face new competition from the regions being opened up by Russian railroads, by

French railroads into Spain, and by British encouragement of cotton production in India. On this letter from Bigelow, Seward jotted an instruction to his secretaries: "Please copy whole, on every other page, for Congress Number." [7]

Bigelow's fear of a war with Britain and France deepened during the spring of '62. He suggested to Seward the wisdom of posting military and perhaps naval attachés at the major legations, as other powers did, in order to keep abreast of the latest advances in military science. Again Seward ordered Bigelow's letter copied, this time to be sent to the War and Navy Departments, although nothing was to come of it until long after Bigelow left the service.[8]

Meanwhile the Confederate, Edwin de Leon, one-time United States consul-general in Alexandria, arrived in Europe. He had $25,000 "to be used by him in the manner he may deem most judicious," Confederate Secretary of State Judah P. Benjamin wrote, "both in Great Britain and the continent, for the special purpose of enlightening public opinion in Europe through the press." At last the Confederate State Department had recognized that it must supplement its demands for help with artful propaganda. But de Leon did his cause little good. He earned Slidell's enmity by opening sealed dispatches he was asked to carry. He spent some $30,000 on French newspapers during the two years he was in Europe, but, outbalancing that, he wrote a pamphlet entitled *The Truth about the Confederacy* which antagonized Frenchmen because it praised slavery, and, worst of all, he expressed in private letters indiscreet if truthful comments upon the ethics of French journalists which Northerners procured and published. At that point, in 1864, he was recalled, leaving Slidell as the ever-present menace.[9]

Towards the end of April 1862, Bigelow was worried by a new outburst of pro-Southern activity. He wrote William S. Thayer, a former reporter on the New York *Evening Post* and now consul-general in Alexandria:

> Slidell has just been elected to the Jockey Club. This is evidence of a strong feeling for the South among the Court people. Gladstone's speech the other day, the course of the London *Post* and *Times* recently and of the *Const* here and an article in the *Debats* on the 24th attributed to Chevalier lead me to apprehend, that any serious disaster to our arms at Yorktown would result in a prompt recognition of the Confederacy by France and England.[10]

He was uncomfortably sure that France and Great Britain were concocting something. What it was he did not know, but he warned Seward that some mischief was afoot, and he set himself more diligently than ever to his extra-consular duties.

He took over from Dayton complete charge of all suspicious letters reaching Northerners in Paris. Of more importance, he made full use of partisans. Foremost among them was A. Malespine, a writer for *L'Opinion Nationale*, who reported to Bigelow at regular intervals upon whatever subject he was asked to look into. Another useful friend was Loubat, a businessman in Paris who frequently called upon Bigelow with a potpourri of fact and fancy. The more reliable bits were offspring of some private connection Loubat had with the Ministry for Foreign Affairs. All too often, however, they were mixed with news concocted by Slidell for the sole purpose of deluding Northerners, for, while Loubat in happy innocence thought he was worming confidences from Slidell, Slidell knew that he would run to Dayton and Bigelow with everything he was told.[11] But Bigelow was no man's fool. Though he did not know that the Confederate deliberately used Loubat, he did know that his friend was more zealous than discriminating. Accordingly, he used the data with caution and found the kernels of truth worth the time spent eliminating the chaff.

He used other partisans for publicity purposes. Juif, his earliest newspaper friend in Paris, was always ready to be of service. Through Juif, Bigelow won another staunch supporter in Peyrat, the conductor of *La Presse*, for which paper Juif wrote. That was because Bigelow listened sympathetically when Juif described to him the financial disgrace looming over Peyrat, that same day asked Henry S. Sanford, the capable Minister to Belgium, for 1500 francs for "extraordinary expenses," and gave Juif 1,000 of them to help Peyrat.[12] Long later Slidell got wind of this and wrote to Benjamin:

> The political director of the French press is well known to me almost since my first arrival in Paris; he was decided in his expression of Southern sympathies and I have no doubt sincerely entertained them. . . . For some time past he has gone beyond the line of his official duties to suppress articles and intelligence favorable to the South and to impose the insertion of those of an opposite tendency. He is needy and extravagant, has lost very large sums at play which have been paid by money obtained from an American banking house with which he had no previous connection.
>
> I think you will agree with me in attributing this sudden and remarkable change of opinion and action to a timely application of Mr. Dayton's contingent fund.[13]

Slidell himself was as busy as Bigelow. When news reached Paris of the defeat of General Banks on the Potomac, he and de Leon helped the imperialist press clamor for intervention to bring an end to the war. The liberal press, urged on by Bigelow, swung into action. *La Presse, Le Siècle,* and especially *Le Journal des Débats* charged the official press with thought only for the South, not for France, and stressed the folly of making war upon the very union France had helped to create. Then Bigelow went to London for a few days late in May to consult with Adams, Weed, George Morgan, cousin of New York's governor, and with Bright and Cobden, about Confederate shipbuilding in England and the steps being taken to combat it. That, of course, was Adams's problem and he was doing his skillful best to handle it, but the time was not far distant when Bigelow would be as immediately concerned.[14]

By the end of May the sense of impending disaster which had perturbed Bigelow for a month, and the mist of half-seen intrigues, too shapeless to grasp firmly and examine, were at least temporarily dispelled. They had been caused, as he had long suspected and as he had warned Bright back in January, entirely by Slidell and James A. Lindsay, Tory member of Parliament and Britain's largest shipowner. What actually happened that spring was that Napoleon, in an interview granted Lindsay on April 11, turned the conversation to American affairs, said that he was prepared to recognize the Confederate States "if Great Britain would set him the example," that he had twice before this asked Britain to join him in such action, that he had received no answer, and would not, therefore, try again. Two days later, according to the reports Lindsay made to Lord Cowley, the British Ambassador to France, the Emperor asked him to seek joint Anglo-French recognition of the Confederacy through private talks with Lord Palmerston, the Prime Minister, and Lord Russell, the Secretary for Foreign Affairs.

Cowley labeled all this "a nasty intrigue" and wrote his chief that Thouvenel, Napoleon's Foreign Minister, had no more knowledge than he of these purported messages to Britain about the Confederacy. Forewarned, Russell refused to receive Lindsay when he returned to London. The self-appointed diplomat perforce contented himself with talking to Benjamin Disraeli, a Conservative leader, and returned to Paris two days later with James Mason — which accounts for the general meeting of Confederate agents of which Bigelow informed Seward, for already Mann, Hotze, Caleb Huse the munitions agent, and James Bulloch the naval agent were gathered at the Hotel Louvre. On April 18 Napoleon talked with Lindsay for a third time. But the golden hour had passed; the Emperor temporized, knowing that Federal forces had attacked New Orleans, and, two weeks later when he heard that New Orleans had fallen, he dropped all thought of immediate action.

Temporarily Lindsay also lost heart and postponed placing before Parliament his motion for recognition of the Confederate States. Slidell, however, continued to believe that recognition was imminent.[15]

Not until after the war did Bigelow know these details. At the time, all that he knew was that Slidell had some connection with Lindsay, that Lindsay tried in vain to commit his government to open espousal of the Confederate cause, and that Slidell was making every effort to unite Europe behind a plan to force an end to the war in America. He knew, as everyone did, that by June talk of intervention was giving way to cries for mediation. Bigelow labeled that "Act II" in the diplomatic war, and believed that it marked the turning point.[16] But he was too optimistic, too happy that a crisis had been weathered. All it meant was that Europe realized the significance of the fall of New Orleans, and that the wary and devious Emperor of France was following his regular pattern whenever Northern successes occurred. The South was still strong in battle and rich in friends. Yet it was encouraging to Northerners to learn that Slidell had offered a hundred thousand bales of cotton to anyone breaking the blockade, and that his offer brought no response although it was made at the height of the cotton famine and the distress of the export trades, when unemployment was greater than it had been for a decade. Rumor had it that Slidell was leaving. "He found his habits of corruption more portable than his fortune," Bigelow wrote Cobden on June 2, "for he brought the one and not the other."

The French press evinced a growing cordiality towards the North, the result of slush funds, Slidell said with a modicum of truth. By July the Orleanist papers were turning to Bigelow for suggestions; within two months the Orleans Prince de Joinville would be writing for the North in *La Revue des Deux Mondes;* and *La Patrie* and even Persigny's *Constitutionnel* were carrying occasional pro-North articles. Typical of the work Bigelow was doing to help create this friendly attitude was his response to three articles in *Le Journal des Débats,* one of them most unfortunate, he thought, the other two excellent, and all, therefore, deserving attention. The article he did not like was upon Northern confiscations of Southern property written by an imperialist, hence a partisan of the South. Bigelow handled that by sending a speech of Sumner's upon the same issue to his friend Alloury, editor of the *Débats,* who published the most pertinent sections. The two articles which Bigelow considered excellent were written by Laboulaye, a regular contributor to the *Débats* and a loyal friend of the Union, who wrote on its behalf without a single, selfish expectation, although he undoubtedly appreciated Bigelow's recognition of his work and his occasional timely gifts of American books. The consul at once sought and gained permission to reprint them in pamphlet form at his own expense, and sent copies to two hundred fellow members of Laboulaye's in the Institute and to diplomats and journalists throughout Europe who had a high regard for the opinions of the eminent Frenchman. Similar in purpose was his handling of an article upon America by Loubat. To insure the public's seeing it, Bigelow guaranteed to buy a thousand copies of L'Opinion Nationale the day the article should appear. By so doing he gave pleasure to editor and author alike.[17]

This knowing who was important, whose words would carry conviction, who was ready to express Northern leanings, and conversely who needed to be answered or silenced, demanded time, diplomacy, and watchfulness. Bigelow's task would have been simplified had he been on easy terms with Ministers and had he been received by Napoleon. But a consul — even a consul like Bigelow who corresponded freely with the United States Secretary of State, the Chairman of the Senate Foreign Relations Committee, Federal Generals, United States Ministers throughout Europe, and leading liberal members of the British and French legislative bodies — could not mingle in high official society in Napoleon's capital. The American Minister could, but he did not. William Dayton did precisely what his instructions called upon him to do but he never exceeded them. During his four years in France he did not visit socially in the homes of more than six Frenchmen of importance, so that even among the English-speaking French his influence was small, his opportunities to gather information were limited. Sanford in Belgium, worried by Confederate successes on the battlefield and in European courts, wrote Bigelow that "he would not be surprised if Mr. Dayton found it necessary to ask for his passports before spring." [18]

Dayton's position was undoubtedly awkward. He had no intellectual attainments to offer to the cultured capital of mid-century France when Guizot, Renan, Taine, Martin, Berryer, Laboulaye, Montalembert, Cochin — all of them men Bigelow knew — were ruling the soirees, the press, and the colleges. Kindly and upright though he was, he had never been singled out, even by his friends, as a man of ability, legal or any other. Moreover, his immediate superior, the Secretary of State, was a man he did not trust and who placed little reliance upon him. Dayton wrote to his friend Thomas H. Dudley, for whom he had procured the consulate at Liverpool: "Don't write too much to Seward. Write only when you have something to say," to which Dudley replied: "I know very well that he does not like either you or me, and that we have nothing to expect from him. He would like very much to get a hold on us, but I have been very guarded in all my dispatches." [19] If on the surface Dayton welcomed the energetic leadership of his consul in Paris, beneath it he was constantly irritated by Bigelow's efficiency and self-assurance. It was no wonder that his handwriting went from bad to worse or that he left, upon his death, a stock of over two thousand cigars. Yet because he was a deeply loyal American, he placed in Bigelow's capable hands transactions another Minister would have jealously retained for himself. For that he deserves credit and respect, especially because he had, at the same time, the wholly natural personal impulse "to put the great Mr. John Bigelow in his proper place," to use the words of his first secretary in a letter to a congressman at home.[20]

Lacking better connections, Bigelow cultivated friendly newspapermen, acquaintances working in the offices of the great, and men like Dr. Thomas Evans, the rotund, ubiquitous American dentist who served the crowned heads of Europe somewhat as barbers had traditionally served their ancestors. Evans knew everyone, was versed in the subtle personal currents behind European politics, and upon request discreetly carried to the right person ideas brewing but not ready for formal utterance. As an instance of his importance, it was to him that the Empress Eugénie was to turn for shelter during the revolution of 1870, and it was he who saw her to safety. Fortunately the doctor and Bigelow had become personal friends during Bigelow's visit to France in 1859; throughout the war they met at many a dinner and included each other in their entertainments.

Yet often in the uncertain summer of 1862 Bigelow felt that he was not doing enough, that his country was not doing enough. He longed for someone from home with whom he could talk freely, who could explain what was happening and why more was not happening. He knew that his propaganda in Europe was constantly met by hostile inquiries about the progress of the armies and about United States finances. French investors were selling American stocks low in '62 because the Legal Tender Act, which substituted paper for gold, had shaken what confidence Europe had in the Union. From Bigelow's personal view, it seemed rather pointless to stay in France when his government was wiping out his capital, which he had expected would last his lifetime, and when what he could do in France to help win the war seemed to amount to so little.[21]

It would have been different had the Emperor been willing to listen to Northern arguments. But he was not. He had sent Persigny to England in June, presumably to talk, among other things, of joint mediation in America. On July 15 when the news of McClellan's defeat before Richmond was published in European papers, he wired Thouvenel, who was visiting in England: "Ask the English government if it does not believe the time has arrived to recognize the South." The next day he granted Slidell his first private audience, a conversation lasting seventy minutes, from which the Southerner departed with a highly satisfied air. Meanwhile, in England, Lindsay had at last formally presented to Parliament his motion urging mediation. On July 23 Slidell asked the French government to recognize his country, and the following day Mason made the same formal demand of Britain. Fortunately Lindsay received little support and was forced, shamefacedly, to withdraw his motion; Lord Russell postponed decision upon Mason's request; Thouvenel persuaded Slidell to withdraw his request as inopportune, and the British Cabinet did not respond favorably to Thouvenel's informal inquiry. So July '62 passed without overt action against the United States.[22]

Yet Bigelow found little cause for satisfaction, because Britain seemed to be taking care not to antagonize the Confederacy. Already one British-built ship, the *Florida*, was sailing under the Stars and Bars, and on July 29 a second ship, the *Enrica*, alias the *Alabama*, succeeded in leaving England in spite of Adams's heroic efforts to stop her. Nor were those two ships, ordered by Bulloch in the spring of '61, the only ones the Confederates were getting. Steadily rumors of more activity spread across Europe. Twice during the summer Bigelow went to London on business partly connected with the Confederate shipbuilding program. But officially his work was in France; and there was little he could do once sure that Cobden and his friends knew the ugly rumors and were aware of the inevitable Union reaction if Confederate plans were allowed to succeed. He could and did warn Governor Morgan that ships were being fitted out in Britain presumably for the purpose of attacking New York Harbor. Bigelow's confidential agent reported Prince Polignac as saying that three ironclads had that in view. "We are already at war with England without knowing it," Bigelow wrote. "She is furnishing the Confederates with all their resources. It is cheaper to fight us that way. . . ."[23] And a similar warning went to Seward, who hastened to pass it on to the Navy Department. Years later the world knew that Lord Russell chose that August to take the lead in urging Anglo-French mediation of the war in America, that he, Palmerston, and Gladstone were privately prepared to act, but that it was Napoleon's turn to hesitate and delay, for at the moment he was wholly concerned with the situation in Italy.

Bigelow professed satisfaction that the war was prolonged until the united North was ready not only to destroy slavery but to conquer its prejudices, and, using the instruments Providence had made, put guns in the hands of the Negroes. But what he chiefly longed for was a major military success. On August 22, he sent Seward a despondent sketch of European officialdom's current opinion of America, the whole letter indicating desire for some assurance of a brightening future. The Secretary could not furnish that. Seward's reply offered, possibly, personal balm, in its implicit acknowledgment of reliance upon Bigelow for political information, for he ended with a cascade of questions upon which the United States Minister should have supplied sufficient data: "Your silence concerning the movement in Italy surprises me. Has it no real significance? Does it produce no anxiety in France? Does the Mexican affair cost no trouble and no money? Is the Government entirely at ease respecting Spain since the recent reply of the Emperor to the new Minister from Madrid? Is it possible that it is alone the United States who are giving uneasiness to France?" However, Seward did not prognosticate an upswing in American affairs.[24]

Sure that the war would be a long one, convinced that slavery would end before it was over, Bigelow, like thousands of Americans, wondered what would be done with the Negroes. More immediately important, what should be done with the Negroes already taken from the South? There had been a time when Bigelow thought that their emigration to Africa or the West Indies was the answer. By the fall of '62, however, he was opposed to any such project:

> . . . It is, I am satisfied now, entirely impracticable and if it were not we cannot afford to part with the labor. One of the causes of our present trouble was the want of labor in the Cotton states, which created the desire to reopen the slave trade. We want all the labor in the South that we have, and a great deal more and history will pronounce any attempt to transport it abroad madness. . . . We should emancipate the negroes as a military necessity, we should then, by legislation, give them, as we profess to give the whites, just so many rights as they can make proper use of and impose just such restrictions as may be necessary to protect the rights of the whites. . . . But the first thing to do is to make the negroes fight for their freedom. . . . So long as we, as a nation denounce the African for fear the Irishman's wages may be reduced, . . . we are committing precisely the same offense which we charge upon the South. The aristocracy of the S. complains of free labor, because it competes with theirs

and whatever superiority it possesses, depreciates the value of their property of that description. We proscribe the Negro upon the same principle to propitiate the Irish.[25]

One postwar method of dealing with the Negroes won Bigelow's support, at least temporarily. It seemed so important to Seward that he gave Bigelow's lengthy description of it to President Lincoln, a rather unusual proceeding with a consular dispatch. Bigelow explained that a German friend, Herr N. Fleischman, thought that the United States should set Florida apart as the home of all Negroes, who would thenceforth be called Floridians. Each of these new Floridians should receive, gratis, a grant of land in Florida and a guarantee of full civil liberties, though none of them should be permitted to bear arms and their Executive should be appointed by the President of the United States. Each of them would have the right to emigrate to the United States whenever he chose, provided he purchased a passport costing five dollars a year, the money to be used for the education of his countrymen. Simply by renewing his passport, he could remain in the United States year after year, unless he committed a crime. In that case, he would be returned immediately to Florida and thereafter refused re-entry into the United States. Bigelow commented upon the plan:

> It has the special merit of giving the Negroes all the civil rights they require without making them citizens of the United States, to which there seems to be an almost universal indisposition, and of giving them a separate national existence without depriving the United States of their labor which the country cannot afford and for which years would be required to provide a substitute.[26]

The problem of white labor, with which the whole problem of the Negro was inextricably mixed, was uppermost in Bigelow's mind during September and October. Discontent in the North was manifestly widespread. Weed wrote that the whole Cabinet might resign. Northern doughfaces were calling as loud as Napoleon for an end to the war. Either Seward would have to accept a French offer of mediation, Weed thought, or there would be a new Secretary of State who would. It was evident that only a signal victory or a vastly increased labor supply could ease the burdened Union and strengthen the will to win. So, instead of tucking away, as many consuls did, circulars from Seward about the advantages of emigration under the new Homestead Act, Bigelow sent them to a number of editors with appropriate remarks, not for publication, of course, but to give the light by which they were to be interpreted. The next day he noted in his diary: "The

Presse this morning had an article on the subject in the sense of my letter." He suggested to Lucas of the *Star* that the unemployed of Britain and France might well go to America. Approximately 400,000 men in France alone, he had been told, were out of work and there must be at least as many jobless in Britain. Land in America was cheap. Wages were high. The United States needed workers. Why should not Lucas urge their going? [27]

Not only did Bigelow publish the circulars but he persuaded other consuls to do likewise, which later caused a biographer of Slidell to remark: "The Consul General in Paris had this document printed broadcast over the Continent and afterwards complacently remarked upon 'the light that it throws upon the mysterious repletion of our army during the four years of War, while it was notoriously being so fearfully depleted by fire-arms, disease and desertion.'" Bigelow wrote Seward of what he had done, and added, though he knew perfectly well that no official circular was to be published without special authorization, that not being sure of the proper way to handle it, he had used his own discretion. "I learn easy, however, and shall be happy to be instructed if I am doing wrong." The only answer from Seward was the pleased comment: "So far you are safe, for you have usurped with discretion and with wisdom. . . . But you must remember that you act at your own peril in such cases." [28]

Answers from French workmen streamed in:

> *M. le Consul:* as I read the *Siècle* every day, I have just read that paper of 3 Sept. in which you communicate the new circular which your government has addressed to you. . . . I am taking the liberty to write to you now that for several years I have wanted to see your beautiful country, that I like especially the form of its government. . . .

> *Monsieur:* For some time I have thought of going to the United States and after the circular of Mr. Seward appeared in the Paris papers, I want to go. . . .

> *To the Consul of the United States of America. M. le Consul:* Yesterday 3 September I learned of your circular concerning the advantages which exist at this time in emigrating to America, which causes me to write to you now to acquaint you with the difficulties there would be in putting into effect the project of emigrating now, for me and several of my friends to whom I have communicated the contents of your circular.

> All my friends and I are farmers or commercial employees, all are single and between the ages of 25 and 38 and able to show good references. . . . I wish, M. le Consul, to ask your kindness

to let me know if we could make the trip at the expense of the United States, for none of us have the necessary resources to take us to the United States. . . ."[29]

These letters and the many like them were all to the good, but they showed that it would take time and tremendous sums of money to organize emigration on a large scale. Was it worth the trouble? While Bigelow was winning some French workmen Hotze was able to write on September 26: "It is difficult to exaggerate the profound impression produced in this country by the brilliant successes of our arms."[30]

Bigelow plumbed the depths of depression on October 2. On the way to his office that morning he met his old acquaintance N. M. Beckwith, the American who had interested him in railroad development, a staunch Unionist who once joined Henry Sanford in talks with Garibaldi concerning the possibility of his serving with the United States army. Beckwith spoke in bitterness and at the moment Bigelow clearly agreed with him, although at a later time he changed his mind and crossed out in his diary the record he had made of their conversation. Beckwith said:

> . . . that someone ought to put a knife in Lincoln. He is the greatest obstacle to the success of our cause and that it is better that one man like him should suffer than so many thousands of men whose blood is manuring the fields of America. This of course was meant as the (?) remedy, but it went to show that the country is rising under its troubles, discipline (?)ing to the demand for a higher order of statesmanship than Lincoln represents. It is a good sign. If such a man could continue to have the support and respect of the people as President it would be (?) omen for the republic.[31]

Three days later the good news came. Slidell himself, Bigelow heard, admitted that his mission was hopeless. The Union success at Antietam and the President's proclamation concerning the coming emancipation of the Negroes in the war zones reached Europe on October 5. In the face of this first official Union statement on slavery, the British Cabinet dared not put into effect its August plan to force mediation, even though Napoleon, nowise affected by either piece of news, was once more eager for joint action. Never again would the British government seriously consider overt interference.

Bigelow rejoiced wholeheartedly in the military victory. But he was less happy about the emancipation statement, because he believed it came a year and a half late and did not show a farsighted recognition of the problems which would inevitably arise. He bluntly wrote Seward that the scheme was "improvident as well as impracticable, necessarily converting the S. if it could be applied into a wilderness." In other words, his first reaction was very like that of most slavery-hating Europeans. He proposed to Seward a corollary to emancipation: ". . . But to secure to the freedman a suitable maintenance; to show him the way to take his labor to market on the one hand, and to protect society on the other from the ignorance, the thriftlessness and the vices which the freedman brings with him out of servitude, laws adapted to his peculiar condition should be passed and agents for their administration be appointed. . . . they might be general laws applicable to all persons answering to his political and social description without reference to race or color." [32]

Specifically he suggested the appointment of local officers with whom all unemployed persons who wished work would register, to whom all employers would go for labor, and who would be empowered to draw up contracts defining the rights and duties of both parties, which a commission would have the right to enforce. If such a set-up were provided, under "a humane man thoroughly acquainted with the habits of the blacks and the legitimate needs of the proprietors, without sharing the common prejudices of slave drivers that the negro was only created to promote the interests of the white man," Bigelow concluded, ". . . I see no reason why the Southern lands should not be better tilled, why the supply of labor should not be more regular and less expensive, why the security of property should not be increased, why the thriftlessness and vice of which slavery is the inevitable parent should not gradually diminish, and why the negro should not in our time be initiated into some of the mysteries of civilization." [33]

The very high regard which Seward had for his consul in Paris is not hard to understand. It was creditable enough that Bigelow, born and bred in New York State, was able after one extended tour of Europe to fit readily into Parisian life, to learn fluent, idiomatic French, and to penetrate the intricacies of European politics in the course of little more than a year and without benefit of a position of prestige. Added to that he had a flair for sensing the type of news Seward wanted fully reported; he used skill and unlimited energy in locating essential facts; and he won hosts of friends for his cause through his personal magnetism. His voluminous correspondence with important officials, unprecedented in a consul, testified to his energy and his indifference to customary routine. So, too, did his extra-consular labors to thwart Confederate diplomacy during the excitement of the *Trent* seizure and the stone blockade, in his handling of Seward's emigration circulars, and pre-eminently in his remarkable influence upon the French press. In October '61 not one Paris paper had openly championed the North; one year later there was only one Paris paper, *Le Moniteur*, the official organ of the government, which had not carried an article favorable to the Union. Moreover, in this first year of his government service, Bigelow had gone beyond the duties formally and informally laid upon him to propose a government-owned and directed railroad system, assignment of military and naval attachés to legations, a Negro state, and a government employment service.

It had been a difficult, anxious year, filled with labors performed in semidarkness. In retrospect the high lights were obvious. First the South had sought, through cotton, French recognition and intervention. That effort failed in February. Then, as the economic distress deepened in Europe, it had sought joint Anglo-French recognition and intervention. That effort collapsed in June. Next came a less exorbitant demand for mediation which might well have succeeded had not Garibaldi's march on Rome held Napoleon's attention until the Northern success at Antietam, coupled with the first Federal statement concerning the emancipation of the slaves, effectively stopped British willingness to act.

Fourth, or third if the effort first for French and then for Anglo-French intervention be regarded as one phase — Bigelow so regarded them — came a plea for an armistice. It was initiated by Napoleon, who formally asked Britain and Russia, in October '62, to join him in urging a six months' truce to the American civil war, during which time he hoped that the blockade would be lifted for the sake of Europe's business. This proposal, long rumored but only published in the papers on November 13, brought newspapermen to Bigelow to get his opinion of the probable Northern reaction. Among them were correspondents for the London papers and Frenchmen like Lucien Prévost-Paradol, the brilliant writer of political leaders for *Le Journal des Débats* (who was soon to be elected to the Institute and later, in 1870, to serve briefly as Minister to the United States, where concern for his country and his own bad health were to lead him to suicide). Bigelow readily assured everyone who approached him that the United States would refuse to consider any such proposal. Anonymously, he wrote a strong article for *l'Independence Belge*, denouncing as unfriendly European efforts to force an armistice and vigorously condemning the masked assistance Britain was continually giving to the

Confederacy. Then in high spirits he wrote to Seward, describing the opening scene in what he called "Act III" of the diplomatic war — the cry for an armistice, milder than the preceding calls for intervention and mediation, but equally futile. For, though Napoleon endorsed it, hoping to replenish French supplies of cotton and to give the depressed French export trades at least a temporary market in America, and though for once French public opinion heartily approved of his policy, neither Russia nor Britain would co-operate. The Emperor's consequent intention to offer his services as sole mediator was foredoomed.[34]

CHAPTER 15

The Turn of the Tide

[*1863*]

NORTHERN representatives dared not relax their efforts even while they took comfort from the fall of Antietam, the President's Emancipation Proclamation, and the November elections, which left the Republicans in control of the House though by a smaller margin. Opinion in Europe might easily undergo another shift. Open assistance to the Confederacy or sufficient underground aid could yet give the victory to the South. Bigelow decided, now that his relations with the French press were cordial and no crisis seemed impending, to undertake a new type of service which he had long contemplated, one which seemed particularly important in view of the outstanding work Henry de Hotze was doing.

Hotze was a brilliant, enthusiastic, hard-working young man, not yet thirty years old. Born in Switzerland, educated in Europe, he became an American citizen in 1855, served as Secretary to the United States Legation in Belgium in 1858 and 1859, and from 1859 to 1861 edited the Mobile *Register*. When war came, he cast his fortunes with the South. Part of 1861 he spent in Britain as a Confederate commercial agent. Hardly had he returned home when the Confederate government asked him to go back to Britain, this time to serve as a propagandist and to do, with far more limited funds, what de Leon was expected to do primarily on the Continent. After reaching London late in January, Hotze wrote leaders for Palmerston's *London Post*, for the *Standard*, the *Herald*, and the *Money Market Review*. Then on May 1 he commenced an undertaking which was to make him, next to Slidell, the Confederacy's most useful agent abroad. He published the first issue of the truly remarkable newspaper, which he called the *Index* and which was ostensibly written by Englishmen for Englishmen. Working in two cheap rooms on a London back street, Hotze did much of the writing, all of the editing, and hired, as part-time workers to whom he paid regular salaries, key contributors to the popular London papers.

Inevitably, having written to his specifications for the *Index*, news-papermen found it convenient to rehash the material and peddle it elsewhere. Inevitably a Southern touch crept into London papers' treatment of American themes and from them passed into the press of Europe.[1]

Within two years Hotze was furnishing some twenty papers in England, on the Continent, and, incredible though it sounds, in the Northern United States with direct, regular correspondence. Later, after de Leon was recalled, Hotze was to add direct propagandizing in France to his activities in England, so that in 1864 he could state with considerable truth: "As it is I do not think that any Government has superior facilities of publicity outside its own territory than we already possess, at least as regards promptness and universality." [2] The North little knew how fortunate it was that Hotze at first received limited funds. Bigelow's task would have been far more difficult had Hotze directed from the first all Confederate propaganda and con-trolled all of its press funds, which must have amounted to ten times the sums Bigelow spent.

By the fall of '62 Hotze's work was already filtering through to the Continent and giving currency to statements which Bigelow knew were false. Hence his desire to prepare a new type of propaganda, a statistical history of the United States, useful to anyone whose interest in America exceeded his knowledge. He had at hand sufficient data to begin the work, for he had requested reference materials in the spring, and the librarian of the State Department had hastened to fill his order, because, he explained: "The fact is that you above all others abroad should be fully supplied with all valuable data relative to this country for you are obviously doing yeoman service for Uncle Sam in a substantial way." [3] By November Bigelow had completed the outline of his book, and on his forty-fifth birthday he signed a contract with Hachette et Cie. for *Les États-Unis d'Amérique en 1863*, the publishers agreeing to pay all costs and to divide the profits.

His plan, as described to Seward on November 21, was to present in compact form a handy reference work, not a synthesized narrative, covering United States political, industrial, and social history based upon as accurate statistics as he could obtain. He would include geography, geology, botany, zoölogy; population and its nativities; agriculture and manufacturing; means of transportation and communication; edu-cation, libraries, the press and churches; an analysis of the form of government; a history of political parties, of finance, of military and naval power; a brief account of each administration; a chapter on

American literature. The book, he explained, was to have nothing controversial in its three to four hundred pages (save only to illustrate the advantages of union over disunion). He believed that an unadorned, realistic presentation, stressing contemporary development and including the latest census returns and government statistics, would counteract Southern misrepresentations. It also would help Seward's emigration projects, and might prove to be of permanent value if revised every four years. That last point was close to Bigelow's heart. As in so many of his earlier projects — prison reform, constitutional revision, his barely started biography of Fénelon — he wanted to commence something which would live after him. Seward heartily approved of the ambitious undertaking and co-operated by having cyclopedias, almanacs, census returns, election figures, and recent executive documents mailed to Bigelow.

Almost beyond credence is the fact that within two months Bigelow completed the immense job of selection, organization, and explanatory text, had the book translated into French, and turned it over to the publisher. Soon twenty pre-sale copies reached him and were sent on to friends. One went to Hargreaves in England, along with a reassuring comment to the effect that the book was not to be read but to be held for reference. The only part Bigelow hoped his friend would read was the introduction, in which he showed that the underlying cause of the present war was the aristocratic feature in the Constitution whereby political power was weighted in favor of men who owned property in persons. He thought that should be interesting to liberals everywhere. And it was interesting to Hargreaves, though it turned out to be the one section to which the historian John Lothrop Motley, who was serving as United States Minister to Austria, took exception when he wrote Bigelow of the value the book was to him. As Bigelow had expected, Hargreaves showed his copy of *Les États-Unis d'Amérique en 1863* to his friends; John Bright saw it and wrote to Bigelow urging an English edition.[4]

Bigelow also sent advance copies to Dayton, Laboulaye, Prévost-Paradol, and other French writers. "Mr. Dayton," Bigelow noted in his diary on March 29, "has not yet acknowledged the receipt of my book in any way." And he added, none too kindly: "I suppose he is afraid of making a mistake as he can't read it." Prévost-Paradol wrote that he wanted to review it for *Le Journal des Débats*, but he was so notoriously lazy and so preoccupied with his own campaign for election to the Chamber of Deputies that Bigelow doubted whether he would find time. Henri Moreau, editor of *La Revue Contemporaine* and close friend of the revered legitimist lawyer, Antoine Berryer, also offered to review it, and to him Bigelow replied with a mixture of cunning and candor:

> I know too well the value of such an attention from you to neglect anything which might encourage you in your purpose and for that reason I have presumed upon my familiarity with the book in question to do what I can to save you time and trouble. [Here followed an explanation of the purpose of the book and a listing of the pages and topics most important for a reviewer to note.] . . . I hope if I have taken a liberty in these suggestions you will pardon it upon the ground that when one's country is in trouble a true patriot cannot afford to be too delicate or too modest in his choice of means to serve her.[5]

By April the book was selling well. Reviews, which gradually appeared in all the important French journals, were uniformly favorable. *Le Journal des Débats* of May 16, for example, described it as "one of the most substantial volumes, richest in documents of all kinds that has ever been devoted to the great republic of the new world. Every aspect is reviewed in this book, which would be of great interest even without that which present circumstances give to it." Even the pro-Southern *Saturday Review* was kinder than Bigelow had expected it to be. A hostile reviewer, who thought it quite unimportant whether America had one state or two or more, who had little faith in democracy and thought that ". . . till the beginning of the present struggle, no history ever deserved more fully the praise of being dull," did concede: "The volume is, indeed, something between a blue book and an instructive pamphlet, and claims no other merits than those which belong to such publications. To such merits, however, it has an undoubted claim. It is a simple, straightforward account of a variety of important matters, and it is full of authentic information." [6] Within a year a Milan publisher brought out an Italian edition without Bigelow's knowledge and without giving him an opportunity to correct the faulty index and the inevitable errors of haste in the text itself. The following year a German edition appeared, which Bigelow had corrected and brought up to date, and that was followed in 1868 by a Spanish edition taken from the Italian translation of the French translation of Bigelow's original copy.

The book was not revised quadrennially and had no lasting value. Yet it would be hard to overestimate its usefulness in the 1860's. It contained every part of Bigelow's original plan except the final section on literature, which he omitted to save space, and omitted reluctantly, for he believed it impossible to understand a people without knowing something of its writings. Without that section, there were

549 pages crammed with exact, detailed information. European writers and lecturers upon American affairs as well as American representatives abroad had good reason to praise Bigelow's recognition of their needs and his prompt and successful effort to help them, for they found in the accuracy, convenience, and inclusiveness of *Les États-Unis d'Amerique en 1863* an indispensable sourcebook and background builder.

While working on his book, Bigelow was comfortably sure that all was well on the diplomatic front. The Emancipation Proclamation, going into effect without any of the feared servile insurrections, won new friends for the North. Seward's courteous but firm rejection in February of Napoleon's offer to mediate between Union and Confederacy seemed to have put an end to such endeavors. The new sources of cotton in India and the increasing effectiveness of the Anglo-French commercial treaty of 1860 gave sufficient new opportunities to industry in both countries to mitigate, to some extent, the hurt caused by the war in America. Journalists who had never been friendly to Bigelow now thought it desirable to make advances. Henry Bowles, conductor of Galignani's *Messenger* and an employee of Hotze's, came to call. Brown, the Paris correspondent of the London *Post*, was at last "evidently disposed to be instructed." Bigelow believed that Europeans were beginning to see that "after all this struggle of ours both at home and abroad is but a struggle between the principles of popular government and government by a privileged class." [7]

Suddenly nervous rumors flooded Paris. Slidell, so the story went, had gained permission to build ships in France, a permission of the utmost importance now that Britain was impeding the Confederate program there. No one knew whether to believe it, but it was enough to put Union men on edge. Actually Napoleon himself had asked Slidell, back in October 1862, when talking of the Confederates' need for ships: "Why do you not have them built as for the Italian government? I do not think it would be difficult but I will consult the Minister of Marine about it." [8] Though Bigelow had no inkling of that conversation, he shed his happy optimism before the end of March. He suspected the French government; he suspected the British government; he believed the ships being built in England nominally for the Emperor of China, and paid, so the rumor went, by a three-million-pound loan, were destined for the South. ". . . I assure you," he solemnly wrote Lucas on March 28, "that for a year past I have looked upon a war between England and America as a mere question of time, provided our domestic struggle continued."

The seeming inevitability of a foreign war made Bigelow long for the status of private citizen in order to serve his country more effectively than he thought he could in his consular capacity. As a minor official he was hedged about by restrictions upon travel and writing for the public and burdened by red tape and detail work which all his life he had found intolerable. A law of 1863 required consuls to issue triplicate invoices in place of the single invoices heretofore deemed sufficient, at once requiring three times the mechanical labor just when trade with France was recovering from the bad years of 1861 and 1862. From 372 invoices for the entire year of 1861, the Paris consulate's work increased in 1863 to some 13,000 invoices — and these for the first time had to be prepared in triplicate, which made in effect 40,740 for the year, or an average of 128 on every weekday, to be listed under thirteen headings instead of the six formerly used. Moreover, Bigelow found it impossible to guard against frauds unless he required samples to be deposited at his office with each invoice. That made more work for him. His staff had been enlarged from two men to four, but it still was too small, and the men he had were underpaid so that he could not, in fairness, demand too much service from them. Before long he was spending two thirds of his own salary to hire additional clerical assistance and translators.[9]

The cost and the confining labor weighed upon him. Then came the last straw, a request from Seward for a detailed report upon the customhouse system of France, an important subject but one which left Bigelow cold. Like coping with triplicate invoices, it might be useful to America, but it was the sort of work to ask of a career man, not of a man who had accepted the consulate as a cover for more pressing war duties and who had been told that the ordinary business of the office would be minimized. If the State Department was satisfied with the French press and no longer felt that it needed careful attention, Bigelow would be delighted to get back to his study of Fénelon; if it was not, he wanted more time for his propaganda work. So he presented his resignation, stating that if it was not convenient to release him, he would of course remain, but in that event he must have a three- or four-month vacation. When he had come to Europe a year and a half ago, he had expected as much leisure as other consuls had, but he had had none.[10]

Seward's reply arrived early in June. There was no place where Bigelow could better serve the United States nor was there "any person who could fill your place satisfactorily. Please reconsider." [11] A week later another note added that the President had seen Seward's first letter dissuading Bigelow and had fully concurred in it. So Bigelow pocketed his frustration and remained. The routine continued, the anxious followings of the ups and downs of Northern fortunes, the constant efforts to serve in spite of the irritating consular work which he detested, the inadequate salary — he received $4800 to Slidell's $12,000 — and the diminishing value of his investments at home.

Office hours necessarily went to consular work. The rest of the day he devoted to what he considered his job. For a second time he set forth the advantages of emigration under the Homestead Act. He sent copies of an article of his own upon the salaries and the postwar opportunities of United States soldiers, together with a circular from Seward upon the subject, to the American consuls at Rouen, Nantes, Marseilles, Lyons, and Berlin, and urgently requested that it be given wide publicity. More directly than any one other Northerner he was connected with the fact that eventually some 400,000 to 500,000 aliens found their way into the Federal Army — a fact which embittered Slidell, because his own attempt, in 1865, to enlist in the Confederate Army Poles residing in Paris, in return for free passage and land grants, was prohibited after Bigelow complained of this violation of the French Foreign Enlistment Act.[12]

In addition to his recruiting activities, Bigelow helped Cobden prepare a speech on French neutrality laws. He worked with J. M. Forbes, brother-in-law of his friend Beckwith, and with W. H. Aspinwall, who had come from America to Britain in hopes of buying up, over the heads of Southern agents, the ships being built for the Confederacy. He suggested American topics for the forthcoming *Biographie Universelle*. He arranged with Laboulaye for a French edition of Fanny Kemble's *Journal of a Residence on a Georgia Plantation in 1838–1839*, though privately he noted: "She must have been a horror on the plantation." He agreed to help Élisée Reclus handle the American section of the *Annuaire des Deux Mondes*. He bought a thousand copies of the proceedings of the Manchester mass meeting of antislavery clerics assembled by the Reverend Thomas Bayley Potter, President of the Union and Emancipation Society of Manchester and later founder of the Cobden Club. And he performed a number of similar acts of encouragement.[13]

Where he got the money for his work is not entirely clear. He spent his private income freely, but it was not large, and he had a wife and five children to support. Often he levied upon Americans in Paris for subscriptions to charities or to the works of worthy French writers. A statement of his account with Sanford, the Minister to Belgium who controlled a fund of $1,000,000 to be used for all special Federal activities in Europe, sheds further light. For the first half of 1863 the record went:

Dr. Cash on hand	705 *fr*	*Cr.* Jan 24 500 copies	75 *fr*
May 11 Rec'd check	1000	Opin Nat	
June 10 Rec'd check	1000	Feb 22 Subscpt to Opin	
	2705.00	Nat 3 mos	13.50
		Feb 29 Pd Leviata for	
		art on Angheys book	
		Iron Furnace	150
		May 12 Paid Malespine	600
		May 28 Subscription on	
		Nationale 3 months	13.50
		June 1 Express for	
		Hearn's pamphlet	6.25
		June 12 Paid Malespine	500
		99 copies of "Etats-	
		Unis in 1863" deliv-	
		ered to Mr. Sanford &	
		to his order 6.50 per	
		copy	643.50
			2001.75
			703.25
			2705.00

Evidently Sanford's discretionary fund was by now at Bigelow's disposal, though the account suggests that Bigelow spent incredibly little compared to Confederate agents in Europe.[14]

Malespine, of *L'Opinion Nationale*, who received 500 francs a month from Bigelow, brought only discouraging reports this summer. Even Dayton worried in June when the Minister for Foreign Affairs, Drouyn de Lhuys, who replaced Thouvenel in October '62, avoided seeing him; when Bigelow passed on the rumor that Slidell had again breakfasted with the Emperor; when it was obvious that Mexico was assuming new importance in French diplomacy; when Malespine said that men in high places expected that at last the Confederacy was to be recognized. Nor was there any comfort in the knowledge that such tales had regularly proved false in the past. This time they might be true, especially as the new French interests in Mexico would make two weak states to the north desirable. Though the joint debt collection undertaken in Mexico by France, Britain, and Spain had ended with the withdrawal of the two latter countries, Napoleon seemed intent upon remaining. And certainly his government tightened up on the press. Malespine found that his offer of an article on America for *Le Monde Illustré* would be acceptable only if its tone was favorable to the South.[15]

During these uncertain weeks Bigelow gave himself a rare luxury.

For several days he concentrated upon a political article, planning his work deliberately, knowing that men had lost their official heads for less serious offenses. Then he had it published in *L'Opinion Nationale* on June 26, and promptly sent copies to Seward with the comment: "[It] . . . may induce you to change your views of my superior fitness for this position, as it will go a long way to convict me of disobedience to a circular of the State Department scarcely a year old." For Bigelow had written a sketch of Seward, describing his importance to the Union and indicating the usefulness he could render as Chief Executive. Seward's answer was mild in word and friendly in tone, for the man was pleased though the statesman disapproved:

> I am glad that you remain at the consulate. I suppose that I can imagine the reason why you wanted to resign, and if I do I am the more convinced that you ought to stay at your post.
> I shall certainly report your violation of your instruction, by your article in the *Opinion Nationale*, to the President, though I will mercifully withhold the deserved punishment. Some good but impatient friends, as you see, are bringing his name forward for re-election. It will show you how just and generous he is that he is able to overlook your crime in putting me in his way, and I think that he will only be the more decided in his conviction that you must stay where you are.[16]

The article about Seward served to put Bigelow's opinion on record and served also, at least during the hours he was absorbed in it, as an escape from the debilitating strain of awaiting dreaded news. Each day of June added to the pall of uncertainty. Northerners in Paris almost despaired when they saw the evident, unexplained joy of their Confederate neighbors, then heard of the receptions Napoleon accorded to Slidell and his English associates, then read of the motion presented to the British Parliament on June 30 for the recognition of the Confederacy. In this second year of the intrigue to win joint Anglo-French assistance, Slidell and Lindsay had been joined by another member of Parliament: vain, sharp-tongued old John Roebuck, who represented the interests of the shipbuilding Laird brothers. Bigelow, with the benefit of private advices from England, knew that Roebuck's motion, though debated day after day in Parliament, could not conceivably pass, and from his sources in France knew with equal surety that Napoleon would not act at this time without British or Spanish assistance. Nevertheless, he was concerned about opinion in Europe and conditions in America. Impatiently he awaited the arrival of William Maxwell Evarts, his friend of the Column Club, at forty-five one of America's renowned trial lawyers, noted for efficiency and cool-headed-ness, from whom he could get inside news about home affairs. At the moment Evarts was in London to give Adams legal advice in his fight to block the Confederate shipbuilding program in Britain. There, his quick grasp of the problems involved, his tact and his legal knowledge, had already earned the admiration of Adams and of the British authorities with whom he consulted, even as those same qualities were later to carry him to added eminence as Senator from New York and Secretary of State under Hayes.

Evarts reached Paris on July 4, the day after the French press carried the startling news that General Lee was advancing into Pennsylvania toward what goal no one knew, and that a Confederate relief force was steadily forging its way to besieged Vicksburg. Evarts had nothing comforting to offer. Gloomily Bigelow listened to his off-the-record account of the men at home: Chase and Seward, though the latter was unable to command good men, were the only statesmen in Cabinet meetings, not even excepting Lincoln. Evarts bitterly denounced democracy, said he did not much care who won the war so long as a unified government was created and an aristocracy gained control. "He is very much disgusted with the govt at Washington and Albany," Bigelow wrote to Preston King, "thinks democracy is the ruin of the nation, that Lincoln is the legitimate fruit of popular sovereignty (whiggery) and that we have got to have our democracy licked out of us, before we shall be good for anything." [17]

The news of July 8 added to their gloom. Latest dispatches from America, dated June 26, told of Lee's continued advance into Pennsylvania, of the apathy of the residents, of the Federal troops' retreat toward Harrisburg. To avoid the deluge of unanswerable inquiries until definitive news could arrive, Bigelow and Evarts entrained for Switzerland. There they read brief notes from America dated July 1 and editorials in the French imperialist press which announced: "The news from America continues to be favorable to the Confederates. All of Lee's army is in Pennsylvania" and added that Grant, apparently, was checked at Vicksburg.[18] Privately Bigelow thought it possible that Slidell had conceived the plan of simultaneous action of Lee across the Rappahannock and Roebuck in Parliament to have, for once, favorable military action at the moment when France and Britain were re-examining their position as regarded America. That, at least, might be the cause of Lee's mysterious drive into the North.[19]

Before more information came from home, another matter brought Evarts and Bigelow back from Switzerland. On July 4, one of the suspect Laird rams had been launched in England. On July 11, Adams presented to the Foreign Office affidavits which he considered proof that the ship ostensibly meant for the French concern, Bravé et Cie., was in reality destined for the South, but he feared that the casual British authorities would let the ship escape as it had the earlier ones. Evarts's knowledge of law was needed in England; Bigelow's knowledge of "sources" was needed in France to learn more of Bravé.

Back in Paris Bigelow found the American colony tense. For months they had been expecting, as ship after ship arrived from home, to hear that one side or the other had finally triumphed at Vicksburg. Everyone knew that word must come at any moment and with it news of the outcome of Lee's bold offensive. Uncertainty frayed the edges of Bigelow's faith. He wrote to Weed on July 15:

> All the news we get here give strength and edge to all yr. apprehensions. The North is to experience a revolution as well as the South. Our system of govt. has failed to provide men competent to the mighty energies of the nation. The people have no way of delegating their powers properly, so that everyone thinks himself fit for any place and there is nothing to prevent his aspiring to any place. Our govt. is all carcass and no brains, all energy, no direction. To make the people feel the necessity for providing a way for choosing men to a public service because of their fitness for that service rather than because of their inability to get a living by any other way, it seems as though no better teacher was to be found than an invading army. And as Nature, the doctors say, always lays a disease in the right place, so Lee could not have begun in a better place than Pennsylvania. When he has regenerated that State, a short visit to New Jersey would be salutory. By that time, I should hope, he would not be needed in N. Y.

Surely the war must make Americans realize the need to educate leaders and make them responsible, even if it took a victory of the South to bring home that lesson. And the Union yet might win. If Lee should invade the North — "If Lee were to march to Philadelphia or Trenton or even to New York he would not succeed; in fact he would fail sooner, than he would have done, if he had remained in Richmond; the army would experience all the difference that a roll or potato experiences on being transformed from the pantry to the stomach."

Two days later came dispatches from America as of July 4. A three-day battle had raged at Gettysburg. Both sides had suffered heart-searing losses. General Meade's communiqué reported that time and again the enemy was repulsed. President Lincoln announced that the battle "promises a great success to the cause of the Union." But it was all alarmingly vague. The brief dispatches could mean anything, as

La Patrie pointed out. *Le Constitutionnel* concluded from them: "The successes of the Confederate invasion are continuing. That is the most natural interpretation of the telegrams dated 3 and 4 July which we received today from New York." *Le Journal des Débats* decided from the same facts that though the outcome was in doubt, it would seem that the Confederates were retreating. That was on Friday, July 17. The next day Paris papers had nothing to add except to note that the London press was suspending judgment upon the battle of Gettysburg until a later mail ship should arrive from New York.

At this very moment Lee might be marching far into the North. President Davis might have moved his headquarters to Washington; or the South might have suffered a crushing defeat. On July 19, Dr. John McClintock was conducting his usual Sunday afternoon service at the American Chapel in Paris when a messenger entered and walked swiftly up to the pulpit. As he handed a telegram to the minister, as the minister glanced through its contents, the congregation sat in anxious silence, sensing that the mail ship had reached Southampton. Turning to them, Dr. McClintock read the words aloud: "Admiral Porter has announced officially that Vicksburg surrendered to the Federal forces the fourth." Then he composedly resumed the service. When the last word of the prayers ended, the excited organist burst into "The Star-Spangled Banner," while Southerners slipped away in sorrow and Northerners remained to offer thanksgiving and praise that at last the Mississippi River belonged to the Union. Though the meaning of Gettysburg was still uncertain, the beginning of the end was in sight.[20]

CHAPTER 16

Confederate Shipbuilding to the Fore

[*1863*]

WHETHER the crisis of the war was past was a question for the
future. For the moment, although the French imperialist press
refused to concede a Federal victory at Gettysburg, and although
the London *Times* persisted throughout July in calling that battle
a draw, the undeniable Northern triumph at Vicksburg sufficed to
check Confederate propagandists. Bigelow was as convinced that the
Confederate hope of waging an offensive war was smashed at Gettysburg as he was that the capture of Vicksburg freed the Mississippi.
So, after arranging for the liberal press to reflect his view — *Le Journal
des Débats,* for example, on July 21 carried a glowing editorial upon
the twin victories — he decided, with twenty months of unflagging
effort behind him, that he could afford a holiday.

Prior to his departure from Paris for a fortnight at the Normandy
shore resort of Luc-sur-Mer, he arranged with Sanford to have a man
capable of spying on French shipyards meet him at the shore. Bigelow
intended to discover what truth there was in the talk of Confederate
shipbuilding in France. No one had yet found him idling when there
was work to be done, and no one ever would. If he approved of Sanford's choice, he intended to send the agent to Le Havre, "which
would be the proper theater of his operations and he could report to
me in person . . . in a way less likely to excite suspicion, than if he
were to visit my office." [1] Except for this man, whom Bigelow hired,
and an annoying letter from Malespine, who frankly wanted more
money, no piece of business disturbed the leisurely vacation.

Bigelow and his two older sons voted to drive to the shore in the
carriage they had recently purchased. The first two days went according to schedule, the boys, one nine, the other eight, eyeing everything they passed, asking innumerable questions, twisting and squirm-
ing in such high spirits that their father had little time or inclination
to read the books he carried with him. On the third day he did start

Boileau's *Correspondence* — Boileau, he noted, "was too entirely occupied with himself and his personal glory to be loved or much respected" — but he stopped reading when they reached François Guizot's
home. Here was an opportunity not to be missed; Bigelow might never
again be in the neighborhood, and he did want to see the home of
the famous statesman-historian, member of the Institute, author of the
History of European Civilization and *History of the English Revolution.*

So he shifted his schedule and, leaving the boys at a hotel, called
for permission to see the gardens of this home which before the Revolution had been an Augustine monastery. His name was recognized;
Guizot himself had written to commend *Les États-Unis,* and he was
at once invited inside. There in the parlor, while awaiting some member of the family, he saw in the *Débats* the good news that Lee had
retreated across the Potomac, that Rosecrans had driven Bragg beyond
Chattanooga, that the Federals were advancing towards Georgia. But
the next column cast a shadow and brought to mind Tilden's prophetic
words in 1860. ". . . To my mortification and grief . . . a fierce and
bloody resistance to the conscription had been made in New York.
. . ." At that moment, before he could read the details, he was invited
into the garden where Guizot and his two sons-in-law, the De Witts,
greeted him pleasantly. The three men had faith in the Union cause
and for that reason were sure to welcome any Union representative.
After a brief, informal conversation, during which they took the measure of this attractive American who spoke their language fluently and
was well-informed upon European problems, their manner became
cordial. Before Bigelow left he had three new friends who were to
help him in his labors.[2] The episode suggests one reason why Seward
thought no one could replace Bigelow: his charm and the range of
his points of contact were not easily matched.

The next morning Bigelow and his sons made an early start. Before
long they smelled the rank salt air, saw the glint of sun-pricked water,
heard the rolling surf smash on the sand. Presently they were reunited
with the rest of the family who had come by train. For two weeks they
could have the sort of family life Bigelow had planned when he left
the *Evening Post.* He had always intended to educate his children at
home under his own direction, but that had become impossible. There
simply had not been time. First Grace, then the boys, then five-year-
old Jenny had gone to day school in Paris, and as the parents usually
were busy in the evenings, the noon hour had come to be the only
time when the family met as a unit. Yet the years in France, so arduous
for the consul, had been happy ones for his family, thanks largely to

Mrs. Bigelow's contagious capacity for activity and enjoyment. She treated her children with a gaiety they adored, and left their training and discipline to their nurse and their father. Her husband's intellectual pursuits and his religious convictions meant nothing to her. She had, however, a quick mind and a strong social sense, so that as Bigelow once wrote, without her his career would have been much the same but his satisfaction would have been much less. "*Mon Dieu! Qu'elle est vive, qu'elle est vive!*" Prince Napoleon once ejaculated,[3] while Bigelow forever marveled at her ability to draw to her receptions, without apparent effort, everyone she wished. Unpredictable, undisciplined, charming and carefree, she complemented her husband. Wherever she was, dull routine was not.

At Luc-sur-Mer the whole family was happy. Little Ernest, born the month Bigelow left the *Evening Post*, quite ruled them all with his funny mixed babbling in French, English, and German. The older children were growing rapidly and were as healthy as Bigelow could wish, except for one serious illness of Poultney's. One of the chief reasons for this holiday was to help the child recuperate and to give the father a much-needed rest, for in June, when Northern hopes were low, he had nursed his son through two weeks of fever, taking full charge of him through the long nights when his anxiety for the child mingled with the burden of his fears for his country. Here at Luc-sur-Mer the family talked wistfully of their home, "The Squirrels," which the older children remembered, of the William Cullen Bryants who were spending the summer there, and of their gardener Kolish — loyal, grumbling, hard-working Kolish, who sent infrequent letters in German or queer English about doings in the village, about quarrels and marriages and lands for sale, about the trees and vegetables he planted or the red raspberries because "they are the most marketable and Mrs. Bigelow likes them best." Details like these Bigelow loved to get. They made him feel that he had a sure anchorage, a haven where he belonged.

Between swims and romps with the children Bigelow found time for long, uninterrupted hours for reading, far preferable to the moments snatched from the busy Paris life. Yet even in Paris he had covered a fair number of books, considering that he never skimmed but gave each one his careful attention. He had gone through the works of Michelet and Mignet, books on Madame de Sévigné and Madame de Maintenon, and every day had read chapters from the Bible and from one or another of Swedenborg's works. The preceding summer when on a brief trip to settle an estate in Toulouse, he had had an opportunity to look up Fénelon's birthplace. That led him to reread Bausset's *Fénelon* and to commence a study of the mystics of the fifteenth, sixteenth, and seventeenth centuries, which he was to continue year after year. In October 1862, when American affairs had seemed satisfactory and no special tasks confronted him, he had decided to continue his own biography of Fénelon, but soon plans for the reference book on the United States had usurped his attention and once more Fénelon had been put aside. Perhaps after this vacation he could get back to it.

Homeward bound after the two weeks' holiday, he continued reading Paul Louis Courier's recollections, amused at the references the popular French author and liberal of an earlier generation made to his uncontrollable laughter and yawning. It sounded so very like himself. As a young man, Bigelow had wondered if he would ever learn not to laugh at the wrong time, and even now in middle age, no presence could deter him from yawning. Neither sleepiness nor boredom caused it; rather, he thought, it was a "reaction of an undue tension of the nervous system during certain hours, which almost every day more or less is my condition." Back in the sweltering city he attended the closing exercises of Grace's school more willingly than most fathers do, and then sought out his friend W. H. Huntingdon, officially a Paris correspondent of the New York *Tribune*, unofficially the genius of the bookstalls.[4]

Early in his consular career, Bigelow had met Huntingdon and found him a gay-hearted, witty American, a booklover and a man of deep, quiet charity. They had become steady companions, book hunting together once a week, gloating over treasures and good bargains. Huntingdon had little money but a rich life in Paris, searching out books for his American and European friends and collecting Franklin items for himself. He was a godsend to Bigelow. He knew everyone in Paris from prince to beggar, liked them all, though possibly with a slight preference for the beggar, and, with an obstinacy which never antagonized, refused all men all titles but "Mr." His letters to Bigelow often began "Dear Biglomat" or "Dear Excellency and Fellow-worm" and were usually impishly and irresistibly funny. His heady love of life was at once relaxing and stimulating; his unselfconscious democracy served as an antidote to the rituals and proprieties which necessarily bound Bigelow's official life, and his tolerant acceptance of the world was a balance to a man too intent upon improvement, upon resisting all temptations. Again on a hot August day they went off for a lazy, eager afternoon, looking at titles which reminded them of other books or past incidents and stopping to talk them over before moving on to the next place. Bigelow came home with extra copies of Swedenborg's *Arcana Coelestia* and *The Apocalypse Revealed*, for though he never commenced the subject, to anyone who expressed interest in Swedenborg he could not resist lending books, and often a loan turned into a gift.

Once more in his office, he found sufficient work for several men. Governor Morgan was contemplating a state hospital for disabled soldiers and wished to know what the French did for their veterans. Bigelow visited the Hôtel des Invalides, compiled and sent a brief fourteen-page description of the hospital covering its origin, the services it rendered, the terms of admission and the daily life of the soldiers there. He emphasized the importance of making residence in such a place a fact to be proud of, and sent with the report authorization to draw from his New York bank up to a thousand dollars as indication of his opinion of the project.[5] Meanwhile the *douanerie*, the report on the French customs system which had contributed to his impulse to resign in May, still dragged along — hard work, time-eating, not absorbing. Within a month it was completed and he could forget it except when high praise from the State and Treasury Departments for its thoroughness, its accuracy and its practical usefulness, as well as their inclusion of it in the Annual Commercial Report at the special request of the Commissioner of Customs, recalled the drudgery involved.[6]

These activities, together with concern about Confederate shipbuilding and triplicate invoices, were, however, so onerous that Bigelow feared he would be physically incapable of keeping abreast of the work. The office must run smoothly, exporters must be able to ship goods promptly, estates had to be settled; yet all the time his essential work was connected with the actions of the Confederates in France. During this August of 1863 Laboulaye asked for material for an article upon American education, and certainly it was important to do anything possible for Laboulaye. Then De Witt, Guizot's son-in-law, called with Moreau, the editor of *La Revue Contemporaine*, whom he wanted Bigelow to know personally. Moreau, it seemed, was studying the diplomatic relations of France and the United States and would appreciate help. Bigelow was delighted to serve the man who had reviewed *Les États-Unis* so favorably. Moreover, friendship with *La Revue* and Moreau could be most useful, for Moreau was a close friend of the ever-powerful lawyer, Antoine Berryer.[7]

Meanwhile the day of reckoning with the Confederate shipbuilders was fast approaching. Bigelow wrote Sanford on August 17 that he thought it time to tell Dayton what they had learned through the secret agent they had posted at Le Havre about Bulloch's activities in French shipyards. It seemed only fair to let the United States Minister to France know what was happening and, too, he might be some help in "getting on the track of the rogues." Four days later Sanford came to Paris to urge further investigation before disclosing anything to Dayton, but at the same time he dodged the responsibility of hiring more agents. His funds were almost exhausted and he wished Bigelow would take over the whole job, possibly getting help from Morse, the United States consul in London.[8]

A totally new problem arose on August 24 to interrupt their planning. Bigelow was introduced to it by a cryptic letter from Sanford asking if the U.S.S. *Macedonian* was at Cherbourg. Bigelow did not know, so he in turn asked Dayton. The Minister thought it had left but was not certain, and that vague information Bigelow wired in reply. Soon Sanford wired back: BE IN YOUR OFFICE AT 5 TODAY. At that hour he appeared, tremendously excited, with news of the great Confederate warship, the *Florida*. This was the much-talked-of ship which Bulloch had ordered in 1861 from the Lairds, an English company. It had been completed in '62 under the less suspect name of the *Oreto* and then had left England to enter Confederate service. Now, Sanford had just learned, it was cruising off Queenstown. Something seemed wrong with its engines for it had not been under steam for the past month. If only they could locate the *Macedonian* and capture the Southern ship!

This was important. Bigelow sought Malespine, who usually had information upon most subjects. But Malespine, just back from Cherbourg, knew only that the *Macedonian* was not there. As a last resort, Bigelow and Sanford called that evening upon Dayton to urge him to help them locate the Federal warship. To their surprise, Dayton calmly told them that though he had no idea of the whereabouts of the *Macedonian*, he had heard during the afternoon from the United States consul at Brest that the *Florida* had just entered that port. If true and if sanctioned by the French government, it was a shocking violation of neutrality. How Dayton could take it so placidly, Bigelow never could understand. But it was a fact that "D. did not seem to think he could do anything. He had called at the Foreign Office but the minister had gone to the country for a week and he had no thought of following him." [9] For the moment the *Florida* was safe, no matter how many Northern war vessels might be hovering off the French coast.

Throughout the afternoon Bigelow had tried to persuade Sanford to tell Dayton of the contract they had discovered for the building of two Confederate warships in France. Dayton, quite as much as they, had long expected Bulloch to move headquarters to France. It was common knowledge that the British government had been more careful ever since Bulloch succeeded in clearing the *Florida* and the *Alabama* from English ports over Adams's vigorous protests. Where earlier a ship was detained only if undeniable proof was submitted that it was intended for a belligerent, since April 1863, "apparent intent" was deemed sufficient grounds for withholding clearance papers. Everyone knew that the *Alexandra* and other Confederate purchases in England were now tied up, and everyone expected the dogged Confederate naval agent to begin work elsewhere. For a month Bigelow and Sanford had been relentlessly tracking down the rumors of Confederate shipbuilding on the Continent, but only recently had they unearthed material signs of Bulloch's activities in France.

This evening, after they had discussed all the possible meanings of the French harboring of the *Florida*, Sanford mentioned that he had heard something of ships being built for the Confederacy in France. Instead of questioning him, Dayton replied offhand that he had heard that rumor weeks ago — he had, in fact, reported it to Seward on August 4 — that he had asked James Putnam, the consul at Le Havre about it, and that Putnam said that there was nothing to it. That was that. Sanford dropped the subject without revealing all he knew or how he knew it, much to Bigelow's disgust, for though Bigelow had as little respect for Dayton as Sanford had, he thought this no time for personal consideration:

> I could not but feel confirmed in the suspicions I had conceived on other occasions and especially when I have proposed to let Mr. Dayton share the responsibilities of whatever is done or left undone for the detection of the parties to this contract for the Confeds. in France, that Sanford wants to beat Dayton in vigilance etc. on his own ground and unseat him as minister and get into his place.[10]

Upon reflection Dayton must have decided to test the attitude of the French government, for two days later he talked with the Minister for Foreign Affairs about a tale he had heard of the sham sale to M. Bravé, a member of the Chamber of Deputies and a partner in Bravé et Cie., Egyptian and Oriental commission merchants, of ships the Confederates had ordered from the Lairds in England. De Lhuys expressed great concern, proceeded to investigate, and was soon happy to report that the truth of the matter was that after the Confederates gave up all hope of ever clearing the ships from England, Bravé had purchased them for his principal, the Pasha of Egypt. "The French

Government has in this matter acted openly, and will, so far as can now be seen," Dayton concluded.[11] Again the matter rested. Bigelow went on with his dreary invoices, arranged for a clipping service on American items from thirteen French journals, broke the news to Malespine that Sanford had no more funds for him, and then softened the blow by authorizing him to translate and publish first a speech of Seward's on the progress of the armies, of which Bigelow himself bought 2000 copies, and then a speech of Sumner's, for which Bigelow paid handsomely after browbeating reluctant Americans in France to order vast numbers of it.

Then one night just as Bigelow was going to bed, Dr. Evans, the dentist, called. It was an unusual hour, but the good doctor had just received word to be at the Emperor's at nine in the morning, which, as he happened to know, was shortly before a Council meeting on American affairs. He wanted the latest news and the Union viewpoint on it, so naturally he turned to Bigelow to be posted. They talked of the Union armies, of the Confederate ships and of Mexico, as fully as Evans wished. Finally he departed and Bigelow, after reading a strangely urgent message from Dayton asking him to call the next morning, retired long past his usual bedtime.

In the morning Dayton reverted to the *Florida*, telling Bigelow that he had been approached by a Frenchman who wanted to institute civil action against the Confederate ship, which he understood to be a privateer, for forcibly detaining at sea his merchantman, the *Bremontier*, and deflecting her from her course. The irate Frenchman believed that his lawsuit would hold the *Florida* indefinitely at Brest, and consequently thought Dayton might be glad to assist him. Dayton said he would help, provided Bigelow believed the suit would be successful. So Bigelow left his own sphere and went to Brest to size up the situation. He was soon convinced that the claim would not be upheld in the courts, but he pointed out that even an unsuccessful suit would advantageously delay the *Florida's* sailing. Hence the case was begun, with Union assistance, if there was any, entirely in the background. In due time Slidell protested the delaying tactics to the ministry, and eventually the case was dismissed on the ground that the *Florida* was a warship, not a privateer, and therefore could not be sued in the civil courts. It was as Bigelow had expected; they lost the case but for almost two months Northern shipping was safe from the *Florida's* depredations.[12]

Bigelow gathered many details about Confederate activities at Brest. He watched water being ferried out to the *Florida*, observed her captain, Maffitt, "pale and haggard, the effect probably of his attack of yellow fever while at Mobile and the constant interruption of his rest since and maybe the Conviction that he is not very creditably employed." He talked with Captain Caverly of the *Anglo-Saxon*, a Federal ship which Maffitt had captured and burned after taking off the officers and crew, and learned from him Maffitt's assertion that the South was getting as much help from New York as it was from England. He learned also, and this fact was significant, that the *Florida* had deliberately sailed by Le Havre and Cherbourg, both good harbors with excellent commercial docks, in order to sail into the smaller harbor of Brest where the only adequate docks were government-owned. To do that Maffitt must have had the previous consent of the French government. Probably, Bigelow suspected, the English authorities had connived in it as well.[13]

Back in Paris on September 7, Bigelow spent most of the day writing long letters to Hargreaves in England, to Morgan, Weed, Seward, and others at home, detailing what he had observed and again warning the Americans of the dangers to New York. He suggested to Seward the wisdom of stationing three or four fast American ships in European waters for the next few months. Frederick Seward, replying for his father, said that Dayton would be given instructions and added: "I am directed to express the acknowledgments of the Department for the continued proofs of patriotism, zeal and discretion in the public service, which your communications afford." [14] To Hargreaves Bigelow wrote: "It is obvious that England and France are intending to act together and do just as much mischief as they can to the United States with the least hazard and expense." For that he blamed the ruling classes, who, if they continued, would sign their own death warrants; the people would take power from their hands:

> You see how I contrive to continue as much of an optimist as ever and to find a certain sort of comfort in everything that occurs or threatens to occur, however deplorable its immediate effects seem to be. These are times when all men, and Americans especially, must walk by faith rather than by sight. We are all walking more or less blindly. No one knows what he is really doing nor what is the real bearing of his efforts. All he can do is try to do right and as much of it as he can, and leave the rest to One who never makes a miscalculation and never wastes a trial or a temptation.[15]

"Walking more or less blindly" was an apt description of what Bigelow was doing. His agent had uncovered enough to assure him that there was Confederate shipbuilding to be seen if only he knew where

to look, but, unable to guide him farther, there he had left him, grop-
ing in a maze of dim half-facts. Then suddenly a small, swarthy, sharp-
eyed Frenchman opened a path. He appeared at the consulate on September 10, bearing a note from Dayton asking Bigelow to hear what
he had to say — Dayton not understanding him — and to decide whether
he was worth bothering with.

P. Trement, a Vicomte apparently, asserted that certain ships being
built in France ostensibly for neutrals were in reality, and with the
permission of the French government, destined for the Confederacy.
This was precisely what Bigelow and Sanford had long suspected: unable to build in England, Bulloch had moved to France. But what they
needed was proof. Bigelow was weary of these fruitless assertions
and conjectures. What basis, he asked, was there for such a statement?
The answer exploded in the room. "Original documents, and, what
is more, I will engage that with my proofs in hand, you can successfully secure the arrest of the ships." It took the whole of Bigelow's
self-control to hide his elation, to sit quietly and demur in the accepted
fashion when his visitor asked for 20,000 francs after his documents had
proved their worth. Somehow he managed to agree calmly enough to
look them over and to have his decision ready on the following Saturday.[16]

Here in his hands was the proof he had so long sought. His own
secret agent, whose name does not appear in Bigelow's papers, had
long since described two suspicious warships under construction in
France for the China trade. But here was concrete evidence that those
two ships had actually been ordered by Southerners. Here was the
news that two other, similar ships had also been ordered by them "to
ply the China and Pacific seas." Here was an application dated June 1,
1863, from L. Arman, the great French shipbuilder and Deputy in the
Chamber, for permission to equip these four 1500-ton corvettes with
fourteen six-inch rifled guns. And here was the necessary authorization, dated June 6, 1863, bearing the signature of Chasseloup-Laubat,
Minister of Marine. Was it possible that a Minister of Marine thought
it natural for merchant ships to be armed before going about their
business? Here was a letter from Emile Erlanger, the banker who
handled the Confederate accounts in Europe, guaranteeing Arman
two fifths payment on the ships. Was it possible that Arman, either
through his business or through his position as a Deputy, did not know
of Erlanger's relations with the Confederacy? Then arose the all-important question: would Arman or Chasseloup-Laubat have dared
to be parties to this transaction without encouragement from a higher
personage?

As a matter of fact, in January 1863 Arman had approached Slidell with an offer to build ships for him. Since Slidell had already talked with Napoleon upon that subject, he naturally inferred that Arman came from the Emperor. In February Slidell asked de Lhuys what France would think of Confederate shipbuilding there. De Lhuys explained that he knew nothing about such matters, that he wanted to know nothing about them, that he would know nothing about them, unless the United States government forced them upon his attention. He suggested that Slidell see the Minister of Commerce, M. Rouher.[17]

The next day, February 23, Slidell called on his old friend, Eugène Rouher, and received a guarded, verbal permission. In April the Confederates ordered four corvettes, two at Bordeaux from Arman and two at Nantes, one from Jollet and Babin, the other from Dubigeon. Early in June, as Bigelow knew, Voruz was allowed to arm them. Later in June, when Slidell had his seventy-minute chat with Napoleon, he found occasion not only to thank the Emperor for that permission but to ask for verbal permission to build several ironclads in France. Napoleon replied that so long as their true identity was concealed, the ships would be unmolested. Shortly before this, without telling Slidell, and without consulting French officials, Bulloch had ordered from Arman two ironclads, unmistakable vessels of war of a size and power that would place them among the most dangerous ships in the world. Arman, it should be noted, was already a good friend of Bulloch's, having kindly assisted him to transfer his Laird rams to the ownership of the accommodating M. Bravé, a transfer which Britain and the United States suspected, though de Lhuys had courteously assured Dayton that it was a bona fide sale. So the Confederates had, by September 1863, at least four corvettes and two rams under construction in France, as well as some smaller ships, and expected to receive delivery in France of two other rams when they were completed in England.[18]

Bigelow did not have a complete picture of the Confederate program. In fact, he did not know the full story until some years after the war when he went through Confederate records deposited in Washington, D. C., in preparation for his history, *France and the Confederate Navy*. But he had all that he needed in the papers Trement had left with him. The following Saturday Trement returned with additional papers which, after some dickering, he agreed to sell together with the first lot for 15,000 francs to be paid after the papers had served their purpose. Among the documents in Bigelow's possession, according to his account, were:

> *First*, the letters of the ship-builders at Bordeaux and Nantes, acknowledging that they were building together four vessels-of-war, of the most formidable description, "for the Confederate States."

Second. A copy of their application for a license to build these ships, which was based entirely upon false representations.

Third. An official copy of the license, which showed, beyond any reasonable doubt, that the Emperor and his Minister of Marine, if no other members of his ministry, were presumptively accomplices in the fraud.

Fourth. I had a letter from the agent of the Confederates (Bulloch), stating that these ships were building for them under his directions; and

Finally. I had the official letter of the diplomatic representative of the Confederate States (Slidell) approving of the contract and guaranteeing the price of them.[19]

Bigelow sped copies of these papers to Seward. Other copies he rushed to Dayton who hastened to reply: "I agree as to the importance of the papers; pay him yourself. I cannot doubt that our Government will indemnify you." Then Bigelow complacently wrote Sanford that he had conclusive proof of Confederate activities in French shipyards, dared not say more in a letter, but wanted Sanford to know that he really need not spend more money for data about ironclads. Bigelow knew all there was to know. He had no share in the conversations with the French government about these revelations, but he followed the course of Dayton's talks with de Lhuys and sent Seward lengthy reports upon the progress of the affair as it appeared to him. He believed that within three months the ships would be afloat unless the French government was forced to act promptly. Apparently he conveyed to Seward some of his own anxiety that the issue be pressed to a conclusion, for by late October Dayton, stung by Seward's dispatch asking him to "lose no time unnecessarily in bringing the transaction to the notice of Mr. Drouyn de L'Huys . . .," reviewed all the steps he had taken which he felt sure would satisfy the President and the Secretary of State.[20]

Meanwhile Bigelow had decided that Antoine Berryer, the seventy-three-year-old lawyer, undisputed head of the bar, orator, member of the Institute, who had been in the Legislative Chamber in 1830, in the National Assembly in 1848 as a legitimist, and now, after years of retirement, was returning to the Chamber to join the opposition to Napoleon, would be the person best able to advise them about further use of the documents. Because of the chain of meetings started by his vacation call on Guizot, he had ready access to the great lawyer through Moreau. Berryer, he found when he spent some three hours with him at his country home, was bitterly opposed to the Confederate and Mexican plans of the Emperor and intended to take a leading part in the opposition when the Chambers convened the following month. This delighted Bigelow, though it was no more than he had expected from Moreau's statements, and he proceeded to unfold to him all that he had learned about the shipbuilding. Possibly Berryer would take public action in the Chambers, which would be particularly effective, as both Arman, the builder of two ships, and Bravé, whose name the Confederates had used to transfer the title to their half-completed Laird rams from England to France, were likewise Deputies. This first meeting, however, consisted only of an exchange of general opinions, valuable to each as a chance to form some estimate of the other.[21]

Bigelow was glowing with good cheer by the end of September. For once the Northerners had the upper hand. While Seward was writing Bigelow: "Your diligence in our matters is very highly appreciated," [22] while Bigelow and Dayton were perfecting their weapon against the unhappy Confederate agents, Slidell and Mason were steeped in troubles. Mason, the accredited representative to England, had left that country in August after the utter collapse of Roebuck's motion, all illusion gone. Shipbuilding there was impossible, hopes for recognition had faded, and the attitude of British Ministers was too slighting to be longer ignored. So far as Bigelow could see, Slidell might as well give up, too:

> Mason had to leave England and if Slidell was half as proud and exacting he would have no excuse for remaining here. I don't believe he has been received with much more attention on this side of the straits, than Mason on the other, only he has had the tact to propagate the impression everywhere, that he and the Empress sleep alternate nights with the Emperor. The London *Herald* speaks of Slidell as being the constant guest of the Emperor. He never had but one private audience with Napoleon and that was at St. Cloud last spring. At Biarritz he was invited to the ball at the chateau with his family and so was every [one] in the place, that could raise a clean shirt. He has . . . received no special attention whatever from the Emperor.[23]

Bigelow could afford to speak contemptuously of the Southerner, though he could not mention that it was Slidell's position in the near future rather than in the past that he had reason to deride. The time was not yet ripe to mention his discovery to friends. First there must be dramatic, public presentation of the evidence, but the method was not yet clear. Soon Berryer solved that problem by suggesting, through Moreau, that Bigelow pay him a retainer to take judicial proceedings against the shipbuilders. At their first meeting Berryer had refused payment for his opinion, calling it a conversation between friends, but now he had satisfied himself of the validity of Bigelow's proofs and was ready to start suit. This was precisely what Bigelow had hoped would result from his visit.[24]

During the fall while Berryer worked on his brief, Bigelow attended to his press tasks, his consular duties, and did what he could to help the lawyer. He exchanged several letters with Cobden about France's continued hospitality to the *Florida*. Cobden suggested that Bigelow might look at the Anglo-French communication to the United States in 1854 upon the outbreak of the Crimean War. This document, according to Cobden, stated their expectation that the United States would "in a spirit of just reciprocity give orders that no privateer under Russian colors shall be equipped, or victualed, or admitted with its prizes in the ports of the United States." Bigelow sent the suggestion to Seward along with his own comments upon its importance, which he showed to Dayton before mailing, and which Dayton endeavored to act upon after Seward expressed the hope that he had done so without awaiting instructions. It was an important point, since, if France maintained that the *Florida* was a belligerent's man-of-war (which it eventually did) and not a privateersman, the Declaration of Paris would be little more than worthless; at any time, merely by issuing commissions in place of letters of marque, any country could convert a privateersman into a warship.[25]

Bigelow continued to make use of Trement, who, in fact, served him on and off throughout the war. In that way he got plans of the ships, models of munitions, expense accounts, and other details which so completely implicated French shipping and financial interests, especially Arman, Voruz, and Erlanger, that on October 23 de Lhuys assured Dayton that authority for the construction of the ships had been withdrawn. "These measures testify, Sir," Dayton informed Seward, "to the scrupulous care which the government of the Emperor brings to the observance of the rules of strict neutrality." Clearly relieved at the happy outcome, Dayton nevertheless was concerned that de Lhuys based his action upon the United States Minister's affirmation of the authenticity of the documents. He hastened to absolve himself in Seward's eyes by noting that he could not, of course, answer for the various handwritings in the letters which Bigelow had procured.[26]

The consul's concerns were less personal. What worried him was that work on the ships continued. Indeed it would not, perhaps, have surprised anyone except Dayton to know that Slidell on November 6, upon learning that the building of the warships might be banned, protested vigorously to the Emperor and that de Lhuys on November 9, fully two weeks after his assurance to Dayton, allowed the Southerner to believe that all would yet be well with the Confederate shipbuilding program.[27]

On November 14 Bigelow presented, to Dayton, Berryer's closely reasoned, unanswerable statement of the case, for which he paid three thousand francs out of funds received from Sanford. Now, he felt, their worries about Confederate shipbuilding belonged as much to the past as his earlier worries about the tone of the French press, which with few exceptions had been favorable to the North throughout the fall. For purely personal reasons, as well as on larger grounds, Bigelow was grateful for the state of their affairs and for the consequent respite he could have from governmental duties. For the next month his family responsibilities had to take precedence over all else. Long since he had received permission from Seward to be away from the office from mid-November to mid-December. The Bigelows were expecting their seventh child, and they intended it to be born in London. By November 18 they had crossed the Channel with the nurse and the two littlest children, and soon they were enjoying quiet visits with Cobden, the Hargreaves, and their other English friends.

Occasionally Bigelow saw Robert J. Walker, the eminent Southerner who had served his country well as Senator from Mississippi, Secretary of the Treasury under Polk and upright Governor of Kansas in '57 and '58. Now in the midst of civil war, he remained loyal to the Union. His presence in England was the result of a suggestion of Bigelow's. Some months before, Bigelow had written Seward, apropos of the Confederate bond issue floated in Europe on March 18, 1863:

> I am surprised that no one thought to collect the evidence of J. Davis' counsel in favor of repudiating the Miss. debt. Slidell has contradicted the statement and there is no means on this side of the Atlantic of proving it. I think it will be worth whatever trouble it may involve to accumulate all the evidence and lay it before the public with as little delay as possible. It would have the double effect of hitting Davis and Slidell who has tried to whitewash him.[28]

Seward read that letter attentively. He knew that without money the Confederates would profit little from Europe's friendship. He knew their funds in Europe had been almost exhausted before they issued these cotton bonds. Emile Erlanger, whose son, incidentally, married Slidell's daughter, cleverly handled the issue at a nice profit for himself, and the loan, generally considered a good investment, was almost at once oversubscribed by British and French partisans of the South. William E. Gladstone, the Chancellor of the Exchequer, apparently invested in it. So Bigelow believed in 1865 when he obtained a partial list of the subscribers and a statement from an ex-Confederate that Dudley Mann had said that the Chancellor subscribed, though others preferred the explanation that the subscriber could not have been the British Minister but was another man of the same name who failed to step forward and identify himself.[29] In any case the cotton bonds were alarmingly successful.

Acting upon Bigelow's suggestion, Seward proposed that Walker go abroad as an agent of the Treasury Department to do what he could to break confidence in the Confederate issue and to sell United States bonds. Walker reached Britain early in the summer and in July published *Jefferson Davis; Repudiation, Recognition, and Slavery*, in which he related how Davis, when a Senator, had frankly favored repudiation of Mississippi State bonds as soon they became a burden. Later he issued another pamphlet on *Jefferson Davis and the Repudiation of the Arkansas Bonds* as well as a series on *American Finances and Resources*.[30] The effectiveness of Walker's work was a source of pride to Bigelow, who felt a paternal interest in the Jefferson Davis pamphlets. Steadily the value of the cotton bonds sank on the European exchanges, and with each major blow at the Confederacy — Vicksburg, the British seizure of the Laird rams, etc. — their value declined still more sharply.

Walker presided at the American Thanksgiving dinner in London on November 26, 1863. Bigelow did not attend it, because his wife was not able to go, but he did join Walker and a group of friends afterwards and listened with amusement to the description of the Southerner's face when he found that the chaplain of the occasion near whom he must sit was a Negro. Another day Walker began talking of the trials of a Southern Unionist. Formerly, he said, when he was in the Senate, his popularity was such that numbers of his constituents named their children after him and he perforce sent them silver cups. Now, as an example of the feeling toward him, he instanced a bitter letter from a former friend denouncing him and saying that he had changed his son's name. "I said rather profanely," Bigelow recorded, "that he should pray to his friend that that cup should pass from him." Yet though he joked about it, he, too, knew the pain of broken friendships; his own wife was from a Southern family, and close relatives of hers had joined the Confederacy.

Another child was added to the Bigelow family on November 30, five days after Bigelow's forty-sixth birthday. Writing to nine-year-old John, Bigelow described how tiny the new sister was, how sweet she was, and how sure he was that she would send her love as Jenny and Ernest did if only they could understand her. It was a crowded, undated letter, full of details which would amuse the children. At the end appeared parental instructions: John was to be sure to tell his brother and sister to use more paper when they wrote, not to crowd words, and never to fail to put the date at the top.

Of course he bought books in London, Longfellow's latest poem, *The Wayside Inn*, Hawthorne's *Our Old Home*, and a memoir of de Tocqueville by Beaumont de La Bonninière. The last was the best in Bigelow's estimation, for Beaumont always interested him because of his anti-imperialism and his studies of American penology, the outgrowth of his visit to America with de Tocqueville in 1831. Bigelow read until two in the morning, unable to put it down, and then noted of de Tocqueville: ". . . His life was morbidly intellectual and that gave him the disease of which he died Consumption. Continued overactivity of the intellectual portion of the brain is sure sooner or later to plant disease in the lungs." He noted of Hawthorne's book, which he was to quote in a consular report soon to be written: "It interests me more than anything of his I have ever seen, perhaps from consular sympathy with allowance for labored descriptions of things not worth describing and of notions elaborated, not worth elaborating. . . ." [31]

Then he prepared for the return trip to Paris with his wife and three youngest children. The month in England had been pleasant but by no means devoid of work. There had been long and frequent consultations with Adams and other officials, meetings with British newspapermen to engender a more co-operative attitude, and one unusually busy day. That was November 27, the day after he heard of the flight of the recently christened *Rappahannock*, an old screw gunboat purchased in England and being repaired there, so it was said, for the China trade. Adams, suspecting from its name that it was owned by Confederates and convinced by other evidence, had protested so bitingly that the English authorities forbade its departure. But at ten o'clock on the evening of November 24 the commander of the ship, the Confederate Captain Campbell, slipped from Sheerness across the Channel to Calais, where he intended to complete repairs. Bigelow relayed that news to Seward and added that two ships, the *Harriet Martin* and the *Agrippina*, both flying the British flag, had been engaged to join the *Rappahannock* in the Azores, there to supply it with armament. He wrote similarly to Dayton, who forwarded Bigelow's letter to the Secretary of the Navy. [32] Then, not content with making a report, which was as much as Bigelow, a mere consul, could be expected to do, he asked a number of consuls in England and France to collect as rapidly as possible and to forward to Dayton from day to day affidavits of witnesses to the escape of the *Rappahannock* or documents relative to its real or supposed ownership. That seemed to him the best method of reinforcing the protests which the Minister would be making to the French government.

CHAPTER 17

Consul and Chargé d'Affaires

[*1864*]

Two DAYS before Christmas Bigelow called at the legation to pay his respects to Dayton. The Minister showed him an affidavit which he had just received stating that the *Rappahannock*, alias the *Victor*, now at Calais, was owned by a British merchant. "Why do they keep sending me these affidavits?" Dayton asked half angrily, half helplessly. His office was getting cluttered with them, and it was not as if he had not protested to de Lhuys; he had, almost a month before, when first told about the ship. Bigelow was disgusted. He had taken the trouble to have consuls keep the legation at Paris constantly posted, but Dayton was too obtuse, or else he was too averse to trouble and responsibility to appreciate Bigelow's forethought.

All told, it was a bad day. Bigelow had asked Captain Winslow of the U.S.S. *Kearsarge*, stationed in a French port, to locate certain data about the *Agrippina* and the *Harriet Martin* and, to save time, to present it to Adams whom he had been ordered to see shortly in connection with other business. Now came a letter from Winslow reporting that Adams refused to receive the facts on the grounds that, as Minister to Great Britain, he could communicate with an officer stationed in France only through the United States Minister to France. In strict propriety that was true. But Bigelow lost all patience:

> Such littleness when so much is at stake disgusts me. If Seward would just send someone out to knock Adams and Daytons heads together till they could forget their two penny personalities and think more of the interests of their country he would do an excellent thing.[1]

The exasperation on all sides, resulting from Bigelow's officiousness or zeal, according to the viewpoint, was momentary, for the triumph of the Union, which was the one abiding concern of Adams, Dayton, and Bigelow, seemed assured by the beginning of 1864. Seward be-

federate shipbuilding program in France. Moreau stated point-blank that a member of the Chamber of Deputies was building ships for the South, that the Minister of Marine had approved an obviously false application for permission to arm them, and that, though the whole affair had long since been brought to the attention of the government, it had not as yet started prosecution. Bigelow secured 1650 copies of this daring pamphlet and judiciously distributed them.[4]

In order to be prepared for some future opportunity for Berryer to speak publicly, should it be necessary for him to do so, Bigelow continued his efforts to place the documents in a newspaper. But publication was not easy. Even if a paper should dare to print the charges, the chances were that the censors would see the proofs in time to forbid the issue. Moreover, Malespine's attitude was unfortunate. As Bigelow explained to Sanford:

> I sketched out for him the plan of 2 or 3 articles [on the ship question] and when I had done, he asked if I wished him to work on the old understanding or as he had been working for the last 3 or 4 months. I asked what he meant. "Why," said he, "when I was paid extra, I could afford to prepare things, when I am not, I take the news, where I find it most convenient at my hands!" . . . the upshot of it was I found if we want anything done specially and at a particular time, that will be the thing that will not be done at the time required in the *Opinion* unless M. has his 1000 frs per trimestre.
>
> I think it is to be regretted too that we have not some person in our pay on the *Debats*. That j [ournal] is not half as useful to us as it might be or as it would like to be I think, if it could afford it.[5]

Malespine was too valuable to be discarded. In March Bigelow paid him 1000 francs (his only public statement about Malespine read: "a faithful and effective friend of ours from the commencement of the war, and the only writer on American affairs for the press here who has never faltered in his republican faith")[6] and *L'Opinion Nationale* carried a strong letter warning the government against releasing the *Rappahannock*.

The all-important Trement papers were yet to be disclosed, however, and by late April their publication once more seemed imperative. De Lhuys's February statement that Arman's ironclads had been sold to Denmark had proved to be inaccurate. Early in April, de Lhuys again had relieved Dayton's anxiety by saying that the ships had been sold to Sweden, but before the month was out that, too, proved to be inaccurate. Sure that he must act now or never, Bigelow consulted at length with Guéroult, the editor of *L'Opinion Nationale*. Shortly thereafter, Guéroult showed an article, written by Malespine under Bigelow's direction, to Arman and to Eugène Rouher, Minister of State. The shipbuilder was distraught when he saw the quotation from his letter stating that the ships were being constructed for the South, begged that there be no scandal, assured Guéroult that all that belonged to the past, that now the ships were going to Chile. Guéroult replied that he would not publish the article if he received a sure guarantee within twenty-four hours that not one of the ships would ever reach the Confederacy. At that point Rouher, the Minister, protested that he needed more time to investigate, but the editor stood his ground. Since no direct answer to his ultimatum arrived on the following day, Guéroult published the article under the title *Les Corsairs du Sud* on Saturday evening, April 30.[7]

The government was furious. It forbade the official press to comment upon the article. It effectively muzzled other papers by a variety of threats. But Bigelow was quite unconcerned; foreseeing the government's reaction, he had rushed a copy to Nantes, where it appeared in the influential *Phare de la Loire* before the government had time to make known its attitude. Seward was delighted when he heard that at last the facts were in the open. He congratulated Bigelow in a confidential note on May 18 and said that the same mail was carrying a letter to Dayton ordering him to give "serious attention" to the subject of the ships, for work on them had been resumed after de Lhuys's first false report of their sale to a neutral country. Three days later in a "private, unofficial and confidential" note to Bigelow, Seward wrote that he had told Dayton in still another letter, "with, I trust, becoming explicitness and earnestness," to get busy about the ships. In fact, he told Dayton that it was up to him to stop the completion of the ships and, in no uncertain terms, he reviewed for the Minister's benefit all the previous instructions he had sent to that effect. Seward did not believe that the ships were going to Chile.

Jules Favre, daring opposition leader in the Chamber of Deputies, was intensely interested when he read *Les Corsairs du Sud*. He arranged to meet Bigelow, pressed him for details of the whole affair, and on May 12 spoke vehemently in the Chambers about the government's toleration of Confederate ships in France. In reply, the Minister of State declared that on May 1 (the day after *L'Opinion Nationale* issued Bigelow's revealing article) the Minister of Marine had written the Minister for Foreign Affairs that not a one of the ships would leave France so long as there was any doubt concerning its destination.[8]

That public statement seemed conclusive, but Bigelow remained suspicious. He had learned from Slidell's private secretary that nine ships were under construction, whereas he knew only of seven. So he asked Seward to have consuls in coastal cities put on the alarm. At Berryer's suggestion, he arranged to have the much-rumored legal opinion of the lawyer-deputy published in *L'Opinion Nationale,* but that came to nothing when the editor was warned that an attack upon Arman was an attack upon the government. Anyway, the government spokesman added, the issue was dead; the ships already had been sold to some Dutch citizens in Amsterdam. Bigelow began to wonder if he ever could believe anything he heard. First Denmark, then Sweden, then Chile, and now the ships were going to Holland! Nevertheless, he passed the tale on to Seward, expressed his delight that Seward was following his suggestion by sending several fast United States ships to European waters, and urged that the United States Minister to Holland be posted. Dayton was equally concerned, for it suddenly occurred to him in June that he had forgotten to get de Lhuys's assurance of a bona fide sale put in writing.[9]

Yet in spite of his anxiety and annoyance about the ships, Bigelow knew that the affairs of the United States were in good shape, while Confederate hopes were fading fast. Bravé had had to sever his connection with the two Confederate ships in the Laird yards after the United States had proved so conclusively that he was acting as a Southern agent that Napoleon refused to countenance the transfer. In May the British admiralty purchased them for the Royal Navy. Moreover, Bulloch was selling his other ships in Britain in order at least to release his funds. Similarly he sold to neutrals the corvettes he held in France, and finally decided, upon Arman's advice, to sell one of the all-powerful ironclads honestly and to hope that somehow the other could be got out under nominal transfer.

Moreover, the press had become hopelessly anti-Southern. In February de Leon lost his job, for it was useless to give him more funds after his indiscreet letters about the "grasping" French were captured by the North and published. At once Felix Aucaigne, the famous editor of *La Patrie,* approached Bigelow. After three years of writing for the South, he was now willing, for $2000 a year, to go to America and send home bi-weekly, pro-North letters to the hitherto inimicable *Patrie.* Similarly Dupont, the editor of *Nation,* a Catholic journal, offered Bigelow control of his paper's editorial policy toward America in return for a loan of 50,000 francs or a purchase of a half-interest in the paper. But Bigelow had never paid out such large, direct sums of corruption money and he saw no reason to begin at this late date. The Emperor was so involved in his Mexican venture that by now there was little chance that he would risk another war under any circumstances.[10]

Judah P. Benjamin, the Confederate Secretary of State, writing to Hotze on January 9, 1864, had freely admitted that the ablest, best-known French newspapers were devoted to the North, and Hotze's subsequent effort to change that picture came too late. Indeed, Bigelow's original task, the creation of a friendly attitude in the French press, was accomplished. He had been the rallying point for all the varied groups in France who wanted the United States to live. It had been his discernment, his tact, and his patience — without which money could have accomplished little — that maintained the faith of liberal French elements in the destiny of the New World republic and that forged in France a reliable and formidable newspaper weapon. The importance of that cannot be denied, even though liberals had no voice in the French government and though Napoleon dismissed with contempt the views of newspaper scribblers, for the Emperor read with utmost care the regular reports of his *procureurs-généraux* upon public opinion, and surely French public opinion was formed in good measure, so far as immediate issues were concerned, by the journals of France.[11]

Bigelow was justly proud of his success in molding opinion. He was justly proud of his major share in making impotent a nascent Confederate fleet. That being so, he was ready to move on to other spheres. There seemed no real need for him to remain at the consulate. Because he had no desire for a lifework in the foreign service, it seemed only fair to turn the job over to a career man. After two and a half years abroad, he yearned to see America once more, and to watch the brightening outlook at home where, to his surprise and mounting respect: "The President is making out for himself a larger place in history than he has any idea of." [12] Besides, he had in mind two definite plans for making more profitable use of his time, one to do with a history of the United States, the other concerned with revising the consular service.

Interest in the latter had crystallized after Seward had written, in October 1863, that he realized how much the business of Bigelow's office had increased:

> . . . and the necessity which exists of additional legislation, rendered necessary by the provisions of the Act of Congress in regard to triplicate invoices. . . . A report, should you have time to prepare it, similar to the excellent and valuable one which you prepared upon the revenue system of France, would be very acceptable. . . .[13]

Before Congress met, Seward wanted recommendations for the improvement of the consular system in general, and in particular wanted to know the problems of the Paris consulate and how its organization compared with the consulates of other nations.

Bigelow worked on this with zest; a request for his opinions on a subject close to his heart was not to be denied. With the report, completed on February 28, 1864, he enclosed a letter to Seward which once more showed the interest he invariably took in the larger aspects of any institution or movement with which he had a practical connection:

> I am quite convinced that no reform of our service is worth attempting, which does not raise the standard of qualification and guarantee a permanent career with reasonable prospects of promotion for those embarking in it.
>
> Under the system of quadrennial changes or even uncertainties an efficient service is simply impossible. Our foreign business is becoming too important to be transacted by talesmen picked up about Washington. The time is at hand, if it has not already come, to change all this. The whole country is ready to recognize the necessity of having more trained and experienced men in our consular and diplomatic service and I see no reason why a solemn effort on the part of the government might not beget a public opinion, which would hedge the service about with the same protection, that guards the military service from vicissitudes.
>
> Next to the restoration of the Union and the extirpation of slavery I can conceive of no more monumental service, which the President and you can render your country than by relieving it of this fatal weakness of its administrative system.[14]

In the formal report itself, he likewise labeled the short, uncertain term of office the fundamental weakness. "No degree of wisdom or patriotism in the appointing power can make our service what it should be while its appointments are regarded as the lawful spoil of a triumphing party. . . ." As a result of that attitude, the officers are untrained and, having no expectation of a lifework in the service, have no inducement to study. "The first steps to be taken towards the organization of an efficient consular body is to raise the standard of qualification; admit to it none but young men; give them a reasonable prospect of promotion; appoint none to high grades who have not gone through the lower, and provide a pension for their retirement after a suitable term in service." An analysis of the French system, the best in the world, Bigelow asserted, showed exactly the kind of civil service he wanted America to establish. The basic requirements to be expected of an applicant under twenty-five should be a college diploma, a knowledge of French, of Kent's *Commentaries*, Wheaton's *International Law*, consular instructions, and treaties with other lands.

As for his particular consulate, he had a number of improvements to suggest. First as to salary: he made $4850, whereas the averages worked out by competent French statisticians for a family of four in the consular service at Paris came to $7422. The expenses of the American office to be paid by the consul out of his salary — clerical assistance, fuel, lights, cleaning — came to $2855.60, and in addition there were contributions to the relief of Americans in Paris and to charities which in his case exceeded $1000 a year. His earned income from salary, legal fees, and a share in the revenues of consular agencies was $6357.24 for 1863. His household expenses, using the rate set by the French ($7422) rather than what he actually spent on his much larger family, together with his office expenses, came to $10,277.60. In other words, a family man without a private income could not accept this position unless he devoted much of his time to private legal work.

And that Bigelow considered an evil. One of his predecessors, he had learned, made $12,000 in one year from private practice and necessarily neglected the government's business. Bigelow was convinced that the Act of 1854, permitting private legal work, should be abolished and an adequate salary paid for full attention to the job. One other suggestion was that the Paris consul be raised to the position of consul-general. Every other large country had a consul-general in Paris, while the United States, for lack of anyone with supervisory power, was unable to develop uniform methods in its European work.

Having made his report, Bigelow wanted to see effective action taken upon it. His consular work no longer of paramount importance, he suggested that "Congress or perhaps the President on his own responsibility might appoint a commission of eminent men (not in Congress) who have had experience in the foreign service to examine and report upon the subject. . . ." As members he suggested William Maxwell Evarts and George Bancroft, and also himself, because he knew no one, and there was no one, who had made so thorough a study as he had of the situation in France.

A week later he gave Seward another reason for requesting four or five months at home. The preceding November before his trip to England, Hachette et Cie. had proposed not only a second edition of *Les États-Unis d'Amérique en 1863*, which *Le Moniteur*, the government organ, had said should be placed in every library in France, but also a six-hundred-page history of the United States for the Duruy series. Bigelow's reaction, a typical one, he noted in his diary on November 5:

The following day someone in the State Department presented a survey which Seward had ordered him to make of Bigelow's report, with a view to revising the United States consular system. In it he remarked, apropos of Bigelow's proposal that the consul in Paris be raised to the status of consul-general:

> In view of the important information which has been communicated by Mr. Bigelow, the present Consul in Paris, the delicacy and responsibility of the duties which he has been called upon to perform, the ability with which he has discharged them, and the eminent qualifications which he possesses, the promotion might be urged upon personal grounds, as the only mode in which the Department could properly signify its appreciation of his services.
>
> But the recommendation is made entirely from a regard to public considerations, whoever may fill the office, for it is well understood that Mr. Bigelow has repeatedly pressed upon the Department the acceptance of his resignation, and only remains in his office at the urgent request of the Department, in view of the difficulty, if not impossibility, of filling his place, should he be permitted to retire. . . .[18]

Not long after this, the position at Paris was elevated to a consulate-general.

Seward himself was extremely interested in Bigelow's list of qualifications for prospective consuls.[19] Since 1853 successive Secretaries of State had vainly sought congressional appropriations to provide for consular clerks. Seward was the first to succeed when in 1864 Congress voted sums for the training of thirteen consular pupils. That was little enough, but it was at least a beginning of a means to develop an informed foreign service. In compiling regulations for the new class of public servants, he leaned heavily on Bigelow's lucid study and then gave it for further study to a House Committee on which sat Thomas A. Jenckes of Rhode Island who more than any other man was responsible for the ultimate establishment of a civil service. But Seward knew that this was not the time to work for an effective civil service system. He knew that the President could get nowhere by appointing such a commission as Bigelow proposed without first having congressional authorization, and he knew how few congressmen and senators were attracted to civil service reform. The history did not interest him; the concept of a civil service commission was too advanced for the time.

In fact, not until two years later, on July 19, 1866, did Congress even authorize a report on the civil service of the United States. And that report was but the first step towards action. On January 29, 1867, HR No. 889 was introduced in Congress: "A Bill to regulate the civil service of the United States and to promote the efficiency thereof." In the report accompanying it, Representative Jenckes, author of the bill, set forth the same evils Bigelow had remarked in 1864, called for a Board of Commissioners to set qualifications and examine applicants, as Bigelow had, and demanded tenure of office during good behavior. He referred to Bigelow's report on the French system as ". . . perhaps, as good an abstract of that system as can be found in any English or American work," and attached a copy of Bigelow's statement to his report.

However, by 1867 congressional rebellion against President Johnson was in full swing and Jenckes could get nowhere. The majority of the House apparently agreed with the flowery outburst of Representative Frederick E. Woodbridge of Vermont, in which he said that he opposed the bill because ". . . it is too good; it smacks of Arcadia. It approaches too near an attempt to bring about the millennium," by which he meant that he for one found the patronage system excellent.[20] In February the bill was tabled. Again in May 1868, and still again in April 1869, Jenckes produced similar bills only to have them meet a similar fate. Not until President Grant temporarily backed reform in 1870 was any forward step taken. At that time and thereafter under the more lasting reform of the Pendleton Act, no one remembered Bigelow's contribution to the earlier impulse to improve the foreign service. Yet he remains connected with the movement, not too indirectly, by his clear presentation of the issue to Seward and by the impression his work made upon Jenckes, who took the lead in the '60's in keeping alive and fostering the spirit of reform until liberals throughout the country were ready to press the issue.

But none of that helped in 1864. Seward, knowing that no reform could be accomplished that summer, wanted Bigelow to keep the consulate and remain in it. The tempers of war-ridden Americans were none too good; the sight of a consul home on a seeming vacation would raise cries of sinecure and complaints that while they were sacrificing, fighting, the government was using their money to give holidays to political jobbers. Seward had heard that criticism too often to want more censure through it. So he wrote: "You deserve relaxation, and you will not abuse it. I will confirm any leave you may take; but I do not think you would do well to come home. . . . That you do not come home is my advice, but it is not to be construed as mandatory."[21]

Bigelow was loyal. He stayed in Europe, but he gave himself sev-

quiring more of my time and attention than in a diplomatic station I might be able to bestow upon them, and who would not be profited by the associations it would surround them with. I have no ambition which a diplomatic career would satisfy even if it were successful, which is more than I could promise myself with any confidence.[24]

Now if he received a new appointment, no one could say that he asked for it.

"While sitting quite alone in my office at the consulate in the Chaussee d'Antin the morning of the 3rd of January, 1865, Mr. Edward G. Buffom . . . the Paris correspondent-in-chief of the *New York Herald*, entered with his face wreathed in smiles and offered me his congratulations." [25] So the news came that was to keep Bigelow in Europe another two years. His resignation of the consulate was accepted in order that he might become Chargé-ad-interim. As soon as Buffom left, Bigelow hastened to read the laws relating to Chargés, for though he had realized that he might be appointed, he had not wanted to read himself into a state of mind to be disappointed if not selected.

Two days later the *Boston Advertiser* of December 24 brought the news that Bigelow's nomination had been made at the special request of Seward and that Sumner's motion of confirmation without reference to committee had been accepted unanimously. That was deeply satisfying. Bigelow wrote Sanford on January 6: "The manner of my nomination and confirmation was as flattering as it well could be. I would rather have the Chargéship on such terms than the full mission in the ordinary way." Paris papers wrote complimentary notes about the new Chargé, letters from friends poured in, but not until January 12, 1865, did he receive official word of his appointment.

An Iowan was in his office talking statistics when the mail packet arrived. It seemed forever before Bigelow could get rid of him and look at the actual commission and the pile of letters that accompanied it. It was good to know that men like Senator E. D. Morgan wanted him as full Minister, though Bigelow would not solicit that position. He made that clear in a number of letters:

I could never enjoy an office that I had solicited. No public distinctions are necessary to my happiness and if they do not come to me I shall never possess any.

In regard to the future disposition of the mission I have nothing to say. I desire nothing so much as that it may go to the best man if he can be found.

I should be flattered by the mission *if it comes to me, because I am thought the best man for it under all the circumstances* but I shall make no interest for it nor authorize anyone to make any for me. I do not think the office would promote my happiness unless I had with it the conviction that I could be more useful in it than elsewhere. The only way I could have assurance of that would be by its falling to me without any personal agency in the matter.[26]

Throughout January he was busy answering congratulations. One simile he evidently liked, for he used it repeatedly with slight variation in wording: "New dignities like trees are always accompanied by shadows proportioned to their height." One shadow was the indefiniteness of tenure. If he remained beyond the next few weeks, he would have to renew his lease; if then a new Minister arrived, Bigelow would be saddled with a useless apartment, but that household worry could not be allayed for several months. Another shadow was the expectation that he would present Americans to the Emperor while he himself, not having been of Ministerial rank, was accredited only to the Minister for Foreign Affairs, not to the Emperor, and had not been presented to him in his new capacity. It seemed an utterly trivial detail, yet amazing numbers of hours and meetings were devoted to solution of the problem, finally solved by the presentation of Bigelow in one room where the Ministers were assembled, followed by his presentations of his compatriots in the next. "*Une question imprévue*," de Lhuys found it. Then there was the question of the proper court costume for the representative of a democracy and the difficult problem of ascertaining who would be acceptable guests to royalty. That had been a delicate matter in the French court since the time that the wife of a horse-dealer in New York had painfully prodded the chamberlain in her effort to break through to the restricted dance floor. "I am an American; we like war, and I am going in," had been her spirited statement.[27]

Bigelow turned over his consular duties to Edward Tuck, carrying with him to the legation his extra-consular tasks. He knew that Mexico would complicate his job increasingly as the war in America came to an end, but he was quite unprepared for the renewal of the ship controversy. He instituted routine inquiries as to the accuracy of the announced destinations of the Arman and Voruz ships, expecting to close the matter there, but again his suspicions were aroused. What Slidell thought of this meddling, he indicated in reporting a conversation with the Count de Paiva, Portuguese Minister to France.

. . . Mr. Bigelow, Mr. Lincoln's Charge d'affaires, with whom he had no previous acquaintance, introduced himself a few evenings since at a soiree for the purpose of saying that the *Stonewall* would probably touch at Lisbon, and that in such case he hoped that the King's Government would not permit the vessel to receive the hospitality of the port. The minister replied that he had no information on the subject, but if Mr. Bigelow would address him a note respecting it, he would communicate it to his Government. The count has heard nothing further from Mr. Bigelow. I mention this incident, not because it has in itself any intrinsic importance, but as illustrating the meddling and undignified manouvres of Yankee diplomatists.[28]

Though Bigelow said no more to the Count, he pushed his inquiries the harder. On January 28, Montagnie, American consul at Nantes who had been most helpful throughout the ship troubles, wired that an ironclad, at first appropriately called the *Sphinx* and supposedly sold to the Danish government, had sailed for Denmark as the *Stoerkodder*, had left Denmark as the *Olinde* and was now in the French bay of Quiberon, receiving a new crew, supplies, and munitions from French and English ships. Months before, Montagnie had advised Dayton of the *Olinde's* sailing, which Dayton in turn had reported to Seward, adding in a later letter: "I accepted the assurances of this government that they should not be delivered to the Confederates, as well from respect to this government as from sound policy." [29] Bigelow was less considerate; Arman's suggestion to Bulloch that they sell one ironclad honestly and route the other indirectly to the Confederacy was not to succeed so easily with Montagnie at Nantes and Bigelow at the Paris legation working as a team. Bigelow at once sent the facts and his suspicions to de Lhuys. The next day, though it was Sunday, he called on the Minister of Marine, Chasseloup-Laubat, who above all others had been implicated in the original permission to the Confederates to build in France. Chasseloup-Laubat was none too comfortable. First he explained that the waters where the ship lay were not under government surveillance, so that he could do nothing. That, apparently, sounded weak even to him, for his next statement was that so far as the French government knew the ship had been bought by the Danish government. Hence, inquiries should be directed to that quarter. Bigelow met that by wiring Bradford Wood, United States Minister to Denmark, for complete data about ships bought by Denmark in France — when delivered, whether resold, and so on. Soon he learned that there had been a contract for purchase of the *Sphinx*, but failure to deliver it until considerably after the date specified had caused Denmark to refuse acceptance. So far as the Danish government was concerned, therefore, the ship was still owned by the French firm.[30]

That news Bigelow communicated to de Lhuys, making sure of a reply by publishing it as an open letter to the Minister for Foreign Affairs. At the same time he asked Wood to secure a copy of the Danish contract. This had immediate effect upon the *Olinde*. On February 4, Perry, United States Chargé at Madrid, wired that the ship had now appeared at Ferrol, Spain, under the suspicious name of *Stonewall*. Two acts now were essential. This ironclad was one of the most powerful ships in the world and could cause serious damage if once on the high seas. Bigelow must try to get French assistance to hold the *Stonewall* at Ferrol and must reinforce that effort by sending American ships to bottle her up. Unfortunately, at the time the United States did not require its ship captains in foreign waters to report their whereabouts to the nearest American legation. Not until Bigelow, profiting from his experience with the *Stonewall*, asked Seward for such an arrangement was it effected. On February 10 Perry wired that the *Stonewall* would probably leave the next day. Action became more imperative. Bigelow located Commodore Craven of the *Niagara* and urged him to sail for Ferrol, but Craven understandably reasoned that his wooden ship was no match for the ironclad, that the help of other ships was essential, so that he first made fruitless efforts to secure reinforcements.[31]

Fortunately the *Stonewall* did not sail at once and there was time for further diplomatic maneuvers. The French government persisted in disclaiming ownership and moreover asserted that they could do nothing about a ship in Spanish waters. Bigelow was sure "that the depredations that the *Stonewall* may occasion us will be the least of the troubles of this government. They don't care how much these steamers worry us provided they do not give us an opportunity of fixing the responsibility for what occurs upon them." His concern deepened when he learned that the chief Confederate agents had gathered in Paris. On the other hand it was clear that the French Ministry did not have a united attitude about the *Stonewall*. Moreover, within a week Perry wired that he could keep the ship at Ferrol temporarily at least, and de Lhuys indirectly assured Bigelow that the French Minister to Spain would make every effort, unofficially, to hold it there.[32]

While Bigelow was still protesting the action or inaction of the French government which had permitted the *Olinde* to sail, he heard from the United States consul at Liverpool that the Confederates were using the *Rappahannock*, still tied up at Calais, as a collecting point for a crew for the *Stonewall*. This was absolutely contrary to French neutrality laws. Bigelow protested in as strong language as diplomacy permitted. "The vigilance you have exercised in the matter is especially commended," Seward wrote of this action.[33] De Lhuys expressed marked concern, insisted that none of the Ministry knew anything about the matter, seemed anxious to conciliate the United States, promised to stop all illegal procedures on the *Rappahannock*, and virtually guaranteed that that ship would cause no more trouble. Nor did it, but on March 24 the *Stonewall* left Ferrol. Luckily for the North, however, the end of the war was in sight by the time it reached American waters. The *Stonewall* had no opportunity to do any damage, and in July 1865 it was surrendered to the United States.

The question of Confederate shipbuilding in France, except for suits to recover unspent funds that the South still held there and to punish violators of the neutrality laws, belonged to the past. The most serious problem of the last two years, since that day Bulloch doubted the safety of building in England and turned to France for help, was no more. Slidell and Bulloch had played their parts astutely, had used every available means towards an end which, had it been reached, might have affected the outcome of the war and certainly would have prolonged it. To Northern agents in Europe, and to none so much as Bigelow, is due all credit for spoiling Confederate plans to break the blockade by securing in France ships immeasurably superior to any the Union possessed. He had kept the *Rappahannock* from sailing. He had secured proof that the Confederacy was hoping to get, with French assistance, four ironclads of the *Alabama* class, four corvettes, and several smaller ships. And he had used that proof with consummate skill, to the end that they were given no opportunity to break the stranglehold of the blockade or even to run through with munitions and medicines which might have staved off collapse.

The problems Bigelow faced in France were comparable only to those of Adams in Great Britain, for those two countries alone had the power to affect the American Civil War. Adams deserved and received the plaudits of his countrymen both during his lifetime and after his death. Though the *Alabama* and the *Florida* sailed from England for the Confederacy, he performed a truly great service in blocking all other hostile plans. Bigelow in France rendered an equal service to his country, though unlike the Minister to England he made his great contribution from an insignificant position. He rarely received equal acclaim, however, and perhaps that was his own fault. During the years when students first pored over the records of the Civil War period, he, who outlived his generation, kept his files unto himself. Furthermore, such material as he considered pertinent to the record he published in discouragingly large volumes, badly indexed. And either because he was too proud or too modest — the line between those two qualities is singularly hard to draw — he wrote his *Retrospections of an Active Life* from the view of what was accomplished rather than from the view of what was accomplished by himself.

CHAPTER 18

Minister to France: Mexico

[*1865–1866*]

ON APRIL 5, 1865, Bigelow wrote in his diary: "Rec'd. my commission yesterday. George D. Pomeroy of New York is my second secretary and Mr. Hay is my first. I am fearful." He honestly did not know whether he wanted the job as Minister, whether he could handle it, whether the continued separation from home would spoil his pleasure in it. Yet he enjoyed the congratulations which poured in. Salmon P. Chase wrote: "I am glad that ability and acquirements have been so recognized and honored. . . ." That was a lot from the Chief Justice of the Supreme Court, whose political friends were no longer Bigelow's. Charles Sumner, Chairman of the Senate Foreign Relations Committee, was obviously pleased. Laboulaye declared: "No one is more capable than yourself in maintaining union between the two countries." Perhaps Seward's private note was the most welcome, for he was in the best position to judge of Bigelow's work. In it he referred to a conversation Bigelow had had with de Lhuys, during which the Foreign Minister had given advance notice of a new Minister to be appointed to Washington. If Bigelow was the first to inform his government of it, de Lhuys had said, perhaps they would realize how acceptable he was to the French and would give him the full mission. "You, however, are entitled to know," Seward wrote, "and he may well be informed, that your appointment as E. E. and M. P. preceded the arrival of your note several days, and so far as I am concerned several months." The only reason that it had not come earlier was that Lincoln, without telling Seward, had offered the position to James Gordon Bennett, and not until the owner-editor of the *Herald* refused, was the path cleared for Bigelow.[1]

By the end of April 1865 Bigelow was accustomed to his new duties. He expected the Mexican entanglement to prove increasingly awkward but to be in nowise comparable to the delicate, highly critical problems with which he had successfully coped through the four, long, wearing years of war. So he looked forward to a pleasant, relatively uneventful ministry devoted to the re-establishment of commercial relations and the strengthening of cultural ties with France, while at home Lincoln and Seward would be leading the united country into peace and prosperity. He saw the course of the future flowing clear and straight. Then on April 26, while he was at Brest on business, he received word of the assassination of Lincoln. The shocking news came in an eighteen-word wire from Paris:

> TELEGRAM RECEIVED AT PARIS BOURSE FROM LONDON AT TWO O'CLOCK. PRESIDENT LINCOLN ASSASSINATED. AN ATTEMPT AGAINST SEWARD FAILED.

Bigelow said later: "It was a clap of thunder from a clear sky. I was glad to be secured of several hours' journey on the cars, surrounded by strangers and left alone to my reflections." His mind was in turmoil; he could not conceive of the assassination of an American President, especially of Mr. Lincoln after he had risen so nobly to the country's needs. Even had Lincoln remained the incompetent he seemed at first to be, there was no place for so dastardly an act in a land where ballots were free. True, rumors of plots against Lincoln's life had been current during the war, but no one had taken them seriously; certainly neither Seward nor the President had been at all concerned when Bigelow passed on details of one plot he discovered in 1862. Yet now, after the war was over, or as good as over, after Lincoln had met every test, had brought the nation through its greatest trial, now some fool or maniac had killed him. Andrew Johnson at this very moment must be President. Bigelow recalled briefly what he knew about Johnson; fortunately the man was far superior to the average run of Vice-Presidents, Bigelow reflected, and with Seward to guide him — thank God for sparing Seward — the country would manage.[2]

He found in Paris milling throngs of people, excited, horror-stricken, their apathy toward America, which had grown up during the past two years when the war across the sea seemed to drag on and on to no apparent purpose, replaced by the liveliest concern. Lincoln now seemed to belong to the common people everywhere. Over and over, shock, sorrow, sympathy were expressed in letters from men and women in every walk of life. Deputations of students filed through Bigelow's office and jammed the streets around the legation in noisy demonstration. Friends and strangers came to pay their respects. Americans besieged him for the details he himself was longing for or asked how they might help. There was little enough for anyone to do.

With his unfailing sense of the appropriate, Bigelow did call together several prominent Americans with whom he planned a formal message from the American colony in Paris which could be sent to Washington. He proposed to the State Department the collection in one volume of all tributes paid to Lincoln in foreign lands — a suggestion which led to an appendix volume to the State Department Papers for 1865. And he wrote a fitting response to the address of the Americans in Paris in which he said, in part:

> Those who like myself are accustomed to search for the hand of God in the phenomena of human life, cannot but feel, as, after much reflection, I am led to feel, that our people were never nearer to Him than at the dreadful moment when we seemed, humanly speaking, most deserted. What revelations that crime has made; what lessons it has taught, and will teach; what prejudices it has corrected; what hostilities it has suspended; what sympathies it has awakened! They are in everyone's mind; they are on everyone's tongue. Even here in a foreign land, and where what we most cherish in our political institutions may be supposed to be but imperfectly comprehended, what American has not been surprised and comforted by the spontaneous and universal demonstrations of sympathy which our national bereavement has elicited from all parties, and from every class, from the humblest and from the most exalted? Such a tribute was never paid to our country before; such homage was never paid to any other American. And why to Mr. Lincoln? Because his death, and the time and manner of it, seemed to have rendered his whole public career luminous, and to make it clear to the most distant observers that our late President, inspired by a love which made all men his brothers, had been building wiser than they knew; that he had been fighting the fight of humanity, of justice, and of civilization; and, finally, that he had been summoned hence to receive a crown of triumph more enduring than that which was preparing for him here.
>
> It is not too much to say that during the long four years of our bloody struggle with this rebellion the world made less progress in comprehending its baleful origin and purposes, and the common interest of humanity in resisting it, than has been made during the brief interval which has elapsed since this dreadful tragedy. By the hand of an assassin that simple-hearted and single-minded patriot has been transfigured, and he has taken his place in history as the impersonation of a cause which henceforth it will be blasphemy to assail.[3]

Throughout May and even later Bigelow's correspondence was crowded with formal addresses and letters of condolence to the American government and to Mrs. Lincoln from groups of workingmen, farmers, liberal intellectuals, from simple women who knew what it was to lose a husband, and from young students who looked upon America as the hope of a democratic world. These, too, he forwarded to Seward, commenting:

> It is difficult to exaggerate the enthusiasm which his name inspires among the masses of Europe at this moment — an enthusiasm before which the ruling classes, however little disposed to waste compliments upon anything tainted with republicanism, are obliged to incline. I think it is generally conceded that the death of no man has ever occurred that awakened such prompt and universal sympathy at once among his own country people and among foreign nations.[4]

He wrote to Thurlow Weed more spontaneously:

> I never saw all classes so entirely moved by any occurrence in a foreign country. And strange to say what has astonished people most is the perfect ease & quiet with which Mr. Lincoln was replaced and the utter uselessness of the crime as a political remedy, which had spread such consternation. The mysterious power of republican institutions was never so highly estimated here as now, never. They are compelled to admit that we have found a political secret which none of the Old States of Europe possess.[5]

Gradually life resumed its normal shape. The war was over; Lincoln was dead; new problems inexorably demanded attention. What concern Bigelow felt this spring was for Seward, his friend of the past six years, and he followed with growing satisfaction the regular notes Weed sent about the Secretary's condition. His own life was affected only in that he gave up his cherished plan of returning home for the summer, while Mrs. Bigelow went to America without him, taking little Jenny along for company. She quite understood that with a new President in office and with Seward on extended sick-leave her husband had to remain at his post, but she declared that she had postponed her visit home from winter to summer, from summer to winter, quite as many times as she intended. Bigelow wrote to Bryant of her coming and added with a very human mixture of pride and homesickness:

> I seem to have no luck in my efforts to fly from work. I quitted the E. Post to find leisure; accepted a consulate, always reputed a sinecure, where for about 2 years at least I first learned what hard work was. I resigned that, when I was suddenly called to the charge of this legation, where most of the time I have been

without a single Secretary, and with more work on my hands,
I venture to say, than was ever imposed upon any Minister here
before in an equal space of time. I suppose I am not fitted to be
trusted with leisure, and am thus, by what seems a run of ill luck,
providentially kept out of mischief.

The circumstances under which I received my present position were quite flattering, but the honor would have given me
much more pleasure some years ago than any political distinction can confer now. Besides I have lived here already longer than
is agreeable to me. I long for the society of my country people.
I have become a convert to the theory of the essential distinction
of races. I do not belong to the Latin race and never can feel that
we started from the same point or are traveling in the same direction. I suppose I must now reconcile myself, however, to a farther absence of two or three years from home, unless I disgrace
myself and am relieved by Mr. Johnson.[6]

He went to London to see his wife off, then settled down to a busy
summer. At first all went well. Grace, at thirteen taking responsibility
for her baby brother and sister, was becoming "a most sensible and
womanly girl." The eleven- and ten-year-old boys, "wild as colts . . .
picked up some acquaintance among the democracy, including an
undercoachman opposite," which was satisfactory to their father until
they picked up "democracy's" language as well. Bigelow enjoyed his
brood enormously, and they enjoyed his rule. As he put it: "I am getting
on as *mater familias* very well indeed by letting everyone do pretty
much as they please, which is a popular regime with all ages, and both
sexes."

Friends in Paris did not let him feel lonely; officials now were eager
to have the American Minister's society. There was the dinner of Victor Duruy, the progressive Minister of Public Instruction — fifty or
sixty people and Bigelow in the place of honor — "Altogether the
pleasantest time that I have ever had at any purely official dinner in
France." Other Ministers honored him similarly. Any Americans for
whom he desired special attentions were assured invitations to the Empress's private ball. The French government intended to make the
American Minister happy, and the degree of their success was evident
in the long, descriptive letters he sent to his wife. In return he wanted
similar letters from her; when they failed to come, he wrote reproach-
fully:

I could not see the people but you could have told me what
some of them said, which you entirely omitted to do. What Weed
and Morgan and such men said to you must have been of great

interest to me and I think I have a right to complain, that while I with all my cares find time to write you long letters with ink, you who have nothing to do but amuse yourself put me off with notes in pencil.[7]

Fortunately "The Squirrels" was rented this summer, for Bigelow intended to take a larger place when his wife returned to Paris and live grandly and beyond his means for the next year. Yet first he would like to feel more sure of his investments at home. Greenbacks had always seemed to him a dangerous resort. Now that the war was over, he thought that the sooner the country returned to specie payment the better:

> When our stores are full of European goods bought at paper prices, when our political divisions become broader as they soon will . . . and when all the political aspirants are in search of something upon which to make a successful political issue with the government it will be difficult to take the first steps towards the restoration of the currency to a specie basis till which Europe will not have faith in us.[8]

However, Bigelow realized that a day which should not be marred by petty thoughts was fast approaching, the first peaceful Fourth of July since 1860. American democracy had survived deadly peril; surely its birth should be celebrated as never before. He decided to give a *fête champêtre* for all the Americans in Paris at the Pré Catalan in the Bois du Boulogne. So 193 ladies, 227 gentlemen, 108 children and nurses — all the Americans in the city — were invited. They made the largest body of Americans ever assembled on the continent of Europe. In the huge, flag-draped tent over 500 people chatted freely as citizens do who are far from home. Older men escorted their wives from group to group; younger people monopolized the dance pavilion, while a wizard off in a special building held the children spellbound. Everywhere good humor marked the circles. Once they all joined together with pride and thanksgiving in "The Star-Spangled Banner." Later they listened to Mr. Home recite a poem on Mobile Bay so eloquently that ladies burst into tears and men tossed their hats in satisfaction — the light, high voices of the children playing in the twilight momentarily forgotten. When the last daylight faded, colored fireworks of eerie, evanescent beauty burst forth one after another, until at last came the grand finale, the American eagle spread across the sky bearing Webster's motto: "The Union now and forever, one and inseparable." [9]

A week later little Ernest had a fever, but he seemed all right the next day. Bigelow wrote his wife about it, and three days later mentioned again that Ernest had a fever. Soon Ernest had been in bed nine days, with "a fever which of course is liable to threaten his brain." The next letter said that he might not get well; the child was unconscious most of the time now. His father sat with him constantly, night and day, scarcely leaving the room for meals. On July 21 the four-year-old boy died. Bigelow asked a friend, the following morning, to locate rooms for him and his four children at Dieppe. He must take them away from the hot city. He should have moved weeks ago because all of them were pale and the baby's legs were pitifully weak. But there had been the *fête* to delay their going, and then illness. He attended a spiritualist séance one evening, hoping vainly for a message. The blessed pressure of work shortened daylight hours, but pressure of pain stretched the nights. Thoughts of the two sons lost twelve years apart through the same illness kept intruding, and concern for his wife alone in America, not yet aware of her sorrow. Write her he must, tenderly, trying to bridge the three thousand miles, not knowing whether his letters would arrive before she set sail, hoping she would be at Liverpool and in his arms before she heard the story.

Meanwhile his work demanded increasing attention. Young John Hay had arrived on July 10, willing and cheerful, quick to help in the distraught household and eager to be of service in diplomatic tasks. But Pomeroy, the second secretary, was useless. Bigelow wrote Seward some time later:

> If you happen to know of any Minister in need of a Secretary who has had a brief experience at the Legation at Paris, I wish you would place Pomeroy's services at his disposal. He left the day my little boy died, and when I was exhausted by the fatigue of two weeks sleepless and anxious days and nights, and when I was making every exertion to get my family into the country, which the doctor said was indispensable to their health. Under these circumstances I wanted, when I went away, to leave the Legation as strong as possible, and Mr. Hay had then but just arrived. Pomeroy seemed to think it more important that he should go than that he should stay, till finally I told him that he might go and stay as long as he pleased. I am not sure but I hoped he would not return. He seems to have taken me at my word.[10]

Bigelow needed a competent staff. The Empire Maximilian was trying to establish in Mexico was proving far more awkward than Bigelow had anticipated. The familiar story of Maximilian and his pathetic wife Carlotta, of the invincible courage of the Mexican republican, Juárez, of the sordid influence of money in Napoleon's fantastic dreams of majesty and power was on the periphery of Bigelow's life, but he was concerned with the effect of the intervention in Mexico upon Franco-American relations.

That problem had originated in 1861 when the Republic of Mexico, having just come through two years of internal strife, found itself unable to pay interest due on loans from foreign countries. European creditor nations determined to collect their monies by force. The United States government was immediately disturbed. Yet it dared do no more than warn Britain and France against intervention in any American land; in 1861 it needed to concentrate its whole energy upon its own survival. In the fall of that year, when Britain, France and Spain turned the threat of a joint expedition to Mexico into an actuality, Seward still could do nothing. He did make it clear that the United States was opposed to a monarchy in Mexico and to permanent foreign settlement there. But he had to select his words carefully, since Britain and France might, if provoked, intervene in the American war and destroy the Union.

Apparently by June 1862 Seward's apprehensions had somewhat abated. In the course of an unofficial, rambling letter to Bigelow, he remarked:

> I do not write nor even talk just now about Mexican affairs. I think it prudent to watch and wait. Between you and myself alone, I have a belief that the European State, whichever one it may be, that commits itself to intervention anywhere in North America will sooner or later fetch up in the arms of a native of an Oriental Country not especially distinguished for amiability of manners or temper.[11]

That comment mystified Bigelow at the time. Five years later, however, when Seward arranged for the purchase of Alaska from Russia, it occurred to Bigelow that the veiled words of this letter must refer to some private understanding which Seward had negotiated with the Czar's government.

Meanwhile, in the spring of '62, Britain and Spain had withdrawn from the joint expedition, consequent to the malodorous Jecker claims and Napoleon's interference in Mexican politics. At that point Frenchmen took alarm and with increasing vehemence opposed the expedition. They began to believe that regardless of the profits Napoleon might make from the venture, they stood to lose. By the summer of 1863, though their troops had invested Mexico City, the French nation was almost unanimously opposed to the overseas war. Nevertheless, Napoleon seemed determined to push his scheme of Empire. In July

1863, against the wishes of the Mexican people, the French people, and the American people, he offered the crown of Mexico to young Maximilian of Austria. He knew that the United States was the only country which might have reason to object; he knew that the United States wanted to object, but he judged rightly that the United States dared not act. The Civil War was still at a critical stage in the summer of 1863; so that, beyond having Dayton once again express the general attitude of disapproval entertained by the United States, Seward kept silent. Not all Americans approved of his course, however; some Northerners bitterly criticized his failure to defend Mexico and waited for an opportunity to strike at him because of it.

It was during this summer of '63 that Bigelow first had occasion to concern himself with Mexico. Two years before, when the *Trent* case filled the headlines, he had gone to Garnier-Pagès for advice and assistance. Now, when Mexico filled the minds of Frenchmen, the liberal Deputy came to him. Garnier-Pagès was convinced that Napoleon would drop the venture if the opposition of his own people, which Garnier-Pagès meant to have strongly expressed in the Chambers, was reinforced by a firm message from Seward. He wanted Seward to emphasize the ideas which Bigelow had been known to express, namely, that the United States was bound to overflow into Mexico, American frontier states were sure to resent the imposition of a foreign government so near to them and might easily act in extralegal fashion regardless of the Federal government's desire for peace, and that, above all else, the French government should remember that the policy of intervention by the strong in the affairs of the weak "would present temptations to all strong governments unfavorable to the prosperity of their own people and fatal to the peace of the world." Such a message, Garnier-Pagès believed, avoiding all reference to the Monroe Doctrine, because that was offensive to Europeans, and saying nothing which might wound French *amour-propre*, lest the people in a surge of patriotism back their ruler at all costs, would go a long way towards persuading the Emperor that the expedition must fail from its very nature. In reporting this conversation to Seward, Bigelow added his own heretical opinion: "Nothing is more unpopular in Europe, and, I may add—the opinion I have always entertained—nothing is more absurd everywhere, than what is popularly known as the Monroe Doctrine." [12]

Seward, however, preferred to watch and wait. He hoped to steer clear of the Mexican question until the American war was over. Again he told Dayton to explain to the French government that the only reason the United States remained neutral in Mexico was that France had given its word that the occupation was merely temporary. To Bigelow he replied stiffly: "The delicacy of the whole matter . . . is such that I must ask you not to speak upon it to any person, however friendly, for me, until you have communicated with Mr. Dayton and have his approbation of what you propose to say." [13] Thereafter when Bigelow had anything to say about Mexico, he spoke privately to friends, or, unrebuffed, wrote directly to Seward.

He gratuitously informed the Secretary of State that he approved of Henry W. Davis's resolution, passed by the House of Representatives on April 4, 1864, which voiced opposition to "any monarchical government erected upon the ruins of any republican government in America under the auspices of any European power." Because the Senate did not concur, Bigelow said, it lacked all the embarrassment of an official commitment and yet served as an effective warning. Again Seward disagreed. He considered that the resolution was poorly timed because the United States was in no position to give force to the words, and he did his best, through Dayton, to satisfy Napoleon of his friendliness, writing:

> . . . This resolution truly interprets the unanimous sentiment of the people of the United States in regard to Mexico. It is, however, another and distinct question, whether the United States would think it necessary or proper to express themselves in the form adopted by the House of Representatives at this time.[14]

Once more Seward had avoided the issue without sacrificing a principle. He wrote to Bigelow that the surest opposition would come through "the ever increasing expansion of the American people Westward and Southward. Five years, ten years, twenty years hence, Mexico will be opening herself as cheerfully to American immigration as Montana and Idaho are now. What European power can then maintain an army in Mexico capable of resisting the material and moral influences of emigration?" [15]

That was precisely what Bigelow had been saying for twenty years, but he disagreed with Seward's implication that therefore they should sit back and let time break the French Empire in Mexico. Bigelow saw no advantage in permitting Napoleon, or his puppet Maximilian who accepted the Mexican crown on April 10, 1864, to become entrenched in the new world. In a letter unusually frank to be addressed by a consul to the Secretary of State, he took issue with what he called the "charming compliments" Seward sent Napoleon through Dayton in his effort to lessen the effects of the House's action: "I think you will find before you get on much farther with this government that you will have to take a more decisive tone with it and require from it less temporizing and equivocation." [16] The Secretary replied on May 21 without the least dudgeon and with the evident belief that Bigelow's opinion merited his full attention. Seward's considered statement of his position went far toward converting Bigelow to his views, though Americans at home increasingly objected to his mildness. He pointed out the futility of a strong verbal stand so long as Union forces were retreating in Louisiana rather than marching toward Mexico. As for the future: "We have compromised nothing, surrendered nothing, and I do not propose to surrender anything. But why should we gasconade about Mexico when we are in a struggle for our own life?" His point was unanswerable.

By the time Bigelow became Chargé d'Affaires in 1865 he had swung completely to Seward's viewpoint and was, in fact, to hold to it longer than did Seward. His first official job relative to Mexico was to demand an explanation regarding the rumored cession of Sonora by Mexico to France. He learned that France had merely been given a lien on mineral deposits there, to secure the French debt. Napoleon himself referred to the tale one evening at a reception, saying, as Bigelow reported to Seward: " 'I am sorry those reports got into the journals about Sonora. There is nothing whatever in them' . . . and added laughing 'What I want is to get out of it altogether.' " To that Bigelow made the uncalled-for reply that he "was of the number of those who hoped that good might result to Mexico from his presence there." [17] The more Bigelow talked with French leaders in 1865 the more he was convinced that the only remaining obstacles to friendly relations between France and the United States was fear of what the United States army would do in Mexico once the Civil War was over. The idea of a large force quietly disbanding was hard for Frenchmen to comprehend. If only, Bigelow now thought — his earlier position quite reversed — there could be some assurance that it was "neither our policy or interest to embarrass the new government in Mexico unnecessarily." [18]

In an informal talk with Achille Fould, Minister of Finance, he made every effort to allay concern over possible Federal action. That same day he wrote Seward that nothing could be gained by hostile action toward France at this time. "My theory is that we are to conquer Mexico but not by the sword." Nonrecognition of Maximilian would begin the conquest. "Emigration will do the rest, faster than the sword and quite as fast as can by any possibility be desired. There is no country in the world in my opinion that can afford to look with such supreme indifference as ours upon European efforts to found an empire in Mexico. They can only succeed upon conditions which would render the spread of our people and institutions in the country impossible. . . ." [19] Hence when de Lhuys expressed concern about Mexico, Bigelow gladly agreed to frequent unofficial talks to settle any difficulties which might arise between France and the United States.

It was painfully evident during the spring that the Foreign Minister wanted United States friendship. Napoleon was being pressed by Maximilian for soldiers, for money. In the coming meeting of the Chamber of Deputies his policy was sure to be attacked by the liberals. Berryer, for one, intended to fight the Mexican venture and asked Bigelow for help in preparing his speech. Bigelow seized the opportunity to lay American antagonism not to a desire for Mexico, not to jealousy of French influence in Mexico, not to a love of the Monroe Doctrine, but entirely to the direct and indirect aid which the French government had given and was still giving to the Confederates. Through Berryer's speech Bigelow hoped to have the *Stonewall* and the *Rappahannock* interned (his conversation with Berryer came shortly before the settlement of the ship question), and to hasten the day when France would withdraw from the Confederacy recognition of it as a belligerent. He had already received assurance that that would happen as soon as widespread opposition in the South ceased. But he wanted action at once to speed the inevitable Confederate collapse. He believed that Lee would surrender once he knew that all the world had deserted the South; Lee was no man to shed blood uselessly. Therefore, through Berryer, Bigelow served notice upon France that speedy disavowal of the Confederacy was a prerequisite to American friendship. He talked in a similar vein to the Minister of State, Eugène Rouher, who later, on June 25, 1865, weeks after France had withdrawn its recognition of the Confederacy as a belligerent, publicly quoted Bigelow as saying:

Without a doubt we do not see with favorable eye a monarchy established in Mexico. Without doubt we prefer republican forms; but we respect the will of peoples and nations; we understand that Mexico, which has for long been ruled by a monarchical form, wished to return to that state; and we shall not go to war over the question of the form of government.[20]

Bigelow had protested that speech at once, denying that he said or even inferred that Mexico wanted a monarchy. What he had said was bad enough: that now that the experiment was begun, "Americans wished it to be fully tried under circumstances best calculated to determine finally and forever whether European systems of government suited the Mexican people." Moreover, he made the serious mistake of adding that to date republican institutions had been so unsuccessful in South America that the United States was disinclined to urge their adoption otherwise than by setting an example. A storm of protest broke forth in America when Rouher's words crossed the Atlantic. "You are already assailed (through me)," Seward wrote on July 24, shortly after Bigelow buried his little son, "about the speech of Rouher. It is no time for you to be away from your post." [21]

Bigelow's situation, unenviable as it was in 1865, was to grow worse; throughout the entire controversy, he was destined to trouble. Prior to 1865, when as a consul he had no official connection with the problem, his belligerent attitude was similar to that of most Americans. But after he took charge of negotiations, from wanting a more vigorous policy than Seward thought necessary, he urged a more temperate attitude than even Seward thought proper. Consequently Bigelow doomed himself, after spending years in relative neglect as a consul because no one could be told all he was doing for his country lest his usefulness be ended, to years of recriminations from a war-minded, articulate element in the United States. They had objected to his carrying out the exact letter of instructions which they believed were not sufficiently strong. They objected far more, therefore, when they learned that he deliberately softened, not once but many times, the spirit of his instructions.

Nevertheless, Bigelow followed his own counsel. By July '65 he was committed to Seward's earlier policy of watchful waiting, to Seward's earlier desire, when the United States government was in peril, to leave the issue "to the arbitration of reason under the instructions of time." He wished that Johnson, four months before "pronounced a disgrace to the country" but "now generally believed to be a much more competent president for the coming emergencies," would forget the Monroe Doctrine and cultivate good relations with Europe for the sake of commerce, markets, and credit. Though Seward constantly warned him of the angry feeling in America towards France, Bigelow failed to appreciate the need to conciliate American public opinion. He was sure that the best way to get France out of Mexico was to leave her alone. "Mexico is bleeding her at every pore, and the more indifferent we seem to Mexico, the less support has the Emperor of France from the national pride of his subjects." As for American pride suffering from the French intervention in the western hemisphere, he wondered ". . . how much better off we would be if Juarez had his own again, or how much worse we would be, if he were restored at the expense of a war or only with the humiliation and consequent alienation of France. . . ." [22] After further reflection he wrote to Seward on August 21:

> My notion of my duty here . . . is substantially this: to say nothing and to do nothing which would require us in honor to compel France to leave Mexico if she did not choose to yield to peaceful arguments; and, on the other hand, to avoid saying or doing anything which would lead the Emperor to suppose we would not resort to force if ultimately necessary for the liberation of Mexico. . . .
>
> I had, and to be frank with you, I have still, a somewhat different view of our true policy towards France. Short of recognizing Maximilian I would give France every possible evidence of our friendship. . . . Till Mexico is populated by emigrants from the United States we do not want any responsibility for her government; when she is, no other government can prevail against the temptations to annexation we can offer.[23]

During the remainder of the summer, while de Lhuys was out of the city, Bigelow had little to do except to read the increasingly anti-French dispatches from America. Late in August he wrote to Thurlow Weed:

> I hope that now that our people think they have discovered that they can whip all creation that they will not feel called upon immediately to go and do it. . . . Hitherto the Monroe Doctrine has only been a side issue upon which it was safe to air our rhetoric at the expense of all the world but it has never yet been met & discussed as a practical question. When it is I am sure the decision will be against war. . . .[24]

Certainly he did his best to ignore his compatriots' belligerency, especially as the Mexican venture was rapidly turning into a tragic farce. De Lhuys, showing the strain of trying to meet American protests, of trying to gain public support in France for Maximilian's Empire, finally admitted in the fall that he would like nothing so much as to collect the debt from Mexico, save the prestige of the French government, and get out without trouble. Early in October he tried to persuade Bigelow, who himself needed little persuading, that a wait-and-see program would serve both countries best; that soon Maximilian would be self-sustaining, whereupon the French could afford to leave and the United States could deal as it would with Maximilian without reference to France. In that case — Bigelow asked suddenly, in an off-the-record chat — would France guarantee to withdraw from Mexico, if the

such fear that a break with the United States was imminent, that, to allay anxiety, the French government was forced to put its proposition concerning the recall of the French troops, already made to Bigelow, in the form of a dispatch to Washington, so that it could be published immediately in the "yellow book," the French equivalent of the United States *Diplomatic Correspondence.* Hence the center of discussion was shifted to Washington where the final steps for the evacuation of the French troops were arranged. In April the French government formally announced that the soldiers would be withdrawn in three equal groups, the first in November '66, the second in March '67, and the third in November '67. This gave satisfaction to America and France alike and relieved Napoleon for more pressing business, since concern over American reactions had, of course, been but one factor in his decision to forgo his Mexican ambitions.

Frictions within Europe demanded his full attention. For several months there had been rumors of an Austro-Prussian war. By April the markets reflected the widespread uncertainty on the Continent. Bigelow was philosopher enough to note that if war came, it would mean an increased flow of men and money to America, which he, for one, would welcome. Moreover, war would bring its inevitable train of rising debts, with the consequence of more concessions to the people in order to get from them additional funds, and so it would further the cause of democracy. In June when the short Austro-Prussian war broke out, visionaries began talking again of the possibility of a United Europe. Bigelow called that a vain hope, at least in the nineteenth century. What government in Europe would surrender the powers of war and peace to any central group? The best to be hoped for, he believed, was that this war might decrease the number of states in Europe and increase the size of the more vital states which might ultimately set up a Confederate States of Europe. When in August the peace terms cut the strangling influence of Austria and ended several small, impotent sovereignties, Bigelow was glad that the peace "has diminished the relative influence of Bonapartism . . . and has given to the best educated nation in the world a political organism through which it can have for the first time its just influence upon other states, and through which its own political and social condition can be more rapidly ameliorated. German influence has been running to waste in late years. There will be less of that hereafter." [30]

Though Bigelow took Europe's war philosophically enough, his own position increasingly dissatisfied him. He had moved into the larger home he had promised himself, but he was not entertaining in the lavish style expected of him. The loss of his boy left him with no taste for social life. Mrs. Bigelow was again the victim of typhoid fever, and he himself was none too well. What free time he had he preferred to spend with congenial men, with Huntingdon and Laboulaye, with Lord Lytton, the erudite if unlovable author of *The Last Days of Pompeii* and numbers of other popular novels, who was wintering in Paris, and with Bon Louis Henri Martin, famous author of the eighteen-volume *History of France from the Earliest Times to 1789*. Bigelow regularly urged Martin to take a vacation in America; however, ". . . he seems to think his life will be too short to finish the work he has to do, if he gives himself that recreation. What a common weakness it is for people — the greatest even — to imagine that what they do or omit to do is of some importance to others than themselves." [31] Bigelow himself found recreation during his ministry only in the hours he spent with these articulate, intellectual friends. And because he so obviously preferred their society to that of any nondescript countryman who came to see Paris, he was criticized.

American tourists in these first postwar years were, as a group, an intolerable lot of *nouveaux riches*, easily impressed, easily rebuffed, shrewd, boasting, and tormented with an insatiable thirst for recognition. They expected good-fellowship from their representatives abroad; else why should they pay them big salaries? Bigelow began to wonder whether any Americans were left in the United States, as senators, representatives, generals, governors, war profiteers, arrived with their wives, all expecting courtesies from the Minister and anxious for private audiences with the Emperor. As young John Hay reported when Bigelow was out of town for a few days: "General Webb is here. So is General Sanford. So are the Générales S. & W. General King's suite still linger at the Hotel Empire. We have a large pile of letters for General Pruyn. Hence, expect him soon. It is, as Loubat says in one of his best bad things (did you ever hear it?) an inondation Générale. . . ." [32] It was utterly impossible to satisfy all the travelers, nor did Bigelow always exert himself to the utmost in the attempt. One unusually persistent woman received the following letter from him:

Madam: You gave me as reasons for desiring to be presented at court statements which were not true. I am not willing to invoke the hospitality of their majesties on behalf of a person who attempts deliberately to impose upon one whose good dispositions towards her she had no right to question. If you think with this explanation there would be any advantage in a personal interview, you can have it tomorrow morning at 11 o'clock at the legation. [33]

One day in July he picked up an American newspaper containing an attack by Congressman Edward Wade of Ohio upon Bigelow's pains-taking efforts to have America properly represented at the coming French Exposition in 1867. Bigelow was furious. When he reached the concluding comment: "Our present representative at the French court is a complete snob," his temper snapped. Sufficiently controlled only to know that he could not trust himself in his present mood, he dashed off an acid retort and sent it to his friend, Senator Morgan, to mail, if he saw fit, to Wade. Morgan wisely pocketed it.[34]

A month before this Bigelow had noted in his diary:

. . . It is a great care to know what to do with the education of boys at their age. I felt lately very much disposed to throw up my mission and go home. I am so discontented with everything about my house, my accommodations are so insufficient & the trouble & expense of getting anything better are so appalling.[35]

Now, on the same day that he wrote to Wade, he sent his resignation to Seward, asking to be relieved by or before December 1:

You know it was my intention, when I left my profession, to betake myself to my books and to private life. I left them to gratify no personal inclination or aspiration, and I have never ceased to pine for the opportunity of returning to them. My health has suffered seriously from my confinement and the cares incident to my position; my children are growing up and re-quire more of my attention than I am able to give them, and will soon be forming habits not suitable for the country in which I hope they are to pass their lives. I have no longer the ambition of youth which might have found in the honors of my present position a compensation for its cares, and, in a word, I am home-sick. I wish to go back to the country in which I was reared, and to those surviving friends who, of course, grow more precious to me as their numbers diminish.[36]

A number of Bigelow's friends had recently died, among them Preston King, Samuel Lucas, Richard Cobden. Thoughts of them were fresh in his mind on the day he wrote his resignation, for it was on that day that he received an invitation to be the first non-British subject to join the Cobden Club.

In his diary Bigelow noted still another reason for resigning: "I am tired of keeping a hotel for Americans and being the slave of others." The most famous frequenter of his "hotel," a man Bigelow personally liked though officially he was disturbed by his presence, was General Schofield, who had arrived late in '65 with a letter from Seward asking

Bigelow to treat him as one who was in the confidence of the government at Washington. Schofield met Napoleon only once, briefly, at a formal reception, but he had long talks with Ministers and other influential Frenchmen upon whom he urged French withdrawal from Mexico. Bigelow was upset when newspapers at home lauded the General and pelted the Minister with criticism of his dilatory policy regarding Mexico. He felt that no one was doing more than he to get France off the American continent quickly, though he insisted upon doing it through friendly measures. Stubbornly he clung to the belief he had had for more than twenty years: "We don't want any territory faster than it will come to us by the voluntary action of its population; we do not mean to fight for the Monroe Doctrine, because it is illogical and absurd for a nation to attempt to propagate democracy by arms." [37]

Schofield's presence worried him, however, and it was an admitted relief, two years later, when Seward's detailed explanation of Schofield's mission proved that the government had in no way distrusted Bigelow. It seemed that in 1865, when Grant was all-powerful in Washington, he, along with General Sheridan and General Schofield, was in favor of using the United States army to drive the French from Mexico. Grant agreed to quarter Sheridan's army on the Rio Grande and then to permit part of it to enlist under Schofield in Juárez's army. To postpone that evil day, Seward sent Schofield to France with much pomp and many vague words about what he could accomplish there. Privately he trusted that before Schofield returned and a contest between the State Department and the Generals broke out, the problem would be resolved, as it was, through the regular diplomatic channels. Until that happened, Schofield had to be kept dangling in Paris.[38]

Schofield had left France months before Bigelow resigned, but there was a constant stream of other Americans for Bigelow to entertain while awaiting Seward's action upon his resignation. In August he heard that General Dix, president of the Union Pacific Railroad, ex-senator from New York, and at the moment naval officer in New York City, had been appointed Minister to Holland. "At last the old man has got a foreign mission and I hope he will be happy. He rolled himself in the dirt for 10 years to get the mission to Paris which he could have had if he had kept out of the dirt." [39] Soon, Bigelow hoped, his own successor would be appointed; he wanted to be out by December 1 when his lease expired. Finally in October the long-awaited letter from Seward arrived. Bigelow's resignation was accepted, General Dix — of all people — was appointed to his place, and Bigelow was requested to remain until Dix arrived. Of course Bigelow agreed and of course he made no comments upon his successor's qualifications. Instead he went on with a recent pastime, collecting Haitian proverbs in which he had first become interested in 1854 and which he was to publish, along with his comments upon them, in 1877.

Suddenly it seemed to him that all the world talked of nothing but his retirement. Unfriendly detractors at home spread the tale that he had been forced out. Among them were old political enemies, newspaper editors who, according to Weed, would never forgive Bigelow for being honored above themselves, and Americans like John Jay and Montgomery Blair who condemned his subservience to the French court — a charge which John Hay considered "too silly for anger" and in connection with which he noted that *La Patrie* was condemning Bigelow for his "ultra-American stiffness in the Mexican question." Hay was to conclude after his own return to America a year later: "I am inclined to think since I returned that Bigelow could not have retained his place very much longer. He did not suspect this when he resigned, though you cannot make any one believe that. His talents and his services are not held at their true value." [40] Bigelow felt the slurs keenly. He sent to Senator E. D. Morgan, his close friend since the days they worked together to encourage emigration to Kansas, a copy of his resignation and an indignant letter:

> It was hardly kind, I think, in the guilty party whoever it was, to allow the impression to prevail that I was recalled and that the President appointed Genl Dix because he was dissatisfied with me.
> The facts cannot be altered and I shall see that history does me justice, but I am sorry that my desire to protect the executive from importunity should have been so ungratefully recompensed. If the President desired to have the credit for a more vigorous policy than I urged here in regard to Mexico he had but to tell Mr. Seward this in the form of a dispatch, publish it and take the benefit of it. I had no right to expect however that after a most faithful and conscientious compliance with my instructions, which has been crowned with entire success, that I should through the direct or indirect connivance of the executive be held up to the world in contrast to my successor as a man who had been wanting in proper firmness in maintaining the dignity and honor of my country. [41]

Bigelow could not understand Seward's failure to announce that the resignation had been voluntary, particularly in view of the obvious sincerity of Seward's note to him on October 8. In it the Secretary of State wrote: "I cannot contemplate the termination of your present public service without recalling the delicate and trying nature of the questions which you have been called upon to deal with, and congratulating the country upon the patriotism, intelligence and zeal which you have so constantly displayed in their treatment." [42] Later, in what Bigelow dismissed as "a curious letter," Seward endeavored to account for the unfortunate confusion concerning Bigelow's resignation:

> When General Dix's appointment was announced I took all the care possible to have it suitably announced that you were recalled at your own request. The press did not care for the latter fact and omitted it. I have tried now to correct the public misapprehension by publishing in advance the letter of credence to the General in which the fact which so deeply concerns yourself is carefully stated. [43]

In view of the gossip, other friends sent condolences, but Bigelow wanted none. He replied to Dr. John McClintock, long-time pastor at the American Chapel in Paris who was now back in America and was shortly to found Drew Theological Seminary: "So dry your tears, my boy, and instead of weeping with those that don't weep, rejoice with those that rejoice." To Hargreaves he explained that he had kept his resignation a secret lest the government be inundated with requests for the mission, that foremost among his reasons for resigning was a desire to have "more time to devote to the offices of friendship and in efforts to render my own less unworthy of those who bestow theirs upon me. I have been toiling some twenty years or more to extirpate public evils; I hope soon to have time and inclination to wage a war of extirpation upon the 'enemies of my own household,' the evils of my heart." And in these days of misrepresentation, he took wry comfort in thought of Jacob:

> People who complain of hard pillows, of hard times, of ill luck, of worldly trials ought to find comfort in the reflection that the pleasantest vision that any man ever had probably, came to Jacob when on his journey . . . he slept at Luz with a stone for a pillow. [44]

He busied himself with binders and packers: all the mirrors and furniture his wife had collected, all the books he had bought, some three thousand volumes, all had to be shipped to America. He did not know precisely what he would do when he reached home. Study and write, of course; live at "The Squirrels" if his preferences, and not his wife's, dominated; and quite likely find some time for interests which could only present themselves once he was back in America. He wrote to E. D. Morgan:

Let me say to you in confidence that when I come home I presume I shall be in receipt of a net income of 8 or 9000 dollars a year. I do not wish to devote any more of my life to money-getting. I mean to live upon what I have, be it more or less, and occupy therein the remainder of my days without direct reference to the pecuniary results of my labor, always supposing that some misfortune does not reduce my resources very considerably below the figure I have named.[45]

Godwin had hinted something of the *Post*, but Bigelow was not interested. Another man suggested a law partnership, but law held no more attractions for Bigelow than it had in the 1840's. John A. C. Gray suggested that he might be run for the Senate, and there were, besides, the literary pursuits which meant so much to him.

However, he could not give much thought to his own plans. Government business continued to require attention. On November 1 Moustier, the new Minister for Foreign Affairs, told Bigelow that plans for the evacuation of the French troops from Mexico had been altered. Instead of withdrawing one third of them this month, one third in March, and the rest during the following November, all of the troops were to be held in Mexico until "spring," when all of them would be withdrawn at one time. Unable to get from Moustier a satisfactory explanation for the sudden change in plan, Bigelow drove to St.-Cloud to discuss the matter with the Emperor. Napoleon received him in a tiny, smoke-filled room, and, after a half-hour's vague conversation during which he nervously smoked three cigarettes, closed the interview by saying that he had advised Maximilian to abdicate but that in any case French troops must remain until spring.[46]

Bigelow informed his government of this development by letter. Seward's reaction, written November 23, crackled over the wires three days later, sent across the ocean through the marvelous cable Cyrus Field had completed only three months before. Paris for the moment became a hotbed of excitement. The message started coming through in code on November 26, before Bigelow was out of bed; and as it continued to come throughout the day and on into the next day, officials had their secretaries call or even came themselves to learn the meaning of this thirteen-thousand-dollar message, the longest yet to be cabled. As rapidly as possible Bigelow decoded it, but he said nothing of its contents save that it was upon a serious matter. Actually in the strongest terms possible Seward refused to accept the Emperor's change in dates for removing his troops from Mexico. He said that the term "next spring" was too indefinite. Moreover, he had no better reason for believing that this new plan would be carried through than he had had for the suddenly discarded one.

All the months of cautious conversations to keep the United States and France from an open break were jeopardized by this cable. Bigelow could not deliver it. What he did do, he recorded in his diary:

> Wrote a dispatch this morning mild and inoffensive as possible. Pereire called, told him what I was charged to do and the risk I proposed to take in making an inoffensive communication in place of the one I was instructed to make, in the hope that I would thus more effectively secure the end intended by Mr. Seward, whose dispatch I described to him. I told him he must see Rouher and secure for my note a reply that would be satisfactory at Washington. He said he would.[47]

The next day he called on Rouher, Napoleon's right-hand man since the death of de Morny. Rouher reiterated his personal belief that France had no choice but to leave Mexico and advised Bigelow to demand a prompt reply to his note. On December 1 Lavalette requested Bigelow to withdraw even the two mild notes he had sent upon the subject, leaving for the record only a verbal communication. In return he guaranteed a favorable answer. The next evening, a Sunday, he proposed officially the formation of a provisional government for Mexico and the withdrawal of all French troops in March, thus setting a specific date which satisfied Seward's chief complaint and providing for the removal of the last French soldier from Mexico six months earlier than the United States had expected.[48]

Bigelow was delighted. As he had ardently desired, amicable and final settlement of the Mexican question was achieved during his Ministry. Immediately he was besieged with expressions of friendship for himself and his country. The entire French Ministry appreciated his rewording of his instructions, especially after the *New York Herald* published the original telegram, for the Frenchmen had been able to ignore Seward's provocative message while making every effort to meet his demands. Pereire suggested an offensive-defensive alliance, or United States annexation of Mexico, both of which Bigelow declined to discuss. Rouher suggested the construction of a United States–French canal at Panama, and though nothing came of that, it was an interesting first mention of an undertaking which was to engage Bigelow's attention thirty years later. However, in America satisfaction was less unanimous. A large group of men would never forget that chiefly through Bigelow's efforts Napoleon had been able to withdraw from Mexico without the overt compulsion of a United States ultimatum, without the public humiliation of bowing to United States force.

Bigelow's last weeks in France sped by. He had to prepare his office for his successor, care for the final packing, make and receive innumerable visits. These were weeks of mixed emotions: anger at some of the articles written about him — "If I don't return . . . to look after my character the *Times* and the *Tribune* won't leave me enough to be worth looking after"; [49] pleasure in the sincere tribute of a parting dinner given him by the American colony in Paris, the first such compliment paid to an American representative in France; dislike for Dix, heightened by unfriendly thoughts that this was the type of man thought worthy to succeed him; a desolate feeling on Christmas Day: "A sad Christmas, children mostly absent, house in confusion with packers and my mind preoccupied with my preparations for departure"; happiness when he thought of the men who respected what he had done these last five years — men whose opinions he respected; and relief, flooding relief, at returning to private life.

CHAPTER 19

Adjustments

[*1867–1873*]

BIGELOW reached New York on a gray, blustering February day, eager to see his old friends, to renew his sense of the country, to discover through talk with men not seen for five-and-a-half years where he would fit in postwar America.

He found his homeland vastly changed. Everywhere he was confronted by huge enterprises, vast accumulations of capital, and immense individual fortunes. In 1861 he had found $10,000 a year, for a large family, affluence; in 1867 it seemed merely sufficient. But what left him troubled, out of the swing, an alien, was the universal acceptance of money as the one standard of value. Later he would blame the new materialism upon the Homestead Act and the consequent influx of "more immigrants than we can assimilate and a population altogether too diffuse for any but a material and numerical progress . . .",[1] but at the moment of his return he was too shocked and shamed by money-grabbing ostentation to ponder its causes.

The war had affected politics as much as it had business and society. In Bigelow's remembered America enmities and wranglings had always been part of political life. Now, however, they seemed the whole of it, exerted in a destructive form that had to be seen to be comprehended. In 1861, in the first tragedy of civil war, at least there had been a cohesive spirit on either side and a devotion to a cause that brought co-operative action. In 1867, the country was "one" in letter, but spiritually it was torn by the bitterness of the political war cry, "Keep the South suppressed."

Avoiding commitments, Bigelow set himself the task of listening. In New York, Thurlow Weed told him that Seward never could be President, that what the country needed was a new party with Admiral Farragut as its leader. Weed was doing his utmost to put his plan across, working with Tilden, Evarts, Blatchford and other Democrats, and he hinted that Bigelow would be assured ten to twelve thousand dollars a year if he would take over the *Commercial Advertiser* as the Farragut organ. Yet when the Admiral called to renew acquaintance, Bigelow maintained his onlooker's view and steered the conversation away from politics.[2]

Then he went to Washington. He sat with Sumner in the Senate when the Presidential veto of the tenure of office act was read and was shocked by the Senate's undisguised contempt for Johnson. Intolerance in New York upon political questions had worried him; in the capital it appalled him. Yet among political leaders of the country, with few exceptions, "Any word of moderation is a ground of suspicion. To require proof of the most malignant and improbable rumor is attributed to political unsoundness." [3]

Nathaniel Banks, once Bigelow's co-worker in the Frémont campaign, now General Banks, told him that the President was going mad; but when Bigelow called upon the President, he was convinced that Johnson's body, not his mind, was collapsing:

> He arose & came forward almost tottering & looking very feeble & wretched I should say that he was not three days off from a typhoid fever. It will be a miracle if he lives a month in my opinion. . . . He said feebly that he was happy to see me; asked when I retd &c. I found his only thought was, how soon I would leave him and after a brief apology for interrupting him I took leave.[4]

Other old friends told him of Johnson's ineptness or evil intentions. Few men besides Seward seemed to respect the President as Bigelow did or to realize, as he had when the Johnson-Congress feud first developed, that "Had the President got on harmoniously with a Congress composed as this is exclusively of Northern representatives it would have been ominous of future and far more serious strife." [5] It is possible that Bigelow's attitude was conditioned by his long removal from the scene of the conflict between Executive and Legislature; yet even after his return, he believed that Johnson's measures, unlike those of Congress, would bear the test of time.[6]

While in Washington, he heard something of the inside story of the war years. Then, after advice from Sumner to settle in Washington and advice from Seward to live anywhere but in Washington, and after examining the costs of New York City houses, Bigelow went to "The Squirrels," vastly relieved to have a place where there was quiet and serenity. For two years he was to savor the life he long had planned — writing, farming, entertaining celebrities like General Grant, who visited near-by West Point, going to the city to exchange views with former newspaper colleagues or to see old Column Club friends.

His chief task during his first summer at home was his famed editing of Benjamin Franklin's *Autobiography*. While Minister to France, he had heard that Franklin's long-lost manuscript might be in that country, but he had tried without success to locate it. Just before leaving Paris he had urged Laboulaye and Huntingdon to continue the search, and while he was yet in England en route for home, Laboulaye reported success. The owner, however, demanded 25,000 francs. Bigelow offered 15,000 francs; then, unable to resist such temptation, he agreed to the exorbitant first price for the manuscript, some letters, and a pastel portrait of Franklin.

Now at "The Squirrels" he sat in his library comparing the standard Sparks edition with the original copy in his hand. As his oldest daughter read slowly from the printed version, he jotted down each discrepancy, doubtless recalling the literary tempest of a quarter-century before when he had denounced Sparks as an editor of Washington. Soon he had over twelve hundred errors, no one significant in itself, but together, as Laboulaye put it, "they give another aspect to the book, for here truly are the most original and the most American expressions of Franklin, which an inept correction has effaced to replace them with platitudes." Of more importance, Bigelow found that the last eight pages had never appeared in print, though through no fault of Jared Sparks. By July he had the text in shape. Before the year was out, he had completed his introduction and placed the whole in the hands of his publishers.[7]

When *The Autobiography of Benjamin Franklin* edited by John Bigelow was issued in the spring of 1868, congratulations poured in from every quarter, except from the London *Athenaeum* whose review was written by the owner of the Sparks plates. Bigelow was delighted by the general reaction. It spiced the calm pleasures of his country life without interrupting its ordered routine. In the hours formerly reserved for Franklin, he now worked on his biography of Fénelon and on articles for the New York Historical Society and for magazines. The daily writing stint completed, he moved from the library to the farm, to the three hundred and fifteen acres he had bought, a half hour's walk from his village home. Cutting wood, draining marshes, blasting rock and removing stone, building a farmhouse, sheds, fences — all that he found useful, productive work. Everything about his place satisfied him, except the smallness of the family residence, and plans to correct that were under way. But before they could materialize he had to use the money earmarked for building to buy up the old homestead at Malden and other essentials for his brothers who had been forced into bankruptcy. Thereafter he contented himself with additions to his house.

The two years at "The Squirrels" were punctuated by brief trips into the world. On those occasions Bigelow would seek out his literary and religious acquaintances in preference to his political friends, for temporarily politics had ceased to charm him. He was ready to campaign for Seward in 1868 if he would run for the Presidency, but he knew there was no chance of that. As for Grant, Bigelow wished the General would realize how much greater would be his reputation if he refused the Presidency.[8] Nevertheless, when Grant accepted the nomination, Bigelow decided to vote for him, but he would do no campaigning. Instead he returned to his literary life, enjoying his new membership in the Century Club, accepting rather indifferently an LL.D. from Union College, writing brief religious tracts for the New Church Society. As never before he studied his own motives, subjectively aware of the disappointment that so often followed efforts to win applause or admiration and of the ineffable joy that followed any exercise of brotherly love.

Yet there was danger in too much introspection. By 1869, again ready for action, Bigelow considered purchasing the *Commercial Advertiser*. He would take young John Hay in with him and teach him free-trade doctrines, he decided, beginning negotiations. But when one stockholder held out for twice what Bigelow was prepared to pay, the plan fell through. Soon he decided to move to Europe to avoid, since he could not improve, contemporary American ideals. Grant, for whom he had voted, was already passing out gifts in a way that made "Johnson's conduct loom up with distinction." In New York the Tweed Ring was so blatantly powerful that most businessmen and politicians, regardless of party, compromised with it. More personally, Bigelow was irritated by newspaper repetitions of the old charges that his policy towards France in Mexico had been weak. Much as he desired, to use his favorite phrase, "to root out his proprium," to look indifferently upon personal reputation, he was too much of the world to succeed. He cared very greatly that he and Seward should appear in a true light, and to that end he engaged in a wordy, fruitless newspaper controversy.[9]

All told, Bigelow was glad to be sailing for Europe on June 1. "The Squirrels" was not equipped as a winter residence, and he had been living in New York, spending too much, constantly being invited out, consulted about politics, asked for help in getting jobs, called on to comment about books and articles on events with which he had been connected. In Germany he could get ahead with some great book, could live more comfortably and could educate his children better at half the cost. But he postponed sailing in order to attend in Chicago a meeting of the Chicago, Rock Island and Pacific Railroad stockholders and to continue West to celebrate the opening of the line at Omaha.

Just as he returned to New York, Henry J. Raymond, founder and editor of the *New York Times,* died. Within a month Bigelow took his place as managing editor, his wife and his friends overcoming his reluctance by the argument, as Henry Ward Beecher expressed it the day of Raymond's funeral, that Bigelow was trained for journalism and though he "might make a great book of some sort, that was an experiment." A few of his friends expressed some misgivings because the *Times,* with thirty-six employees, was enormous compared to the *Post.* Bigelow had no doubts on that score; "It is proposed that I should edit the *Times* not that the *Times* should edit me," he wrote Sumner.[10] And most people expected him to do just that. The *Commercial Advertiser,* congratulating the *Times,* recalled how Bigelow had put the *Post's* finances in order, and added:

He is not the man to "play second fiddle" in the editorial orchestra. He will wield the *baton* or there will be no music from his French horn. The world knows Mr. Bigelow is an accomplished writer. His State papers show that, his literary and political writings are models.

The *Independent,* a Radical Republican paper, wrote the most glowing tribute:

It was an eminent loss to journalism when Mr. Bigelow laid aside his editorial pen. In any list of six of the ablest editors of this country Mr. Bigelow's name must have an honored place. It was under his administration of the *Evening Post* that that journal rose to its first great political eminence and financial success. We mean no disparagement of the *Post's* present able conductors when we say that their sheet was never more rich, sparkling and readable than when Mr. Bigelow daily lent to it the point of his own keen pen. Tall, manly, and elegant in person; courtly and affable in manners; statesmanlike in the cast of his mind; clear, terse, and ringing in his style; positive in his convictions; unimpeachable in his character and motives: — Mr. John Bigelow will find himself the successful occupant of a chair which he ought not willingly to exchange for a foreign ministry or a United States senatorship.

Other papers spoke favorably of him as an able writer, and a man of strength and integrity. In addition, the *Commonwealth* noted: "There were some also who felt keenly his assaults, who have not even now forgotten their sting." [11]

Bigelow's first editorial on August 3 discussed the uses and abuses of journalism, indicating that the *Times* would have no space for sensationalism, rumors, or personal attacks used as weapons to defeat ideas. Setting a journalistic standard unknown in New York, Bigelow concluded:

The American Press is responsible, to a very considerable degree, for the administration of this Government. The laws of our Congress and the policy of our Executive are, and necessarily must be, largely shaped by the Fourth Estate. This was never more true perhaps than now. If the Press is true to itself our government will always and under whatever party dispensation be a success, and our legislation always wise and humane.

He abolished the "Minor Topics" — "I was sick of the twaddle"; he dismissed the day editor who was out to make trouble, having desired to become managing editor; he made other changes on the staff. He was the head and he intended to have full control.[12]

The grumbling began. Bigelow's notions of journalism appeared antiquated to some of his colleagues and his demands impossible to meet. He himself found working to midnight contrary to the habits of a lifetime, and the cold antagonism in the office oppressed him. Soon the position which he had accepted with mixed eagerness and doubt became a chore. George Jones, chief stockholder and guardian of the Raymond interests, objected to the changes in the staff, to the rigorous correction of reporters' English, to the mounting costs of the paper, and most of all to Bigelow's efforts to mold opinion rather than to cater to it. Bigelow's inside track to the White House was excellent, Jones thought, for through it he could give people what they wanted; but to use a newspaper as Bigelow was, to campaign for a national university which would bring together outstanding scholars of all fields, was pointless.[13]

Yet it was Bigelow's relationship with Grant that made his brief interlude on the *Times* unhappily memorable. He had met the General occasionally during the past two years, and found, as soon as he became the editor of an important organ, that Grant sought him out whenever he came to New York. Hence Bigelow's editorial of August 7, on taxes, was commonly accepted as a semiofficial announcement of government policy, and when it was learned that Grant saw Bigelow in

New York on August 19, another exposition of the President's views was shortly expected. Jay Gould saw in this his opportunity. For several months he had been quietly bulling gold with the intention of cornering the market. Through Abel Corbin, the President's unprincipled brother-in-law, he had approached Grant, impressed the impecunious President with his wealth and power, and convinced him that the nation's welfare depended upon a rise in the price of gold and maintenance of cheap, plentiful currency until the fall crops were moved. By mid-August he was almost ready for the final plunge, but first the country must be told that the government intended to boost the price of gold.

Thereupon Gould had his fellow conspirator, Corbin, prepare an article to be planted in the *Times* on "Grant's Financial Policy." He asked James McHenry, the railroad magnate, an acquaintance of Bigelow, to present the article to Bigelow as written by "one in the intimate confidence of the President." Bigelow accepted it on face value, knowing nothing of Gould's connection with it, of the months of intrigue that had brought Grant around to the Gould-Fisk views, or of the gigantic plans to corner gold. Presuming that the article must have value, else McHenry would not have said that Grant himself hoped to see it in the *Times*, he ordered it put in type even before reading it. He often did that, finding it a timesaver to wait for the proof sheets before correcting well-recommended contributions. However, as soon as he glanced at the proof of this article, he knew that something was wrong. Quickly he passed it to Caleb C. Norvell, the financial editor and an old-timer on the paper, who confirmed his fear that the article was a "plant," intended to bull gold. Norvell deleted the last paragraph, which predicted that gold would rise to 135 or 140, and added a sentence to the effect that the government might sell 5-20 bonds for gold. Undoubtedly the wiser course would have been total suppression. Yet Bigelow was satisfied with the emasculated editorial which appeared on August 25, because it kept McHenry friendly to the *Times* without, Bigelow believed, compromising the paper.[14]

What followed is familiar. On September 23 gold soared to 162½ and the next day, an ill-famed Friday, Wall Street was in turmoil. Ugly rumors of what was behind the crisis swept through the turbulent crowds. At Bigelow's order, the *Times*, lashing the conspirators, demanded that the government put a stop to the talk that the Treasury and the Executive were in the plot and would not interfere. It carried another strong editorial on September 25; other papers issued equally vigorous and even more damning charges against the government, and abruptly that day the government sold $4,000,000 in gold. The price dropped; the corner was smashed.

At the height of the Black Friday excitement, Bigelow and Jones had their final clash. As of September 25, Bigelow ordered his name removed from the payroll. Angry, disillusioned, faced with the fact that journalism was no longer for him, he saw nothing to do but to pocket his feelings. Only to personal friends did he admit that he had made a mistake, that if he had followed his convictions rather than the well-meaning advice that was showered on him, he would have avoided two unpleasant months. "Richard's himself again," he wrote to Huntingdon on October 3, and to Mrs. Eames he wrote:

> I was a fool, I admit it, but do me the justice also to admit on your part that there was never so great a fool who got over his folly quicker. I was in the *Times* just two months by the calendar, but it seemed two centuries by my feelings. . . . I was never in such an uncongenial position in my life. The surroundings of the office were such as a man like Raymond would naturally make — I believe in moral spheres — and I discovered the first day that I had no sympathy with anything about the concern.

How he was implicated in the Black Friday conspiracy Bigelow was not to know until in 1874 when in Brentano's he chanced upon Frederic Hudson's *Journalism in the United States from 1690 to 1872* and looked in it to see if he was mentioned. There for the first time he learned that Gould had sent him the editorial which he issued in revised form on August 25, 1869, for he was abroad when the scandal was aired in Congress.[15] Bigelow, all unknowing, had been caught in a web of trickery; and the *Times*, without intent, had been of service to the conspirators. In 1869 what Bigelow knew of the scandal he summarized in a letter to Mrs. Eames. Obviously he had no idea, then, that he personally was connected with it.

> The recent raid of Jay Gould & Co on the gold market has been very disastrous to individuals but to the country at large it has revealed the endless mischief incident to our variable standard of value and has converted thousands who could only be converted through their cupidity and selfishness, to a conviction that a fixed standard was the best, and that the quicker the legal tender act was repealed the better for all. There was an attempt to get Grant into the gold ring formed to run up gold and there is no doubt that he was near being caught but I don't think he was longer in discovering the trap than most honest men would have been, I believe that it is no longer questioned that he did discover it in time and avoided it.[16]

Nor did other editors even hint at the charge of conspiracy (which was to be made six years later) in their explanation of Bigelow's sudden retirement. He caused "dissatisfaction among the old *attaches* of the paper, while his management lacked that vigor and skill which the journal needs," said the *Daily Democrat*. The New York *Spirit of the Times* thought that he had "outlived the years of stern and anxious work." Other papers repeated those charges or mentioned his "ruthless slaughter" of old employees. On the other hand, the Philadelphia *Morning Post* thought: "Perhaps there never was a managing editor so *critically criticized* as Mr. Bigelow has been . . .," while many agreed with the Syracuse *Journal:* "In some respects he would have elevated American journalism, and short as was his period of control, the *Times* during the last ten days of his control, had already begun to exhibit the effect of his conscientious editorship and wide knowledge of men and affairs." *The Citizen and Round Table* summed up its opinion in a sentence: "It seems that straightforwardness and directness of purpose are not always palatable." [17]

Long before the talk died down, Bigelow was silently engrossed in organizing documents relative to his ministry.

But such a life, he realized, could not continue long. Either he must take a job merely to make money, which he had promised himself never again to do, or he must cut expenses. The latter was almost impossible. For some years the cost of educating and providing comfortably for his six children, ranging in age from one-year-old Flora to Grace who was now eighteen, would be a heavy burden. The sensible solution, as he had realized in 1869, was to move where his income would purchase more then it could in America. So Bigelow decided to go to Germany, and on April 30, 1870, the family sailed from New York.

For the next three years Berlin was to be home. There Bigelow watched with the keen interest of a man versed in French domestic conditions the brewing of the Franco-Prussian war. He had little sympathy for the French. He thought their government rotten and their upper classes weak. The Germans, on the other hand, won his admiration. ". . . The German race is destined gradually to dominate the Latin race just as the Northern states have dominated the Southern in the U. S. . . . it is the order of Providence that in due time Russia should go to the Bospherus, Austria to the Mediterranean and Prussia to the Atlantic and Mediterranean." By September 3 Berlin was celebrating the surrender of MacMahon and the capture of the Emperor Napoleon III. Bunting waved from every building; shouting crowds surged through the streets; that night huge torches lighted the city as the rejoicing swelled. The historian, George Bancroft, serving as Minister to Germany, looked out upon the scene weighted with consequence for the future, and remarked, merely, that it beat the *Arabian Nights*.[18]

Bancroft and Bigelow, acquaintances of almost thirty years standing, were frequently together in Berlin. Bancroft introduced Bigelow everywhere, especially to congenial English-speaking Germans of official and university circles. Dr. Karl Abel, a youthful, quick-witted scholar, a philologist and Berlin correspondent of the London *Times*, became a close friend. So, too, did George de Bunsen, liberal, free-trade member of the Reichstag, later to be ostracized and ruined by Bismarck. Frequently Bigelow took trips with one or the other of these friends, attended lectures and parties with them, and through them met Germans whose interests paralleled his. He became acquainted with the historians Johann Droyson, Theodor Mommsen, Ernst Curtius, Leopold Ranke, and the scientists Herman Helmhotz and Justus von Liebig.

The more Bigelow saw of these Germans the more he was impressed by the thoroughness of their education, their application and their high resolve. Many of his opinions he relayed in letters to Whitelaw Reid for use in the *Tribune*. He explained why he thought that the United States, Russia, and Germany would be the three great nations of the twentieth century; he described the progress of the war of 1870 as it appeared to an American inside Germany; he sent a pamphlet on Germany's military system "as the U. S. by her system of comparatively general if not universal education is better prepared than any other nation to profit by this example. . . ." And he commented: "If I were the conductor of a public journal in America I should set to work at once to educate our people up to the idea of making a knowledge of the arts of war a part of every young man's education." [19]

In July 1871, when the Franco-Prussian war was a fresh memory, when Europe was still a hotbed of international and intranational fear and suspicion, and before the Third French Republic was formally established, Bigelow published his provocative *France and Hereditary Monarchy*. The thesis was dynamite coated with objective, dispassionate words. Bigelow's intent was to discredit Thiers, the mainspring of the new French government, and to deplore the effects of the Catholic Church and of a hereditary monarchy. Had he inveighed against Thiers, or against the Church, or against inherited power, he would have aroused opposition; but when he attacked all three, in a biased, easy-to-read booklet of eighty pages, he was seeking serious trouble.

In brief, he charged Thiers with more concern for his own authority than for republicanism, with such fear of the people that he used the National Assembly, elected solely on the issue of making peace with Germany, to set up a new government instead of calling for the election of a Constituent Assembly, and with designs to re-establish the Bourbons and to maintain such cordial relations with the Papal hierarchy that it would in effect control France. He used the treatment meted out to the Paris commune in the spring of '71 as confirmation of his thesis. The time had come, he declared, when Frenchmen must choose their form of government. To help them reach the right decision, he said, his book was written, and he strongly advised the election of a chief executive at frequent intervals, separation of Church and State, and compulsory civil and military education as "the means of contending successfully with the powers of superstition and priest-craft, by which the great mass of her people are held in thrall." [20]

The effect of the book was not what Bigelow had expected. His French friends were indignant. They disliked his thesis, his attitude, and the timing of his pamphlet. His English friends were scarcely more cordial. Americans on the whole viewed the book more calmly, as they could afford to do, but some reviewers thought Bigelow had turned communist or else utterly failed to comprehend the evil of Parisian radicalism and the irresponsible leadership they believed Paris invariably had given to revolutionary movements, while Catholics resented his diatribes against their Church.

Bigelow had as great a desire for approval as most men have; yet he was glad that he had published his views. The exposure of an evil which he believed, rightly or wrongly, the world could not afford to ignore was more important to him than approval. He was convinced that a clash between Protestantism and Catholicism was inevitable, and he feared that the center of the struggle would be America, where, because of the large Irish immigration, the two religious groups were more evenly balanced than in any European country. For that reason, a year later he added to his anti-Catholic utterances an article entitled "Was St. Peter Ever at Rome?" which appeared anonymously in the *Galaxy* after *Harper's* and *Scribner's* preferred not to handle it. The question at issue was: "Have all the nations of the earth for the last eighteen centuries been the victims of a gigantic fraud?" Bigelow did not presume to answer in so many words, but he marshaled all the evidence which European scholarship had recently unearthed to support the affirmative, and he presented it solely to awaken his countrymen to what he conceived to be the danger of Catholicism to democracy, the danger of exalting ends over means.

Somehow the months went by and the great book he had intended did not materialize. The fact was that he was temperamentally unfit for years of patient concentration on one topic. There were too many interesting people, too many new ideas and viewpoints to distract his attention. It was not in him to stand apart from the issues of the day; he could not forgo companionships; he could not neglect his children, nor could he curtail the time he devoted to his personal religious study. His adolescent sons, now away from him in German schools, must have the opportunity to profit from the experience he had gained through trial and error; they deserved the sort of advice he in his youth had missed. It took time for him to decide what to emphasize and to express his thoughts in terms meaningful to them. In summary, he told them that no man or boy could predict results; no one could control anything but his motives; therefore they alone should be the subject of continuous scrutiny. If from the pursuit of worthy motives, honor and power should result, they should be prized as offering larger opportunities for doing good. But position and power as ends in themselves or sought for unworthy motives were as chaff. "Knowledge is not truth unless sought from good motives and for good purposes." [21]

Shortly after the boys were enrolled in school, he sent them specific guidance for their daily lives. The sum of the advice which he had received in 1831 when at thirteen years of age he departed for college was not to gamble. That advice he passed on to his sons, commenting: "I regard gaming as the most depraving of the vices to which one can become addicted. . . . The gambler's pleasure is purchased only by the corresponding misfortune of his neighbor." To that he added rules governing physical and mental health: retire early, do little mental work in the evening, avoid coffee, tea, beer, and tobacco, take a cold bath daily.

God gives us daily all the strength we require for our daily duties. This allowance is so divinely apportioned to our needs that whoever resorts to stimulants to increase it, commits precisely the offense by which Adam fell and repeats the folly of the unbelieving Israelites who disobediently stored up Manna beyond their daily needs only to breed worms and offensive odours.

Beware of the ambition of reading fast or much. It is the most certain way you can adopt of being a long time in learning a very little. You should read to get new ideas and not distractions. [On whatever you read meditate and reflect.] Reading without meditation is like eating without digestion.

Among all the forces and graces of your characters be sure that truthfulness ranks with the first. . . . The great need throughout the world today in every calling, in public and in private life, is truthful men who are proof against all temptation to deceive and betray.

Beware how you talk about yourselves. You can converse upon no topic upon which you are likely to appear to so little advantage, upon which you will find it more difficult to avoid wilful misrepresentations, or upon which what you have to say is less likely to edify your audiences.

As to their friends: "Cultivate no society that does not receive you socially upon equal terms." Within that group seek the older, abler, and better-educated lads whose company will stimulate and bring out the best in you. In games and work alike keep always a clear distinction between the important and the unimportant.

Accustom yourself to yield in unimportant matters and to give pleasure whenever you can by self-denial. But be rock adamantine, where the rights of others are entrusted to your care or where a duty is involved.[22]

Though like Polonius a shrewd man of the world who had tasted success and knew the means to reach it, Bigelow differed vastly from that noble lord, for Bigelow spoke with a morality that decried expediency. His were the words of a man who had found something more to life than wealth or position or reputation. His point of view and his acts were, in fact, increasingly determined by his religious beliefs. On November 9, 1871, he noted in his diary:

I wish to consecrate the rest of my life to efforts to make my fellow creatures realize *1st* that they are accountable for their conduct to God and not to priests or popes — that is my idea of the true Church and *secondly* that they owe loyalty to all who compose the community in which they live and not to any one man dynasty or race; and that is my idea of a Republic.

After two years in Germany Bigelow began to think of all he was missing at home, of all the activities useful to himself and to others in which he might engage. He decided that the place for him was in his own country working with his own countrymen. Just where in America that place would be, he was no more sure than he had been in 1867. Probably Washington would suit them best. In an amusing letter to Mrs. Eames he described the problem thus:

I do not feel sure that Washington will suit us but what can one do. I can't bear the idea of settling in New York where wealth only is power nor in Boston where everyone in society seems always undergoing a sort of competitive examination to show how much less book learning he has than his examiners, nor Baltimore where the talent of the people is exhausted in eating and drinking or in Phil. where it seems to be exhausted in sleeping. Still less can one endure any of the smaller towns where all the gaiety consists in sewing societies lectures by Greeley and Geo. F. Train monthly prayer meetings and occasional funerals.[23]

However, upon returning to America in the spring of '73, he went directly to "The Squirrels," there to relive, in a sense, the literary-country life of 1867 and 1868. He made progress in arranging his Haitian proverbs and in distilling his own philosophy into his interpretations of them. He wrote upon a variety of contemporary problems for the *Evening Post* and the *Tribune*. As in '67 his major literary work centered about Benjamin Franklin. He took his edition of Franklin's autobiography, which ended in the year 1757, appended to it carefully selected passages from Franklin's writings to complete the story of his life, and in 1874 issued in three volumes *The Life of Benjamin Franklin Written by Himself*. The work won immediate acclaim as well for the standard it set in accuracy of editing and biographical writing as for the subject matter.[24]

But Bigelow had not as yet, eight years after the war, found a niche that fully satisfied him.

CHAPTER 20

In Politics with Tilden

[*1870–1885*]

B Y 1874 Bigelow was again active in politics; for the next decade state and national issues were to take first place in his interests.

His personal attitude towards Grant had shifted to hostility in 1870 after the President refused to appoint Bigelow's son to West Point on the grounds that he must reserve his appointments for the sons of "deserving veterans." Yet in 1872 Bigelow returned to America just long enough to vote a second time for him. He disliked Grant; he disliked "his fondness for segars, for presents, and for rich and honorable friends"; he thought his action in regard to Santo Domingo inexcusable; yet he believed that by and large he had made a good record as President. His administration had cut the debt, had settled the Alabama claims, had dealt firmly with the Mormons, wisely with the Indians, and had passed the Fifteenth Amendment.[1]

Though Bigelow's sympathies lay with the liberal Republicans, with Schurz and Curtis and Adams, he was too well-versed in politics to think that they could lead a successful revolt in 1872. Bigelow's letter upon that subject so impressed Senator Morgan that in January, without permission, he had it published in the *Times* and had marked copies sent to every Senator and Representative. In it Bigelow predicted the sure defeat of the liberals not only in the next election but for a long time to come if they joined forces with the Democrats. The Democrats would use them, he said, but would use them for their own ends. Even if the impossible happened and the party won, the reformers would find themselves eclipsed, a minority of nonentities in a triumphing party of politicians. He thought 1872 not the time to bolt parties or to form new ones, not when the masses, still proud of their soldier-President, were sure to re-elect him. Nor were the Democrats prepared to make good use of political power. Give them four more years, Bigelow urged, to purge themselves of outworn aristocratic elements and to develop a positive policy. By 1876 the Civil War would be far in the past; then the old, old issues of sound money, the tariff, and the proper sphere of government would cause new alignments. Men who had left the Democratic party in order to fight slavery would have reason to return to their old loyalty and once again the historic majority party would be ready to take control.

When the Greeley boom developed and the liberals supported him, Bigelow was torn between amusement and disgust:

> Greeley is an interesting curiosity which everyone likes to see and to show and in whom we all feel a certain kind of national pride, but I do not think anyone can seriously believe in his fitness for any administrative position whatever. If they do, they know as little of him as he knows of himself.[2]

And when Grant routed Greeley in November '72 Bigelow was glad, because that, he believed, dealt the final blow to Southern interests, which had hoped to regain through the ballot what they had lost on the battlefield.[3]

Yet within two years Bigelow was ready to join any anti-Grant movement. By 1874 he could no longer stomach the graft of the administration or the third-term talk which he considered outrageous in principle and in present fact utterly evil. First he worked within his own party, trying in February 1874 to have Senator Morgan get Grant himself to quash the dangerous third-term talk. Nothing resulting from that, he went to Tilden, who was seeking the Democratic nomination for the governorship of New York. With a shrewd appeal to patriotism, party, and Tilden's own political future, Bigelow persuaded him to insert into the state Democratic platform the anti-third-term plank which Bigelow had written. So, two years before Grant's term expired, the Democrats raised an issue upon which thousands of Republicans could unite with them. It was a clever move of Bigelow's and he made the most of it. He secured the Republican *Evening Post's* neutrality upon the issue and the active support of the *Tribune*, prevailing upon it to open its columns to anti-third-term articles, most of which Bigelow wrote.[4]

He was still a Republican, however. He felt flattered in September 1874 when told that a unanimous nomination as a Republican candidate for Congress was his if he gave the word. Yet eleven days later when the offer was repeated, he refused it. Upon reflection he had realized how slim were his chances of defeating a Democrat in his district as well as how near he was to bolting the Republican party, for Tilden now controlled the New York Democrats, and where Tilden was, Bigelow felt sure there would be honesty. Only recently he had written to the *Post* that Tilden "had the audacity a few years ago to proclaim to his party that public office was a trust not a perquisite." [5] Moreover, he was indignant at the continued silence of the New York Republicans upon the third-term issue. In declining the Republican nomination, he wrote:

> . . . I could not with propriety accept any candidature involving even an implied approval of the election of any President of the U. S. for three consecutive terms. I think it was a grave error in the State convention to remain silent upon that subject, especially after the action taken by the Convention at Utica and I think it ungenerous not to say ungrateful in the President to embarrass the party to which he owes all his important positions in life, by persisting in his ominous silence on this subject.
>
> Messrs Conkling, Morgan and the other eminent statesmen whose counsel prevailed in our State Convention may have had light which justified them in letting things drift; I have none and I do not propose to drift one inch in that direction. Were all the wisdom and all the statesmanship and all the patriotism of all the Presidents from Washington to Grant concentrated into a single candidate — and I do not say they are not in Grant — I would not connive at his reelection for a third term. I celebrate the anniversaries of 1776 not the anniversaries of 1775 — the first year of popular not the last year of dynastic rule among us. You are sufficiently well-acquainted with me to know that I could not consent to run with only one of my party traces drawing. I dare say you think me more nice than wise. Perhaps I am. Whether I am or not, you will readily find a candidate not so nice and a great deal wiser. That will be the sort of man you should nominate for this canvass.[6]

Two days later he again called on his good friend Senator Morgan, the Republican National Chairman, to outline once more his plans for blocking a third term, but Morgan, though interested, was reluctant to commit himself. Hence when the November state election brought Tilden a smashing victory, Bigelow was delighted. Its significance, it was generally conceded, went far beyond New York State, for Tilden's success, coupled with the nation-wide gains of the Democrats, pricked the third-term bubble. To Mrs. Eames, Tilden's friend as well as his own, Bigelow wrote on November 20:

> The prominance he has as the governor who upset Grant's apple cart in the largest and most influential State in the Union, renders his nomination for the Presidency almost inevitable. If elected, he will so organize the Democratic party that they may

reasonably count upon the control of the country for the next twenty years — or at least till the struggle between Romanism and Protestantism comes upon us. . . .

Significantly, Whitelaw Reid congratulated Bigelow upon Tilden's victory: "No man," he wrote, "has done more than you to bring about the result." [7]

In retrospect it seems inevitable that Bigelow was to find through Tilden the opportunity for useful work for which he had come home. As early as November 8, 1874, his change of party allegiance was foreshadowed in a letter to a friend in which he wrote: "Though there are not many men in the country who had more to do — humanly speaking — with the organization of the Republican party than I had, I cannot say that I contemplate the prospect of its defeat with regret. The fact is its raison d'etre has ceased." [8] He believed that in the coming years men would divide politically according to their positions upon financial questions. If so, he would be with the Democrats whose economic theories he had always endorsed. Moreover, his friend Tilden was now national leader of the Democratic party. It did not matter to Bigelow that Tilden was cold and self-centered while Bigelow was warmly interested in his fellows, that Tilden was rich and liked wealth while Bigelow was not and cared not, that Tilden had channeled his life into one deep current while Bigelow had let his flow out in ever-widening circles. Nor did it matter that Tilden devoted the full strength of his intellect to the knowable and the practical while Bigelow looked upon the material world through his conception of the Unknowable. What bound them together was a common political philosophy shared for thirty-five years: belief in democracy, equality of opportunity, a government of laws that kept centralization to a minimum, and in economical, efficacious, honest administration.

Tilden had won the governorship on the strength of his successful battle against the Tweed Ring and on the expectation that he would continue to fight crookedness throughout the state. Few citizens, however, expected him to attack New York's oldest, most notorious ring, which regularly, year after year, extracted fortunes from the Erie Canal — the Canal Ring, headed by Denison, Belden, the Lords, and Johnson. But they did expect some action from him. At first they were disappointed. It was characteristic of Tilden to begin his term quietly and to make no idle threats against any entrenched interest. In thirty years of a successful law practice he had learned the value of caution and the importance of proof.

So he moved slowly, while privately and at his own expense he engaged an engineer, Elkanah Sweet, to dig up data about the Canal

Ring. Then suddenly, dramatically, satisfied that he had precise facts and a sure strategy for their use, he declared war. In a vigorous message to the legislature on March 19, 1875, he denounced the Ring and called for the immediate creation of a nonpartisan investigating commission, authorized to subpoena witnesses for private examination and granted a $30,000 appropriation for expenses. Once he received legislative sanction, he appointed two Republicans and two Democrats to the Commission: Bigelow, whom he asked to be Chairman, Alexander E. Orr, Daniel Magone, Jr., and John D. Van Buren, Jr.

To them was left the task of determining the validity of Tilden's charges. For almost a year the four Commissioners labored. The first part of their job involved a physical strain which few men of Bigelow's fifty-seven years would care to undertake. Day after day they examined construction projects along the Canal, on one occasion walking ten miles in the face of a freezing northwester, on another putting in a stretch of eleven hours with time out only for a hastily swallowed sandwich. In vain contractors tried to steer them to display walls, or earnestly warned them of the smallpox on a near-by houseboat. These four men intended to measure up to the hopes of reformers. Through Elkanah Sweet they were initiated into the mysteries of canal engineering and construction. With their own hands they learned to take apart new walls and to measure the worth of the crumbling stuff that passed for cement, to detect at a glance the walls that had an imposing facing but no lining or headers, to spot the places where workers were tearing down honest bulwarks to be replaced by cheaper, shoddy makeshifts.[9]

In June, their personal examination completed, they started taking private testimony in the Senate library in Albany, and on July 31, after three-and-a-half months of working five days a week to uncover a deliberate, long-established thieving business in which "the horizon of fraud recedes on every side as we approach it," their first report was completed. It was only a partial report, however, and the findings were kept from the public and the Ring's friends. Eleven other partial reports were submitted to Tilden before the final one was ready on February 14, 1876 — so long had it taken to collect specific proof that the canal system cost $28,500,000 more than it had earned, that specifically named state officers and contractors had robbed New York. The Commissioners offered a simple remedy: prosecute the thieves, center responsibility for canal work, and pass penal laws to cope with any future corruption.[10]

From Bigelow's viewpoint, their work merited the superlative of his vocabulary: it was useful. Though he had learned a lot about canal building that he had no desire to know, though the stolen money was never fully recovered nor were the Ring's leaders properly punished, at least temporarily corruption was ended, the Ring was deflated, citizens of the state were aware, for the moment, of their responsibility for the honesty of their government, and Tilden, hailed throughout the country as an effective reformer, was well on his way to the White House.

Whether Tilden would become a candidate for the Presidency was, so far as Bigelow could see, entirely dependent upon one factor, his health. In April when Bigelow began work as a Commissioner, he heard that Tilden had recently had a touch of paralysis. Yet "in spite of these warnings, it seems to be impossible to turn him from his course of life which is self-destruction. His mind is insanely absorbed with his public duties. . . . He seems to require their excitement as much as the inebriate requires his brandy. The moment he is compelled to suspend thought & talk upon those subjects, his face grows pale his eyes lustreless, his features expressionless & he has the exhausted air of a man pining in vain for sleep. . . . The danger of his becoming a drivelling paralytic in the midst of his great work is now quite imminent." [11]

No one could make Tilden lessen the pace. His friends could worry about him, could prescribe exercise, relaxation, pills — usually he would be willing to try the pills — and could try to relieve him of some of his burdens. It was on that score that in July 1875 E. K. Apgar, Deputy Secretary of the Treasury, urged Bigelow to run on the Democratic ticket for the position as New York's Secretary of State. Bigelow's first reaction was a shocked refusal. He saw no advantage to himself or to anybody else in such action. He was still officially a Republican and as a Republican he had been appointed to the Canal Commission. He could expect little support from Democrats if he shifted his party just in time to run for office. He would certainly alienate many of his Republican friends. Worst of all, he might undermine public confidence in the impartiality of the Commission, which at the time of this conversation was not half through its work, and thereby ruin its opportunity to do good. All of that was true, Apgar conceded, but Tilden wanted the counsel Bigelow could give if he was Secretary of State. Moreover, Tilden meant to capitalize upon a reputation as a reformer; with Bigelow's name on the ticket, people would be convinced that the reform program was to continue. Bigelow might also, Apgar urged, swing to Tilden the vote of New York liberal Republicans. Finally Bigelow agreed to think it over. [12]

On September 4 Tilden broached the subject but nothing was settled. Two days later, on Monday, September 6, while Bigelow was on the cars headed for Albany, he was told by General Sharpe that the Republican leaders wanted to nominate him as Comptroller at the convention scheduled to meet on the eighth. "It is impossible," said Bigelow, briefly outlining his reasons. Sharpe thereupon departed, only to return a few minutes later with Chester Arthur, Collector of the Port, who likewise urged Bigelow to accept or at least not to give a final "no" at the moment. Again Bigelow refused, this time explaining in detail why he could not accept such a nomination. Since he made his refusal without reservations, he saw no need to state that the Democrats had already approached him about the top place on their ticket and that he would accept their nomination as Secretary of State unless he and Tilden decided it would hurt the Investigating Commission. So far as he was concerned, negotiations with the Republicans had been begun and ended within an hour.[13]

They, however, thought otherwise. The next morning Hugh J. Hastings wired him: CONVENTION WILL NOMINATE YOU BY ACCLAMATION FOR COMPTROLLER. WILL YOU ACCEPT? Bigelow's reply — UNDER NO CONCEIVABLE CIRCUMSTANCES — brought Sharpe to his Albany office that afternoon. Bigelow *had* to run, said the General; G. W. Curtis, E. D. Morgan, and the other leaders would not take "no" for an answer. It was a hard moment for Bigelow. Morgan had been much closer to him for the last twenty years than Tilden; yet the choice had to be between issues, not personalities. For the third time Bigelow refused the Republican offer. He repeated that his close relations with Tilden were imperative to the success of the Commission and to the cause of reform. Should he enter into active political opposition, he could not co-operate with Tilden nor could another be appointed to his place on the Commission at this late date without jeopardizing its success. Moreover, his acceptance of such a nomination would redound to his dishonor and to the Republicans' hurt. How could they answer the cries of "cheap politics!" which would greet this apparent effort to transfer to the Republican party the credit for uncovering the Canal thieves? That credit, he told Sharpe, belonged to Tilden, without whose "firmness and courage we should none of us have accomplished anything." [14]

If Bigelow's refusal to serve on their ticket annoyed Republicans, his acceptance ten days later of the Democratic nomination for the Secretaryship of State incensed them. Bigelow became the chief target for campaign abuse. He had the Ring crowd and all the friends of Presidential aspirants other than Tilden ranged against him. A blow at Bigelow was a blow at Tilden. Moreover, strict party Democrats objected, with cause, to an erstwhile Republican getting preference to themselves, and the Catholic vote, closely allied to Tammany, was sure to turn against this man who time and again had put himself on record as an opponent of Catholicism. Nor did Republicans let the anti-Tilden and Catholic Democrats do all the fighting. They asserted truthfully that Bigelow had accepted as a Republican the Chairmanship of the Canal Commission and now, within six months, was seeking another position as a Democrat. They berated him for dangling the Republicans for a month solely to cripple their organization, letting them think he was with them all that time before declining their offer of the Comptrollership. That, of course, was untrue. The most they had a right to say was that he failed to inform them of his intention to run for the Democrats, which was a piece of information he could not easily divulge since the position was formally tendered to him only after the Republican convention had adjourned. Nevertheless, liberal Republicans, former friends like Carl Schurz and G. W. Curtis, sneered at the self-seeking motives beneath his lip-service to reform.

The *New York Times* led the attack upon him in a series of vicious, personal slanders which perfectly illustrated the type of journalism Bigelow had tried to eradicate just six years before from that very paper. Not once did the editors analyze his record or give the slightest basis in fact for the statements they issued. Instead they indulged in an orgy of mud-slinging and innuendo. On October 4 they said: ". . . Mr. Bigelow stuck to the Republican party only so long as he could gain anything by it. . . . He 'ratted' as soon as he believed the other party was destined to win." Four days later they added another touch to their picture of the "miserable renegade": ". . . If they knew as much about him as we do, they would know that he is utterly unfitted to hold any place of trust or responsibility. They will find it out sooner or later, as we found it out — to our cost." The next day they took a fling at his diplomatic career, which no reading of the record could sustain:

> He simply sold himself to the highest bidder. . . . A foreign mission is the bait which tempted him, but people who remember the ridicule Mr. Bigelow brought upon the office of American Minister in Paris will not be anxious to see him sent back to repeat his exploits. Public opinion must be strangely demoralized before it can set the mark of its approval on a man who has betrayed every trust confided in him, and who finished his career by an unheard-of act of treachery.

On October 14 after Bigelow had set up no defense which they could attack but had quietly continued his regular duties on the Commission, the *Times* declared: "His entire conduct through this canvass proves him to be utterly destitute of principle. . . ." The week before election they redoubled their efforts to defeat him by elaborating their earlier hint of their own misfortune with him. Why, they asked, was he double-crossing the Republicans? ". . . There is no gold conspiracy or 'Black Friday' to help along just now. We must say, however, that when an opportunity of that kind did once present itself, Mr. Bigelow made the most of it." Vote for Frederick Seward, the Republican candidate and son of Bigelow's greatest benefactor, they urged, "rather than for John Bigelow, an unprincipled intriguer, and the great abettor of the gold panic of 1869." So, six years after the event and five years after a complete Congressional investigation of Black Friday, Bigelow was for the first and last time charged with improper dealings with the gold conspirators.[15]

The *Tribune*, for the most part, kept out of the conflict. It endorsed Bigelow as "a gentleman of the highest personal character; a Republican throughout the war and long afterwards, and a man of spotless record," but it was left to the *Evening Post*, like the *Times* a Republican paper and like the *Times* acquainted with Bigelow as an editor, to defend him. It should be noted, however, that in this campaign the *Post* wanted the Democratic ticket elected as a sign from the people that they approved a reform program regardless of party affiliation. Yet in any case Bryant would not have permitted malicious, unfounded vilifications of Bigelow to appear in his sheet. When on September 17 Bigelow received the unanimous Democratic nomination, the *Post* took its stand:

> Mr. Bigelow's varied accomplishments, his wide experience in public affairs, his high personal character and his freedom from every sort of "entangling alliance" which so often hampers men of good reputation when they enter into active political life, all mark him as preeminently fitted for the service of the people in a place of great responsibility.

Bryant admitted that Bigelow would be attacked for his political shift, but, he said, so far as his paper was concerned, "We have sufficient confidence in his judgment, prudence and fidelity to right to rest assured that since he has accepted the nomination offered to him he has acted for the best, and is entitled to the vote of every honest man in the state." Later, when the *Times's* offensive was in full swing, Bryant took pains to correct the morning paper's inaccuracies, to state precisely when and why Bigelow declined the Republican offer of a nomination, and to point out the irony of a Republican attack upon the past record of a man whom they had eagerly sought for their own ticket.[16]

On October 28 Bigelow delivered his only campaign speech.[17] The *Post* carried most of it in its news columns and on November 1 repeated, in an approving editorial, Bigelow's defense of his return to the Democratic party:

> Because I joined with those of my way of thinking in 1856 to resist the extension of slavery into free territory, and to maintain the integrity of the Union and the supremacy of the majority, does it follow that, after these ends are fully secured, I am to continue voting with the same men to maintain and perpetuate a worthless currency, to perpetuate a system of administration that has destroyed our foreign commerce, that has paralyzed our domestic trade and industry, and threatens the national credit?

November 3 was Election Day. Bigelow sat with Tilden until three o'clock the following morning and then went home, convinced that he was defeated, and too weary to care. The morning papers, however, conceded his victory though with a majority of only 14,500 over Frederick Seward. For the next two years Bigelow was to be New York's Secretary of State.

The duties of his new office were sufficiently light for Bigelow to devote much of his time first to the completion of the canal report and then to Tilden's campaign for the Presidency. Into the latter he poured all his energy and skill. The story has been told and retold — how Democrats and Republicans campaigned in the name of reform; how Samuel J. Tilden won the Democratic nomination and Rutherford B. Hayes the Republican; how both sides covered pivotal states with speeches, letters, money; how an unprecedented means was devised to count disputed returns; and how Hayes was inaugurated the nineteenth President of the United States on March 4, 1877. That Tilden was the choice of the people and received the requisite number of electoral votes is commonly conceded, but precisely how justice miscarried is not known. Was Hewitt too conciliatory for his job as Democratic Chairman? Did Tilden muff his great chance through lack of decisive courage? Did Grant capitalize on fears of army intervention? Was Chief Justice Bradley, when he cast the deciding vote for Hayes, corrupt? What Bigelow thought he for the most part told later in his biography of Tilden, in his editions of Tilden's writings, and in interviews. To him, Tilden was "Mr. President," and bitterly he wrote of the crime of '76, yet he could not place the blame for it upon any one person. In his estimation Congress, Hewitt, and Bradley shared the blame — and Tilden, too, he reluctantly admitted.

During the campaign itself Bigelow's place was behind the scenes, writing, publicizing, advising. Before the Democratic national convention met on June 27, 1876, he worked with Abram S. Hewitt, Manton Marble, Philip Dorsheimer, and others to insure a clear path for Tilden. He sketched an account of Tilden's life for Watterson's *Louisville Courier Journal*, wisely emphasizing the governor's lifelong opposition to centralized government, because Southerners who did not know much about Tilden would predominate at the convention. He served on the state committee which in April planned New York's part in the coming convention, and he was frankly delighted with the success of his intricate maneuver to get the right men on the committee for contested seats in order to assure Tilden the united backing of his native state.[18] In a heavy preconvention correspondence he renewed contacts with Southern and Northern Democrats with whom he had worked in the '40's and '50's. Moreover, through his efforts numbers of Republicans shifted to Tilden. Bryant, however, whose name and pen would have meant the most, he could not turn. Personally Bryant favored Tilden and probably voted for him, but the *Post*, long since deteriorating financially, could not afford to break with its party. Bryant's daughter Julia, in a letter to her uncle dated July 23, 1876, remarked to her father: "I imagine he is disappointed that Hayes came out so well in his letter & leaves him no excuse to support Tilden. His heart I am sure, is with the latter." [19]

After the formal nomination it became evident that personal attacks upon Tilden were to be directed primarily against his Civil War record, his income tax returns, and his connections with railroad rings. To these three issues, therefore, Bigelow turned his attention. It was upon him that Tilden depended to dissipate rumors of his business dishonesty; it was Bigelow who wrote the telling article upon Tilden's Civil War record and inserted it as Chapter XI in Cook's popular campaign biography, the whole of which Bigelow undertook to correct and polish. And it was he who with Hewitt finally forced Tilden to answer the damning charges that he had falsified his income tax returns during the war.[20]

That task was one of the hardest, because in August, when the tax story reached sizeable proportions, Tilden was in no shape to take positive action. For two years he had been working without respite and the strain was telling. He temporized, quibbled, talked pros and cons with the repetitiousness of an exhausted man who dared not trust his own conclusions. Moreover, he could not postpone the selection of his successor at Albany, which consumed what strength and time he could spare from the larger issues of the campaign. He wished

Hewitt, whom he had chosen as his manager, to run for the governorship; but Hewitt had not lived in the state long enough to be eligible. Hewitt in turn endorsed Dorsheimer; others advocated C. N. Potter; and still others, including Bigelow, favored Lucius Robinson, the Comptroller. It was up to Tilden to make the final decision. Bigelow, who saw Tilden almost daily to discuss with him all pending questions, steadily urged the selection of Robinson because, weak though he might be, he was less apt to drop the reform program than any of the other favorites. Hewitt's preference for Dorsheimer Bigelow labeled "one of the illustrations I fear of Hewitt's weakness"; he could see no advantage in Dorsheimer over the Canal Ringer, Doc Denison. Finally Tilden accepted Bigelow's reasoning, and that problem was settled.[21]

Until then, Tilden had tried to ignore the tax scandal. He had told Bigelow on August 29 that the whole thing was irritating beyond words; he could not find his records and he hated to take the time to prepare an answer. Hewitt, despairing of getting help from his chief, hired Judge James P. Sinnott, who had been Tilden's confidential law clerk during the years in question, to write out a statement for him. Sinnott in turn asked Bigelow to put the facts in shape, and Bigelow in his turn made Tilden assist them. Once the cautious old lawyer set himself to it, he worked laboriously to insure a thoroughly unexceptionable statement — and other issues suffered from neglect. Bigelow began to doubt whether Tilden would hold out until November. The necessity of making quick decisions and of stating himself without reserve seemed too taxing. Added to that, the death of his brother in September was an ugly reminder of his own bad health. Three days after Moses Tilden's funeral, Bigelow poured his fears into his diary:

> Last night read proofs of Sinnott's letter which has occupied 2 or 3 men about three weeks of continuous work to do what should not have consumed more than a day. The matter has worried the governor until he is scarcely fit or able to do anything. He cant write or control himself. He finds fault with everyone about him makes the most childish complaints of others for his own omissions & commissions. I begin to have some misgivings whether he will prove equal to the labors of the Presidency.[22]

Hewitt was equally concerned. He needed from Tilden closer cooperation, a more positive lead, and money. In September he told Bigelow that Tilden would never have been nominated had he not been expected to contribute generously to the campaign funds. Hewitt and Peter Cooper had given all they could, indeed they had advanced $70,000 beyond their pledges, but the party still lacked sufficient funds to cover legitimate expenses in such pivotal states as Florida. Bigelow himself could afford only $500 for the national committee and $250 for the state fund, but he could use his influence with Tilden. Bluntly he told him "that he just must make up his mind to give Mr. Hewitt what he thought reasonable & leave to H. the responsibility for the use of it and for the defeat of the ticket if to be defeated through a misuse of the money. I said that he at least must not have the responsibility of defeat for not supplying what he could perfectly well afford if the Chm who was his friend & a man of probity said it was necessary." But Tilden would not make a definite pledge; though eventually he contributed approximately $100,000, he seriously hampered his manager, who had to run the campaign without a definite budget.[23]

On November 7 — a dismal, rainy day — Tilden, Hewitt, Bigelow, Colonel Pelton and others tallied electoral votes in the Everett House as the wires flashed in returns. By midnight, when they parted company, they knew as surely as did Hayes in Ohio that the Democrats had won. The morning papers, except for the *Times*, confirmed their belief. That paper said first that the outcome was in doubt. Later, at 6:30 A.M., it held that the odds favored Hayes, for so close was the contest (the *Times* gave Tilden 184 electoral votes and Hayes 181 votes, with 185 the requisite minimum for election) that the four votes from the unreported state of Florida would determine the issue. That state the *Times* expected to go Republican. Later that same day Republican headquarters announced: "Hayes has 185 electoral votes and is elected."[24]

The Democrats were dumbfounded. At the moment they knew nothing of the fateful telegram which had gone out in the quiet of early morning to Republican leaders in Louisiana, South Carolina, and Florida: HAYES IS ELECTED IF WE HAVE CARRIED SOUTH CAROLINA, FLORIDA AND LOUISIANA. CAN YOU HOLD YOUR STATE? ANSWER AT ONCE. Planned, it is generally agreed, by John C. Reid of the *Times* — though Daniel Sickles later claimed credit for writing the telegram and for signing Zach Chandler's name, he being too drunk to be consulted — that query, apparently emanating from the Republican campaign manager, served to marshal all the carpet-bag forces of the boss-ridden states. When Bigelow heard of the telegram, he, like other Democrats, accused Chandler and Reid of conspiracy, for the telegrams were charged to the *New York Times;* he denounced Reid as a thief, and took pains in at least five later publications to give his opinion of the Crime of '76.[25]

By nightfall on Wednesday it was evident that the election would go to the man who carried the three notoriously corrupt Southern states. On November 14, J. Stokes Boyd of Florida wrote Bigelow that the Democrats had carried Florida, but that for lack of ten thousand dollars to hire honest watchers he had no way of guaranteeing a fair count. Cynical Democrats observed that only a stupid man would hope for a fair count in Florida and advised a display of force. Even Tilden momentarily toyed with such an idea when on November 16 he suggested to Robinson, the governor-elect of New York, the wisdom of appointing General McClellan as his adjutant. Bigelow, present at that meeting, opposed such a move; rather, he advised, appoint another and hold McClellan in reserve to be shifted into the position if need arose. And in his journal he noted: "The fact that we have to contemplate such emergencies, is a melancholy commentary upon the anniversary we have been celebrating. [Thanksgiving.] The chances are by no means inconsiderable that our form of govt. may not survive another 4th of July without serious modifications, the results perhaps of bloody strife." [26]

The more Tilden contemplated physical strife, however, the more he shrank from it. Rather lose the election, he determined, than subject the country to another war. Obviously the question of his future would depend upon how the Florida, South Carolina, and Louisiana votes were counted. Those three states had each submitted two sets of returns, an original tally made by Carpetbag Republicans in favor of Hayes and a Democratic recount which gave the victory to Tilden. The problem was to determine who had the Constitutional authority to decide which set was valid. Republicans and Democrats could not agree. Did the President of the Senate (in 1876 a Republican), standing before the two Houses of Congress, choose which set of returns he would open? Or was he authorized by the Constitution merely to open everything placed upon his desk, to announce the contents, and leave to Congress decisions concerning validity? Unfortunately the Constitution was not clear upon that point. Tilden, with relief, put aside all thought of a bold, definite step during December in order to join Manton Marble and Bigelow in their self-appointed task, the writing of *Presidential Counts*, a short book which was intended to prove that the right to count electoral votes rested solely with the two Houses meeting in joint session, after they, not the President of the Senate, had determined which of the votes conformed to law. If at any stage the two Houses did not concur, then the election, by law, was to be made by the House of Representatives — which in 1876 was controlled by the Democrats. It was a lawyerlike brief which made sense to Tilden, however much opponents might disagree with its conclusions, and the labor on it gave him deep satisfaction. But it was inexcusable for a Presidential candidate to give his time to the preparation of such a document at the very moment that his election depended upon his immediate actions, particularly when he was so halting a writer that he wasted precious hours writing over and over and over every sentence that he composed. Had he let Bigelow and Marble handle the legal precedents while he made an aggressive, public, political fight for his rights, *Presidential Counts* might have proved the crowning touch to Democratic strategy.[27]

When not absorbed in the analytical introduction or the summary of the booklet, Tilden conferred with Democratic friends from all parts of the country and had Bigelow and other lieutenants do likewise. Even Republicans came to protest the iniquity of their party's claim. But the hybrid advice — to do nothing, to go to Washington and force the issue, to buy up a state electoral board (Florida, Tilden told Bigelow, was offered for $200,000),[28] to work through Conkling, Blaine, and other anti-Hayes Republicans — left Tilden with so many possibilities to consider that he continued marshaling precedents while time slipped by.

In January Congressional leaders feared that the deadlock would continue into March and that the nation would be left without a President. So they suggested turning over the entire dispute to a special commission empowered to make final decision upon the questions at issue. Hewitt believed such a tribunal the only way out of the *impasse*, and was ready to accept it if Tilden acquiesced. As soon as a detailed plan was formulated, he mailed a copy to Tilden and then on January 14 came to New York to discuss it with him. As proposed, there were to be five Representatives and five Senators, half of them Republicans and half Democrats, and, from the six senior Supreme Court Judges, five were to be chosen by lot. Since three of the judges were Republicans and three of them were Democrats, the lottery might well decide the election. Hewitt asserted in his "secret history" written two years later that only C. N. Potter was present at his conference with Tilden upon the plan. If so, Hewitt must have been referring to a first formal statement to Tilden, for Bigelow, writing four days after the Sunday morning conference, noted that after breakfasting with E. L. Godkin and calling upon a sister, he went to Tilden's house where he found Hewitt and learned the details of the contemplated tribunal.

Bigelow expressed dislike for the plan in no uncertain terms:

In order to guard against a deadlock one of the judges is to be withdrawn by lot. The scheme reminds me of the aleatory device of the Hollanders described by Huet the Bishop of Auranches for the election of a burgomaster. The electors laid their heads upon a table and a louse was put upon the table in the center & the head he chose for refuge was the choice for burgomaster. The Govr decided against it but I do not know if Hewitt is not too much afraid of trouble to give the project up, for he thinks it is the best that can be done. I told the Gov. I thought our case a very simple one & required no resorts to expedients. The vote had always been counted by the two houses; no vote had ever been counted in which they did not concur; if they could not unite upon the Constitutional majority of Electors, the Constitution provided a remedy in the House of Reps. This was all simple we had nothing to do & all these efforts to provide new tribunals were simply contrivances to relieve the Reps. from the difficulties of their position at the expense of our party.[29]

But although Tilden refused to countenance the lottery aspect, he had no alternative to suggest for the general scheme of an electoral commission. He insisted upon several changes in detail, he obviously disliked the plan as a whole and consistently refused to approve it, but though told explicitly by Hewitt that if he objected to it the Democrats would refuse it, he said nothing. Tilden was an apostle of caution.

So the Electoral Commission began its meetings with Supreme Court Justice Bradley, a Republican, substituted at the last moment for his colleague Davis, a Democrat, who refused to serve on the ground that his sudden, unexpected election as Senator from Illinois would preclude all possibility on his part of maintaining the impartiality expected of him. On Wednesday, February 7, as Bigelow was rushing for a 5 P.M. train for New York, he heard that the Commission, by an eight-to-seven party vote, had refused to go behind the returns in Florida, had refused to consider whether the votes had been honestly cast and counted, which alone would have made possible a Democratic victory in that state. Instead of catching his train, Bigelow hastened back to the Governor's Mansion and spent the evening with Tilden discussing "the pleasant places in Europe for him to visit next summer." Their escapist planning was interrupted by a call from Senator Stockton of New Jersey, who remarked that Bradley "is not particular about the means with which he compasses his ends." The next day Tilden told Bigelow that he had been offered the vote of one Republican judge for $200,000 and had refused to consider it. But beyond that they said little about the workings of the Commission.[30]

Nevertheless it was on their minds. Bigelow wrote Pelton, Tilden's nephew who was representing him in Washington, "to recommend the Dem. judges to retire from the Commission on the ground that a vote of the majority had put out one of their eyes; had deprived them of the light necessary to decide properly the questions submitted to them & therefore they should decline to receive any more references." [31] Tilden, however, made no move; the Tribunal continued to sit, and with the awarding of the Louisiana vote to Hayes, by the persistent eight Republican to seven Democratic votes, the last hope of the Democrats flickered out. Bigelow was with Tilden when the formal word came that Hayes had been counted in, and he stayed with him throughout the bitter week of the inauguration. Watching his friend, he could not avoid feeling that the result was fortunate for Tilden if not for the party. Though Tilden's political ability preeminently fitted him for the Presidency, and his plans to restore harmony between North and South, to revive the old reverence for the Constitution and to improve the credit of the country were admirable, his miserable health might well have proved disastrous.

Indeed, in the final analysis and in spite of the blame he attached to a number of other men, Bigelow believed it was Tilden's own infirmity which cost the Democrats the election. "Tilden should have taken the field, so to speak, immediately after the election, gone to Washington, moved amongst, inspired, and directed them. If that had been done, his election would have been a matter of course. But it was impossible." [32] Impossible, Bigelow concluded, for a man who had to carry a medicine chest everywhere he went, whose massages and doses and diet needed careful supervision, whose whole body protested any undue exertion.

After a spring devoted to state politics and after making it clear that he would not be a candidate for re-election as Secretary of State, Bigelow accompanied Tilden to Europe. When they landed in Ireland, they heard of the railroad strikes and the riots which had swept the East. What interested Bigelow was Tilden's reaction, indicative at once of the attitude he would have taken had he been in office and of the strain he would have undergone:

> Tilden thinks we are both to be congratulated for being spared the necessity of meddling with a question so beset with difficulties and bad feeling. He criticizes the action of the Federal government in sending troops to do a duty which should have been discharged by State authorities until proved to be incapable of it and doubts whether anyone can do his duty and not make more enemies than friends.

In October they returned to America with the Hewitts. On shipboard the food was bad, the conversation worse, and for the first time Bigelow recorded in his diary marked hostility to Hewitt on his and

Tilden's part. Though they had seen Hewitt frequently enough in Paris to indicate a fundamentally cordial relationship, they found his garrulous egotism impossible to escape on shipboard. That, as much as Tilden's gnawing desire to blame someone for his defeat and his old feeling that, next to Bayard and Thurman, Hewitt was responsible for the fiasco of '76, brought from him an irritable outburst shortly before the end of the voyage in which he said ". . . it was easy to see how the electoral business was bedevilled with such a man at the head of the National Dem. Com. professing to be his mouthpiece in Congress. . . . T. says nothing that any one every [sic] does on Hewitt's recommendation whether in business or elsewhere that does not result in disaster." [33]

Yet neither Tilden nor Bigelow was given to useless recrimination. Nearly forty years before, Tilden had taught Bigelow the proper reaction to defeat: start at once to organize for the next campaign. Having worked on that principle throughout the intervening years, neither man was apt to change. They had to maintain the state organization, find a way to counteract the success of the Canal Ringers in the fall elections, study the possible effect of the split between the Kelly and Tilden Democrats upon the state and national campaign of 1880, and meet the damaging publication of the cipher telegrams so that Tilden would emerge unsmirched both for his own and the party's sake. As each of these political problems became acute, it came to be Tilden's custom to send for Bigelow to get his views, to receive editorial assistance upon anything to appear in print, and to have at hand an utterly loyal friend with whom he could talk freely.[34]

At first Bigelow thought Tilden had no intention of running in 1880; later he was convinced that Tilden would run if sure of success. There was little hope of a Democratic victory until 1884, however, and by that year Bigelow was positive that Tilden would not and should not run. As early as March 1884 he favored a firm, open withdrawal from the contest before the New York state convention was called to name delegates to the national convention. Only by so doing could Tilden give the party time to groom a worthy candidate.[35] In June, after Randall and Converse visited first Bigelow and then Tilden to insist that the ex-governor run for the Presidency, Bigelow again advised Tilden to issue an absolute and immediate withdrawal. Pressed by Bigelow, Tilden did dictate a note which would suffice, Bigelow thought, though it smacked too much of a man willing to be drafted. However, it was the firmest expression he could get from Tilden; so he proceeded to "polish" it.

A week passed and still Tilden delayed mailing it. At that point

Daniel Manning, long-time follower of Tilden and friend of young Governor Grover Cleveland, who had Presidential aspirations provided Tilden did not desire the nomination, came to Bigelow in dismay. Roswell P. Flower was sewing up Tilden delegates to the state convention scheduled to meet on June 18, so that if Tilden decided at the last moment not to run, Flower would be their second choice. If Flower's plan succeeded, Cleveland would be out of the running and Tilden's old reform program, which Cleveland was continuing and developing, would be wrecked. Cleveland wanted Tilden to withdraw before the convention met, and he wanted him to do it in such a way that Cleveland would become his heir. Manning told Bigelow, or so Bigelow understood, that if that happened, Tilden could name any or all of the Cabinet. As Bigelow had already advised this course and knew that the necessary letter of withdrawal was sitting on Tilden's desk, he gladly accompanied Manning to Tilden's to force the issue. On June 10, eight days before the convention met, the letter was mailed. Published on June 12, it gave Manning and the Tilden Democrats a go-ahead signal in their plan to put forward the aggressive young Governor of New York.[36]

Bigelow had little to do with the campaign of 1884, family business necessitating a brief trip to England; yet it was he, Tilden said later, who made possible Cleveland's election by persuading the old leader against his judgment to withdraw when he did. For that reason Tilden expected Bigelow to get political preferment. There was, he knew, always the possibility that Bigelow would display some unaccountable perversity, as he had a number of times when he could have, but had not, picked up a fortune by stooping in a fashion acceptable to most men. There was an unworldly streak in Bigelow which Tilden could not fathom. For example, in May 1884, Mayor Edson offered Bigelow the city chamberlainship at $15,000 a year, no mean salary to Bigelow; yet Bigelow turned it down merely because he had a poor opinion of the mayor's integrity. Again, in October 1884, while Bigelow was in London, he was invited by cable to run for the city comptrollership on a ticket headed by William R. Grace. He cabled back: "Impossible," and commented in his diary that there would be as much disgrace in holding that position as in the far more profitable one he had turned down in the spring. When he returned home he told Tilden what he thought of the offer and then discovered that Tilden, unable to comprehend Bigelow's scruples, had been behind the whole idea.[37]

Certainly, however, Bigelow would not object to a place in the Cabinet. Tilden was sure that he would have the naming of at least one member; so, shortly after the election, he asked Bigelow which he preferred to be, Secretary of State or of the Treasury. Bigelow replied that he was "less unfit for State." Another time Tilden asked how he would like to be Minister to England. But he might as well not have asked. Cleveland proceeded to make his appointments quite without reference to Tilden. That both Tilden and Bigelow felt disappointed was to be expected; that Bigelow would take it more philosophically was likewise to be expected. He had resources within himself and sufficiently varied interests to be able to stand aside from politics. But politics were Tilden's life; to find himself slighted, shelved, by a man whom he considered his inferior, was galling.

After most positions were filled, Cleveland finally asked Tilden whom he would recommend for the Treasury. The choice soon narrowed to Bigelow or Manning, the Tilden Democrat who had managed Cleveland's campaign. Bigelow refused to be considered. Manning, too, was loath to accept the office. Tilden settled the matter in his usual indirect way. He wrote a letter to Smith Weed, who was in Washington acting as his personal liaison officer, which he wanted read to Manning. In it Tilden recalled the promises made concerning his influence with the new administration. He pointed out that unless Manning accepted the Treasury Tilden would have no friend in the Cabinet. If, however, Manning persisted in his refusal, Tilden thought Bigelow "the best substitute. He is an accomplished man, accustomed to deal with great public questions, utterly unselfish and unambitious, without any tendency to inferior associations and would command the confidence and support of the financial classes." Manning clearly was Tilden's first choice, but that was quite unimportant to Bigelow seventeen years later when he was clearing out old papers of Tilden's and came across a penciled copy of the letter. Rather, he was touched, for, he said, it was the first time in their lifelong friendship that he had ever heard of Tilden "uttering by tongue or pen a compliment to or about me." [38]

By mid-February 1885 Manning had accepted the Treasury position and Bigelow had given up thought of any position from Cleveland. But not Tilden; while Bigelow completed his edition of *The Writings and Public Speeches of Samuel J. Tilden* and began a biography of Bryant, who had died in 1878, Tilden guided Manning in the conduct of his department. In May he suggested Bigelow as Assistant Treasurer, stationed in New York. The work was light and the position one of dignity. When told of Tilden's action, Bigelow expressed interest — though he said that he would prefer to be Minister to Italy. The Treasury position would not be available for some months, the salary was less attractive, and, though he did not mention it to Tilden, he had very much enjoyed his winter in Italy in 1881 and would like another one there. Tilden said he would see what he could do.

Outside of the Treasury, however, Tilden's influence was small. He told Bigelow one evening: "I tried very hard to induce him [Cleveland] to give you a place 'who' said Tilden with some emotion 'did more to put him in his present position than any other man in the country.' He no doubt referred to my part in persuading him against his own judgment and wish to publish his letter of withdrawal before the election of delegates to the State Convention, instead of waiting, as he had proposed to do, until the Convention met. I also persuaded him to write a letter in favor of the ticket which was of great advantage to it." In talking to Manning about placing Bigelow in the Treasury office, Tilden stormed that Bigelow "was the worst used man in the United States." Tilden, however, was on the way out; no longer did politicians have to consider his preferences, and only Manning chose to.[39]

In November Bigelow went to Washington to help W. C. Whitney, Secretary of the Navy, prepare a report upon the causes for the inefficiency and abuses rampant in the navy and to suggest remedies. The result so delighted Whitney and won such wide acclaim that he declared he intended to buy two thousand shares of stock, divide the profits with Bigelow, or, if the speculation went amiss, take unto himself the loss. While in the capital, Bigelow saw Manning and learned that the Assistant Treasurership would be offered to him in about a month. Another day he was invited to dinner at the White House. Only Whitney and himself, "Miss Cleaveland" — as Bigelow invariably spelled the name — and the President were there, thus giving Bigelow his first opportunity to measure the President. After dinner Cleveland had him marching up and down the hall, discussing efforts to purify the public service. The next day Bigelow jotted down his verdict:

> He is evidently trying to do his best, but his ignorance, his inexperience, his immaturity of mind, his total lack of social *savoir faire* and withal the illusions bred of his extraordinary and unaccountable success, were constantly coming to the surface. I did little but listen for I was all the evening trying to ascertain to what stage of maturity I was to adapt my remarks. He is learning all the time however; he seems to keep himself remarkably free from misleading influences; he does not seem to have any special sympathy for flatterers and whatever faults he commits are his own.[40]

In December Bigelow was formally tendered the Assistant Treasurership. He had every intention of accepting it, but the more he considered the responsibility of giving his personal guarantee for the safety of the government funds, the more he thought of the boring hours he would spend signing checks, the more he balanced that against the small salary, the heavier grew his heart. Even Tilden changed his mind when he realized how Bigelow felt; indeed, he even offered to pay him $4000 a year for four years if he refused the job.[41]

On December 19, shortly after his sixty-eighth birthday, Bigelow dispatched a formal refusal to Cleveland. He had shut the door to politics, and probably very wisely so, for by 1885 another generation was in the saddle. His contemporaries, those few men still alive who had known Van Buren and Silas Wright, were now observers, critics, honored advisers — elder statesmen. They were not wanted in the daily strife.

CHAPTER 21

A Library and a Canal

[*1886–1910*]

IN HIS seventieth year Bigelow started weaving into a new pattern threads of capacity and interest which he had spun in the course of five industrious decades. For the quarter-century following 1886, during which he followed keenly a succession of civic and national issues, his major, and most fitting, occupation was the development of the New York Public Library. The task demanded modesty, for in time no one in all the thousands who would use the library would remember his share in making easier their search for knowledge. It demanded at once leadership and co-operation. It demanded a knowledge of politics, the press, books. In its early stages the enterprise was helped enormously by having at its head a man who had mixed in state politics for twoscore years, who knew when and how to seek newspaper support, who had been collecting books as long as he could remember and knew how the world's greatest libraries were conducted. Bigelow had the heart for the job, as well as the qualifications. It was, to him, a privilege to be permitted to share in such a contribution to the civilization of his country. The project satisfied his old yearning to be connected with something that would long outlive him. Moreover, he saw in it an opportunity to fill the void he had so often remarked in American cultural institutions; in time New York would have a vast repository of the world's knowledge, available to all, forced upon none.

The idea of a free library was not a new one in America, nor was it, on Bigelow's part, a sudden interest produced upon his appointment as a Tilden executor. A half-century before, when as a lonely, ambitious boy of eighteen he first lived in New York City, his craving for books had been whetted as much as satisfied in the small library of the New York Historical Society. For that he had been glad to pay a nominal fee, but he never forgot that even a nominal fee was prohibitive to many young men. Twenty-five years later, on his first trip to Europe, he had interrupted his studies of religious leaders of a by-gone day to make a careful record in the Sorbonne and the British Museum of methods of storing books, types of slips used in getting access to them, procedures in dealing with readers.[1] He had not thought it odd that he should take time on his vacation to note practical details of library management even though he had no specific use for the knowledge. It had seemed mere common sense to learn whatever might eventually be applicable in America. The Astor Library in New York City, which had opened its doors in 1854, might develop into a large and useful institution, or possibly a new city or national museum might be established along the lines he and Bryant urged regularly in the *Post*.

During that same trip he had tried to arrange for American purchase of the Campana marbles. Later, during his consulate and Ministry, he had found moments in his busy life to write to wealthy friends at home whenever he heard of collections of books which, if brought to America, might one day find their way to a still unborn national library. In 1871 he almost inspired William B. Astor to organize a document room in the Astor Library.[2] About the same time he urged William H. Aspinwall, the leading trustee of the Lenox Library, established in 1870, to make that institution a center for the conservation of manu-scripts. He recommended the same idea to E. D. Morgan, suggesting that he start by purchasing the Stevens collection of Franklin corre-spondence. To Calvert Vaux, no longer the struggling architect who had helped him remodel "The Squirrels" but the noted designer of New York's Central Park, he described his dream of a manuscript repository and for the time being won Vaux's enthusiastic support for placing such an institution in the Park.[3] Nor was Tilden unaware of Bigelow's belief that a large public library was the noblest memorial a wealthy man could raise unto himself. That Tilden decided to leave such a memorial Bigelow knew even before Tilden's first will was drawn in 1882; so that on trips to Europe Bigelow was constantly on the alert for books and works of art which would improve Tilden's collection.

In April 1884 Tilden asked Bigelow to help him revise his will; with some $5,000,000 at stake to be used for a library, it was important that the will be foolproof. Bigelow, having no faith in himself as a lawyer, suggested that they consult their friend Charles O'Conor, and the elderly jurist, retired yet still famous, came to New York to assist. In this, his final will, Tilden appointed three executors, Andrew H. Green, his partner, already well known in New York for his work on the public school board and the Park board, later called the "father of

Greater New York" for his leadership in the consolidation of the five boroughs; George W. Smith, his confidential secretary for twenty years, and Bigelow. By its terms New York was to have a public library; that old dream of Bigelow's, which he himself could never have made real, was to have substance. Bigelow experienced deep satisfaction, tempered with puzzled wonder that Tilden would deliberately leave to others the joy of creation:

> How strange that he should deny himself the pleasure of appropriating this money to the welfare of those for whom it is ultimately designed. Can the pleasure of holding money be so much greater to anyone than of giving it away when it is not needed. He had it tied up in his old will so that the income of his estate should accumulate sufficiently to replace all that would be required for his legacies bequests and devises before the General Trust should come into action. This O'Conor satisfied him was impracticable. He meant to hold on to it as long as he could. He allows the Executors $5,000 a year each. He said Green thought that a small allowance. So it is for the work but the privileges of directing the disposition of so large an estate to beneficent uses is itself worth paying for.[4]

A few days after Tilden's death, after his burial in the little hillside cemetery at New Lebanon in August 1886, where the relatives, according to Bigelow, showed rather more than Christian fortitude, the will was read in the presence of the three executors and the next of kin, Tilden's sister and his brother Henry's six children. On October 20 it was submitted for probate. George Tilden, on behalf of the heirs, at once sought its invalidation on the grounds that it was indefinite and uncertain in naming the beneficiaries and that it substituted the will of the trustees for that of the testator by authorizing them to determine how best to use the legacy on behalf of the public. Nevertheless, the executors went ahead with their plans. The will ordered them to incorporate as the Tilden Trust at the earliest possible moment. To that end they petitioned the legislature on January 4, 1887. On March 26 the permissive legislation was passed, but it carried an amendment, over the executors' repeated protests, that nothing in it should be construed to affect the rights of the heirs or next of kin.[5]

According to the will the three trustees now had ninety days in which to add a minimum of two trustees to their number and to elect a President, a Vice-President, a Treasurer, and a Secretary. In April, Green, Smith and Bigelow met by agreement, each bringing a list of candidates for the other trusteeships. Not one name appeared on any two lists. Green wanted Paul Dana to whom Bigelow was absolutely opposed because Dana was a newspaper editor and would be tempted to publicize, to the detriment of the library, any disagreements they might have. Green's other candidate was unsatisfactory both to Smith and Bigelow because he, like Green, was a trustee of the *Staats Zeitung* and the two men might find it convenient to swap votes on their trusteeships. Yet Bigelow was willing to accept him if Green would accept one of Smith's candidates. But Green was adamant. He had strong personal objections to every man Smith suggested. Ten days passed; the deadlock continued; neither Green nor Smith would accept any man on the other's list. Finally, to Bigelow's delight, they agreed upon his candidates as least objectionable: Stephen A. Walker and Alexander E. Orr, Bigelow's erstwhile fellow investigator of the Canal Ring. Bigelow noted in his diary: "Expecting to be obliged to surrender both the men of my choice for the sake of harmony I secured harmony by taking both." [6] On April 26, the day after the new trustees were elected, the five men met to name their officers. Bigelow became President, Green Vice-President, Smith Treasurer, and Orr Secretary.

Thereafter, until the litigation of the will should end — and they expected it to drag on perhaps until 1890 — the trustees had to mark time. Bigelow went to Paris for the summer where he continued the job of editing Franklin's writings, which he had commenced in 1886. Already the first two volumes had been issued; by fall another six were made ready for the publisher, and in 1888 appeared an important contribution to the world of letters, a ten-volume edition of Benjamin Franklin's works, the most complete and carefully edited set then available.

Bigelow did not forget the library, however. It occurred to him "that it would be within the province of the free library for which Mr. Tilden made provision in his will . . . to issue drawings, designs, patterns, of every kind of industry in which art is an important element so that the young worker in Pottery or in Brass or in Steel or in the precious metals or in music and so on may be able to take home with him from our library any of the models drawings and illustrations which money can purchase which would offer him any assistance in perfecting his tastes or in suggesting ideas." [7] But before any definite plans could be made, the Tilden will case had to be settled. In January 1889 the trustees won the first round; in November of that year the State Supreme Court reversed the decision. An appeal and another waiting period followed. During it, in February 1890, George Tilden proposed an out-of-court settlement by an equal division of the estate between heirs and trustees. Bigelow refused to consider it. Instead he called in his old friend Daniel Magone, pumped him for information about possible candidates for the Court of Appeals, explained the importance to the people that an unbiased judge be elected, and offered up to $1000 to cover any expenses Magone might have in keeping him informed of political developments. Another year went by. In May 1891, Mrs. Hazard, the sole heir of Tilden's now deceased sister, offered to surrender her claim to the trust in return for $975,000. Because that would assure the library approximately $2,000,000, would divide the heirs, and would put Smith Weed, Mrs. Hazard's counsel, on his side, Bigelow voted to accept the settlement. The following month the contest with the remaining heirs reached the Court of Appeals, but no decision was expected until fall.[8]

Meanwhile the trustees could make tentative plans, knowing that in any event they would have at least $2,000,000. In July Bigelow sent to Orr the detailed sketches for a library building which he had lovingly drawn and redrawn through the years, now with the help of one architect friend, now of another. The time had arrived to get the experts' opinion of them, but not the time, he warned Orr, to publicize that these plans were afoot, for Bigelow's drawings were clearly intended for the Reservoir site, on Forty-second Street between Fifth and Sixth Avenues, which belonged to the unsuspecting City. So, almost a year before Green read into the minutes of the Tilden Trust a proposal to investigate the Reservoir site, his fellow trustees had been considering it.[9]

Finally on October 27, 1891, the five-year-old contest over Tilden's will terminated. The huge fortune he had labored to amass went to relatives who had meant little to him. He had clung too long to his money. Just as the Presidency had been taken from him on a technicality, so a large part of his memorial was taken from him. What New Yorkers thought of the decision was plainly illustrated by a law passed two years later providing that no gift for charitable or educational uses "shall be deemed invalid by reason of the indefiniteness or uncertainty of the persons designated as the beneficiaries." Yet perhaps it was as well for New York that Tilden's will miscarried. Had the trustees received $5,000,000 they would have added a third to the City's relatively small libraries, whereas with less than half that sum they were led to consider a co-operative enterprise.

Green formally raised that issue in May 1892, when he reported to his fellow trustees that the Lenox Library had approached him on the subject of a union. He was in favor of it, he said, or else of an alliance with the Scientific Societies of New York. Moreover, he advocated asking the City to erect a building for them, and, possibly, to deed them Reservoir Square on Fifth Avenue. Bigelow publicly described his hopes in an article appearing in *Scribner's Magazine* in September '92. He wanted the Trust and the City to co-operate, the City to erect a library building on the site of the old reservoir, the materials of which could be used in the foundation, thus cutting costs, and the Trust to equip and run it. He suggested that the structure be in the form of a cross stretching from Fifth to Sixth Avenues and from Fortieth to Forty-second Streets, permitting, he emphasized for the benefit of the ever-zealous Park Commissioners, four sizeable park squares. Inside he envisioned good light in all rooms, thanks to the shape of the building, space for 1,500,000 books, special literary rooms, scientific laboratories, general reading rooms. As an alternative, should the City refuse to assist them, he proposed either consolidation with an older library or concentration of their funds upon complete collections within a limited range of subjects, preferably in the physical sciences because they were neglected by other city libraries.

Shortly thereafter Seth Low, President of Columbia University, proposed a union of the Tilden Trust with the Columbia library. Bigelow replied that he doubted whether the new site of the college, on the heights north of the city, would be practicable for the public, or whether the university would care to provide the same facilities for the general public as for its students. The idea was not dropped, however, until two years later when the trustees finally voted against any such merger. Meanwhile, negotiations with the City were continued. Early in January 1893 Mayor Gilroy informally advised Bigelow that the time had come to request from the City the old City Hall and to ask that it be removed to the reservoir site for use as a library. And, Gilroy added, get the press back of it. Forthwith the trustees submitted such a request, hastened to their newspaper friends for support, and waited in high hope.[10]

In February '93 an act to donate the old City Hall to the Tilden Trust received its first reading in the Legislature. It received, too, stunning opposition. Andrew H. Green, one of the Tilden Trust's three-man "plan and scope" committee, supported by Paul Dana of the *Sun* who was also President of the Park Board and by the architect Calvert Vaux, suddenly objected. Consequently at a stormy session of the Tilden Trust in March the "plan and scope" committee was discharged. In May Orr proposed that the Chair appoint in its place a one-man committee to have complete and sole charge of all negotiations. The motion was carried unanimously, Green being absent that day; and Lewis Cass Ledyard — recently elected a trustee to succeed Stephen A. Walker, deceased — was appointed by Bigelow. Ten months later, in January 1894, the Board held its next meeting. Green moved to rescind the motion of the preceding May, but no one seconded him. Harmony had departed from the Board of the Tilden Trust.[11]

The annual election of officers in April made the split more obvious. Only four members were there, Smith being unable to attend. After the first ballot was cast, Green, as teller, announced the result: two votes for Bigelow (Orr's and Ledyard's); two votes blank (Green's and Bigelow's). No one having a majority, a second ballot was taken with the same result. *Sotto voce* Ledyard said to Bigelow: "You must vote." On the third ballot, three votes were cast, but the teller simply refused to announce the result. As the last President, Bigelow thereupon took over Green's task and calmly announced his own election, by three votes and one blank, to the Presidency of the Tilden Trust for the coming year. The Vice-President was next elected and he, too, received three votes, Orr's, Ledyard's, and Bigelow's, and one blank. But this year the Vice-President was not to be Green. Orr succeeded him and from then on Bigelow, Ledyard, and Orr tended to work closely together.[12]

Ledyard's unceasing efforts to get the old City Hall for the Tilden library eventually came to nothing, but his subsequent labors to unite the Tilden Trust with the Astor Library were completely successful. Early in '94 he commenced talks with John Cadwalader of the Astor Library, looking to collaboration. By autumn he was as enthusiastic about such a merger as Green. Smith, on the other hand, preferred to merge with the New York Historical Society and the National Academy; Orr was strongly opposed to the Astor plan, while Bigelow was content to go along with any proposal that looked to the establishment of a library in the near future. Eight years, he noted, had passed since Tilden died and as yet his memorial was not begun. Upon Green's formal request, Bigelow appointed a committee to meet with a committee from the Astor Library. On it he put Ledyard, the proposer of the alliance; and with him shrewdly appointed Orr, who was most strongly opposed to it, and Green, who favored it but constantly needed placating. In January the Tilden Board accepted the proposals submitted by the joint committee. In February the Astor Library followed suit. Meanwhile the Lenox people approached Bigelow with renewed expression of interest in a union. Another series of conferences was instituted, and by April the outline for merging the three groups was clear.[13]

The next step was to select officers for the new consolidation. The Tilden Trust objected to a Lenox man at the head, fearing that would mean retention of the Lenox site; and two of them, Bigelow and Green, objected to Bishop Potter of the Astor Library on the score that he might be offensive to non-Episcopal groups. Ledyard thought that Bigelow alone could be elected. And on May 27, 1895, while Bigelow was in Europe on one of his frequent trips, he became President of the United Libraries and a member of two of its three committees, the executive and library book committees. That his election became unanimous only after the trustees of the three Foundations forced Green to shift his vote was no shock to Bigelow.[14]

The new Free Public Library — Astor, Lenox and Tilden Foundations — began work in earnest in the fall of 1895. At Cadwalader's suggestion they chose as director Dr. John S. Billings, eminent creator of the Surgeon General's Library in Washington, a connoisseur of the handling of books, and at the time engaged in organizing the Pepper Laboratory of Hygiene at the University of Pennsylvania. They appointed their President, their Vice-Presidents, Bishop Potter and John Kennedy, and three members to be named by Bigelow, to a committee on library site. Until that was determined, they could make no further headway. Bigelow immediately filled the committee by choosing one man from each of the three original groups; next he held several long conferences with Dr. Billings who thereafter joined him in urging the reservoir site. Before long the full committee approved. Yet though empowered to make the final decision, they decided to hold an open meeting at the Century to hear any objections to that site which any trustee might care to make; it seemed good policy to them to avoid all appearances of railroading through their preference. As was expected, Sturgis and Green objected, the former adamant for the Lenox site, the latter, who notoriously favored any site but the reservoir, earnestly urging them to postpone consideration of location until they had decided whether they were to be solely a reference library or a lending library as well. But the majority, eager to settle the matter, approved of the reservoir area. Bigelow was supremely content. He might be seventy-eight years old, but he still knew how to set a course:

> Having the new library on the site of the Reservoir has been the supreme idea in my mind as trustee of Mr. Tilden for the last four years. I first made it popular with the assistance of Mr. Flagg in the *Scribner's Magazine* three or four years ago and I have kept my gun pointed in that direction ever since from a conviction that that is the place first in every respect for it and there is no other that ranks even second to it. Ledyard's management of Green through his vanity has been superb.[15]

Consummation of the plan took time. In April the legislature sanctioned it, in June the governor signed the bill, and finally in December the Aldermen agreed to the removal of the reservoir. Still the Park

Commissioners' approval and an appropriation of funds from the Board of Estimate had to be secured. By the time the last red tape was cut, Bigelow was past seventy-nine. Then indeed he could rejoice. In his diary, in a firm, clear hand, he reviewed the history of the past twelve years as a result of which: "I now begin to feel that the institution which has been my chief earthly concern for the last dozen years or more is destined to live and move and have a being." [16]

Under Billings and his enthusiastic staff, the library soon was functioning with remarkable vigor in the Astor and Lenox buildings. Donations and purchases swelled their material resources. In the '90's they acquired the Emmet, the Ford, and the Gould collections. Lesser gifts came from other trustees and friends, among them Bigelow's collection of Congressional documents prior to 1850, the largest private collection in the country, he thought, to which he had the government add, so far as possible, all later publications. Now all that the library needed was a home in which to expand. So throughout '97 the trustees discussed building plans, about which both Billings and Bigelow had fixed ideas. Unfortunately they were diametrically opposed; and so angry did Bigelow get, at one conference, that he could not sleep that night for thinking of it. Indeed, he never became resigned to certain of Billings's cherished ideas which were incorporated into the plans — namely, the artistically dark rooms which necessitated artificial lighting and the placing of the main reading rooms on the top floor so that readers had to walk up two long flights or be hauled up in lifts — a waste of library funds — while books had to be raised one flight to reach them. Bigelow thought the convenience of serious readers more important than the discouragement of loafers. [17]

The trustees hoped that by 1901 or 1902 the library would be open to the public, but it was November 10, 1902, before even the cornerstone was laid. On that occasion, on a brilliantly clear afternoon when the sharp lines of near-by buildings etched themselves against the sky, Bigelow arose, tall, erect, easy in carriage despite his eighty-five years and the extra pounds he had lately put on, and presided with evident dignity and pleasure. [18]

The following year Andrew H. Green died. Bigelow, knowing that Ledyard and Green had not been on speaking terms, could not resist saying to Billings in what he thought was a joking manner, "I wish you would tell Ledyard I expect him to prepare a minute for our record of Mr. Green." Whereupon, at the next meeting of the Board, Ledyard arose and solemnly read an incredible eulogy, crediting Green for instituting and pushing through the legislature the first act authorizing the consolidation of the library corporations of New York City, praising his active part in all their counsels, and so on. "Not a word of this could Ledyard have believed," Bigelow noted in his diary. The memorial address was formally placed in the minutes and then, only then, did Bigelow discover that Ledyard had signed it with Bigelow's name. ". . . Ledyard had, rather maliciously as I thought, got the joke on me," Bigelow commented. And Ledyard had done just that, even better than he thought, for that memorial, added to Green's habit of proposing formally actions long informally entered upon, gave him a place of honor in the minutes of the Trustees which later formed a chief source for the standard history of the library.[19] Andrew H. Green was unquestionably a foremost citizen of New York, but he was certainly not an easy man to work with. He and Bigelow never teamed well together in the sixty-five years of their acquaintance, not even in the early days when they both taught in Green's sister Lucy's school. Indeed, Bigelow's personal dislike for Green was such that when he learned that his name had been used without authorization as a Vice-President of the Andrew H. Green Memorial Association, he ordered it removed with a few tersely explicit comments.[20]

To replace Green, Cadwalader nominated Archbishop Farley "on the ground that the Catholics were entitled to this representation." Bigelow, who was never made speechless by anger, explained with great courtesy that sectarian distinctions were not among the qualifications essential in members of library boards. Privately he decided to oppose the election of Farley. It seemed to him that the Board could act more harmoniously without a member who accepted the Index, the Catholic Church's list of books forbidden its communicants. Before doing so, he thought it proper to write to the Archbishop to ask, were he elected, if he would "assist in the indiscriminate circulation of books, the reading and even the possession of which by the worshippers of his communion is forbidden under severe penalties by its head. . . ." Two days later, on December 23, Farley replied, according to the copy Bigelow made in his journal:

THE HON. JOHN BIGELOW *Prest etc*
NEW YORK

MY DEAR SIR
Your very kind favor of 21 inst. is much appreciated and the contents noted.
Wishing you all blessings and joys of the happy Christmastide, I am with much respect and esteem

Very truly yours
JNO N. FARLEY
Abp. N. Y.

"It does not," Bigelow noted, "overflow with information upon the subjects for which I asked light." [21] Further correspondence in January, however, satisfied Bigelow that the Archbishop would be a welcome associate and he became a trustee.

The construction of the library was discouragingly slow. Bigelow was convinced that he would not live to see it in operation. Years passed before the building was completed. Then, in the presence of six hundred guests, on May 23, 1911, Directors, Trustees, and civic dignitaries marched two by two to a platform erected in the high arch facing the Fifth Avenue entrance. At the end of the procession, William Howard Taft, President of the United States, walked beside John Bigelow, ninety-three-year-old President of the Board of Trustees of the New York Public Library.[22] Alone among that gathering, old John Bigelow could remember what New York had been like seventy-five years earlier for young men who sought knowledge through books, and as he arose to make his address, he alone knew how deeply moved he was to witness the successful outcome of this chief interest of his old age.

In his seventies and eighties and nineties, Bigelow was no more able to limit himself to one field of activity than he ever had been; he liked too much to be in the thick of things, as his interest in the Panama Canal showed. This is not the place to recount what is known of the creation of the Panama Canal, for Bigelow did not play a major or official role in that great enterprise as he did in the library. He was, however, the confidant, the adviser, the encourager, of Philippe Bunau-Varilla in the long series of maneuvers that culminated in the Hay–Bunau-Varilla treaty in 1903. At every step of the negotiations he was kept informed; to his files came immediately copies of every important letter and telegram that Bunau-Varilla sent, and frequently the young Frenchman turned to him for strategic advice. The little Bigelow recorded about the Canal, therefore, has the double interest of throwing some further light upon Bunau-Varilla's activities and of illustrating once more Bigelow's own political acumen and his unquenchable spirit of youth.[23]

At first glance it seems strange that he, a man of unshakable integrity always more concerned with motives and means than with ends, wholeheartedly approved of what he believed to be deliberate interference by the United States in the domestic life of a weaker nation. Yet it is less strange when his strong convictions, his fervent, rather than coldly judicious advocacy of causes, and his loyalty to friends are added to the account. Indeed, he shared none of the scruples over the United

States's role in the Panama Revolution which bothered some contemporary and many later Americans. He found the course of Theodore Roosevelt so admirable, in fact, that in 1904 he made it his business to see Alton Parker, the Democratic candidate for the Presidency, to persuade him not to center his attack upon the Republican record on the canal. Bigelow, like Bunau-Varilla, was convinced, first, that an interocean canal was essential to the economic welfare of the world; second, that it must not be postponed in view of the increasing threat Japan presented to American safety; third, that only the Panama route was feasible; and fourth, that the corrupt government of Colombia would not be content with its fair share, but would hold up negotiations at least long enough to take over the New Canal Company's concession, thereby grabbing what legitimately belonged to the shareholders of the company.

Bigelow's interest in the Canal dated from 1886, the same year that saw the beginning of his long task as one of Tilden's executors, when he visited the De Lesseps canal enterprise at Panama as a guest of the Panama Canal Company and as a representative of the New York Chamber of Commerce. Baron de Lesseps, hoping for favorable publicity through the visit of a party of distinguished Americans and Frenchmen, urged his guests to inquire into any aspects of the work which interested them. Bigelow needed little urging. He filled his notebooks with detailed descriptions of machine shops, derivative canals, construction projects; he asked workmen and executives all the questions he considered pertinent and carefully recorded their replies. He found especially helpful the recently appointed chief engineer, Philippe Bunau-Varilla, an attractive youth of twenty-seven, utterly devoted to his task. On the other hand he was appalled at the death rate among the laborers, the corruption and waste, the jealous lack of unity among the top men. After his return to New York he prepared a report for the Chamber of Commerce in which he neither condemned nor extravagantly praised the company. Rather he tried soberly to describe its plan, its progress to date, the difficulties it faced, and the state of its finances.[24] His thirty-page letter received high commendation from newspapers grateful for an honest layman's reaction and to Bigelow's surprise won him an honorary membership in the Chamber of Commerce, which placed him in the company of such men as Cyrus W. Field, Carl Schurz, John Ericsson — who thirty-five years before had built an engine for Bigelow's *Evening Post* and later constructed the famous *Monitor* — and of William M. Evarts, his old Column Club friend and more recent political foe.

For the next twelve years he gave little thought to the Panama

Canal. When not traveling, he was busy in New York with the library, the Metropolitan Museum and other civic matters. He was an incorporator and trustee of the New York Law School — "our" law school, he always called it — which was founded by George Chase in rebellion against the introduction of the Langdell method into the Columbia Law School, and which for a number of years enjoyed an enviable reputation. He brought out new editions of his life of Franklin and his ten-volume edition of Franklin's works. He wrote *France and the Confederate Navy*, biographies of Bryant and of Tilden, *The Bible that was dead and is alive again*, *The Mystery of Sleep*, and many brief magazine articles.

He did not forget young Bunau-Varilla, however; the friendship between the elderly man and the brilliant youth ripened into almost a father-son relationship. In 1891, five years after Bigelow's visit to Panama, Bunau-Varilla came to him in discouragement. The outlook for the Canal seemed hopeless. The company was bankrupt and de Lesseps, charged with graft, was facing trial in Paris. Bigelow promptly advised Bunau-Varilla to write a book. "I have often observed," the Frenchman later recalled Bigelow as saying, "the deep and lasting influence of a true relation of a great event in which one has taken part even though at the time passions and error disfigure your action. That book will be a document which will serve for the defense of the work to which you are attached. It will also serve as a defense of yourself." Bunau-Varilla took his sage friend's advice. The next year *Panama: Past, Present, and Future* appeared, whereupon Bigelow judiciously undertook to distribute copies of it among American statesmen, journalists, and representatives of steamship interests. Much later Bunau-Varilla commented: "Never have I known counsel more happy or prophecy more surely realized," for that book, he said, became the basis for converting the Walker Commission to the Panama route.[25]

Yet months stretched to years before that happened. Meanwhile in France, in England, in Russia, Bunau-Varilla tried in vain to get financial backing, acting as a private individual, a stockholder but not an officer of the New Canal Company which had taken over the de Lesseps concessions. In the early 1890's he made no effort to get American help; in view of the general indifference to an isthmian canal, America seemed barren ground to the French propagandist. It was left to an American, William Nelson Cromwell, the astute legal representative of the New Canal Company, to seek American converts to the Panama route. He had some measure of success, though it was nothing like that of Senator John T. Morgan of Alabama, an early and persistent advocate of a canal in Nicaragua, who finally, in 1897, succeeded in having Congress create a canal commission to examine the possibility of a Nicaraguan canal. Bigelow followed Senator Morgan's campaign for the Nicaragua route with little more than average interest, expecting nothing to come of the canal commission, and he had, apparently, almost no knowledge of Cromwell's activities until later on, when he obviously had no use for him or his ambitions or his methods.

Then suddenly came the Spanish-American War, and with it an end to American apathy toward an interocean canal. Soon it was a foregone conclusion that President McKinley would not only urge the prompt construction of an isthmian canal in his annual message to Congress in December 1898 but would frankly tell Congress to adopt the Nicaraguan route. That expectation satisfied most Americans, among whom only a scattered few gave more than a passing thought to the Panama route. It filled Bunau-Varilla with alarm, however. If America chose the Nicaraguan route, which he believed inferior in every respect, the Panama Canal would never be built, for two isthmian canals were out of the question. At once he urged his American friends, among them Bigelow, to do what they could to combat the new threat.

On November 9, therefore, several weeks before the President's message was due, Bigelow wrote to John Hay proposing that McKinley refrain from endorsing the Nicaragua route until he had investigated the Panama route with equal care. He followed up his letter first by advising Bunau-Varilla to come to America to help in the approaching battle of the routes and then by moving to Washington for the winter, shortly after his eighty-first birthday in November 1898, in order to use what influence he had on behalf of the Panama Canal. It seemed to him that he had some success. The President reported to Congress on December 5 that the canal commission would soon complete its investigation; he showed obvious expectation that the Nicaragua route would be adopted, but he did not, in so many words, demand the creation of a canal across Nicaragua as many people had expected him to do. Bigelow wrote in his diary:

> I perceive that the President in his message practically follows the advice I gave to Hay in a letter a few weeks ago to content himself with urging the importance of a transcontinental canal, but not to make himself the partisan of the Nicaragua route until he had taken as much pains to inform himself about the Panama route and [as] he had taken to inform himself of the other.[26]

The following month when the Senate passed the Nicaragua Canal Bill, Bigelow for some reason felt no concern; the ultimate decision, he noted merely, would rest with the President. So he continued seeing his friends, John Hay who personally leaned to the Nicaragua route but had no strong convictions on the subject, Wayne Parker who frankly said he preferred the Panama route, the Pinchots, the Bancrofts, Henry Adams. ("He is an inspired prophet or crazy," Bigelow noted of Adams, incidentally. "He says Russia and Germany must be regarded as one in casting the horoscope of the future. That all the Latin States France included are going out with the tide. . . . he said that the time approaches when the world [will] belong to Russia and the United States.") He saw, in fact, as many people as he could whose friendship for the Panama route seemed worth cultivating. On March 8, Panama advocates won a major victory when Congress suddenly appropriated $1,000,000 for an investigation of all proposed routes instead of voting immediately for the Nicaragua scheme. William N. Cromwell took to himself credit for that action. So also did Bunau-Varilla, who then divided it with his friends Lieutenant-Commander Asher Baker and John Bigelow, writing: "Thanks to Mr. Bigelow, light fell on the Government itself through the intermediary of Mr. Hay. Thanks to Lieutenant Baker it penetrated the two recognized heads of the House." Probably all of them, and others as well, influenced the action of Congress. Certainly Bigelow seemed not surprised by the appropriation. The following day he made a highly typical notation in his journal:

Now 1st Yesterday Congress appropriated $20 millions of money to carry out a treaty stipulation for the extinction of the Spanish title to the entire group of Philippine islands. 2. The President in his message in recommending an interoceanic canal omitted to recommend specifically and exclusively the Nicaragua route and 3. Yesterday Congress appropriated $1 million of dollars to be used by the President to investigate all Isthmian Canal routes, especially the Nicaraguan and Panama routes, while the Bill for a canal in Nicaragua was rejected. These three coincidences make me suspect that the difficulties of being a prophet may be exaggerated.[27]

During the next years, while the Walker Commission carried on its comparative investigation of the two routes and Bunau-Varilla won the support of Senator Mark Hanna and the engineer George Morison by his exhibitions based upon the book Bigelow had told him to write in '91, Bigelow continued to urge the Panama route whenever opportunity arose and wherever he happened to be. Early in 1901 when Bunau-Varilla made a whirlwind lecture tour across the United States, Bigelow managed through George Parsons, the engineer of New York's subway, to get his friend a twenty-minute hearing before the hostile

New York Chamber of Commerce, which, though too short a time to win converts, was good publicity nonetheless. Shortly thereafter he wrote to Bunau-Varilla, who had returned to France, that he must issue a frank and disarming statement upon canal finances, since much of the antagonism that Bigelow ran into resulted from fear of the costliness of the Panama route. Bunau-Varilla complied in his "Second Appeal to the French People," then wrote to Bigelow: "It is I believe decisive from the point of view for which you told me to make special effort." [28]

Frenchmen, however, did not respond to the appeal. Thereafter Bunau-Varilla's attention centered exclusively upon getting American support. Finally, in January 1902 after the New Canal Company agreed to sell out to the United States for $40,000,000, the Walker Commission formally advocated the Panama route, and the battleground shifted to Congress. Cromwell made enormous efforts to convert Congressmen, but his story belongs elsewhere. Bunau-Varilla labored heroically. Bigelow again did his bit to help, this time by arranging a dinner party to take place just after the Walker Commission approved the Panama route, for the purpose of introducing Bunau-Varilla to Paul Dana of the *Sun.* Soon Bunau-Varilla acknowledged his gratitude in his endearing if effusive manner, calling the *Sun's* first editorial on behalf of the Panama Canal, "a fruit of the tree which your friendship has planted. . . ." [29]

Mark Hanna swung his full support to the Panama route, apparently honestly convinced that it was to the best interests of the United States, and the Senate passed the Spooner amendment providing for a canal at Nicaragua only if the New Canal Company and Colombia failed to make satisfactory financial arrangements with the United States. The problem then became one of negotiating with Colombia. Its representative, Dr. Concha, was not amenable; and on December 1 he departed from Washington, leaving the more co-operative Dr. Herrán to negotiate with Secretary Hay. The very following day Bigelow happened to send to a personal friend who might possibly be interested — to John Hay — a letter which he had received from Bunau-Varilla denouncing Colombian immorality in its rumored plan to take over the Canal Company and get the French Company's $40,000,000 as well as its own just fees. He enclosed with the letter a copy of a cable Bunau-Varilla had sent to President Marroquín of Colombia warning him that if he did not take prompt action, the United States would drop the Panama route. Hay returned the letter to Bigelow, but kept the cable. [30]

Ensuing United States negotiations with Colombia were complicated by Colombian misconceptions, remoteness, and domestic problems, which were, unfortunately, to prove insurmountable. In January 1903, its representative signed a treaty — the Hay-Herrán treaty — granting to the United States rights in Panama in return for the payments previously proposed by Bunau-Varilla to President Marroquín and very possibly shown to Hay by Bigelow.[31] Two months later the United States Senate ratified the treaty, but in August the Colombian Senate rejected it.

Bunau-Varilla almost despaired. President Roosevelt had been a good friend to the Panama route, but he could not afford to let matters drift longer; an election was coming up in which he had to show some definite accomplishment to catch the imagination of the people. Bigelow was not especially surprised, therefore, when he went to New York to meet his expected guests from France, Mme. Bunau-Varilla and her daughter, to find Philippe Bunau-Varilla with them, or to hear that his friend had decided at the last moment that his wife needed his escort and help in collecting their young son who had spent the summer with the Bigelows in Maine. Privately Bunau-Varilla explained to Bigelow that he would be in America only for eight or ten days:

> . . . to see that the Washington govt. makes no mistake in dealing with Columbia in the next half dozen days. The time limit for the ratification expired at midnight last past. He professes to have no doubt that the treaty will be ratified but he thinks it may be at the end of a revolutionary crisis, though he believes that the treaty will see daylight again in five or six days.[32]

The eight or ten days Bunau-Varilla expected to stay in America lengthened into as many weeks. He was desperately busy; the work of his lifetime depended upon his immediate actions. He saw Dr. Amador, leader of a group of would-be revolutionists in Panama, who was seeking financial assistance in New York. He saw John Bassett Moore, Professor of International Law at Columbia University and a close friend of Roosevelt, and followed that with a letter which Moore might conceivably pass on to his friend. In it he repeated his well-known belief that if Colombia refused to ratify the treaty Panama might revolt. He observed:

> But it is most probable that the explosion of this sentiment will only take place if it be encouraged beforehand by the United States; if it should receive a financial subsidy and a moral pledge that the new government will be recognized by America and protected from Columbia's soldiers immediately after the proclamation of independence.[33]

He saw Francis B. Loomis, a personal friend and now fortunately Assistant Secretary of State. On Saturday, October 10, he even conferred with the President.

After that meeting he went to "The Squirrels" for the weekend, where his family were Bigelow's guests, and described his plans in detail for Bigelow's benefit. The summary which Bigelow made of those plans and of the actions to which they gave rise was shown to Bunau-Varilla by Grace Bigelow in 1913, after her father's death. What Bunau-Varilla had to say of his old friend's accuracy, she immediately wrote out and attached to the diary:

> Mr. Bunau-Varilla was very much pleased to read these pages which he pronounced to be admirably accurate except for a few points which seem to have been confused in Mr. Bigelow's memory.

Those confusions were the date of the arrival of the U.S.S. *Nashville* at Colón, and Bigelow's belief that Roosevelt and Hay were fully informed of Bunau-Varilla's plans for the revolution — a belief Bigelow always held. Roosevelt denied it in a letter to Bigelow on January 6, 1904, writing:

> Of course I have no idea what Bunau-Varilla advised the revolutionists, or what he said in any telegrams to them as to either Hay or myself, or from anyone authorized to speak for us. He is a very able fellow, and it was his business to find out what he thought our government would do. I have no doubt that he was able to make a very accurate guess, and to advise his people accordingly. In fact, he would have been a very dull man had he been unable to make such a guess.[34]

A year later, nevertheless, in the course of a letter to Hay, Bigelow gaily referred to ". . . the Minister of the French King who lent Franklin $15,000,000 to do for our colonies what you and Bunau-Varilla — I do not add the President, *il ne faut pas decouvrir le Pape* — did for Panama."[35]

Perhaps Bigelow had misunderstood the Frenchman. In 1913 when Congressional investigation of events leading to the Panama revolution was in full swing, Bunau-Varilla told Miss Bigelow:

> . . . that far from unfolding his plans to anyone belonging to the American government, he strictly abstained from it in his personal relations with members of this government. He limited himself to study the dispositions of the American government on the Panama question and he modelled his action on these observations.[36]

Certainly Bunau-Varilla and Roosevelt told the same story. Yet perhaps Bigelow had not misunderstood the Frenchman. More likely he made the wholly natural mistake of failing to see any signal distinction either of a practical or moral nature between privately exchanged words and private, nonverbalized understandings. The record he made in his journal within a week of Bunau-Varilla's conversation with Roosevelt states:

> Bunau-Varilla was up over Sunday, has seen the President and the Ass't Secretary of State; unfolded to them his scheme for proceeding with the Isthmian Canal without much more delay, and which he has been talking over with me in case, the Columbians failed to ratify the treaty. It is in brief to have Isthmians revolt from the Columbian govt. declare their independence over the territory embraced only by the Watersheds of the Chagres and Rio Grande Rivers issue a Proclamation to that effect, adopt the Constitution of Cuba at the same time, and give Dictatorial powers to the President who is an old and trusty friend of B-V., have the U. S. send vessels to protect the Railway as it did during the uprising four years ago and forbid any fighting on the Canal territory which would protect the new state from any hostility that could do it any harm, etc. &c. B.-V went down again Monday [to New York] and the same [day] left for Washington to ascertain whether the govt of the U. S. would carry out this programme. He is under the impression that it will unless the Columbian Congress changes front and renders such a revolt unnecessary to the Isthmians.[37]

A week later, on October 19, Bunau-Varilla was again at Highland Falls. What happened there and thereafter, so far as Bigelow understood it, is best told in his words:

> Bunau-V. returned from Washington this morning. He has seen the Secretary of State during his absence, for the first time to talk with him. He recd from [   ] the assurance that if safety of the R.R. is threatened a sufficient naval force will be at both extremities of the RR to protect it &c &c &c. B-V. read me the Proclamation of Independence which will be issued, and his wife and Grace [Bigelow] have gone to Jenny's house Stonyhurst (which is deserted . . .) to make the flag which is to be unfurled. The[y] went there to be perfectly a l'abri des curieux. The proclamation will be followed by reading the Constitution of Cuba mutatis, mutandis. The proclamation declares B-V. an honorary citizen of the Republic for his great services first as chief Engineer of the Canal and afterwards in turning the attention of the U. S. to Panama from Nicaragua as the most practicable

waterway between the two Oceans. He proposes that immediately by plebescite the people shall send delegates to a constuent [sic] assembly adopt the Constitution elect a president and provide an organization for a government. B.-V. is to be appointed at once the diplomatic representative of the Republic of "The Isthmus of Panama" in Washington. This will enable him to exert a directing influence over the Canal Commission sitting at Washington. He makes himself responsible for 500,000 personally as a necessary lubricator. . . . he has a letter from Obaldiah [sic] recently apptd Governor of Panama which leaves no doubt of his sympathy with the revolt. . . . B.-V. has prepared detailed instructions for the enterprise from beginning to end which he will entrust his friend Amador to execute. He sails I believe on Wednesday B.-V. does not expect more than 10 days to elapse before Panama becomes the Capital of an independent State, and will fly a flag of her own made at Stonyhurst.[38]

Two days later he continued his narrative:

Sunday night after the children retired Grace & Mr. & Mrs. Bunau-Varilla sat up in the library until 11:30 making the flag for the new State or nation rather, to be called the Isthmus of Panama. B.-V. had bought the material, all of silk during the morning in town. The next day B.-V. went to town. He returned this morning and tells me that he handed over to Amador all the material for inaugurating the revolution on the Isthmus and promised to give the insurgents a credit in New York probably with the Seligman's of $100,000 providing everything is done precisely as he has given written instructions to do, including his designation as Minister to the U. S. The establishment of the New Govt. must be established within ten days or not attempted. . . .

B.-V. returned to the City this evening and expects to return on Friday. Congress is to meet in Extra Session on Novr. 9th ostensibly to act on the reciprocity treaty with Cuba but I fancy the emergency likely to rise between this and the 10th of Novr. was more distinctly in the President's mind when [he] signed the call [to Congress] though he said nothing about it in his message.

The Bunau-Varillas moved to the Hotel Amsterdam in New York on October 30. Four days later Bigelow opened his Gramercy Park home. That same day, November 3, the revolution in Panama went off according to schedule. Thereafter events moved fast. Hay wired recognition of the new Republic on November 6, an example of indecent haste which Bigelow quite approved. Soon Bunau-Varilla's credentials as Minister to the United States arrived and he departed for Washington to represent his new government. Satisfied that the interests of

America, the Canal Company, and the citizens of Panama had been well-served, equally sure that Colombia was receiving its just rewards for its selfish, grasping effort to block the world's progress, Bigelow in New York eagerly awaited word that all was settled. It came at midnight, November 18, in a telegram sent that evening from Washington at 7:35 P.M.:

I ARRIVED TODAY AT SIX FORTY AT THE END OF A NINETEEN YEARS CAMPAIGN THE PERILS OF WHICH HAVE BEEN LESSENED BY YOUR WISDOM THE BITTERNESS OF WHICH HAS BEEN SWEETENED BY YOUR FRIENDSHIP I HAVE SIGNED CANAL TREATY WITH SECRETARY HAY. BUNAU-VARILLA.

CHAPTER 22

Elder Statesman

[*1886–1911*]

THE BACKDROP of continental resources wrought upon by patient, inventive genius portended a glorious climax to the late nineteenth century. But as the scene unfolded, the Babel swell of the new immigration and the vast shifts in economy — which came too fast to be understood or assimilated in comfort — brought, instead, a new, upsetting note in politics and letters, where eager praise clashed against bewildered, bitter protest. A long list of able politicians had each his passing moment during the quarter-century between 1886 and 1911, while a few men, their pockets bulging with America's wealth, played a major part in every act and left to nondescript masses anonymous walk-on roles. These were the decades when Bigelow reached his seventieth, his eightieth, his ninetieth anniversaries; the decades when a senile Lotos-land obscured those few of his great contemporaries whom death had not effaced, yet when his interests ranged from the free library in New York City to the Panama Canal, from "The Blinding Influences of Sin" to "What Shall We do with Our Ex-Presidents?" Each added year brought to him new interests, or raised again issues of his youth upon which as an old man he once more took a fearless stand.

He found much in the new America puzzling: the organized labor movement, the continuing strength of the tariff lobbyists, the widespread fear of big business. He could not understand that the Manchester liberals' creed was antiquated. Nor could he understand, any better than he had in 1867, the prevailing emphasis upon material possessions. Why anyone wanted vast wealth he did not know; nor, for that matter, why anyone hated poverty — which was perfectly understandable, because display of riches bored him and he had never known poverty. From Tilden's view Bigelow was a dilettante who never would make money, but from the view of the average man Bigelow did well enough. Retiring at forty-three years of age, thereafter living within the income of small salaries, royalties, and the interest on his capital, he gave a minimum of time to his investments, yet handled them shrewdly enough to increase his annual income from less than $10,000 in 1867 to more than $43,000 in 1910.[1] Able to satisfy all of his material wants, which were not many — he found, for example, that ordinary chicken wire made as satisfactory doors as expensive fine-wire screens behind which to lock his books, and when he traveled his lunch from preference rarely cost more than twenty cents — he knew that members of the great middle class in America could provide equally well for themselves. Why they strove for more he could not understand. Some of his contemporaries, similarly situated, looked cynically upon their fellows. Bigelow, however, sustained by faith in his country and belief in a guiding Providence which wastes no motion, concluded that the flaw of materialism was but a phase in the process of growth. Yet he was not a fatalist; by his creed every citizen must try to scrape the evil from himself and his country if the high promise of early America was one day to be realized.

Obviously his patterns of thought had not changed; indeed, with advancing years they inevitably became rigid. What did not atrophy was his capacity to modify conclusions in the light of new evidence. That, perhaps, more than any other quality in him, explains why he stimulated and inspired younger men, why they entertained for him at once an affectionate regard and a healthy respect. Possibly that capacity to discover new aspects of truth, so rare in an old man, resulted from his unusual physical vigor combined with his established habit of reflecting not only upon the people he met and the books he read but upon the new regions he visited.

Thirteen times after his seventieth birthday he made trips to different parts of Europe — on one of them, in 1888, serving as United States Commissioner at the International Exposition at Brussels. Moreover, both before and after his seventieth year, he traveled throughout America, until he knew its regions and customs far better than did most of his countrymen. In 1874 he had taken a railroad trip through the Southwest. In 1880, when he was sixty-two, he had spent two winter months exploring mines in Nevada, riding in sub-zero weather in a springless, public "jerky" across mile after mile of winter-thinned sagebrush, pushing on through a blizzard to examine the Lookout and Silver Wreath mines. To be sure, that trip had yielded him a cold and a bad investment; but it had given him also a new insight into the free and easy, independent society of a gambling region. Early in '82 he had gone to Mexico and thence to Yucatán, curious to see the land about which he had ghost-written a book forty years before. In the fall of that same year, he had traveled West once more to inspect a ranch in Wisconsin in which he had invested. Two more Western tours had followed, in '83. On the first he had gone to California, as the guest of William H. Osborn of the Illinois Central Railroad, and had returned by way of Arizona where at last he understood why Frémont used to urge a canal linking the desert to the Gulf of California. The second trip had taken him across the vast stretches of the Northwest, as one of Henry Villard's guests invited to witness the last spike driven into the Northern Pacific Railroad. On that notorious tour of celebrities, he had found the repetitious, ornate ceremonies so boring, the profusion of cigars and wines so vulgar, that in Portland and Seattle, dodging his eminent companions, he had quietly divided his days between talks with Westerners, fishing, and idling in Pacific Coast bookstores — so far away, so different from his beloved Parisian haunts.

Yet he never regretted going. These trips through America, though they did not shift his focal point from the Eastern Seaboard-Western European world, did give him new awareness of the complexities of regional issues which needed to be considered in the formulation of national policies. And after his seventieth birthday, he continued to travel in America, constantly renewing and deepening his sense of the whole country. Time and again, during the last fourth of his life, he left New York to go to Massachusetts, Maine, West to the Pacific, South as far as the Panama Canal. Sightseeing he found a bore, but talking with people whose lives were cast in other lines was an ever-new adventure.[2]

New York, however, was always headquarters. Much of his time was spent at "The Squirrels" or at his city home at 21 Gramercy Park — conveniently close to Tilden's house and a present from Tilden, who purchased it in 1881 while the Bigelows were in Europe, then deeded it to Bigelow's eldest daughter to forestall the protests he knew his friend would make.[3] By the turn of the century Bigelow was a familiar figure on the streets of New York. People used to point out the tall, stout, well-dressed old gentleman when he took his customary walk from his home to the serene little New Church on East Thirty-fifth Street or drove in his modest tandem to visit friends and, likely enough, to stop en route at a bookstore. They liked his alert cheerful glance, his healthy good looks, the way he made a little ceremony of his bows to friends and acquaintances among a younger generation. And they were highly amused, sometimes, when they saw him stop short at a street corner to shake his cane angrily at a swerving truck.

Several hours of each day he sat at his desk writing letters to Cleveland, McKinley, Roosevelt, Taft, as one President succeeded another; to John Hay, Elihu Root, senators, newspaper editors — all of them men he knew — expressing a strong opinion, answering their queries, volunteering strategic advice. Indeed, his life between his seventieth and his ninety-fourth years was so varied and crowded that it is hard to keep the picture clear. Roughly, his interests fell into four categories: civic projects, national and international issues, his family, and his religion.

Americans had always placed education high on their list of civic projects, as they did during the quarter-century of Bigelow's old age. They had always asserted their right to direct the educators of their children, refusing, in this institution so closely affecting each individual life, to surrender their democracy to the expert. True to the American type, Bigelow held strong opinions on current pedagogy. True to himself, he expressed them openly, boldly, in strong terms. More often than not he disagreed with the theorists, for, like most people whose intellectual interests continue to develop in manhood, he never ceased to regret the waste and misdirection which he felt had been his portion in school. His opinion of any educational project was largely determined by the answers to two questions: Was it a private, voluntary activity, or was it superimposed by government? Did it turn out individuals or conformists? He held the conviction, in common with almost all Americans, that a high level of education was essential to democracy, that ". . . the average civilization of the whole of a nation is the true measure of its civilization. To train a few hundred out of 40 million to be great writers and artists, leaving the remaining millions in the densest ignorance and hereditary stupidity is not civilization." [4]

Unlike most Americans, however, he believed that such a level could be achieved only by providing opportunities for self-improvement, never by forcing people to support schools. Throughout his adult life he considered government control or even regulation of education evil. As a youth he had argued in the columns of the *Democratic Review* against required schooling and against all class legislation, in which he had included free education of the poor. Sixty years later, in 1906, he again objected to cooping up youngsters in the healthy morning hours, to leveling them off and teaching them conformity, when from the sturdy independence of the poor had always come America's leaders.[5] In 1909, when he was ninety-two years old, he bluntly refused to support a movement for a Federal Children's Bureau, and when its advocates wanted to know why the nonagenarian was opposed, he told them:

> More than fifty years ago I condemned state pedagogy in an editorial in the *Evening Post,* and as yet I have learned nothing to change my mind. One of the first of the deplorable consequences of the system was to provoke sectarian difficulties about schoolbooks. That was followed shortly by the exclusion of the Bible from the curriculum of the public schools. As a consequence the children who frequent them never hear of the Bible where they are sent expressly and exclusively to be educated . . . and they leave those schools as ignorant of that Saviour as a Fegee Islander or a Hottentot. . . .
> Had the state not meddled with the schools all the freedom secured by those early immigrants, would be enjoyed still by their descendants. Now the proscription in New York is worse than that from which our ancestors fled. . . .
> The greatest danger to all governments always has been the possession of too much power. That is an appetite which grows by what it feeds on, and the more power a government gets the more it needs to sustain itself. Our common schools cost us probably three times as much as would be required to educate their pupils in a far wiser way than they are educated at present. Did the American parentage raise the money voluntarily for educational purposes, they would have something to say about the way it should be spent and what kind of religion or morals should be taught in their schools nor would there be any lack of means to secure far better facilities for it than we now possess, in my opinion.[6]

His attitude was rooted in the old Jeffersonian belief that where government was least, progress was greatest, where government kept out, men stepped in, accepting among their responsibilities that of helping their fellows to find their own interests and to develop their capacities. Therefore he approved of private efforts to bring knowledge to the underprivileged. He had tremendous respect for two educated women he knew who went South to make their knowledge available to Negroes. And because he had always believed that the inherent capacity of Negroes and whites was the same, because he believed that democracy could not flourish if any group was suppressed, he agreed to serve as President of their newly-formed Board of Trustees of the Calhoun Colored School in Alabama. When he visited the school in March 1893 he was impressed by the vocational

training given to three hundred pupils and by their rapid achievement of literacy, while the evasions which kept these educated Negroes
from voting and buying land at fair prices strengthened his resolve
to work for them. For similar reasons, also in 1893, he accepted the
presidency of the Armstrong Association to use what influence he had
to raise funds for the Hampton Institute in Virginia.[7]

However, helping the less fortunate to help themselves was an adult
occupation, in his opinion, and not a device to arouse interest among
privileged youth in sociology courses. Hence in the same year — he
was seventy-five then — when he was one of fifty New Yorkers gathered to hear President Seth Low of Columbia University describe his
plan for sending students to live in the slums in order to learn what
problems the poor faced and to raise standards there, he labeled it
charlatanry:

> If he wanted to lift these people out of the slums to a better
> life, instead of sending the young men of wealth down to live
> with them he should advise rather that the rich young men bring
> the slummers home to live with them. . . . If they don't invite
> the slummers to return their visits, they break down no barriers
> between the rich and the poor, on the contrary they insult the
> slummers by treating them as outcast objects of charity thereby
> increasing rather than weakening the antagonism between the
> two classes.
> Then Mr. Low and his associates seem to entirely overlook the
> interests and welfare of the young men whom he proposes to
> expose to all the hideous influences of slum life. . . . Which is
> better to degrade our young men to the average of the slummers
> or to bring the slummers one by one or as fast as is possible out
> of the slums and raise them to the average of decent people.
> This mode of dealing with the slummers seems not only to
> involve a fearful waste of health and character but what is worse
> to lead to a fearful development of self-righteousness, than which
> nothing is more fatal to the growth of genuine Christ-like char-
> acter. . . .[8]

One form of compulsory education did receive Bigelow's endorsement, the one form never adopted in America. That was military education. He had keenly felt the lack of it in his own education upon
the outbreak of the Civil War. In the '70's when he saw how Germany
profited from such a program, he had campaigned unsuccessfully for
enforced military training in the United States. And in the '80's after
serving on the Boards of Inspectors at West Point and Annapolis, he
tried a second time, and again without success, to win converts to a

national program of military education. Nevertheless, he remained convinced that the time would come when the arts of war would be treated as an essential in every American's education, when their study would be made compulsory as the only way to insure lasting freedom to the nation.

Another educational device, in his opinion perhaps the most important, he found deplorably limited in America. That was the free cultural institution, in existence for those who wanted it but forced upon no one. Hence he delighted in museums like the Metropolitan Museum of Art, which he served as a trustee from his seventieth to his ninetieth year, and in libraries like the New York Public Library, in whose development he played a major role. Similarly he found value in endowed colleges and graduate schools, such as the New York Law School, of which he was an incorporator and a trustee from 1891 to 1907. To a lesser degree he was interested in the erection of monuments and other memorials with which the New York Art Commission was concerned; he was a member of the Commission from his eighty-second to his ninety-fourth year. Bigelow believed that if Americans had constantly before them the features and names of their useful citizens, they might remember to cherish their heritage of freedom and be inspired, not to imitate the past, but to conserve and add to the nation's reservoir of values.

So he had helped to arrange for a statue of Seward on lower Fifth Avenue. More earnestly, he worked to create a memorial to William Cullen Bryant, "the only man in the United States who cannot be replaced, whose death would leave the country substantially poorer in genius in character in moral courage & purpose . . . ," he had noted in his diary six years before Bryant died, adding:

> Longfellow is a melodious poet but had neither the learning nor the philosophy or wisdom or statescraft of Bryant. Whittier is not the artist nor the scholar nor the statesman that Bryant is. Holmes is witty but not wise. His wit edits him instead of him editing his wit. You have never found Bryant lending his genius to glorify or ennoble anything not essentially noble.[9]

In 1884 he succeeded in having Reservoir Square renamed Bryant Park, the first public honor tendered Bryant by the city in which he had lived so long. Six years later he issued a biography of Bryant, not to compete with Godwin's more scholarly account, he said, but to let the average man know what manner of man was this gentle poet and aggressive editor who for fifty years championed liberalism as his century conceived it. He elaborated plans for a statue of Bryant in

Central Park. Later he shifted them to Bryant Park after it was selected as the site of the new Public Library, to which books from Bryant's collection, chosen by Bigelow, had been donated. There Herbert Adams's statue of Bryant was eventually erected just west of the library on a terrace facing Sixth Avenue. Similarly he tried to have a noble memorial to Tilden erected appropriately near the library which Tilden had helped to make possible, on the east and west sides of Forty-second Street at Fifth Avenue. That location, however, and others which Bigelow sought were turned down until in 1911 a site at One Hundred and Twelfth Street overlooking the Hudson was agreed upon.[10]

Numbers of other projects looking to practical improvements within a brief span of time engaged his attention. One such undertaking was the drafting of the New York Constitution of 1894, upon which Bigelow worked as a Tammany delegate. He had no special love for Tammany, though he was a New York Democrat, but he had no objection to machines *per se* or to bosses, as he had explained back in 1881 in a long, tempered letter written from Italy to his good friend Lawrence Godkin, when Godkin with Carl Schurz and Horace White took over the management of the *New York Evening Post:*

In politics as in war organization is the first element of success. . . . So in politics I think history will show that whenever the Machine ceases to work the people not only are making no progress but are declining to a lower level of civilization. The difficulty with Russia, with Turkey, with Tunis and all the Anthropomorphous Civilizations of the world is that the people have no machines, or if they have, cannot get them into position so that they will work. What in fact is the *Evening Post* but a "Machine" organized for the effective employment of a much larger sum of money for the number interested, than has ever been at the disposal of the Tammany or Conckling machines, in directing public opinion in the way supposed to be best calculated to promote the personal interests of its proprietors. And what better definition than that, can be given of any machine. It seems to me that in quarreling with the *machine ad qua* we are imitating our remote ancestors who ascribed their diseases to the stars or to witchcraft. Machines are incidents not causes. We have to go farther back for a remedy for the degradation of our politics. Does not our difficulty rise primarily from the fact that the greatest rewards and highest prizes within easy reach of the great body of the American people are political. Wealth excepted, we have no standard of merit of anything like national acceptation, which has not a strictly political origin, which is not more or less the reward of party services and subject in a corresponding degree to party vicissitudes. One of the consequences of this is that all that is most selfish, most presumptuous and most unscrupulous rushes either into politics or mining. . . . But this I venture to believe is a transitory state. Every day it seems to me political prizes become of less relative value. Every day the class that can afford to be indifferent to them is enlarging. . . . When those who do not want office shall be in the majority, and that time I am sure is approaching, we shall hear no more complaints of the machine nor have the least difficulty in establishing an effective civil service. But I do not see how we shall ever be able to dispense with the boss in politics any more than with the chief of police unless we are willing to see society fall an easy prey to the dangerous classes, who are always equipped with machines and are skillfully bossed; and they will continue to be in the U. S. at least so long as its eminent citizens are not ashamed to publicly proclaim their right to pay off their private debts with public offices. . . .

I worked at killing machines a good many years and as I flattered myself not without a certain amount of success, but I came to the conclusion at last, that killing machines was a good deal like beheading ghosts or slaying Harlequin. All N. Y. boasted of its success in putting an end to the Tammany-Tweed machine and yet the same Tammany machine with Boss Kelly at its head was at the funeral and occupied front seats. You may succeed in destroying the Conckling machine but can only do so with the aid of the Blaine machine which will replace it. And you will have to continue the work of Sisyphus with a stone just as heavy — some think a good deal heavier — than that you have been rolling *in saecula saeculorum.*

Now the way to spoil the ghost business is to extinguish superstition; and the way to fight the machine in politics when it must be fought, is to give the people other and higher standards of merit than the successful management of an Alderman's canvass and to vary and multiply the prizes from which an honorable ambition may find inspiration. Increasing wealth constantly elevating standards of public instruction and the public press are bringing about these results if not as fast as some of us would desire, quite as fast as could fairly be expected, with due allowance for the half million of foreigners whom we have to take into the national stomach and digest every year.[11]

In 1892 Bigelow was strongly sympathetic with Edmund Kelly's new organization built to combat Tammany, but he refused to join it. "You hope," he wrote, "to counteract the influences of one political machine operating upon the plane of the wage-earning class which does most of the voting by creating another which is to be operated on the plane of the wage-paying class which does most of the scolding but comparatively little of the voting. . . . A Club that would have any chance of coping with Tammany Hall must be composed of the class that does the voting or are in direct and sympathetic relation with them. . . ." [12] So, though he disliked some Tammany practices, he tolerated that Society as a necessity and readily accepted its invitation to be a delegate to the Constitutional Convention of 1894.

Bigelow thought it high time to improve New York's basic law, which had been only slightly revised since he had helped the Radicals write it in 1846. Yet, though able men labored diligently throughout the summer, he was vastly disappointed in their resulting draft. He thought that it failed to correct old weaknesses; it failed to write into the Constitution more liberal provisions such as woman suffrage; it seemed to him that it succeeded only in strengthening an aristocracy. He believed that was because the majority of the delegates were Republicans, who, "as a party entertain a traditional distrust of the people and are always trying to concentrate power in the hands of privileged classes." Consequently he refused to serve on the committee appointed by his friend Joseph Choate, the presiding officer, to recommend the proposed Constitution to the people.[13]

Between 1886 and 1911 Bigelow's interests ranged far beyond New York state. For example, he protested vigorously in 1886 against the apparent disposition in Congress to end the treaty with Hawaii. It could not be long before the Pacific would be spanned by steamers, he asserted, and then Hawaii would be essential as a coaling station and naval depot. If the United States abrogated its treaty, Britain, Germany or Japan, or all three, could be counted upon to take over the islands with the consequences that the United States would lose out in the coming race for the Pacific.[14]

He followed the fortunes of Cleveland — sure, at the very time of his personal disappointment in not receiving Executive appointment, that ". . . Cleveland is a fair expression of the average intelligence and the morals of the nation and that is the best possible description of a good President of a Republic. I think he may have rough sledding for a year or two but in the end he will probably win the confidence of the Nation as Jackson did." Three years later, however, he called Cleveland an infatuated ass when he lost the election and his chance to put through a free-trade program because of what Bigelow considered a stubbornly tactless pre-election challenge to protectionists. Yet when Cleveland returned to the White House in 1892, Bigelow rejoiced that "the restoration of the Democratic party by overwhelming majorities has I hope delivered the country for a generation at least from the grasp of the reckless scoundrels who were bankrupting the country." His hope, again, was short-lived. A year later he saw his party gradually breaking apart, losing its pre-eminence, he thought, through Cleveland's obtuseness:

> He seems to think he has nothing to do as President, but to make up his own mind as to what Congress should do; send them a message to that effect and pay no attention whatever to what they may think he ought to do. He either has no talent or makes no effort to prepare the minds of Congressmen for acting in concert with him.

When Cleveland undertook to mediate the British-Venezuelan dispute in 1896, Bigelow thought him anything but courageous:

> This on the eve of his application for a gold loan is one of those fatuous proceedings for which Cleveland has a peculiar gift. . . . The apprehension and disorder financially and politically wrought not only here but throughout the world is incalculable. If we are spared a war with England in consequence it will be mainly because of the sudden diversion of her attention by the congratulatory message sent by Kaiser Wilhelm to the Govr. of the Transvaal Republic.

He wrote furiously to William H. Russell, his old newspaper friend in England:

> It was the most inauspicious, inopportune, as well as brutal exhibition of Jingoism that ever emanated from the head of a responsible government. . . . Our Constitution has confided the war-making power to Congress. President Cleveland does not appear to have yet read the Constitution so far as that; and besides entirely misconstruing the language and import of President Monroe, he assumes the "Monroe Doctrine" to be a part of the formulated and established determination of the American people.

The Monroe Doctrine had been a red flag to Bigelow since the days of his Ministry to France. It never ceased to upset him: "It seems to me such a silly pretension when we own less than a quarter of this continent, that I cannot understand how men occupying the positions of Statesmen can trust themselves to lean upon it any more than they would lean upon the sharp end of a spear. Our people in Washington will have to climb down from this eminence one of these days." [15]

Yet he considered Cleveland far preferable to the next Democratic candidate. Back in '86 he had recorded dislike for "that horrid Bryan of Idaho and Chicago" who had called upon him in Washington one day and after ascertaining that Bigelow intended going to the Episcopal church the following Sunday, had insisted upon escorting him and sharing a pew. After the service Bigelow had bidden him a hasty adieu and had gone home alone, later noting: "It somewhat impaired the effect of a good sermon by Bishop Potter on the Magi who after they had seen the infant Jesus *returned home another way*." In 1896 he saw little choice between that same Bryan and McKinley; so he advocated a third party, as he had in 1848, as he was again to do in 1908 when he wanted Governor John A. Johnson of Minnesota to be run. In '96 he thought the new party should call itself the Democratic-Republican party, in order to unite men of both major political creeds to meet a crisis which he considered almost as grave as that of 1848–1860. He was distressed that his old party, the party of sound finance, "should now be led by a sort of Jack Cade and flying an anarchical flag which is only suitable for a horde of banditti. . . . The bond of union is that some people in the East are richer than others in the South and West, that Capital is crushing Labor and that the government should equalize the burdens of the people etc etc. This craze has got possession of a numerous class in the South and West." Therefore he voted for Palmer and Buckner, the third party Democrats, the Gold Democrats, and for Republican Congressmen and Assemblymen.[16]

In his opinion even McKinley was preferable to Bryan, though with him in office Bigelow looked forward to four bad years for the nation. However, at his gloomiest he never expected anything so bad as the War with Spain, which he condemned as roundly as he had the Mexican War a half century before:

> This war has made me nearly sick — it was so utterly inexcusable in its purposes and undertaken with such an ignominious lack of preparation. . . . We shall spend 100,000,000 before this year is out upon the war, and if successful will get as our compensation what we would hardly have accepted as a gift two years ago if the people had been consulted. When I was in Paris in 1863 I received a proposition from Prim, through an agent, to sell Cuba to our Government for 3,000,000 dollars. . . . I declined to entertain the proposition . . . because I looked upon the acquisition of Cuba with its population as a calamity.

He wrote to Mrs. Pinchot advising that she keep her son Amos from enlisting: "Enough lives have been sacrificed already to gratify the vanity and ambition of a few politicians in Washington and their newspaper parasites." Similar letters went to other friends, and to his son, John Junior, a West Point graduate in active service, he suggested writing a book "to illustrate the wickedness as well as the folly of attempting to carry on a political and a military campaign at the same time and with the same weapons." [17]

Once the fighting ceased, he wrote to his old friend Whitelaw Reid, shortly after Reid had been appointed one of the Peace Commissioners, to explain why he believed it constitutional to acquire territory even if it were never to be given statehood and to suggest offering Spain $20,000,000 for the Philippines, precisely the sum later agreed upon. He had already written similarly to John Hay, his former secretary, now McKinley's Secretary of State, who replied on September 4: "I fear you are right about the Philippines, and I hope the Lord will be good to us poor devils who have to take care of them. I marvel at your suggesting that we pay for them. I should have expected no less of your probity; but how many except those educated by you in the school of morals and diplomacy would agree with you?" But the purchase of the friars' rights in the Philippines and the ruthless suppression of the natives were different matters. To James Brooks, his assistant in consular days, who wrote angrily of the Philippine maneuvers, the octogenarian replied with grim jocularity:

> Be patient my friend we are founding an empire and don't you forget that the men who founded the Roman Empire were suckled by a wolf. Tantae molis erat Romanum condere gentum. That kind of molis is greater than ever now. It takes wolfs milk to build empires against the wishes of the native born inhabitants.
>
> Oh yes I know all about the Constitution and the rights of man and all that sort of thing. Why shut up Brooks you are getting old and are falling out of the procession.[18]

For the first time in his life, Bigelow deliberately stayed home on the following Election Day, after expressing opposition to both McKinley and Bryan so strongly that the *Times* softened his comments almost beyond recognition before publishing them. Nor was he more content when Roosevelt stepped into the Presidency upon McKinley's death. Now in his eighties, clinging to the liberalism of his youth, recalling his own life of unlimited work, Bigelow was impatient with legislation limiting hours of work, irate at Roosevelt's sympathetic dealings with striking coal miners, shocked by talk of limiting incomes, and furious at Roosevelt's play for votes through trust-busting gestures. But what roused him to action was the President's mediation of the Russo-Japanese war. In 1897 he had refused an invitation to the Mohonk Conference on international arbitration. His reading of history had taught him how fortunate the United States was that its wars had not been arbitrated. It had taught him, too, that no tribunal could prevent war if a powerful country was bent upon it. To that belief he continued to hold. In 1905 he thought that the President should favor the continuation of the Russo-Japanese war until the hand of the Romanovs was so weakened that the Russian people could come into their own. Only the bankers wanted peace, he asserted — and the businessmen who sought the friendship of Japan.[19]

So he drafted a letter to Roosevelt in June, writing, in part: "The Master who is a Silent Partner to all wars, is not worrying about the holders of Russian Securities in St. Petersburg and Frankfort and Paris and London or in Wall St. He is not worrying either about the slaughter of his creatures that is staining the soil of Manchuria. . . . He is thinking rather of the government and institutions to be provided for the training of countless future generations to qualify them for a higher seat in his Kingdom." As to Russia: ". . . If the lessons of history are to be trusted, restlessness, agitations, revolutions must be the warp or the woof of her history until her people rule her government instead of being ruled by it." Finally, he asked the President if he cared ". . . to place your administration in like relations to the people of Russia — now struggling hopefully for a free and enlightened government — that the English and French governments occupied towards ours in 1863–4 when they were trying to force President Lincoln to purchase peace by a surrender of more than half of our national territory to be desecrated to the perpetuation of Chattel Slavery." [20]

But he decided against sending the letter when his friend William Mackay Laffan of the *Sun* convinced him it was useless in face of the President's fixed intention to mediate in order to build closer ties with Japan. The following month, however, after John Hay died and Elihu Root replaced him as Secretary of State, Bigelow sent Root a revision of his earlier letter, this time minimizing his references to Providence and the Silent Partner.[21] Bigelow was sure that the new Secretary, unlike Hay, would dominate the government and by sheer personal superiority would force Roosevelt to defer to him. However, peace negotiations continued. In September 1905 upon the conclusion of the Portsmouth Conference, Theodore Roosevelt was hailed throughout the world as a peacemaker, though not by old John Bigelow who had never been one to jump on bandwagons.

Let men prate of peace; he knew it meant little. It was embarrassing one April Sunday in 1907 to have the pastor of the New Church nominate Bigelow to accompany him to the coming Peace Congress and to have the congregation approve by a unanimous vote before Bigelow could get the floor. Sturdily Bigelow rose to explain that he must decline because he was not in sympathy with "Carnegie's Vanity Fair at the Hague." [22] Two months later he presented to the public, in a paper entitled *Peace Given As The World Giveth*, his reasons for refusing to attend any peace conferences of a contemporary nature. It won the applause of a few men like C. F. Adams, but not of many. Bigelow maintained that the result of the Portsmouth Conference was enough to quell anyone's interest in arbitration devices. Look at the casualties in Russia before and after Roosevelt wrote the peace, he urged, citing figures; look at the destruction of property; note to what extent that man-made peace increased the sufferings of the masses of Russians whose only hope of amelioration of their condition had lain in a weakening of Czarist power through a prolonged war. Because of Roosevelt's interference the Czar was continuing to terrorize the democrats among his subjects in a way "that can only terminate in Revolution." [23] Bigelow's brief pamphlet, remarkable in sprightliness and vigor for a man only a few months from ninety years of age, closed with a newspaper quotation of tortures inflicted upon Russian mutineers, and the sentence:

> During the very week in which the prison cells of St. Petersburg were the theaters of these peaceful amenities, shiploads of foreign notabilities were imported into the United States to participate in an international revel in honor of our apostolate of peace.
> > Peace indeed!
> > Peace given as the World giveth.
> > Creating a desert and calling it peace.[24]

He wrote to James Ford Rhodes:

> . . . Was that *a peace* which simply delivered the Czar's Kossacks from the grasp of the Japs to be turned loose upon the Czar's subjects, where they provoked the shedding of more blood and the waste of more property than could have resulted from a five years continuation of a war to the finish . . . ? [25]

The more Bigelow thought of the surging hope that an organization could bring peace to the world, the more he was convinced that high tariffs precluded any possibility of peace. Shortly before his pamphlet on the Portsmouth Treaty appeared, he had written an interview for the *New York Times* about the war in which the United States was presently engaged, the war between breadwinners and capitalists. In it he stated:

All our labor troubles and our wars between the bread-winners and the capitalists are attributable to our tariff legislation, by which a good share of the property of eighty millions of people is practically confiscated for the benefit of the three or four million who participate in the profits of such confiscations.

Although Bigelow had long been antagonistic to labor unions and labor weapons, although he still disliked them, he could try to understand them, old as he was, and he could modify his views where he saw new light. He now admitted that there was much to be said for labor and he began to develop his plan to bring peace to the two great economic classes in the United States, without which, he believed, his country could not effect a lasting peace between nations.[26]

As was to be expected, his plan was based upon the elimination of protective tariffs. He told a Tariff Reform Committee in 1909 when the Payne-Aldrich Tariff was under discussion:

All appeals for a revision and a reduction of the tariff are like appeals to inebriates not to drink to excess, to burglars not to burgle so much, to thieves not to steal so often, to swindlers not to swindle the chief of police or the judges of the criminal court. In each and every case these appeals are not merely a toleration of crime but an excuse for it. . . .

When your Reform Committee is prepared to take a firm stand against any tariff upon imports . . . I shall be happy to join you and to do what I can to promote the success of your labors. In such a work I should have the satisfaction of knowing that I was not even indirectly countenancing a vicious system of taxation, also that I was helping to put our statesmen upon an inquiry for sources of revenue that are not tainted with every crime, save murder, of which highwaymen have ever been condemned by the laws of God or man.[27]

Finally he presented his plan in *The Folly of Building Temples of Peace with Untempered Mortar; The Necessity of Building Temples of Peace with Tempered Mortar.* He was past ninety-two years of age when he wrote that, but he had not yet stopped fighting.

The clamor for peace, of which we hear so much of late, is only a clamor for "the peace that man giveth." It means, to those making most noise and professions about it, little more than a change of weapons with which to fight. The predatory classes nowadays make war by securing the protection of a tariff for their own industries, of which the unprotected millions have to bear all the burden. It is the sham coat of arms of Vanity Fair assumed from the peerage with *Pace in bello* for its motto.[28]

Talk of peace, of arbitration, he declared, was sheer hypocrisy so long as the United States conducted a commercial war through its tariffs against 90 per cent of its own citizens, and against all other commercial lands; so long as it maintained a new aristocracy wielding power and privileges far exceeding those of Southern slaveowners in other days; so long as it permitted the tariff to form unnatural class divisions in America and consequent bitterness among the oppressed majority.

In place of the tariff he proposed making the state the partner of every individual or corporation to whom it gave any share of the people's capital, by which he meant any share of the nation's natural resources or any special service from the people's government. Every charter granting land or a right of way to a transportation company, a telephone, telegraph or gas company; every patent whereby the State guaranteed protection to an inventor; every homestead carved from public lands, should carry with it an agreement to pay the State a percentage of profits. Were that done only with new undertakings, he noted, there could be no complaint of retroactive legislation. Gradually, as income from new enterprises came to the State, it could afford to reduce the tariff until in approximately fifty years protective tariffs would be nonexistent. Meanwhile industries dependent upon the special privilege of a tariff would have ample time to redirect the use of their capital and equipment.

Then, Bigelow believed, peace among Americans might become possible. Then Labor would be satisfied with its position, for consumers' goods would be markedly cheaper and the cost of government would come, as he thought it should, not from Labor's pocket by indirect taxes but from the surpluses remaining to capitalists after they had deducted a fair reward for their time, ingenuity, and risks. Nor should capitalists object to sharing their surplus, since it was the people's government which gave them the encouragement, assistance and the stable society without which they could not exist. Moreover, under his plan he believed that the incentive to enter business would not be lessened, because the Jeffersonian government which he envisioned would need only a small share from any one enterprise and that only after it was well established. Then Government, Business and Labor, that is, Americans, would be partners, not watchful antagonists. Then, at long last, Americans, having added economic unity to their political unity, might with some assurance of success take part in eliminating the causes of war over a still larger area. Visions of peace, Bigelow had always believed, had their place, but the practical man must look to the means by which they could be realized.

CHAPTER 23

Of the Double Tribe of Joseph

[*1886–1911*]

A SUMMARY view of John Bigelow's career exemplifies the influence religion can have upon a man who finds "God's House" everywhere and who does not keep his beliefs in mothballs with a frock coat for use on Sundays only. For decades it had been his custom to read in the Bible before breakfast each morning, to ponder what he read and to make marginal jottings in an effort to grasp the truths behind the incidental narratives. For help he turned primarily to Swedenborg's twelve-volume *Arcana Coelestia*, a work he read with painstaking attention four times during his life. Its significance for him was strikingly illustrated in 1909, when he was asked to list the ten books he considered most influential in his education. Only the Bible and the *Arcana Coelestia* was he sure of including. Possibly Maria Edgeworth's novels belonged on the list, Tocqueville's *Democracy*, Macaulay's articles in the *Edinburgh Review*, and possibly also Guizot's *History of Europe* and *History of France*, but Bigelow could not decide. Two books alone, out of all those he had read and enjoyed and been influenced by, had been supremely essential. Yet it irked him to be called a Swedenborgian, though he attended the New Church regularly and frequently wrote for the *New Jerusalem Magazine*. He was a Christian, he said, and no more a Swedenborgian than he was a Newtonian or Kantian, "unless it be that I read Swedenborgian writings more frequently than Newton's or Kant. S. not only never founded a sect but he most explicitly refused to countenance any attempts of the kind by his friends and students. He simply expounded the Bible."[1]

Bigelow had little use for dogma or ritual in the New Church or in any other. He thought that formal creeds tended to block spiritual growth. Prayers for gifts from God invariably disturbed him; they smacked too much of setting men's judgment above God's. He considered prayers for rain, such as he heard in his Highland Falls church, a relic of paganism. In his ninety-fourth year, after reading the prayers in Robert Louis Stevenson's *Letters from Vailima*, he commented: "They seem all to expect a great deal from the Lord promising but little in return." [2] He continually deplored the authoritarian basis of Catholicism and with much in Protestant churches he took issue. To his brother who had written him in 1880 that the Presbyterian Church in Malden "has gone into the hands of the rabble," he had replied:

> As the Christian church was started and passed its early youth at least among the rabble, I do not quite understand why its return to the rabble should prove any special grievance. . . .
>
> I find it to be the great deficiency and shortcoming of the Protestant Church nowadays, everywhere that it never comes in contact with the "rabble" though in spiritual matters I fear we are all a rabble much of the time.[3]

The religious exercises to which he devoted himself regularly, though only his intimates were aware of their importance in his life, consisted of prayers for guidance, attendance at church to offer praise and thanksgiving, study of the Bible and meditation upon such concepts as the distinction between Father and Son, which he had long since come to accept as the distinction between principle and fact, there being a principle in every fact, and every fact or event being the offspring of a principle. In all of his waking hours it was his ambition, he recorded, to keep in the foreground of his mind: ". . . that all of what I call my possessions, my property, my education, my talents such as they are, my position in the world, my influence are only committed to me in trust but are no more mine than the Sun or the Moon are mine and hence the folly and dishonesty and injustice of taking any credit to myself for anything I am empowered to accomplish. . . ." Perhaps he stated his beliefs most simply in a letter written in his eighty-second year to his son who had expressed religious doubts:

> . . . I imagine however that the root of them all is that you have not realized the vital truth, that all causes are spiritual and all phenomena, effects; that a man consists of what he wills and loves — purely spiritual all — and that his body is merely an agent through which his will and loves manifest themselves. . . .
>
> . . . All power is spiritual and everything that lives and moves owes its life and motion every instant to supplies from that infinite and inexhaustible fountain. No one has ever seen, tasted, smelt or felt of power, but death is the instant result of a suspension of a supply of that power which we commonly call life.[4]

In that spirit and with that faith he had accepted his wife's death in 1889, when the close bonds of thirty-nine years of wedded life were snapped. For months she had suffered from Bright's disease, and after a vain effort to seek a cure in Europe, Bigelow had brought her home. There she had turned to him for every comfort and, what gave him abiding joy, she had turned also to his God. To the children away from home he sent constant reports upon her health, but when the end came, the simple wire, WHAT WAS MORTAL OF YOUR MOTHER DIED THIS MORNING AT 7:15 O'CLOCK, bespoke the distance his faith had carried him since that despairing time thirty-seven years before when his first child died.[5]

Complete assurance of eternal life reinforced Bigelow's interest in the world around him. Because he believed that a Creator put him in the world, he accepted as a corollary that the Creator meant him to make the most of it. As a youth Bigelow had wanted renown and money earned through socially useful means. As an old man he wanted to serve God by serving his fellows. In other words, somewhere in his fifties or sixties he won a long fight to give credit for his successes to God rather than to himself; though his desire to be useful remained constant throughout his life, his religion shifted the relation of his ego to his acts. A specific, if minor, example of that was his turning over to another biographer pictures he had carefully selected and saved for his biography of Tilden, together with the remark in his journal: "I would have preferred to reserve these illustrations for my own work but I am unwilling to obey such a motive." Yet he had no priggish desire to outdo others in godliness. He wrote in "The Golden Rule": "We are commanded to love the Lord our God with all our heart and soul and mind, but we are to love our neighbor only as ourself." Later in that essay he remarked: "The struggle to be first is the expression of earthly pride; the struggle to be last is the expression of self-righteous conceit." Once he quoted or paraphrased Swedenborg to the effect that "No man who is not content with this world, is likely to be content with any other. The unhappiness of this as of the next world comes from warring with our environment here." Certainly Bigelow was content with this world. He had no intention, merely because he was old, of forgoing any of his interests. What if by the time he was eighty the friends of his youth were gone? What if many of the friends of his middle years were dead and if each successive year cut into the remainder of his circle until not one friend was left to recall with him the zestful years of their young manhood or their later battle against the extension of slavery? Without dwelling on his aloneness, he could love their memory and go on to form new friendships among a younger generation.[6]

Among them were Mark Twain, whose views on the tariff exactly matched his own, Henry M. Alden, whose personal philosophy was so very similar, George Haven Putnam, Worthington Ford, and other men of letters whom he often saw in New York or, on a summer Sunday, at "The Squirrels." John Hay, whom Bigelow had loved ever since he proved such a godsend to the bereaved Minister in Paris in 1865, never let much time go by without seeing him or writing to him. Back in '68 Hay, then Minister to Austria, had written:

> You and Mr. Adams worked while you were in harness. I am not sure but that a serious man could always find work in either of those two missions. But equally sure am I that no two other American diplomatists can catch each other's eyes without mutual guffaws, unless they have a power of facial muscle that would put the Roman augurs to shame.[7]

Almost forty years later Hay pleased his old friend even more by sending him a copy of a speech he had made as Secretary of State in Jackson, Michigan, in honor of the Republican party's semi-centennial anniversary. In it Hay remarked: "We are not claiming that we monopolize the virtues or the patriotism of the country. I know far better men than I am who are Democrats." That sentence was underlined in the copy he mailed to Bigelow and in the margin Hay had noted: "This means you."[8]

Through Hay, Bigelow came to know Henry Adams though with the older brother, Charles Francis Adams, Jr., he had more intimacy, for they frequently exchanged bits of historical information or wrote to express agreement or disagreement with each other's historical conclusions. More attractive to Bigelow was William James, the son of another contemporary, Henry James, Sr. (Bigelow recalled him as saying "that he was not so much confounded by the idea of God but what puzzled him was, who were we.") "Of all the men at Harvard that I know of, he is the one with whom I think I should most enjoy an intimacy," Bigelow wrote in his eighty-eighth year. So two years later when William James lectured at Columbia University on "Pragmatism, Monism, and the Universal Unity," old John Bigelow drove up to the Heights to hear him. Let a man have something to say, and Bigelow was interested. Himself a pillar of propriety, he never lost a friendly feeling for Oscar Wilde, who had spent several days with the Bigelows at Highland Falls in 1882. Bigelow admitted that even that early the man had proved himself an epicurean in the worst sense of the word, with no ambitions which the pleasures of this world could not satisfy and with an undisciplined moral nature totally unrelated to his intellect. Yet when he read of Wilde's imprisonment in 1895, he condemned it as persecution, and five years later he felt quite sad on hearing of his death, and recalled:

> I saw a good deal of him while in this country. He was frequently a guest at my table. I took him once to the Century. Some of the older members there regarded him as a trifler and a poseur, but we had not a man in the club who could talk so cleverly or entertainingly as he did. . . .[9]

E. L. Godkin, whose nature, so contrary to Bigelow's, was, perhaps, best revealed in his favorite poem, "The Wallflower" — "To thee alone the privilege is given Proudly to root thyself above the rest As Genius does, and from thy lofty tower Send fragrance to the very breath of heaven" — was a close friend. Back in 1870 when Bigelow heard that Godkin had been offered a professorship at Harvard, he had hastened to write: "Tell them to require each student to take a copy of the 'Nation.' Do not profess history for them in any other way." In the '90's the two men were frequently together, the critic's acid comments stimulating to the genial, older man. When Godkin retired from the *Post* in 1899, disheartened, writing Bigelow: "My sober belief is that Croker provided a government more satisfactory to the people than anybody else . . .," Bigelow noted in his diary with the gentle humor of a man whose ambition is behind him:

> Alas poor Godkin. He is prematurely superannuated. I converted him to the Blickersdorf typewriter, I converted him to Homeopathy as administered by our Dr. Dillingham, but I could not cure his propensity to tea tippling, nor make him believe that our country could get on without following his advice entirely nor that there was a Being that had more to do with the directing the policy of nations than he thought he ought to have.[10]

Not all the acquaintances of Bigelow's old age were writers. He knew Nikola Tesla, who astounded him with wild talk of Martians signaling the world, of a plant he intended to construct from which he could talk to anyone without wires, of a light he planned for New York's first subway "which would require no trimming or feeding and would never be tired of burning."[11] He often saw J. Pierpont Morgan, Joseph H. Choate, Charles Evans Hughes, Andrew Carnegie, Elihu Root, men with whom he clashed on political, economic and religious beliefs, yet men who were later to establish in his honor a memorial at Union College. Moreover, there were colleagues on trusteeships, friends in the New Church society, farming neighbors at Highland Falls, who were dear to him, besides his large family of children and grandchildren. Given so varied a circle, the old gentleman rarely felt lonely, rarely reminisced. The present still offered him sufficient attractions.

"Old age it seems will tell as well as blood," he noted with composite humor and pride when he recorded the unusual applause which greeted his first appearance at the Century after his ninetieth birthday. Two years later he received a larger ovation upon attending a dinner in honor of Johann von Bernstorff, the new German ambassador to the United States. When Bigelow, distinguished in presence as ever, arose to leave early, cheering and clapping burst forth, the band swung into "Auld Lang Syne," and the spontaneous tribute continued while he crossed the length of the room. "If I had been twenty years younger," he observed later, "I hope I should have been modest enough to be embarrassed." As it was he was touched and very happy.[12]

His formal honors did not so much impress New Yorkers — his LL.D. degrees from Racine College, Union College, New York University, the fact that he was an early member of the American Academy of Arts and Letters, President of the Century, President of the Board of Trustees of the New York Public Library, member of the Art Commission of New York, long-time trustee of the Metropolitan Museum of Art and the New York Law School. Nor was it the fact that after his ninetieth year he had the strength to write anti-tariff booklets, religious essays, to edit his *Retrospections of an Active Life* and *The Letters and Literary Memorials of Samuel J. Tilden*, all of them useful if biased works. It was the elasticity of his mind, the keenness of his humor, the frankness of his pen that they delighted to honor.

It was also the link he made between two centuries, the fact that this virile old man had known New York in 1835, had seen its population increase from 250,000 to 2,500,000, had heard the dialects of generations of emigrants sound hesitantly for a moment and then give way to the dominant tongue, had seen economic life, social life, home life, revolutionized. He gave them a sense of continuity, especially on the rare occasions when he told tales of old New York. Then it was evident that in 1835 as in 1905 America's largest city had been noted for relish of speed, pride in variety, pre-eminence in commerce and finance. Most New Yorkers, it would seem, had always admired strong talk and prompt action; had cherished the ideal of the self-made man, resourceful, dependable, a force in the community; had denounced vested interests yet bowed down before them, and had condemned in opponents a carelessness in use of means which they condoned in themselves. To be sure, definitions of abstract terms had shaded into new meanings in the course of three wars, economic revolution, vast migrations and immigrations; yet old John Bigelow could prove that most of his fellow citizens had always believed in co-operative action, in political democracy and constitutional government, had been perennially proud of themselves and dissatisfied with themselves, proud of their achievements, and determined that their sons should surpass them.

Bigelow, like the city, had changed more in incidentals than in fundamental pattern. It did not take much imagination to see, in the strong, furrowed face of the old man the strikingly handsome youth of 1835, and to sense from the easy movements of the nonagenarian the graceful assurance of his middle years. His hair was white, his teeth were wearing thin, he knew that he was slightly deaf though others seemed unaware of it, yet his eyes were bright, for time could not quench his joy in living, his relish of a hearty laugh, his eager curiosity before a new idea. That was primarily what New Yorkers respected in him, that and his public spirit. But after his ninety-third birthday he knew that he was failing. A trip to Europe early in 1911 brought no relief from a bloody discharge, and after the ceremonial opening of the library in May, he collapsed, for two weeks hovering near death. Yet he rallied, and, his mind as clear as ever though his body was weak, he set to work once more, after dictating answers to the hosts of friends who had sent messages to him in his illness. He mailed a revision of his most personal writing, *The Bible that was dead and is alive again,* originally written for his family, now to be made public at the insistence of his pastor. By August he was again in his library at "The Squirrels," preparing the fourth and fifth volumes of his *Retrospections.* And on the twenty-ninth of that month he responded to notification that he had been elected to the Union Society of the Civil War with a crisp letter which young John Bigelow would have admired:

> . . . Practically all but the slave-holders in our country served in the Civil War as bearers of arms or tax-payers, while few of your Union Society are old enough to have done either, or to know by experience anything of the crisis through which their forebears passed, and who therefore in such a Society are but as sounding brass and tinkling cymbols. Such an organization today has the air of being more animated by politics than by patriotism, and of playing at dominoes with the bones of one's parents. I do not care to take a hand in such a game.[13]

In the fall he made his usual move to Gramercy Park, continued reading, dividing his time between religious books and a further study of DeWitt Clinton, and in his journal he commented upon his reading

in his strong, clear hand. He wrote to his fellow library trustees urging
once more an appropriation for a special room for storing manuscripts
— a room established three years later and where his papers now are
kept. Often he reflected upon his effort to follow up the resolution
of the Episcopal Convention of 1910 which looked to closer unity
among the churches. He had invited leading Baptist, Presbyterian,
Methodist, Episcopal, and New Church pastors to meet in his home in
order to discuss the calling of an international conference upon religious unity. He hoped that these men, among them young Dr. William
T. Manning of Trinity Church, would carry on that important work
and would persuade other men of their faiths to give more attention
to Ezekiel 37:15–28. He continued to study the political scene, as he
had for seventy years. Sure that the Democrats would return to power
in 1912, he urged his party to select a sound-money, low-tariff Southern candidate. Again he suggested, as he had periodically for the last
forty-five years, that ex-Presidents be made senators for life. Practical
to the last, he wrote to the mayor and to the Reverend Charles H.
Parkhurst urging regular garbage removal and improved methods of
street cleaning by use of river water, patterned upon the system of
Paris.[14] A few weeks later, after a brief illness, he died in his ninety-
fifth year, on December 19, 1911.

John Bigelow was satisfied with the label "Author" in *Who's Who*.
He was, however, less a literary figure than a public servant, an American Agricola, perhaps, called to a succession of jobs into each of
which he put the whole force of a sagacious intellect and a persistent
will; then, the job completed, quietly withdrawing. Never did he
seek personal advancement or gain in the position he held. Every
major task which he undertook in his long life had a significance larger
than individual profit, and in each of his undertakings, big or little,
the success of the job was more on his mind than the success of John
Bigelow. He held no position which from its very title gives a man a
line in history texts, and it would be idle to speculate upon his place
in history had American politics in the years just after the Civil War
been other than a stamping-ground for rabble-rousers or had Tilden
been inaugurated President and made Bigelow, as he undoubtedly intended, his Secretary of State.

Bigelow's chief specific claim to a place in American history lies in
his service in France during the Civil War, where his energy, diplomacy and perspicuity brought about the active friendship of liberal
and intellectual groups, the wreckage of Confederate plans to build

a fleet, and the preservation of Franco-American friendship during the delicate negotiation over the Mexican empire.

In the long run his work as a publicist was of equal importance. From 1841 to 1911 his pen had active service in the cause of democratic principles and, what is more, in the cause of democratic practices. As prison reformer, as journalist and publicist, he labored before the Civil War for specific social, political, and economic improvements. After the war, as canal commissioner, adviser to Tilden, as private citizen, he labored similarly. Rarely did he verbalize a theoretical point of view. Nor did he speak as a prophet to future generations. For seventy years, however, down in the market place he urged his fellows ever to take one more step along the road of democracy to the end that the individual, unhampered by discriminatory legislation and with a minimum of restrictions, could have freedom to lead a full life.

He had his weaknesses and idiosyncrasies. There was little humility in him. He was strong-willed, sometimes opinionated. His judgment of men was strongly colored by his personal relations with them. His judgment of institutions was occasionally shadowed by his religious views, most markedly evident in his intolerance of Catholicism. His dedication of himself to the cause of democracy did not prevent him from being, personally, an aristocrat. His shrewd ability to satisfy his modest wants blinded him to the hardships of the less fortunate. Yet with all that, he was a man of singularly balanced qualities of mind and spirit.

A picture emerges from the long record of activity, from the complex personality at once introspective and co-operative, intellectual and practical, of a well-used life which achieved the goals of the nineteenth-century American — to give loving care to a family, to serve God devoutly, to be a success in business, and to influence public affairs — and which, like some deep-rooted tree, had time to reach full development and fruition.

Notes

(Mr. Bigelow's *Journal* and all correspondence not otherwise described are in the John Bigelow Papers, New York Public Library.)

FOREWORD

1. *Memorial Addresses Delivered before the Century Association, March 9, 1912*, pp. 12, 18; *Commemorative Tributes of the American Academy of Arts and Letters, 1905–1941*, pp. 50 ff.

CHAPTER I

1. E. A. Bigelow, *Historical Reminiscences of the Early Times in Marlborough, Mass.*, pp. 125 ff.
2. H. W. Brainard, *The Ishams in England and America*, pp. 183 ff.
3. N. B. Sylvester, *History of Ulster County, N. Y.*, Pt. II, pp. 74 A, B, E; 34, 42; *Valentine's Manual of Old New York*, New Series, vol. II, pp. 349–357; vol. VI, p. 45; Brainard, *op. cit.*, pp. 274–276.
4. Bigelow, *Retrospections of an Active Life* (hereafter cited as *Retros.*), vol. I, Ch. 1; to David Bigelow, November 21, 1879.
5. Bigelow to Braxton Bigelow, October 7, 1907; *Journal*, September 13, 1900; March 23, 1905; April 18, 1906; *Retros.*, vol. I, pp. 18, 28–29.
6. *Catalogue of Washington College*, 1835, pp. 5–10.
7. *Catalogue of Books in the Library of Washington College*, 1832; S. Reznick, "A Schoolboy of 1830," *New York History*, vol. 17, April 1936, pp. 135–136; *Retros.*, vol. I, p. 29.
8. T. C. Brownell, *Farewell Address to the Students of Washington College*, December 16, 1831.
9. *Retros.*, vol. I, pp. 32–33.
10. *Annual Report of the Trustees of Union College*, 1832, 1834, 1835; F. B. Hough, *Historical Sketch of Union College*, p. 5.
11. M. Westover, *Schenectady Past and Present*, pp. 30–31.
12. *An Abstract of the Laws of Union College*, p. 16; *Annual Report . . . for 1835*, pp. 7–8.
13. Cited in a bulletin prepared in 1913 by the John Bigelow Memorial Committee, which Mr. Oswald Garrison Villard kindly showed to me.
14. *Annual Report . . . for 1835*, p. 6; Union College, *Nominae Senatus Academici*, 1843.

15. J. Rotundo, "Eliphalet Nott," *New York History*, vol. 13, April 1932, pp. 166–172; A. Raymond, *Union University*, vol. I, pp. 154–156.
16. *Retros.*, vol. I, pp. 35–36.
17. Bigelow to Mrs. E. S. Van Winkle, June 15, 1907; *Retros.*, vol. I, p. 37.
18. Bigelow to Braxton Bigelow, October 7, 1907; *Retros.*, vol. I, pp. 37–39.

CHAPTER 2

1. *Retros.*, vol. I, pp. 39–40, 53.
2. N. F. Adkins, *Fitz-Greene Halleck*, pp. 272–275; *Retros.*, vol. I, pp. 52–53.
3. *Retros.*, vol. I, pp. 55–56; Bigelow to Mrs. Eames, November 21, 1867.
4. Bigelow to W. M. Evarts, February 7, 1896; *Retros.*, vol. I, pp. 41–46; B. J. Lossing, *History of New York City*, vol. II, pp. 436–438.
5. Bigelow to Mrs. Eames, November 21, 1867.
6. Bigelow, MS Notebook, "Reflections, Hints, Suggestions," 1839.
7. *Ibid.; Journal*, January 2, 1891.
8. *Retros.*, vol. I, pp. 55–56; F. Saunders, *New York in a Nutshell*, 1853, pp. 15–16.
9. Asa Greene, *A Glance at New York*, 1837, pp. 175, 180–182.
10. J. G. Wilson, ed., *Memorial History of the City of New York*, vol. IV, p. 370; Greene, *op. cit.*, p. 38; *Journal*, entries for 1843–1845.
11. Written *circa* 1842; sent to Bigelow in 1907 by a niece of the writer.

CHAPTER 3

1. Greene, *op. cit.*, pp. 130–137.
2. F. L. Mott, *A History of American Magazines*, vol. I, pp. 785–809.
3. *Retros.*, vol. I, p. 59.
4. *Democratic Review*, August 1841, pp. 133–142, October 1841, pp. 360–382; *Retros.*, vol. I, pp. 59–62.
5. To Fanny Campbell, dated only "July," 1845.
6. *Democratic Review*, September 1842, p. 225.
7. *Ibid.*, pp. 232–233.
8. *Journal*, May 24, 1908; J. T. Lee, "Authorship of Gregg's *Commerce of the Prairies*," *Mississippi Valley Historical Review*, vol. 16, No. 4, p. 466.
9. *Journal*, entries for December 1843.
10. *Ibid.*, January 1, February 24, 1844.
11. P. Horgan, "Josiah Gregg Himself," introduction to *Diary and Letters of Josiah Gregg*, pp. 26–27; *Diary . . . of Josiah Gregg*, edited by M. G. Fulton, pp. 150 ff, 176 ff, 180 ff.

12. Lee, *op. cit.*, pp. 456–457.
13. *Journal*, June 9, 1844.
14. Cited in P. Horgan, "The Prairies Revisited: A Re-estimation of Josiah Gregg," *Southwest Review*, Winter 1941, p. 162.
15. Horgan, *op. cit.*, p. 27. Mr. Horgan comments, possibly unaware that Bigelow wrote the review: "The critic simply was not intelligent enough — one of those who in combing a book exhaustively can snare everything but the point; this would be the author's conclusion, mourning his work in memory of his intention." Yet before the next edition of the book appeared, Gregg again sought Bigelow's help.
16. *Democratic Review*, June 1844, pp. 639–646.
17. *Journal*, June 20, 1844.
18. *Ibid.*, November 25, 28, 1843.
19. Newspaper comments, *Journal*, November 30, 1843; *Democratic Review*, January 1849, p. 84.
20. D. T. Lynch, "Party Struggles 1828–1850," *History of the State of New York*, edited by A. Flick, vol. 6, no. 3; *Journal*, July 5, 1844.
21. *Journal*, August 28, July 28, 1844.
22. *Ibid.*, entries for summer 1844.
23. *Ibid.*, October 11, 15, 20, 27, 1844.
24. *Ibid.*, December 15, 1844.

CHAPTER 4

1. *Retros.*, vol. I, p. 66.
2. C. Z. Lincoln, *Constitutional History of New York*, vol. II, p. 138; *Journal*, April 30, May 11, 1845.
3. O. F. Lewis, *Development of American Prisons*, p. 327; C. M. Young, *Women's Prisons Past and Present*, p. 4.
4. D. Dix, *Remarks on Prisons . . .*, edition of 1845, p. 43.
5. Lewis, *op. cit.*, pp. 324, 327; Prison Association of New York, *First Annual Report*, December 1844, and *Report for 1846*.
6. Lincoln, *op. cit.*, vol. II, p. 38; Dix, *op. cit.*, p. 17.
7. Young, *op. cit.*, p. 9; Prison Association of New York, *Report for 1846*, p. 48.
8. *Journal*, September 7, 1845; L. Sherwood to Bigelow, December 19, 1845; R. Cook to Bigelow, December 15, 1845.
9. *Journal*, March 15, 1846; *Retros.*, vol. I, p. 68.
10. Mrs. Farnham to Bigelow, January 15, 19, June 21, August 4, 1846. Bigelow reviewed the book in the January 1847 *Democratic Review*.
11. July 22, 1846.
12. March 7, 1847; November 17, 1846.
13. Powers to Bigelow, March 20; Eldredge to Bigelow, March 3;

Journal, entries for March, May 1847; Prison Association of New York, *Third Annual Report*.

14. New York State Legislature, Act of May 13, 1846; Young, *op. cit.*, p. 10; Powers to Bigelow, September 9, 27, 1847; *Evening Post*, January 11, 1848; Prison Association of New York, *Fourth Annual Report*, p. 27.

15. Mace to Bigelow, January 28, 1848.

16. Bigelow to Small, February 14, 1846; Powers to Bigelow, December 23, 1847; *Annual Report of the Inspectors* . . . , January 19, 1846, pp. 1–5.

17. *Annual Report of the Inspectors* . . . , January 6, 1848, pp. 3–4.

18. New York Senate Document No. 17, January 21, 1848, p. 3.

19. Powers to Bigelow, February 14; Mace to Powers, February 21; New York Senate Document No. 22, *Report on Indebtedness of Sing Sing*, February 8, 1848.

20. Bigelow to Rowell, March 6; Powers to Bigelow, March 7, 8, etc.; Rowell to Bigelow, March 14, 18, 23; *Evening Post*, March 21; Mace to Bigelow, March 21, 1848.

21. New York Senate Document No. 69, March 17, 1849.

CHAPTER 5

1. Bigelow, "Prospects of the Legal Profession in America," *Democratic Review*, January 1846, pp. 26–30; on Bigelow's law partnership, *Journal*, April 30, 1845.

2. *Journal*, October 20, 1844.

3. Bigelow to Eames, July 7, 1845; *Journal*, September 7, 1845; Mott, *op. cit.*, p. 505.

4. Bigelow, "Eldon," *Democratic Review*, July and August 1845, p. 104.

5. Bigelow, "The Priest — The Wife — The Family," *Ibid.*, pp. 131, 135–136.

6. Bigelow, "Reciprocal Influences of the Physical Sciences and of Free Political Institutions," *Democratic Review*, January 1846, p. 4.

7. Bigelow, "Political Patronage," *Democratic Review*, September 1845, pp. 163–172.

8. Bigelow to Mrs. A. E. Semple, May 12, 1911.

9. Bigelow, "Territorial Aggrandizement," *Democratic Review*, October 1845, pp. 243–248.

10. *Democratic Review*, January 1849, pp. 83–84; *Evening Post*, March 4, 1850; O'Reilly to Bigelow, January 7, 1845; C. C. Cambreleng to Seeley, April 20, 1846.

11. *Retros.*, vol. I, p. 70; Bigelow, "History of Constitutional Reform," *Democratic Review*, June 1846, pp. 403–421.

12. Bigelow, "New York Constitutional Convention," *Democratic Re-*

view, November 1846, pp. 339–348; *Journal*, December 4, 11, 12, 14, 16, May 6, 1846.
13. Bigelow, "History of Constitutional Governments," *Democratic Review*, March 1847, p. 202.
14. D. Loomis to Bigelow, December 13, 1848, quoting a comment of Bigelow.

CHAPTER 6

1. *Memoirs of Anne Lynch Botta,* esp. articles by Kate Sanburn and Grace Greenwood.
2. *Journal*, February 7, March 21, 1847; *Retros.*, vol. I, p. 73; Bigelow to Eames, December 14, 1848.
3. *Journal*, January 9, 1904, February 7, 1847.
4. D. T. Lynch, *op. cit.;* Alexander, *A Political History of the State of New York,* vol. II, pp. 127 ff.
5. Bigelow, *William Cullen Bryant,* pp. 72, 110, 115.
6. Miscellaneous correspondence in Bigelow Papers.
7. *Retros.*, vol. I, pp. 73–75.
8. *Journal*, (?) 1846; *Retros.*, vol. I, pp. 75–78; Bigelow to O'Conor, April 24, 1878.
9. "The New Home of the *Evening Post:* Supplement," April 13, 1907.
10. Statistics in Bigelow Papers; *Retros.*, vol. I, p. 75.
11. Lossing, *History of New York City,* vol. II, pp. 522–523; Bigelow Papers.
12. Allan Nevins, *The Evening Post,* pp. 236–238; *Evening Post,* "One Hundredth Anniversary Issue," p. 5; stenographic account of an interview which Mr. Oswald Garrison Villard had with Mr. Bigelow on November 21, 1897, lent to me by Mr. Villard, hereafter referred to as O. G. Villard Interview.
13. Bigelow to Bryant, July 19, (fall) 1849. Bigelow had no time for journalizing. There are no entries in his diary between October 7, 1848 and December 17, 1850.
14. *Evening Post,* May 29, 1849.
15. *Ibid.*, February 17; March 1, 7, 8, 12; April 14; May 29, 1849.
16. *Ibid.*, August 11, 17, 21, 24, 1849.
17. *Ibid.*, October 23, 1849; see also September editorials on the course of the Barnburners.

CHAPTER 7

1. Bigelow, *Jamaica in 1850: or, Effects of Sixteen Years of Freedom on a Slave Colony,* Ch. I.
2. *Journal*, December 17, 1850.
3. Dana's comment, cited in J. S. Pike, *First Blows of the Civil War,* p. 298; Sidney Olivier, *Jamaica the Blessed Island,* pub. 1936, p. 143; Bigelow to Eames, April 20, 1851; *Journal*, May 4, 1851.

4. Bigelow to Sumner, May 24, 1850; see also May 20, 29, in Sumner Papers, Harvard Library.
5. For example, the *Evening Post,* July 18, 22, November 13, 1850.
6. *Evening Post,* December 5; *Journal,* December 18, 1850.
7. *Retros.,* vol. I, pp. 104–105; *Journal,* December 18, 1850.
8. Bigelow to Sumner, April 23, 1851, in Sumner Papers, to Whitelaw Reid, February 23, 1871; *Journal,* April 27, 1851.
9. *Retros.,* vol. I, contains a large number of letters from Sumner.
10. February 22, 1851.
11. April 5, 1851.
12. Bigelow to Sumner, July 1, 1851, in Sumner Papers.
13. *Evening Post,* January 1852, esp. January 9, January 18, October 26, 1853; February 17, 1853; April 15, 1853.
14. Nevins, *The Evening Post,* p. 231.
15. *Ibid.,* p. 233. Sparks believed that there was "an editor's and publisher's project" on hand to issue a new edition of Washington's writings and "that the best preliminary steps would be to ruin my edition." See H. B. Adams, *The Life and Writings of Jared Sparks,* vol. II, p. 502. There is no evidence to indicate that Bigelow had any such intention.
16. Sparks's letters appeared in the *Evening Post* on April 2, 3, 6; Bigelow's retorts on April 15, October 1, 1852.
17. *Evening Post,* February 9, 1849.
18. Bigelow to Mrs. Eames, December 5, 1889.
19. In order, *Evening Post,* January 31, February 6 and 11, 1852; E. L. Pierce, *Memoir and Letters of Charles Sumner,* vol. III, p. 272, and Bigelow to Sumner, February 27, 1852, in Sumner Papers.
20. Alexander, *op. cit.,* vol. II, p. 171.
21. Bigelow to Sumner, September 5, 1852, in Sumner Papers.
22. Statistics in Bigelow Papers.
23. *Evening Post,* April 7, May 3, July 5, 1853; "The New Home of the *Evening Post:* Supplement," April 13, 1907, pp. 2, 9; "One Hundredth Anniversary Issue," p. 14.
24. Reprint in *Evening Post,* April 27, 1853.
25. *Evening Post,* July 14, 23, 1853; statistics in Bigelow Papers.
26. Bigelow to Benton, July 16, 1853.

CHAPTER 8

1. Passport in Bigelow Papers.
2. *Retros.,* vol. I, p. 97.
3. *Journal,* December 17, 1850.
4. *Ibid.,* February 9, 1889; MS expense books.
5. *Journal,* March 23, April 18, August 18, September 14, November 20, 1851; *Retros.,* vol. I, pp. 98, 163; to John Bigelow, Jr., May 11, 1909.

6. Bigelow, *The Bible That Was Lost And Is Found*, pp. 5–13.
7. *Journal*, February 10, 1853.
8. Bigelow to Sumner, dated only "Thursday," [June 1854], in Sumner Papers.
9. Bigelow, *The Bible That Was Lost And Is Found*, pp. 2 ff, 14 ff, 26 ff, 44, 52, 116 ff.
10. Bigelow, *Emanuel Swedenborg Servus Domini*, pp. 53–55, 65.
11. *Ibid.*, LV.

CHAPTER 9

1. Wilson, *Rise and Fall of the Slave Power*, vol. II, pp. 409–412; *Evening Post*, January 1854; Alexander, *op. cit.*, 190 ff.
2. *Evening Post*, May 23, 1854; Bigelow to Russell, May 19, 1904.
3. Wilson, *op. cit.*, vol. II, pp. 410–411; Pike, *op. cit.*, p. 237; *Evening Post*, May 30, 1854.
4. Wilson, *op. cit.*, vol. II, pp. 411 ff; F. Curtis, *The Republican Party*, pp. 177 ff, 202 ff.
5. For example, see the *Evening Post*, June 1, 8, 16, 1854.
6. *Ibid.*, June 26, July 19, on the South; September 8, 15, 20, October–November 1854, on New York politics.
7. A. Crandall, *The Early History of the Republican Party*, pp. 44–53; R. Bartlett, *John C. Frémont and the Republican Party*, p. 5.
8. *Retros.*, vol. I, p. 142.
9. *Ibid.* They met in "early" February; hence presumably before the convention.
10. Bigelow to Chase, February 26, 1856, in Chase Papers, Library of Congress.
11. *Evening Post*, June 17, 18, 1856.
12. Pike, *op. cit.*, pp. 322, 344; Bartlett, *op. cit.*, p. 15; Bigelow to Sumner, August 22, 1858, in Sumner Papers; *Evening Post*, June 19, 20, 1856; Curtis, *op. cit.*, pp. 258 ff.
13. Folder of Frémont items in Bigelow Papers.
14. *Evening Post*, August 18, 1856.
15. C. C. Phillips, *Jessie B. Frémont . . .*, p. 212; *Retros.*, vol. I, p. 144.
16. Unnamed author (W. H. Bartlett), *The Life of Frémont*, p. 32.
17. S. M. Smucker, *The Life of John Charles Frémont*, p. 57.
18. C. W. Upham, *Life, Explorations and Public Services of . . . Frémont*, preface, p. 260.
19. *Retros.*, vol. I, p. 143.
20. James C. Derby, *Fifty Years among Authors, Books and Publishers*, pp. 676–678.
21. Nevins, *Frémont, Pathmarker of the West*.
22. *Ibid.*, pp. 450–451; F. H. Harrington, "Frémont and the North Americans," *American Historical Review*, vol. 44, July 1939, pp. 842–848. *Evening Post*, August 6, 5, 1856; the Reverend Henry Field to Bigelow, September 15, 1856.

23. C. C. Phillips, *op. cit.*, p. 214.
24. *Retros.*, vol. I, p. 145; *Journal*, July 14, 1890; W. E. Smith, *The Francis P. Blair Family in Politics*, vol. I, p. 399.

CHAPTER 10

1. *Evening Post*, March 7, 1857.
2. For these and following details of the move to Highland Falls, see MS account books and inventories.
3. *Evening Post*, September 30, 1851.
4. Nevins, *The Evening Post*, pp. 237–238, 426–430; O. G. Villard Interview; *Retros.*, vol. V, pp. 368, 370.
5. Mr. Poultney Bigelow to author, October 1944.
6. McMaster, *History of the American People*, vol. VIII, pp. 283–290.
7. Italics as they appeared in the *Evening Post's* reprint.
8. *Evening Post*, August 14, 1857.
9. M. Myers, *New York Money Market*, pp. 141–144; McMaster, *op. cit.*, pp. 291 ff; Alexander, *op. cit.*, vol. II, p. 245.
10. *Evening Post*, October 9, 1857.
11. P. Foner, *Business and Slavery*, pp. 139–140; editorials in *Evening Post*, October 1857.
12. *Evening Post*, October 15, 1857; *Retros.*, vol. I, p. 176.
13. McMaster, *op. cit.*, vol. VIII, pp. 297–299.
14. *Evening Post*, January 23, 1858.
15. *Ibid.*, October 23, 1857.
16. *Evening Post*, November 12, 1857; January 2, February 5, April 3, 28, 1858.
17. Bigelow to Bryant, February 11, 1858.
18. *Evening Post*, February 4, 1858.
19. *Ibid.*, July 31, 1858.
20. *Journal*, May 4, 1851.
21. Bigelow to Bryant, October 12, 1857; June 12, 1858.

CHAPTER 11

1. *Retros.*, vol. I, p. 181.
2. *Ibid.*, pp. 192–193.
3. *Retros.*, vol. I, pp. 198 ff, and *Journal*, for 1859–1860, are the sources for this section.
4. Bigelow to Bryant, undated.
5. Duyckinck, *Cyclopaedia of American Literature*, rev. ed., vol. II, pp. 810–812.
6. *Journal*, January 24, 31, 1860; *Retros.*, vol. I, pp. 251–253; *Evening Post*, "One Hundredth Anniversary Issue," p. 4.
7. *The Diaries of John Bright*, edited by Philip Bright, p. 248.
8. Bigelow to Bryant, March 20, 1860.
9. *Journal*, April 8, 1860.

10. *Retros.*, vol. I, pp. 270–272.
11. *Ibid.*, pp. 284–289, 279, 264.
12. Bigelow to G. W. Reed, July 10, 1860.

1. P. Godwin, *Life of . . . Bryant*, vol. II, p. 137.
2. *Evening Post*, June 25, 1860.
3. *Ibid.*, June 27, 1860.
4. Bigelow to Sumner, June 27, 1860, in Sumner Papers.
5. *Evening Post*, September 5, 1860, on Seward; October 30 on Buchanan; see also October 27, 29 on Buchanan; September 27, 29, November 8 on secession.
6. *Retros.*, vol. I, p. 180.
7. *Evening Post*, October 9, 1860; Bigelow, *Letters and Literary Memorials of Samuel J. Tilden*, vol. I, pp. 137–138.
8. *Retros.*, vol. I, p. 292.
9. Bigelow fully developed this argument as the cause of the war in *Les États-Unis d'Amérique en 1863*.
10. *Retros.*, vol. I, pp. 319–320.
11. *Journal*, January 16, 1861.
12. *Ibid.*, January 23, 28, 29; March 21, 1861. Godwin's account of the sale, written forty years later for the *Evening Post*'s "One Hundredth Anniversary Issue," is full of inaccuracies. He asserted that he was managing editor at the time, which he was not; that the sale was in return for his gift to Bigelow of the Paris consulate, which, he said, Lincoln promised Godwin after the inauguration. There seems to be no contemporary evidence that Godwin was offered the consulate or even seriously considered for it. Bigelow categorically denied the whole tale in his *Journal* and in the O. G. Villard Interview in November 1897.
13. *Evening Post*, February 22, 1861.
14. *Ibid.*, March 27, 1861.
15. *Ibid.*, May 8, 1861; *Retros.*, vol. I, pp. 365–366.
16. *Journal*, March 8, 12; September 14, 1861.
17. Wilson, *Memorial History of the City of New York*, vol. III, p. 487; *Journal*, April 15, May 6, 1861; *Retros.*, vol. I, pp. 349–351.
18. *Journal*, June 13, 30, 1861.
19. *Ibid.*, entries for July 1–12; *Retros.*, vol. I, p. 369.
20. Bigelow to Hargreaves, July 27, 1861.
21. *Retros.*, vol. I, p. 364; *Journal*, August 14, 1861.

CHAPTER 13

1. *Evening Post*, May 25, 1853. See also November 20, 1854; March 8, 1855.
2. *D.A.B.*; B. J. Hendricks, *Statesmen of the Lost Cause*, pp. 140–141.

3. Dayton to Bigelow, October 2, 1856.
4. B. Willson, *America's Ambassadors to France*, p. 263.
5. *Retros.*, vol. I, p. 365.
6. L. M. Case, *French Opinion on the United States and Mexico*, p. 10.
7. *Journal*, September 2, 7, 1861; Bigelow to Kolish, September 5.
8. *Ibid.*, September 8, 1861.
9. See *Official Records of the . . . Navies in the War of the Rebellion* (hereinafter cited as *ORN*), series II, vol. 3, pp. 214 ff, 221 ff; May 21, July 14, 1861.
10. E. D. Adams, *Great Britain and the American Civil War*, vol. II, p. 231, footnote; C. Villiers, *Anglo-American Relations*, p. 182.
11. *Journal*, September 10, 1861.
12. Bigelow to Hargreaves, September 24, 1861.
13. F. Owsley, *King Cotton Diplomacy*, pp. 62–64; Dayton to Seward, September 7, 1861, in Dayton Papers, Princeton Library; *Journal*, September 14, 1861.
14. Bigelow, "Report on Consular Service," 1864, p. 79, in Bigelow Papers.
15. *Ibid.*, p. 100.
16. Bigelow, *Some Recollections of the Late Edouard Laboulaye*, p. 1; R. West, *Contemporary French Opinion on the American Civil War*, p. 20.
17. *Journal*, October 5, 1861; Bigelow, *Some Recollections of . . . Laboulaye*, pp. 3–4; Seward to Bigelow, October 21, November 20, 1861.
18. West, *op. cit.*, pp. 40–53; H. Moreau, *La Politique Française en Amérique*, pp. 80–81; Cowley, *Memoirs*, p. 226.
19. C. F. Adams, "The *Trent* Affair," *Massachusetts Historical Society Proceedings*, vol. 45, November 1911, p. 92, for Adams to Motley; *Retros.*, vol. I, pp. 398–399, for Adams to Seward.
20. *Retros.*, vol. I, pp. 385–386.
21. Bigelow to Mrs. Eames, June 11, 1846.
22. *Journal*, July 8, 1871, on Weed's errors in describing the genesis of Scott's letter.
23. *Retros.*, vol. I, pp. 387–390.
24. Jordan and Pratt, *Europe and the American Civil War*, pp. 36–37.
25. J. A. Hobson, *Richard Cobden, the International Man*, pp. 350–351; Motley to Dayton, December 17, 1861, in Dayton papers; Weed, *Memoirs*, vol. I, p. 654. C. F. Adams, in "The *Trent* Affair," followed Rhodes in crediting Sumner and Blair for the release of Mason and Slidell but later accepted Bigelow's version. See *American Historical Review*, vol. 15, July 1910, p. 886.
26. Adams, *op. cit.*, vol. I, pp. 264–265; F. W. Seward, *Seward at Washington*, vol. II, pp. 54, 57.
27. *Ibid.*, 77; F. W. Seward to Bigelow, April 8, 1862, in Consular Correspondence MS, National Archives.

28. *Retros.*, vol. I, pp. 442–443.
29. *Ibid.*, p. 510.
30. Bigelow to Sumner, January 30, 1862, in Sumner Papers.
31. Jordan and Pratt, *op. cit.*, p. 208; Bigelow to Bryant, January 28, 1862.
32. Bigelow to Seward, January 17, 28; to Hargreaves, February 1, 1862; J. F. Rhodes, "Letters of John Bright," *Massachusetts Historical Society Proceedings*, vol. 45, November 1911, pp. 148–159.
33. See Yancey and Rost to Hunter, as late as October 5, 1861, in *ORN*, series II, vol. 3, pp. 278–280.
34. *ORN*, series II, vol. 3, p. 216; Owsley, *op. cit.*, pp. 61, 70, 75; Callahan, *Diplomatic History of the Southern Confederacy*, pp. 119–123.
35. For description of Dayton, Owsley, *op. cit.*, p. 298; Bigelow to Bryant, October 15, 1861.
36. Owsley, *op. cit.*, Chs. 1 and 2; Adams, *op. cit.*, vol. II, pp. 3–17, 203.

CHAPTER 14

1. B. Willson, *John Slidell;* B. J. Hendricks, *Statesmen of the Lost Cause*, pp. 283–292.
2. To Hunter, February 11, 1862, *ORN*, series II, vol. 3, pp. 336–342.
3. Jordan and Pratt, *op. cit.*, pp. 234–235.
4. Willson, *op. cit.*, p. 47; Owsley, *op. cit.*, p. 85.
5. On Slidell see *ORN*, series II, vol. 3, p. 372; on Bigelow, *Retros.*, vol. I, p. 470; Dayton to Clay, March 10, 1862, in Dayton Papers.
6. *Evening Post*, January 18, 1853.
7. To Seward, February 21, 1862, Consular Correspondence MS, National Archives.
8. To Seward, April 8, 1862, *Ibid.*
9. Benjamin to Mason, April 12, 1862, *ORN*, series II, vol. 3, pp. 384–386; Owsley, *op. cit.*, pp. 177–181; for de Leon's account of his activities, see *Thirty Years of My Life on Three Continents*, vol. II.
10. April 29, 1862.
11. Slidell to Benjamin, August 20, 24, 1862, *ORN*, series II, vol. 3, pp. 518–520.
12. *Journal*, May 9, 11, 1862.
13. Slidell to Benjamin, April 7, 1864, *ORN*, series II, vol. 3, p. 1078.
14. *Retros.*, vol. I, p. 532; *Journal*, May 12; Owsley, *op. cit.*, pp. 318–320; Bigelow to Seward, June 10.
15. Owsley, *op. cit.*, p. 304; L. M. Sears, "A Confederate Diplomat at the Court of Napoleon III," *American Historical Review*, January 1921, pp. 259 ff; Adams, *op. cit.*, vol. I, pp. 289–307., vol. II, pp. 18–23. See also Slidell to Benjamin, April 14, 18, May 15, June 1, 1862, *ORN*, series II, vol. 3, pp. 391, 419 ff, 428 ff, and Mason to Benjamin, April 21, *Ibid.*, pp. 397 ff.

16. To Seward, June 15, 1862.
17. To Alloury, dated only "June," 1862; *Retros.*, vol. I, pp. 512, 538; *Journal*, August 30, September 28.
18. *Journal*, January 16, 1865; *Retros.*, vol. I, p. 549.
19. Dudley to Dayton, March 26, 1862, in Dayton Papers; W. L. Whittlesey, "William Lewis Dayton, 1825," *Princeton Alumni Weekly*, vol. 30, no. 30.
20. Willson, *op. cit.*, p. 56; G. H. Putnam, *Memoirs of My Youth*, pp. 215–219.
21. *Retros.*, vol. I, p. 502; to Trimble, July 30, 1862.
22. Adams, *op. cit.*, vol. II, pp. 17–32; Owsley, *op. cit.*, pp. 341–350; *Memoirs of Dr. Thomas Evans*, edited by E. A. Crane, pp. 123 ff, eulogistic, not always accurate, recollections; Slidell to Benjamin, July 25, 1862, *ORN*, series II, vol. 3, pp. 479 ff.
23. To E. D. Morgan, August 22, 1862.
24. September 19, 1862, Consular Correspondence MS.
25. To Bowen, "September," 1862.
26. Bigelow to Seward, July 31, Seward to Bigelow, August 14, 1862, Consular Correspondence MS.
27. *Journal*, September 22, 1862, on Weed; *Ibid.*, September 3, on use of the circular; Bigelow to Lucas, September 2, 1862.
28. Willson, *op. cit.*, p. 203; Bigelow to Seward, October 10, 1862; Seward to Bigelow in *Retros.*, vol. I, p. 563.
29. In Bigelow Papers.
30. To Benjamin, in *ORN*, series II, vol. 3, pp. 534 ff.
31. *Journal*, October 2, 1862.
32. To James Bowen, October 6; to Seward, October 7, 1862, Consular Correspondence MS.
33. To Seward, *op. cit.*
34. To Seward, November 13, 1862; Seward to Bigelow, December 2, 1862; Godwin, *Life of Bryant*, vol. II, p. 182; Adams, *op. cit.*, vol. II, pp. 45–49; Case, *op. cit.*, pp. 7, 257.

CHAPTER 15

1. J. F. Jameson, "The London Expenditures of the Confederate Secret Service," *American Historical Review*, vol. 35, no. 4; Hendricks, *op. cit.*, pp. 390–394; Owsley, *op. cit.*, pp. 167–173.
2. Jameson, *op. cit.*, p. 824.
3. J. E. Werty to Bigelow, May 5, 1862; for Hotze's activities, see *ORN*, series II, vol. 3, pp. 534 ff.
4. *Retros.*, vol. I, pp. 619, 627.
5. Rough draft dated only "March," in Bigelow Papers.
6. *The Saturday Review*, May 23, 1863; *Journal*, May 24, 1863.
7. Adams, *op. cit.*, vol. II, pp. 100–107; Jordan and Pratt, *op. cit.*, p. 214; *Retros.*, vol. I, p. 600. According to L. M. Case's docu-

mented study, the war in America continued to hurt French cotton manufacturers and export trades.

8. Bigelow, *France and the Confederate Navy*, p. 130. Published in 1888, this book printed for the first time parts of the captured Confederate correspondence.
9. Bigelow, "Report on Consular Service," February 1864, in Bigelow Papers.
10. *Retros.*, vol. II, pp. 3 ff; *Journal*, May 14, 1863.
11. *Retros.*, vol. II, pp. 8 ff.
12. Willson, *op. cit.*, pp. 201 ff.
13. *Journal*, May–June 1863; Owsley, *op. cit.*, pp. 518–520.
14. On Sanford's fund, see Thos. A. Scott, Acting Secretary of War, to Dayton, October 14, 1861; and Dayton to Malespine, December 4, 1863. Malespine appealed to Dayton for payment, Bigelow being out of town. Dayton replied: "Mr. Bigelow and Mr. Sanford both I think have some discretion in these matters. I have none." Dayton Papers. For Bigelow's account, see Bigelow to Sanford, June 12, 1863.
15. *Journal*, June 23–25, 1863.
16. *Retros.*, vol. II, pp. 25, 31.
17. *Journal*, July 4, 14, 1863; to King, "July," 1863.
18. *Le Constitutionnel*, July 12, 1863.
19. *Retros.*, vol. II, p. 26; to Thayer, July 4.
20. To Appleton and Company, July 21, 1863.

CHAPTER 16

1. *Journal*, July 24, 1863.
2. *Ibid.*, July 27.
3. Thayer, *Life and Letters of John Hay*, vol. I, p. 223.
4. *Journal*, August 1863.
5. To Morgan, July 8, August 17, 1863.
6. F. W. Seward to Bigelow, December 7, 1863, Consular Correspondence MS.
7. To Seward, August 26, 1863.
8. *Journal*, August 22, 1863.
9. *Ibid.*, August 24.
10. *Idem.*
11. To Seward, August 27, in *State Department Papers*, 1863, pt. I, pp. 762 ff.
12. *Journal*, August 28, 31, 1863.
13. To Weed, September 7; *Journal*, August 31, September 1, 1863.
14. October 7, 1863, in Consular Correspondence MS.
15. *Retros.*, vol. II, pp. 52 ff.
16. Bigelow, *France and the Confederate Navy*, pp. 1–5; to Dayton, September 10; *Journal*, September 10–12, 1863.

17. Slidell to Benjamin, January 11, March 4, in Bigelow, *France and the Confederate Navy*, pp. 133 ff, 150 ff.
18. *Ibid.*, pp. 136 ff; Bulloch to Mallory, May 16, *ORN*, series II, vol. 2, pp. 423 ff; Slidell to Benjamin, April 20, Bulloch to Mallory, June 30; contract for rams, July 16, *Ibid.*, pp. 741 ff, 444 ff, 464 ff.
19. Bigelow, *op. cit.*, pp. 16 ff.
20. Dayton to Bigelow, in Willson, *America's Ambassadors to France*, p. 267; Bigelow to Sanford, September 14, 15; Dayton to Seward, October 22, *State Department Papers*, 1863, pt. I, p. 797.
21. *Journal*, September 16, 18, 1863; Bigelow, *op. cit.*, pp. 21–27.
22. *Retros.*, vol. II, p. 76.
23. Bigelow to Weed, September 29, 1863.
24. *Journal*, October 1, November 11, 1863; to Dayton, October 21.
25. *Retros.*, vol. II, pp. 79, 82 ff, 91 ff; Bigelow to Seward, October 9, and Seward to Dayton, October 24, Consular and Diplomatic Correspondence MS.
26. October 23, in *State Department Papers*, 1863, pt. I, p. 800.
27. Slidell to Benjamin, November 15, *ORN*, series II, vol. 3, p. 956.
28. *Retros.*, vol. I, p. 642.
29. Bigelow, *Lest We Forget . . .*; *Retros.*, vol. III, pp. 185 ff, 192, 217 ff, 281; *Journal*, December 14, November 6, 1865.
30. J. H. Kiger, "Federal Governmental Propaganda in Great Britain during the American Civil War," *Historical Outlook*, vol. 19, no. 5; A. Taylor, "Walker's Financial Mission to London, 1863–1864," *Journal of Economic and Business History*, vol. 3, pp. 296–320.
31. *Journal*, December 4, 14, 20, 1863.
32. *ORN*, series I, vol. 2, pp. 510 ff; for proof that the *Agrippina* was a Confederate ship employed in such tasks, see *ORN*, series II, vol. 2, p. 440.

CHAPTER 17

1. *Journal*, December 23, 1863.
2. Dayton to Seward, January 21, *State Department Papers*, 1864, pt. III, pp. 21 ff; Slidell to Benjamin, March 5, July 11, August 8, 1864, *ORN*, series II, vol. 3, pp. 1045 ff, 1169 ff, 1186 ff.
3. *Journal*, January 14, 17; Bigelow, *France and the Confederate Navy*, pp. 31 ff, 36; Dayton to Seward, February 14, 1864, Diplomatic Correspondence MS.
4. H. Moreau, *La Politique Française en Amérique 1861–1864; Retros.*, vol. II, p. 144.
5. To Sanford, dated only "Monday," 1864.
6. Bigelow to Sumner (Fall) 1863, in Sumner Papers.
7. Bigelow to Seward, April 29, May 3, 1864, in Consular Correspondence MS; Bigelow, *France and the Confederate Navy*, pp. 37 ff.

8. Bigelow to Seward, May 6, 13, 1864, in Consular Correspondence MS.
9. Bigelow, *op. cit.*, pp. 28 ff; to Seward, June 8; Dayton to Seward, April 7, March 11, 16, June 8, 1864, in Diplomatic Correspondence MS.
10. Bigelow to Seward, March 11, 24, June 10, *Retros.*, vol. II, pp. 161, 165 ff, 192 ff.
11. Villiers, *op. cit.*, 114; for Hotze's account of his work, see *ORN*, series II, vol. 3, pp. 1090 ff, 1115 ff, 1142 ff, 1177 ff; for an attempt to establish the determining factors in Napoleon's foreign policy, see Case, *op. cit.*, pp. 13, 297 ff, 403 ff.
12. *Retros.*, vol. II, pp. 153–154, March 4, 1864.
13. October 23, 1863.
14. To Seward, March 3, 1864.
15. To Kolish, November 13, 1863.
16. To Seward, March 10, 1864.
17. To Sanford, April 22, 1864.
18. Unsigned memorandum, March 23, 1864, in Consular Correspondence MS.
19. F. W. Seward to Bigelow, July 26, 1864.
20. Cited by Representative Schenck, February 6, 1867, *Congressional Globe*, 39th Congress, 2nd Session, p. 1036.
21. *Retros.*, vol. II, p. 191.
22. *Ibid.*, pp. 216 ff; to W. B. Isham, October 21, 1864.
23. *Retros.*, vol. II, pp. 145, 386; *Journal*, October 9, 1864.
24. *Retros.*, vol. II, p. 244.
25. *Ibid.*, p. 251.
26. In order, to W. Isham, January 7; to E. D. Morgan, January 17, *Retros.*, vol. II, p. 270; to J. Brooks, January 27, 1865.
27. *Retros.*, vol. II, pp. 299 ff.
28. Slidell to Benjamin, February 24, 1865, *ORN*, series II, vol. 3, p. 1263.
29. Dayton to Seward, October 19, November 4, 1864, *State Department Papers*, 1864, pt. III, pp. 551 ff.
30. Bigelow, *France and the Confederate Navy*, pp. 57 ff; Bigelow to Seward, January 30, 31, February 3, *State Department Papers*, 1865, pt. II, pp. 209 ff.
31. Bigelow, *op. cit.*, pp. 61–62; *Retros.*, vol. II, pp. 285–298; Bigelow to Seward, February 10, and Seward to Bigelow, February 27, *State Department Papers*, 1865, pt. II, pp. 224 ff, 231 ff.
32. Bigelow, *op. cit.*, pp. 70–76; *Retros.*, vol. II, pp. 332–339; *Journal*, February 1865.
33. Seward to Bigelow, March 23, in *State Department Papers*, 1865, pt. II, p. 249.

CHAPTER 18

1. *Retros.*, vol. II, pp. 424, 429, 434, 442.
2. *Ibid.*, pp. 519, 523 ff; *Journal*, July 16, 1865.
3. *Retros.*, vol. II, pp. 541–550; Bigelow to Seward, October 28, Seward to Bigelow, November 18, 1865, in Diplomatic Correspondence MS.
4. *Retros.*, vol. II, pp. 578 ff.
5. May 12 (1865), in "Personal Miscellany," Library of Congress.
6. *Retros.*, vol. II, p. 557.
7. To Mrs. Bigelow, May 26, June 8; to W. H. Russell, May 31, 1865; *Retros.*, vol. III, pp. 47–49.
8. To William Isham, June 8, 1865.
9. *Retros.*, vol. III, pp. 104–107.
10. *Ibid.*, pp. 151–156.
11. *Retros.*, vol. I, p. 499.
12. *Retros.*, vol. II, p. 45; *Journal*, August 26, 1863.
13. *Retros.*, vol. II, p. 48.
14. "Present Condition of Mexico," *State Department Papers Relating to Foreign Affairs of the United States*, 1864, pt. 3, p. 597.
15. *Retros.*, vol. II, pp. 182–183.
16. *Ibid.*, p. 180.
17. To Seward, February 9, 1865.
18. To Sumner, February 24, 1865.
19. To Seward, February 14; *Journal*, February 14, 1865.
20. *Retros.*, vol. II, pp. 426 ff; vol. III, pp. 67 ff.
21. *Retros.*, vol. III, pp. 69–72, 121.
22. Callahan, *op. cit.*, p. 57, citing Seward; on Johnson, *Journal*, July 16, 1865; on Mexico, to (?), dated only "July," 1865, and to Seward, August 2, 1865.
23. *Retros.*, vol. III, pp. 151–156.
24. To Weed, August 29, 1865.
25. *Retros.*, vol. III, pp. 200 ff; Seward to Bigelow, November 6, December 16, *State Department Papers*, 1865, pt. III, 429, 489.
26. *Retros.*, vol. III, pp. 287 ff, 368 ff.
27. Case, *op. cit.*, p. 402; *Journal*, January 6, 1866.
28. *Retros.*, vol. III, pp. 305 ff; Bigelow to Seward, January 11, 1866, *State Department Papers*, 1865, pt. III, pp. 802 ff; *Journal*, January 25, 1866.
29. To Seward, March 7, 1866.
30. To Seward, February 23, May 18; to Bancroft, dated only "May"; to J. W. Edmunds, June 1; *Retros.*, vol. III, pp. 506 ff, August 25, 1866.
31. To Bancroft, October 30, 1865.
32. *Diaries and Letters of John Hay*, pp. 248–249.

33. January 24, 1866.
34. *Journal*, July 6, August 12, 1866.
35. *Ibid.*, June 4, 1866.
36. *Retros.*, vol. III, pp. 468 ff.
37. *Journal*, July 8; *Retros.*, vol. III, pp. 569 ff, September 25.
38. *Journal*, December 10, 1896; Callahan, *op. cit.*, p. 62.
39. *Journal*, August 9, 1866.
40. *Diaries and Letters of John Hay*, pp. 251–252, 265.
41. October 19, 1866.
42. *Retros.*, vol. III, p. 571. Similarly December 8, 15, 1866.
43. Seward to Bigelow, November 27, 1866, in Diplomatic Correspondence MS.
44. Bigelow to McClintock and to Hargreaves, *Retros.*, vol. III, pp. 575, 592 ff; *Journal*, October 19, 1866.
45. *Retros.*, vol. III, pp. 606–607.
46. *Ibid.*, pp. 598–600; *Journal*, November 1, 7, 1866.
47. *Journal*, November 28; *Retros.*, vol. III, pp. 611 ff.
48. To Seward, December 3, *State Department Papers*, 1866, pt. I, pp. 368–369.
49. To Weed, December 14, 1866.

CHAPTER 19

1. *Journal*, October 5, 1873.
2. *Ibid.*, February 15, 1867.
3. *Retros.*, vol. IV, pp. 47–49.
4. *Journal*, March 1, 1867.
5. Bigelow to E. D. Morgan, May 17, 1866.
6. *Retros.*, vol. IV, p. 40.
7. *Ibid.*, pp. 11–30, 87–89, 225–226.
8. Bigelow to Beckwith, July 19, 1867.
9. *Journal*, November 1, 21, 25, December 4, 18, 21, 1868, on *Commercial Advertiser;* March 3, 1869, on Johnson. *Retros.*, vol. IV, pp. 251–257; *Journal*, January 24, 27, February 27, March 3; *New York Tribune*, February 22, 27, and *New York Times*, March 10, 1869, on the newspaper controversy.
10. *Retros.*, vol. IV, pp. 289–290, 294, 319.
11. Clippings in Bigelow Papers.
12. *Journal*, August 29, 1869.
13. *Ibid.*, September 24, 1869.
14. House Report No. 31, 41st Congress, 2nd Session, March 11, 1870; for Bigelow's version, *Congressional Record*, 43rd Congress, 1st Session, March 20, 1874.
15. Bigelow to Sumner, February 25, 1874.
16. Bigelow to Mrs. Eames, October 31, 1869.
17. Clippings in Bigelow Papers.

18. *Retros.*, vol. IV, p. 408; *Journal*, August 28, 1870.
19. Bigelow to Reid, February 15, 1871.
20. Bigelow, *France and Hereditary Monarchy*, p. 72.
21. *Journal*, March 16, 1871.
22. *Retros.*, vol. IV, pp. 535–543. *Journal*, August 9; September 12, 1871.
23. Bigelow to Mrs. Eames, January 10, 1872.
24. E. H. O'Neill, *History of American Biography 1800–1935*, p. 60.

CHAPTER 20

1. *Retros.*, vol. V, pp. 11–15; Bigelow to Mrs. Eames, January 10, 1872; to Whitelaw Reid, November 22, 1871.
2. *Retros.*, vol. V, p. 34, June 14, 1872.
3. Bigelow to Hargreaves, dated only "December," 1872.
4. *Retros.*, vol. V, pp. 137–138, 159, 166, 168–169; Bigelow to Tilden, September 18, 21, 27, 1874; *Journal*, October 7, 1874.
5. *Evening Post*, September 3, 1874.
6. *Retros.*, vol. V, pp. 165–166.
7. *Ibid.*, p. 170.
8. *Ibid.*, pp. 170–173.
9. Flick, *Samuel Jones Tilden* . . . , pp. 267 ff; *Journal*, entries for April 1875.
10. Bigelow to George de Bunsen, June 20, 1875; *Retros.*, vol. V, pp. 210–212, for excerpts from the first report; Bigelow, *Letters . . . of Tilden*, vol. II, pp. 407–422.
11. *Journal*, April 24, 1875.
12. *Retros.*, vol. V, p. 209.
13. *Journal*, September 4, 1875.
14. *Ibid.*, September 6, 7, 1875; *Retros.*, vol. V, pp. 247–255.
15. *New York Times*, October 21, 24, 1875.
16. *New York Tribune*, September 8, similarly September 15, 16, 23, October 29, 1875; *Evening Post*, September 20, 22, 23, November 1, 1875.
17. *Retros.*, vol. V, pp. 219–228, gives the whole speech.
18. *Journal*, April 28, 1876.
19. In Bryant Papers, New York Public Library; Nevins, *The Evening Post*, pp. 402–405.
20. Flick, *op. cit.*, pp. 286, 309; *Journal*, August 29, 1876.
21. *Journal*, August 27, September 11, 12, 13, 1876.
22. *Ibid.*, September 20.
23. *Ibid.*, September 18; Flick, *op. cit.*, p. 303.
24. Nevins, *Abram S. Hewitt*, p. 322.
25. *Journal*, June 9, 1901, gives Sickles's version; March 13, 1894, relates Miller's account of Reid's participation.
26. *Retros.*, vol. V, p. 288; *Journal*, November 22, 1876.

27. The document is in Bigelow, ed., *The Writings and Speeches of Samuel J. Tilden*, vol. II, pp. 385 ff. On the writing of it, see *Journal*, January 4, 1877.
28. *Journal*, February 9, 1877; *Retros.*, vol. V, pp. 298–299.
29. *Journal*, January 18, 1877. For Hewitt's account, see *Selected Writings of Abram S. Hewitt*, edited by Allan Nevins, pp. 155–194.
30. *Retros.*, vol. V, p. 298; *Journal*, February 7, 1877.
31. *Journal*, February 20, 1877.
32. *Retros.*, vol. V, p. 303.
33. *Journal*, July 27, on strikes; March 17, late October, on Hewitt.
34. For Tilden's letter on the cipher dispatches, written by Bigelow, see Bigelow, *Life . . . of Tilden*, vol. II, pp. 175 ff.
35. Smith, *F. P. Blair Family in Politics*, vol. II, p. 489; *Journal*, December 3, 26, 1879; Bigelow to E. Reemelin, March 8, 1884.
36. *Journal*, June 4, 16, 1884; Bigelow, *Life of . . . Tilden*, vol. II, pp. 280–281.
37. Flick, *op. cit.*, p. 483; *Journal*, May 25, 27, October 22, November 9, 1884.
38. *Journal*, November 23, 1884, November 22, 1902; Bigelow, *Letters and Literary Memorials of . . . Tilden*, vol. II, p. 676.
39. *Journal*, May 19, 26, 1885.
40. *Ibid.*, November 17, 1885.
41. Bigelow to Mrs. Eames, December 1, 28; *Journal*, December 22, 1885.

CHAPTER 21

1. *Journal*, February 25, 1860.
2. *Ibid.*, June 25, 1871.
3. *Ibid.*, May 19, dated only "June," 1873.
4. *Ibid.*, April 10, 1884.
5. *Ibid.*, March 26, 1887. For the Tilden will case, as well as for the establishment of the library, H. M. Lydenberg's *History of the New York Public Library* is most valuable.
6. *Journal*, April 25, 1887.
7. Bigelow to D. F. Haynes, September 11, 1888.
8. *Journal*, February 17, September 17, 1890, May 31, 1891.
9. Bigelow to Orr, July 1, 1891.
10. Bigelow to Seth Low, October 5, 1892; *Journal*, January 18, 1893.
11. *Ibid.*, entries for February, March, May, 1893, January 1894; Lydenberg, *op. cit.*, p. 50.
12. *Journal*, April 24, 1894.
13. *Ibid.*, "October," 1894, November 25, 1894, January 10, 11, 16, 1895; Bigelow to Kennedy, January 11, 1895.
14. *Ibid.*, April 15, 16, June 2, 11, July 10, 1895.
15. *Ibid.*, January 2, 27, 30, 1896.

16. *Ibid.*, April 15, 1897.

17. Bigelow to Julia Bryant, June 22, 1899; to Senator Hill, January 24, 1892; *Journal*, November 24, 1896, on gifts to the library. *Journal*, dated only "July"; November 19, 1897; May 25, 1907, on disagreement with Billings.

18. New York Public Library, *Ceremonies on Laying Its Cornerstone*, November 10, 1902.

19. *Journal*, December 12, 1903. See Lydenberg, *op. cit.*; his purpose, of course, was to trace the development of the library's resources rather than to examine the personalities of the trustees.

20. Bigelow to Isaac Seligman, March 3, 1906.

21. *Journal*, December 21, 24, 1903.

22. Lydenberg, *op. cit.*, pp. 417–418.

23. For the best analysis of the steps leading to selection of the Panama route, see D. C. Miner, *The Fight for the Panama Route*. On Bigelow's share, see Bunau-Varilla to Bigelow, February 25, 1903, February 17, 1904.

24. Bigelow, *The Panama Canal — Report of the Hon. John Bigelow . . .*, March 1886; *Journal*, entries for February 1886.

25. Bunau-Varilla to Grace Bigelow (no date), 1889, in Bigelow Papers.

26. Bigelow to Hay, November 9, 1898; DuVal, *Cadiz to Cathay*, pp. 143–144; *Journal*, dated only "November," 1898; December 9, 1898.

27. *Journal*, January 23, 1899; Dennett, *op. cit.*, p. 366, on Hay; *Journal*, February 16, 1899, on Adams; Bunau-Varilla, *Panama: The Creation, Destruction and Resurrection*, p. 161; *Journal*, March 4, 1899.

28. *Ibid.*, February 10, March 12, 1901; Bunau-Varilla to Bigelow, May 14, 1901.

29. Bunau-Varilla to Bigelow, May 13, 1902.

30. Copies in Bigelow Papers: cable, November 23, 1902; Bunau-Varilla to Bigelow, November 28, 1902; Hay to Bigelow, December 2, 1902.

31. Copy in Bigelow Papers, December 19, 1902.

32. *Journal*, dated only "September," 1903. For Bunau-Varilla's public statement, see *Panama . . .*, pp. 288–289.

33. Bunau-Varilla to J. B. Moore, October 3, 1903, carbon copy in Bigelow Papers labeled by Bunau-Varilla "Copy for Hon. John Bigelow."

34. Cited in D. C. Miner, *op. cit.*, p. 359, footnote.

35. Bigelow to Hay, May 15, 1905.

36. In *Journal* for year 1903; actual date, Wednesday, February 19, 1913.

37. *Journal*, October 16, 1903.

38. *Ibid.*, October 19, 1903. Stonyhurst was the home of Bigelow's second daughter, Mrs. Charles Tracy.

CHAPTER 22

1. MS account books.
2. Bigelow's *Journal* contains full descriptions of each trip.
3. Mr. Poultney Bigelow to author, October 1944.
4. Bigelow to Mrs. Eames, June 2, 1887, referring to France.
5. Bigelow to the Reverend William H. Mabie, April 24, 1905.
6. Bigelow to Dr. R. A. Benson, July 10, 1909.
7. *Journal*, January 22, March 29, June 31, 1893, dated only "January," 1894.
8. *Ibid.*, March 2, 1893.
9. *Ibid.*, January 2, 1872.
10. Bigelow, *William Cullen Bryant*, introduction; *Journal*, June 11, 1891; Bigelow to Randolph, November 4, December 6, 1911.
11. Bigelow to Godkin, June 8, 1881.
12. Bigelow to Kelly, February 24, 1892.
13. *Journal*, October 15, 1894.
14. Bigelow to Senator James P. Beck, April 24, 1886.
15. Bigelow to Huntingdon, March 1, 1885; *Journal*, December 6, 1892; December 12, 1893; January 2, 1896; January 5, 1896; May 17, 1900.
16. *Journal*, January 25, 1886, on Bryan; July 13, 1908; August 2, October 16, November 4, 1896; Bigelow to Bourke Cochran, August 19, 1896.
17. Bigelow to Russell, June 5, 1898, on the War with Spain. (The offer from Prim was in 1866, through Tremont, who had supplied Bigelow with details of Confederate shipbuilding. See *Retros.*, vol. III, pp. 496, 591.) Bigelow to Mrs. Pinchot, July 5, 1898; to John Bigelow, Jr., August 3, 1898.
18. Bigelow to Reid in *Journal*, July 15, 1899; Hay to Bigelow in Thayer, *Life and Letters of John Hay*, vol. II, p. 179; Bigelow to Brooks, June 29, 1899; *Journal*, December 25, 1906.
19. *Journal*, October 26, 1900, on the *New York Times;* August 28, 1900, October 6, 1902, July 19, 1905, on Roosevelt's program; Bigelow to A. K. Smiley, May 27, 1897, and *Journal*, June 5, 1905, on international arbitration.
20. Draft dated June 5, 1905.
21. *Journal*, July 19, 1905; Bigelow to Bunau-Varilla, July 15, 1905.
22. *Journal*, April 7, 1907.
23. *Ibid.*, June 17, 1907.
24. Bigelow, *Peace Given As the World Giveth* . . . pp. 85–86.
25. Bigelow to Rhodes, December 12, 1907.
26. *New York Times*, May 26, 1907; see Bigelow, *A Substitute for the Tariff upon Imports*, 1908.
27. *Free Trade Broadcast*, vol. II, no. 7, October 1909.
28. Bigelow, *The Folly of Building Temples of Peace with Untempered Mortar* . . ., p. 40.

CHAPTER 23

1. *Journal*, March 18, 19, 1909; Bigelow to John Bigelow Jr., January 12, 1893.
2. *Journal*, January 1, 1911.
3. Bigelow to David Bigelow, March 30, 1880.
4. *Journal*, March 15, 1863; March 3, 1890; Bigelow to John Bigelow Jr., July 8, 1899.
5. February 8, 1889.
6. *Journal*, August 16, 1893; Bigelow, "The Unfailing Moral Standard," in *Toleration and Other Essays,* pp. 75, 76; Bigelow to Mrs. Eames, December 5, 1889.
7. *Retros.*, vol. IV, p. 179.
8. *Journal*, July 14, 1904.
9. *Ibid.*, October 7, 1903, on Henry James Sr.; Bigelow to John Bigelow Jr., May 11, 1903, on William James; *Retros.*, vol. V, p. 130, to John Bigelow Jr., August 6, 1882, *Journal*, May 27, 1895, December 1900, on Oscar Wilde.
10. *Journal*, September 13, 1902, contains a copy of a letter from Mrs. Godkin citing the poem; Bigelow to Godkin, September 25, 1870, in Harvard Library; *Journal*, October 29, 1899.
11. *Ibid.*, February 10, 1901.
12. *Ibid.*, December 8, 1907; February 5, 1909.
13. Bigelow to Col. H. H. Andrew, August 29, 1911.
14. Bigelow to the Trustees of the New York Public Library, October 3, 1911; *Journal*, March 16, September 24, 1911, on religious unity; first letter on the candidate in 1912 to H. Watterson, November 6, 1908; Bigelow to the Mayor of New York and the Reverend C. H. Parkhurst, November 10, 18, 1911.

Bibliography

MANUSCRIPTS

John Bigelow Papers, New York Public Library

These papers consist primarily of letters to and from John Bigelow from 1841 to 1911 (some copies) and of his *Journal*, in 40 volumes, begun in November 1843 and continued, with some lapses, into October 1911. The only long breaks in continuity are from October 7, 1848 to December 17, 1850, from September 20, 1853, to April 24, 1859. Written with the utmost freedom, Mr. Bigelow's *Journal* is marked throughout by a dual interest in public affairs and in his own intellectual-emotional life. He usually differentiated gossip from reliable sources and personal observations to an extent that there seem to be only two major points recorded as fact upon which his testimony has been challenged: his published account of the purchase of Alaska votes; his unpublished account of the Panama Revolution. Many, but by no means all, of his entries from 1843 to 1879, as well as some later ones, appear in his *Retrospections* or other published works. Footnote references have been made to the *Journal* only when the material, either in part or in entirety, is not available in print.

The papers also include transcripts of his consular and diplomatic correspondence, 1861–1866, a copy of his "Report on the Consular Service" in 1864, address books, account books, drafts of articles, material relative to the election of 1856, the Brussels Exposition of 1888, the Panama Canal, and miscellaneous pieces.

Salmon P. Chase Papers, Library of Congress
William L. Dayton Papers, Princeton library
E. L. Godkin Papers, Harvard University library
Charles Sumner Papers, Harvard University library
U. S. Department of State Papers, in National Archives, Washington, D. C.
> *Consular Correspondence.* Dispatches from and instructions to the consul in Paris. 1861–1864
> *Diplomatic Correspondence with the U. S. Minister to France.* 1861–1866

PUBLISHED MATERIAL BY JOHN BIGELOW

"Roman Lawyers in the Augustan Age," *New York Review*, July 1841, pp. 111–139

"Anthon's *Classical Dictionary*," *United States Magazine and Democratic Review*, August 1841, pp. 133–142

"Anthon's Dictionary and Defence," *ibid.*, October 1841, pp. 360–382

"Lucian and His Age," *ibid.*, September 1842, pp. 225–245

"Constitutional Reform," *ibid.*, December 1843, pp. 563–576

"*Commerce of the Prairies*," *ibid.*, June 1844, pp. 639–646

"Eldon," *ibid.*, July and August 1845, pp. 94–104

"The Priest — The Wife — The Family," *ibid.*, July and August 1845, pp. 127–137

"Hurlbut's *Essays on Government*," *ibid.*, September 1845, pp. 189–195

"Political Patronage," *ibid.*, September 1845, pp. 163–172

"Territorial Aggrandizement," *ibid.*, October 1845, pp. 243–248

"Prospects of the Legal Profession in America," *ibid.*, January 1846, pp. 26–35

"The Reciprocal Influences of the Physical Sciences and of Free Political Institutions," *ibid.*, January 1846, pp. 1–16

"The Progress of Constitutional Reform in the United States," *ibid.*, April 1846, pp. 243–256

"History of Constitutional Reform in the United States," *ibid.*, June 1846, pp. 403–420

"The New York Constitutional Convention," *ibid.*, November 1846, pp. 339–348

"*The Rationale of Crime*," *ibid.*, January 1847, pp. 49–55

"Constitutional Governments," *ibid.*, March 1847, pp. 195–204

Jamaica in 1850: or, the Effects of Sixteen Years of Freedom on a Slave Colony. New York, George P. Putnam, 1851

Memoir of the Life and Public Services of John Charles Frémont. New York, Derby and Jackson; Cincinnati, H. W. Derby; 1856

Les États-Unis d'Amérique en 1863. Paris, L. Hachette et Cie., 1863. (Translated into Italian and Spanish, and revised for a German edition in 1865.)

Autobiography of Benjamin Franklin; Edited from his Manuscript with Notes and an Introduction by John Bigelow. Philadelphia, J. B. Lippincott & Co.; Trübner & Co.; 1868

Some Recollections of the Late Antoine Pierre Berryer. A Paper Read before the New York Historical Society on Tuesday, February 16, 1869. New York, privately printed, 1869

"Father Hyacinthe And His Church," *Putnam's Magazine*, January 1870, pp. 96–113

Beaumarchais the Merchant. Letters of Theveneau de Francey, 1777–1780. New York, Charles Scribner & Co., 1870

"Terms of Peace Proposed by the Great Powers," *Scribner's Monthly*, January 1871, pp. 290–297

"A Breakfast with Alexandre Dumas," *ibid.*, March 1871, pp. 597–600

France and Hereditary Monarchy. London, Sampson Low, Son, & Marston; New York, Charles Scribner & Co.; 1871

"Was Saint Peter Ever At Rome?" *Galaxy*, August 1872, pp. 231–238

"Our First Centennial And How It Was Celebrated," *ibid.*, May 1873, pp. 671–675

The Life of Benjamin Franklin Written by Himself. 3 vols. Philadelphia, J. B. Lippincott & Co., 1874

"How Mayor Havemeyer Took His Pie," *Harper's Weekly*, January 16, 1875, p. 51

"DeWitt Clinton as a Politician," *Harper's New Monthly Magazine*, February 1875, pp. 409–417; March 1875, pp. 563–571

Mr. Tilden's War Record: An Authoritative Statement by Mr. John Bigelow. New York, privately printed, 1876

The Wit and Wisdom of the Haitians. New York, Scribner and Armstrong, 1877

"Mr. Seward and Mr. Motley," *International Review*, July and August 1878, pp. 544–556

"Oration," *Bryant Memorial Meeting Of The Century, Tuesday Evening, November 12th, 1878*, pp. 21–64. New York, The Century, 1878

"Franklin's Religious and Moral Character Examined," *New York Observer*, June 19, 26, July 3, 1879

Franklin. A Sketch. Boston, Little, Brown & Co., 1879; reprinted in *Encyclopaedia Britannica*, 9th edition, pp. 711–719

"Thomas Jefferson," *Encyclopaedia Britannica*, 9th edition, pp. 613–616

"La Fayette," *ibid.*, pp. 201–203

Emanuel Swedenborg Servus Domini. Introduction to Samuel M. Warren, *Compendium of the Theological Writings of Emanuel Swedenborg*, 3rd and revised edition. Philadelphia, J. B. Lippincott & Co., 1879; published separately, New York, G. P. Putnam's Sons, 1888

"A Visit to the Republic of San Marino," *Harper's New Monthly Magazine*, February 1880, pp. 365–372

A Masterly Statement. Why Mr. Tilden Did Not Seat Himself. His Course in 1876–77 Vindicated. Reprint from *Nashville Banner*, April 12, 1880

"The Early History of Charles James Fox," *Harper's New Monthly Magazine*, February 1881, pp. 419–433

"The New French Minister of Public Instruction," *ibid.*, March 1882, pp. 559–567.

"The First Century of the English Mission," *Frank Leslie's Popular Monthly*, July 1882, pp. 1–10

"The Railway Invasion of Mexico," *Harper's New Monthly Magazine*, October 1882, pp. 745–757

Molinos the Quietist. New York, Charles Scribner's Sons, 1882

"The Heir Presumptive to the Imperial Crown of Mexico," *Harper's New Monthly Magazine*, April 1883, pp. 735–749

"Some Recollections of Charles O'Conor," *Century Magazine*, March 1885, pp. 725–736

"Thomas Jefferson's Financial Diary," *Harper's New Monthly Magazine*, March 1885, pp. 534–542

"Galileo and the Doctrine of Correspondences," *New-Church Messenger*, April 15, 1885, p. 2

"Some Recollections of Lord Houghton," *Harper's New Monthly Magazine*, November 1885, pp. 952–957

The Writings and Speeches of Samuel J. Tilden. 2 vols. New York, Harper and Brothers, 1885

Panama Canal: Report of the Hon. John Bigelow Delegated by the Chamber of Commerce to Assist at the Inspection of the Panama Canal. New York, Press of the Chamber of Commerce, 1886

"Unpublished Letters of Benjamin Franklin," *Century Magazine*, June 1886, pp. 260–272

The Complete Works of Benjamin Franklin Including His Private As Well As His Official and Scientific Correspondence, and Numerous Letters and Documents Now for the First Time Printed, with Many Others Not Included in Any Former Collection also the Unmutilated and Correct Version of His Autobiography Compiled and Edited by John Bigelow. New York and London, G. P. Putnam's Sons, 1887–1888

"Franklin's Home and Host in France," *Century Magazine*, March 1888, pp. 741–754

France and the Confederate Navy 1862–1868. New York, Harper and Brothers, 1888

Some Recollections of the Late Edouard Laboulaye. New York, privately printed, 1889

William Cullen Bryant. Boston, Houghton, Mifflin & Co., 1890

Resist Beginnings or, The Blinding Influence of Sin. New York, Wm. H. Alden & Co., 1890

"The Confederate Diplomatists and Their Shirt of Nessus. A Chapter of Secret History," *Century Magazine*, May 1891, pp. 113–126

"The Tilden Library: What Shall It Be?" *Scribner's Magazine*, September 1892, pp. 287–300

"The Southern Confederacy and the Pope," *North American Review*, October 1893, pp. 463–475

The Bible that was dead and is alive again, That was lost and is found. New York, privately printed, 1893; revised and public edition under title, *The Bible That Was Lost And Is Found.* New York, New-Church Board of Publications, 1912

The Life of Samuel J. Tilden. 2 vols. New York, Harper and Brothers, 1895

"What is Gambling?" *Harper's New Monthly Magazine,* February 1895, pp. 470–480

The Mystery of Sleep. New York, Harper and Brothers, 1897; enlarged and revised, 1903; memorial edition, New York, New-Church Press, 1924

"Von Bunsen's Recollections of His Friends," *Century Magazine,* October 1899, pp. 849–857

The Supreme Court And The Electoral Commission: An Open Letter To The Hon. Joseph H. Choate. New York and London, G. P. Putnam's Sons, 1903

Democracy in America, by Alexis de Tocqueville, translated by Henry Reeve, with a critical and biographical introduction by John Bigelow. 2 vols. New York, D. Appleton & Co., 1904

Lest we Forget: Gladstone, Morley and the Confederate Loan of 1863. New York, privately printed, 1905

The Useful Life. A Crown to the Simple Life as Taught by Emanuel Swedenborg. With an introduction by John Bigelow. New York, Charles Scribner's Sons, 1905

"Franklin as the Man," *Independent,* January 11, 1906, pp. 69–72

"How Frémont Came To Be Nominated," *Leslie's Weekly,* June 14, 1906, p. 574

Our Ex-Presidents: What Shall We Do For Them? What Shall They Do For Us? New York, privately printed, 1906

Peace Given As The World Giveth Or The Portsmouth Treaty And Its First Year's Fruits. New York, Baker & Taylor Co., 1907

The Proprium or What of man Is Not His Own, as Revealed in the Bible and Expounded by Emanuel Swedenborg with an Introduction by John Bigelow. New York, New-Church Board of Publications, 1907

The Panama Canal and the Daughters of Danaus. New York, Baker & Taylor Co., 1908

A Substitute for the Tariff upon Imports and a Provision for an Equitable Distribution of the Wealth of Nations, Suggested in a Letter Written to His Excellency, Charles E. Hughes. New York, privately printed, 1908

The Letters and Literary Memorials of Samuel J. Tilden. 2 vols. New York and London, Harper and Brothers, 1908

"The Sewage-Polluted Hudson," *Survey,* October 23, 1909, pp. 131–132

Retrospections of an Active Life. Vols. 1–3, New York, Baker & Taylor Co., 1909. Vols. 4–5, Garden City, Doubleday, Page & Co., 1913

"Is There Existence After Death?" *In After Days: Thoughts on the Future Life.* New York, Harper and Brothers, 1910

The Folly of Building Temples of Peace with Untempered Mortar; The Necessity of Building Temples of Peace with Tempered Mortar. New York, B. W. Huebsch, 1910

Toleration and other essays and studies. Posthumous. New York, New-Church Press, 1927

OTHER PUBLISHED WORKS

Adams, Brooks. "Seizure of the Laird Rams," *Massachusetts Historical Society Proceedings,* vol. 45, December 1911, pp. 243–333

Adams, Charles Francis. "The *Trent* Affair: an Historical Retrospect," *ibid.,* November 1911, pp. 35–148

Adams, Ephraim D. *Great Britain and the American Civil War.* 2 vols. New York, Longmans, Green & Co., 1925

Adams, Henry Brooks. *Civil Service Reform.* Boston, Fields, Osgood & Co., 1869, reprinted from *North American Review,* October 1869.

Adams, Herbert B. *The Life and Writings of Jared Sparks.* 2 vols. Boston and New York, Houghton, Mifflin & Co., 1893

Adkins, Nelson F. *Fitz-Greene Halleck.* New Haven, Yale University Press, 1930

Alexander, de Alva S. *A Political History of the State of New York.* 4 vols. New York, Henry Holt & Co., 1906–1923

Auchampaugh, Philip G. "Politics and Slavery," *History of the State of New York,* edited by A. Flick, vol. 7, pp. 61–98, New York, Columbia University Press, 1933–1937

Bancroft, Frederic. *The Life of William H. Seward.* 2 vols. New York and London, Harper and Brothers, 1900

Bartlett, Ruhl J. *John C. Frémont and the Republican Party.* Columbus, Ohio, Ohio State University, 1930

Bartlett, W. H. *The Life of Col. Frémont.* New York, Greeley and M'Elrath, 1856. Author unnamed; work often credited to Greeley.

Block, Marguerite B. "Scientist into Seer: The Psychological Problem Presented by Swedenborg," *Review of Religion,* vol. II, May 1938, pp. 412–432

The New Church in the New World. A Study of Swedenborgianism in America. New York, Henry Holt & Co., 1932

Botta, Vincenzio, ed. *Memoirs of Anne C. L. Botta.* New York, J. Selwin Tait & Sons, 1894

Bradley, Joseph P. "A Memorial of the Life and Character of Hon. William L. Dayton," *New Jersey Historical Society Proceedings,* second series, vol. 4 (1865), pp. 69–118

Brainard, Homer W. *A Survey of the Ishams in England and America.* Rutland, Vermont, Tuttle Publishing Co., 1938

Bright, John. *The Diaries of John Bright.* London, Cassell & Co., 1930; New York, W. Morrow & Co., 1931

Brownell, Thomas C. *A Farewell Address to the Students of Washington College.* Hartford, H. & F. J. Huntington, 1832

Bulloch, James D. *The Secret Service of the Confederate States in Europe; or, How the Confederate Cruisers Were Equipped*. 2 vols. London, R. Bentley & Son, 1883

Bunau-Varilla, Philippe. *Panama: The Creation, Destruction, and Resurrection*. New York, McBride, Nast & Co., 1914

Bush, George. *Professor Bush In Reply To Mr. Emerson on Swedenborg*. Introduction to *The Memorabilia of Swedenborg*, part I, nos. 9 and 10. New York, John Allan; Boston, Otis Clapp; 1846

Callahan, James M. *The Diplomatic History of the Southern Confederacy*. Baltimore, Johns Hopkins Press, 1901
 Evolution of Seward's Mexican Policy. Morgantown, West Virginia, West Virginia University, 1909

Carman, Harry J. and Luthin, Reinhard H. *Lincoln and the Patronage*. New York, Columbia University Press, 1943

Case, Lynn M., *French Opinion on the United States and Mexico, 1860–1867*. New York and London, D. Appleton-Century Co., 1936

Century Association. *John Bigelow. Memorial Addresses Delivered before The Century Association, March 9, 1912*. New York, Century Association, 1912

Chester, Alden, with Williams, E. M. *Courts and Lawyers of New York*. 3 vols. New York and Chicago, American Historical Society, Inc., 1925

Cowley, Henry. *The Paris Embassy during the Second Empire*, edited by his son. London, T. Butterworth, 1928

Crandall, Andrew W. *The Early History of the Republican Party 1854–1856*. Boston, R. G. Badger, 1928

Curtis, Francis. *The Republican Party*. 2 vols. New York, G. P. Putnam's Sons, 1904

Dana, Richard Henry. *The* Trent *Affair: An Aftermath*, reprinted from *Massachusetts Historical Society Proceedings*, March 1912. Cambridge, 1912

Davis, Elmer. *History of the New York Times 1851–1921*. New York, the *New York Times*, 1921

De Leon, Edwin. *Thirty Years of My Life on Three Continents*. 2 vols. London, Ward & Downey, 1890

Dennett, Tyler. *John Hay: from Poetry to Politics*. New York, Dodd, Mead & Co., 1933

Derby, James G. *Fifty Years among Authors, Books and Publishers*. New York, G. W. Carleton & Co., 1884

Dix, Dorothea. *Remarks on Prisons and Prison Discipline in the United States*. Boston, Munroe & Francis, 1845

Donovan, Herbert D. *The Barnburners*. New York, New York University Press, 1925

Dougherty, J. Hampton. *Constitutional History of New York State*. (Rev. ed.) New York, Neale Publishing Co., 1915

Duniway, Claude A. "Reasons for the Withdrawal of France from Mexico," *American Historical Association Annual Reports,* vol. I, 1902, pp. 315–328

DuVal, Miles P., Jr. *Cadiz to Cathay.* Stanford, California, Stanford University Press; London, H. Milford; 1940

Duyckinck, Evert A. *Cyclopedia of American Literature,* rev. ed., edited by M. Laird Simons. 2 vols. Detroit, Paine, 1882

Eliot, Samuel. "Civil Service Reform," *Journal of Social Science,* vol. I, June 1869, pp. 112–119

Evans, Thomas W. *Memoirs of Dr. T. W. Evans.* Edited by E. A. Crane. New York, D. Appleton & Co., 1905

Fite, Emerson D. *The Presidential Campaign of 1860.* New York, Macmillan Co., 1911

Flick, Alexander. *Samuel Jones Tilden: a Study in Political Sagacity.* New York, Dodd, Mead & Co., 1939

Foner, Philip S. *Business and Slavery.* Chapel Hill, North Carolina, University of North Carolina Press, 1941

Godwin, Parke. *A Biography of William Cullen Bryant.* 2 vols. New York, D. Appleton & Co., 1883

Goodwin, Cardinal. *John Charles Frémont: an Explanation of His Career.* Stanford, California, Stanford University Press; London, H. Milford; 1930

Greene, Asa. *A Glance at New York.* New York, Asa Greene, 1837

Gregg, Josiah. *Commerce of the Prairies: or, the Journal of a Santa Fe Trader.* 2 vols. New York, H. G. Langley, 1844. (Edited from Gregg's account, by John Bigelow.)
> *Diary and Letters of Josiah Gregg,* edited by Maurice G. Fulton, with an introduction by Paul Horgan. 2 vols. Norman, Oklahoma, University of Oklahoma Press, 1941–1944

Harrington, Fred H. "Frémont and the North Americans," *American Historical Review,* vol. 44, July 1939, pp. 842–848

Harris, Thomas. *The Trent Affair.* Indianapolis and Kansas City, Bowen-Merrill Co., 1896

Haworth, Paul. *The Hayes-Tilden Disputed Presidential Election of 1876.* Cleveland, Burrows Brothers Co., 1906

Hay, John. *Lincoln and the Civil War in the Diaries and Letters of John Hay,* selected and with an introduction by Tyler Dennett. New York, Dodd, Mead & Co., 1939

Hendricks, Burton J. *Statesmen of the Lost Cause.* Boston, Little, Brown & Co., 1939

Hobson, John A. *Richard Cobden, the International Man.* London, T. F. Unwin, 1918.

Horgan, Paul. "The Prairies Revisited: a Re-estimation of Josiah Gregg," *Southwest Review,* vol. 36, winter 1941, pp. 145–166

Hough, Franklin B. *Historical Sketch of Union College.* Washington, Government Printing Office, 1876

Hudson, Frederic. *Journalism in the United States, from 1690 to 1872.* New York, Harper and Brothers, 1933

Jameson, John F. "The London Expenditures of the Confederate Secret Service," *American Historical Review,* vol. 35, July 1930, pp. 811–824

Jordan, Donaldson, and Pratt, Edwin J. *Europe and the American Civil War.* Boston and New York, Houghton Mifflin Co., 1931

Kiger, John H. "Federal Governmental Propaganda in Great Britain during the American Civil War," *Historical Outlook,* vol. 19, no. 5, May 1929

Lee, John T. "The Authorship of Gregg's Commerce of the Prairies," *Mississippi Valley Historical Review,* vol. 16, March 1930, pp. 451–466

Lewis, Orlando F. *The Development of American Prisons and Prison Customs, 1776–1845; With Special Reference to Early Institutions in the State of New York.* Albany, Prison Association of New York, 1922

Lincoln, Charles Z. *The Constitutional History of New York from the Beginning of the Colonial Period to the Year 1905.* 5 vols. Rochester, Lawyers Cooperative Publishing Co., 1906

Lossing, Benson J. *History of New York City.* 2 vols. New York, G. E. Perine, 1884

Lydenberg, Harry Miller. *History of the New York Public Library, Astor, Lenox and Tilden Foundations.* New York, the New York Public Library, 1923

Lynch, Denis T. "Party Struggles 1828–1850," *History of the State of New York,* edited by A. Flick, vol. 6, pp. 61–87. New York, Columbia University Press, 1933–1937

McMaster, John B. *A History of the People of the United States.* 8 vols. New York, D. Appleton & Co., 1885–1913

Miner, Dwight Carroll. *The Fight for the Panama Route.* New York, Columbia University Press, 1940

Moreau, Henri. *La Politique Française en Amérique 1861–1864.* Paris, E. Dentu, 1864

Mott, Frank L. *American Journalism 1690–1940.* New York, Macmillan Co., 1941

   A History of American Magazines 1741–1885. 3 vols. New York and London, D. Appleton & Co., 1930–1938

Myers, Margaret. *Origins and Development of the New York Money Market.* New York, Columbia University Press, 1931

Myers, William Starr. *The Republican Party: A History.* New York and London, Century Co., 1928

Nevins, Allan. *Abram S. Hewitt: with Some Account of Peter Cooper.* New York and London, Harper and Brothers, 1935

   The Evening Post: A Century of Journalism. New York, Boni & Liveright, 1922

Todd, Herbert H. *The Building of the Confederate States Navy in Europe*. (Summary of Ph.D. thesis, 1940.) New York, Vanderbilt University, private edition, 1941

Union Alumni Monthly. 1909–1916

Union College. *Annual Report of the Trustees of Union College*, 1832, 1834, 1835

    An Abstract of the Laws of Union College. (No date)

    Circular and Catalogue of Union College. 1834

United States Navy Department. *Official Records of the Union and Confederate Navies in the War of Rebellion*. Washington, Government Printing Office, 1894–1922

United States

    House Executive Document No. 73, 39th Congress, 1st Session, March 20, 1866, *The Conditions of Affairs in Mexico*. 2 vols.

    House Report No. 8, 39th Congress, 2nd Session, January 31, 1867, *Civil Service of the United States*

        No. 31, 41st Congress, 2nd Session, March 11, 1870, *Gold Panic Investigation*

    Senate Document No. 474, 63rd Congress, 2nd Session, 1914, *Diplomatic History of the Panama Canal*

    State Department Papers Relating to the Foreign Relations of the United States, 1861–1867. Washington, Government Printing Office

Upham, Charles W. *Life, Explorations and Public Services of John Charles Frémont*. Boston, Ticknor & Fields, 1856

Valentine's Manual of the City of New York, edited by Henry C. Brown. New series, vols. II, V, VI. New York, Old Colony Press, 1917–1918

Van Pelt, Daniel. *Leslie's History of Greater New York*. 3 vols. New York, Arkell Publishing Co., 1898

Washington College. *Catalogue of Books in the Library of Washington College*. Hartford, 1832

    Statement of the Course of Study and Instruction Pursued at Washington College. Hartford, P. Canfield, January 1835

Weed, Thurlow. *Life of Thurlow Weed, Including his Autobiography and a Memoir*. 2 vols. Boston and New York, Houghton, Mifflin & Co., 1884

West, W. Reed. *Contemporary French Opinion on the American Civil War*. Baltimore, Johns Hopkins Press, 1924

Westover, Myron (ed). *Schenectady Past and Present*. Strasburg, Virginia, Shenandoah Publishing House, Inc., 1931

Whittlesey, Walter L. "William Lewis Dayton, 1825," *Princeton Alumni Weekly*, vol. 30, May 9, 1930, pp. 797–820

Willson, Beckles. *America's Ambassadors to France (1777–1927)*. London, John Murray, 1928

John Slidell and the Confederates in Paris (1862–1866). New York, Minton, Balch & Co., 1932

Wilson, Henry. *History of the Rise and Fall of the Slave Power in America*. 3 vols. Boston, J. R. Osgood & Co., 1872–1877

Wilson, James G. (ed). *The Memorial History of the City of New York*. 4 vols. New York, New York History Co., 1892–1893

Young, Clifford M. *Women's Prisons Past and Present and Other New York State Prison History*. Elmira, New York, Summary Press, 1932

Index

draft New York Constitution of 1894,
323, 325; remarks on "machines," 323–
324; on Monroe Doctrine, 326; on
Bryan, 327; on Spanish-American
War, 327; on the Philippines, 328; on
Theodore Roosevelt, 328–329; and
Portsmouth Treaty, 329–330; on tariffs,
331–332; religious beliefs, 333–335;
friends of the last years, 335–338; on
Oscar Wilde, 337; on E. L. Godkin,
337; honors, 338; death, 339–340; esti-
mate of, 340–341
Bigelow, John, Jr., 108, 211, 226
Bigelow, Lucy Isham (mother of John),
4–6, 10, 27, 88
Bigelow, Poultney (first son of John),
86–87
Bigelow, Poultney (third son of John),
108, 197
Billings, John S., 302, 303
Biographie Universelle, 189
"Black Friday," 265–266, 281
Blaine, James G., 287, 324
Blair, Francis P., Sr., in campaign of
1856, 99, 100, 102, 103, 106; favors
Bates for 1860, 127–128
Blair, Montgomery, 143, 144, 146, 254
Blatchford, Richard M., 259
Boggs, William, 60, 61
Boileau, Nicolas, 196
Bossuet, Jacques, 124
Boston Advertiser, 228
Bouck, William C., 31
Bowen, James, 146
Bowles, Henry, 187
Boyd, J. Stokes, 285
Bradley, Joseph P., 282, 288
Bragg, Braxton, 196
Bravé et Cie., 193, 201, 205, 207, 218
Breckinridge, John C., 135
Bremontier, 202
Bright, John, meets Bigelow, 127; during
Civil War, 132, 152, 162, 171, 185
Brooks, Erastus, 128, 129
Brown, John, Bigelow on, 124–125, 127;
Seward on, 124
Brown (journalist in France), 187
Brownell, Bishop Thomas C., 7, 8
Bryan, William J., 326–328
Bryant, Julia, 127, 283
Bryant, William Cullen, 16, 23, 62, 64,
68, 75, 76, 82, 84, 87, 91, 99, 110–111,
120, 122, 126, 143, 159, 197, 296; recom-
mends Bigelow, 26, 28; in campaign
of 1844, 35; interested in prison re-
form, 42, 46; beliefs, 52–53, 57; takes

Bigelow as partner, 56–57, 60–61; and
campaign of 1848, 59; in Europe 1849,
1853, 1857–1858, 63, 80, 108–109; on
Compromise of 1850, 70–71; and Kan-
sas-Nebraska Act, 94–95; and Anti-
Nebraskans, 96–97; joins Republican
party, 98; and campaign of 1860, 128,
130, 134, 135, 137, 138; on Bigelow,
281; in campaign of 1876, 283; death,
292; memorial to, 322–323
Buchanan, James, 103, 108, 121, 151; and
Lecompton issue, 119; Bigelow on,
120, 127, 137
Buckner, Simon B., 327
Buffom, Edward G., 228
Bull, Ole, 21
Bulloch, James, 171; orders ships in Eng-
land, 152, 175; transfers work to
France, 199–201, 204–206; fails in
France, 214, 218, 232
Bulloch, Mrs. James, 152
Bulwer, Sir Henry, 227
Bunau-Varilla, Philippe, 305, 306; battles
for Panama Canal, 307, 308, 309, 310;
assists Panama Revolution, 311–315
Bunau-Varilla, Mme. Philippe, 311, 314
Bunsen, George de, 268
Burr, Aaron, 62
Bush, George, 90, 91
Bushnell and Gall, 12–13, 14, 15
Butler, Andrew P., 83
Butler, Benjamin F., 12, 35, 40, 58; for
third party in 1852, 80
Butler, Charles B., 13
Butler, George, 18

CADWALADER, JOHN, 301, 302, 304
Calhoun School, 320–321
Cambreleng, Churchill C., 58
Cameron, Simon, 143
Campaign of 1840, 30–31; of 1844, 33–35;
of 1848, 58–60; of 1856, 98–107; of 1860,
134–138; of 1868, 259–260; of 1872,
273–274; of 1876, 282–289; of 1880,
290; of 1884, 291–292; of 1896, 327
Campbell, Captain, 211
Carlotta, Empress of Mexico, 240
Carnegie, Andrew, 330, 337
Cass, Lewis, 58, 59
Cassignac, 166
Caverly, Captain, 203
Chandler, Zachariah, 285
Charleston Mercury, 81–82
Chase, George, 307
Chase, Salmon P., 140; and Kansas-Ne-
braska Act, 94–95; possible candidate